Modern Perspectives on Islamic Law

Modern Perspectives on Islamic Law

Ann Black

Associate Professor of Law, TC Beirne School of Law, The University of Queensland, Australia

Hossein Esmaeili

Associate Professor of Law, Flinders Law School, Flinders University, Australia

Nadirsyah Hosen

Senior Lecturer, University of Wollongong, Australia

Edward Elgar

Cheltenham, UK • Northampton, MA, USA

Published by
Edward Elgar Publishing Limited
The Lypiatts
15 Lansdown Road
Cheltenham
Glos GL50 2JA
UK

Edward Elgar Publishing, Inc.
William Pratt House
9 Dewey Court
Northampton
Massachusetts 01060
USA

A catalogue record for this book
is available from the British Library

Library of Congress Control Number: 2012955226

This book is available electronically in the ElgarOnline.com Law Subject Collection, E-ISBN 978 0 85793 447 5

ISBN 978 0 85793 446 8 (cased)

Typeset by Columns Design XML Ltd, Reading
Printed and bound in Great Britain by T.J. International Ltd, Padstow

Contents

Foreword

This is an unusual book written by academics at three Australian universities. They are respectively, a Muslim in the Sunni tradition, a Muslim in the Shia tradition, and a non-Muslim woman. Their different traditions and gender perspectives inform the book throughout. The purpose of the authors is to examine Islamic law by offering a contemporary view that is, as they put it, rational, ethical and comparative. In particular, they believe that there are no theological reasons why Islam should be in contradiction with what have become increasingly accepted international principles in the fields of human rights, democracy, the rule of law, civil society and pluralism.

Whatever the outcomes of the political movements loosely characterized by terms such as the 'Arab Spring', it is plain that Islam continues to play a vital role not just in the Middle East but also across the wider world. The discussion on which the authors embark therefore is a crucial one, but it remains controversial in many respects – even the appropriateness of the enquiry can be in dispute. The authors approach the subject from a position of informed respect. Readers will find an analysis that includes historical perspective, reference to religious writings and scholarship, and a discussion of the Sharia as it applies in various different contexts. Divisive issues such as the ban in some countries of the wearing of the burqa are tackled, with a careful reference to the arguments for and against.

Fundamentally however, the issue is a more general one. While the relationship between law and religion in the Western world is, as the authors point out, more or less settled, the same is not true in the Islamic world. However, a simple distinction between the religious and the secular no longer seems adequate. This book makes its own characteristic contribution to that important and ongoing debate.

By the Honourable Sir William Blair
Judge, High Court of England and Wales
September 2012

Preface

This book presents an in-depth analysis and a practical approach to Islamic law from a contemporary perspective. The authors intend to give both a practical and a theoretical scholarly discussion of the most important areas of Islamic law, as it is studied and practised not only in Muslim countries today but also by Muslims who live in non-Muslim countries, particularly in the secular Western nations.

Apart from drawing on the experience of authors from three different law schools and states in Australia, the authors provide a juxtaposition of different cultural perspectives and traditions – Middle Eastern, Southeast Asian and European Australian; different religious traditions – Sunni, Shia and non-Muslim; different languages – Indonesian, Persian and Arabic, three of the major Muslim languages; and different gender perspectives, all of which reflect the diversity within Muslim societies, and Muslim communities in the West.

An article based on Chapter 1 was published in the *Connecticut Journal of International Law*. (See Hossein Esmaeili, 'The Nature and Development of Law in Islam and the Rule of Law Challenge in the Middle East and the Muslim World' (2011) 26(2) *Connecticut Journal of International Law*, 329–66.) A shorter version of Chapter 3 was published in the *Journal of Islamic State Practice in International Law*. (See Hossein Esmaeili, 'Islamic Law (Sharia) in Modern Democratic Nation States' (2011) 7(2) *Journal of Islamic State Practice in International Law* (UK), 23–36.) The authors acknowledge that Chapter 4 develops concepts and material first published in *Griffith Law Review* in 2009. (See Ann Black and Nadirsyah Hosen, 'Fatwas: The Role in Contemporary Secular Australia' (2009) 18(1) *Griffith Law Review*, 405–27.) These chapters are published with the permission of these journals. We thank those journals for giving permission for us to republish some parts of the original articles in this book.

For the record, Ann Black was responsible for Chapters 5 and 6, and shared responsibility for Chapters 4 and 10 with Nadirsyah Hosen. Hossein Esmaeili was responsible for Chapters 1, 3 and 8. Nadirsyah Hosen was responsible for Chapters 2, 7 and 9. However, we present this book as a collaboration representing the diversity of the authors' experiences and strengths in scholarship on Islamic law.

We would like to thank those who have helped during this project. We jointly thank Kate Wheldrake for her editorial assistance. We also would like to thank Edward Elgar, who was supportive of the book from the outset and more recently Alex Pettifer, Laura Seward and John-Paul MacDonald for their editorial work and encouragement.

Hossein would like to thank Nadir and Ann, who have been great collaborators and good friends. Also, he would like to thank Kate Wheldrake and Alyssa Sallis for their research assistance, and colleagues at Flinders Law School for their help and support. Hossein acknowledges the financial support of the Faculty of Education, Humanities and Law for the final preparation and editing of this book. Hossein would also like to thank his family for their patience and support – Shokoufeh (his wife), and children Nikki, Hannah and Sarah.

Ann greatly values the opportunity to have collaborated with two highly respected Islamic scholars, Hossein Esmaeili and Nadirsyah Hosen, and that together we worked to achieve something distinctive in our different reflections on the role of Islamic law today. She also is grateful to be married to Rob, who has been a tower of strength through good and difficult times, and to her children, Peter, Suzi and Katherine, who remind her of the blessings that only a family can bring.

Nadir would like to thank Hossein and Ann for this wonderful collaboration, to colleagues at Legal Intersection Research Centre, Faculty of Law, University of Wollongong for their continuing support, and to his family for their unflagging love. Special thanks to his father, the late Professor K.H. Ibrahim Hosen, from whom he learnt *usul al-fiqh*, *fiqh muqarin*, and above all, the love of knowledge.

Prologue

> [Give the good news to] [t]hose who listen [to different views and perspectives (*qawl*)], and follow the best [of those views] … [that] those are the ones whom God has guided, and those are the ones who are indeed people of wisdom (*ulul al-bab*).[1]

Islamic law is the world's third major legal system, after the common and civil law systems. Although the Quran and Sunna are the original sources of Islamic law, the Islamic legal system has evolved many other sources, methodologies and perspectives. Like any other legal system, the Islamic legal system has developed over many centuries in various Muslim societies, incorporating local cultures and customs as well as some limited state decrees and particularly the work of Muslim jurists. In the words of Joseph Schacht, 'Islamic law represents an extreme case of "jurists' law"; it was created and developed by private specialists; legal science, and not the state, plays the part of a legislator, and scholarly handbooks have the force of law'.[2] Islamic law is therefore neither common nor civil law, but is juristic law.

Traditionally, Islamic law consists of both revelation and reason. After the death of the Prophet Mohammad (633 AD), the revelation of Islamic law by God to humanity ceased. Humanity now relies on reason to understand Islamic law. According to Allama Muhammad Iqbal (d. 1937), humanity needed the guidance of Prophets when it was primarily controlled by passion and instinct. However, from the time of the Prophet Mohammad, people achieved the ability to reason, and this is why the Prophet Mohammad is the final (*khatam*) Prophet. Iqbal concludes that the nature of revelation (*wahy*) is reason. This means that human beings, since the time of the last Prophet, must involve reason and human experiences in developing the legal system of Islam.[3] However, do we still need to follow reasoning suggested by Muslim scholars a hundred or even a thousand years ago to solve our contemporary problems? This book examines Islamic law by offering a contemporary perspective that is rational, ethical and comparative. For this reason, we have given our book the title *Modern Perspectives on Islamic Law*.

The rational approach of this book is an effort toward a renewal of classical traditional Islamic thought on the basis of rational thinking.

There are no theological reasons why Islam should be in contradiction to human rights, democracy, the rule of law, civil society and pluralism. The book is an attempt, within an Islamic legal context, to demonstrate that Islam, as a religious, cultural, political, ethical and economic worldview, could deal with the rapidly modernizing and ever-changing world that we live in today. This does not mean that it neglects revelation and reason in the classical sense, but rather it uses classic Islamic legal discourse as a vehicle to respond to some modern issues. The authors do not neglect classical Islam's richly textual basis, as such a collection of knowledge provides valuable tools to respond to questions and problems in the contemporary Islamic world. At the same time, the authors do not treat these classical works as the only source of authority, but as important for the legal reasoning (*ijtihad*) of each scholar devoted to reaching solutions to challenges in their respective contexts.

The ethical approach of this book means that rationality alone is not enough as ethics is one of the core elements of Islamic teachings. Islamic teachings are not confined to acts of worship and prayer and to a set of moral counsels. As Islam has dealt with people's relations with God, it has also given the broad lines of human beings' relations with each other. It has, in various forms, dealt with individual rights and obligations too. The authors take the view that there is an intersection of Islamic law and ethics as reflected in our discussions of economics, family law, criminal law and contemporary debates. The authors also use a comparative approach: evaluating the practice of Islamic law in different times, regions, schools and places, and also connecting Islamic law to other legal systems (common law and civil law). All of these approaches bring together the modern perspectives indicated by the title.

The approach taken by this book encourages *ijtihad* (independent legal reasoning) in order to revisit many concepts and issues in Islamic legal tradition. *Ijtihad* in modern times may require collaboration between religious leaders and scholars from related disciplines. It is a collective effort leading to various opinions and options. For instance, when scholars discuss a controversial subject such as human cloning, rather than simply stating whether such a practice is forbidden (*haram*) or permitted (*halal*), they should consider other observations and views, particularly professional views, such as those of scientists, medical practitioners and lawyers. This will result in more comprehensive advice being given on a particular subject.

It has often been understood that certain traditional civil and social laws of Islam are drawn from the simple life of the pre-Islamic Arabs, and are mostly based on their customs and usages. At the time of the Prophet, the Islamic legal system consisted of two main types of laws:

those which pre-dated Islam and were approved by Islam (*akham ta'idi*); and those developed by Islam (*akham ta'sisi*). As the Islamic legal system has developed over the centuries, many more interpretations and distinctions have developed in response to the changing needs of society. The body of rules that we consider 'Islamic law' today may be based on the original two sources of law, but the majority of rules that apply were developed over 15 centuries of juristic interpretation, scholarly work and occasional pronouncements by authorities. Therefore, some Islamic law rules and principles are based on facts and circumstances that existed many centuries ago. In this sense, contemporary Muslim scholars must find a way to determine which Islamic legal principles should be maintained, and which ones should be adjusted in response to social changes. Islamic principles support the flexibility and adjustability of principles to the requirements of time.

In the classical or traditional sense, a study of Islamic law requires an examination of both principles of the study of Islamic jurisprudence (*usul al-fiqh*) and the study of Islam to infer legal and religious principles (*fiqh*), which is the subject of an extensive literature in English and other languages. A historical approach is useful to understand the text of Islamic law, but this book focuses more on the context of Islamic law today: modern times. The authors take the view that the adaptation of Islamic law according to time and circumstance is necessitated by changes in society, and the influx of various cultures and material conditions. As will be shown, this new *ijtihad* can lead to reform of Islamic law, as has occurred in some Muslim countries and through some juristic works. Such reforms also allow Muslims living as minorities to better accommodate Islam within a non-Muslim majority setting.

The book starts with an analysis of the nature of Islamic law, its concepts, meaning and sources, as well as its development in different stages of Islamic history. The first chapter discusses some of the most important and fundamental contemporary issues of Islam and Islamic law, such as the relationship between religion and law; the divine aspects of law; the sacredness of certain legal principles; and the traditional and modern sources of Islamic law. Any attempt to interpret, analyse and reform Islamic legal systems to accommodate modern societies must start with a comprehensive understanding of these fundamental and basic concepts. This is followed by accounts of how Islamic law is being practised today. Key modern institutions are discussed, such as the parliament, judiciary, *dar al-ifta*, political parties and other important organizations. While some elements of Islamic law are practised at individual level, others require the involvement of institutions or communities. Consideration of Islamic institutions is a good example of 'Islamic law in action' rather than 'Islamic law in books'.

It continues by analysing some key concepts in our modern times: nation-state, citizenship, *ummah*, *dhimmah* (recognition of the status of certain non-Muslims in Islamic states) and the rule of law. Fifteen centuries ago, when Islamic law was introduced in Medina, the concept of state and the rule of law had not been developed. Today, Muslims live in both Muslim and non-Muslim countries. As a citizen, a Muslim should follow the law of the land, but as a Muslim, they must follow Islamic teaching, particularly its requirements and restrictions: the parameters of *halal* and *haram.* This is one of the most challenging issues facing modern Muslims. It is concluded that the overwhelming majority of Muslims living in non-Muslim countries (including in the West) take Islam and its legal system in broad terms of belief in God, the humanitarian message of Islam and the practice of rituals and Islamic personal law within the boundaries of the existing legal system where they live, rather than as an exclusive ideology. It is also acknowledged that mainstream Muslims in Western countries are rightly concerned with the acknowledgement of their identities, the practice of their faith and the preservation of their traditions, family life and values.

For Muslims everywhere, Islamic law is living law. The practical importance of Islamic law to everyday life relates to the role of fatwa in contemporary Muslim societies, a topic too important to ignore. Muslims at grass root levels require guidance from Muslim scholars on an array of relevant Islamic issues ranging from ritual, social interaction and technological advances to problems associated with business, schools, the workplace or the government. The book investigates how in recent times more and more fatwas are issued collectively rather than emanating from an individual scholar. Collective fatwas are a modern phenomenon that did not exist at the time of the Prophet and his companions, nor was there the plurality of fatwas that are issued today by Islamic organizations, state and non-state muftis via both digital and non-digital media. The on-line environment that gives ready access to fatwas is a reflection of the modern global world.

As will be shown in the book, changes in social life also affect relationships at personal levels. The family is considered a very important unit within all Muslim communities. Modernization of Islamic family law has taken place since the nineteenth century, but this has not been uniform. Owing to increased level of education and prosperity, Muslim women seek new roles and the recognition of rights they believe are inherent in Islam. While adherence to the principles and edicts of Islamic family law remains strong and central to Muslim identity at an individual and community level, colonization and other factors resulted in the codification Islamic family law in many Muslim nations. In the era of nation-states, governments have given Sharia courts greater oversight of family matters, with court registration and judicial approval required for a growing range of matters. Acknowledgement, too, of international norms has meant that principles of equality and nondiscrimination inform family law reforms in many Muslim countries. It makes family law a perfect vehicle to appreciate the contemporary role of *ijtihad* across the Muslim world and in the West, where it continues to inform the lives of Muslims in secular lands.

While the Sharia courts are the most visible mechanism for dealing with family law matters and other disputes, Islamic law has always sanctioned and supported other modes of alternative dispute resolution. Amicable settlement through mediation and arbitration continues to have relevance for Muslims today, not only in Muslim nations but also in non-Muslim countries, where there has been considerable recent debate on whether Muslims should be allowed to establish Sharia tribunals to resolve conflicting issues between Islamic family law, especially in matters of divorce and inheritance, independently from Western law.

The next chapter focuses on relationship between Islamic law and economics. The idea of non-interest banking and other related financial products and institutions is introduced, along with discussion of how Islamic law could potentially provide options and possibilities that are relevant to the debate on the current global financial crisis in United States and Europe. This is followed by a chapter that reviews the historical background of theories of property and inheritance in Islamic law, and considers the basic principles of Islamic trust (*waqf*) law under Islamic law. The book investigates the institutions of property, inheritance and *waqf* as economic instruments in the history of the Middle East, and examines the relationship between these institutions and the rule of law in Middle Eastern and Muslim countries' legal systems. Unlike family law and inheritance law, Islamic property law is in its early stage of development. *Waqf*, unlike trust in common law, has at its heart a charitable purpose, has acted as a social security mechanism, and has significant potential to be further developed in Islamic economic law.

On Islamic criminal law, the book re-examines the classic rules of *hudud*, *diyah*, *qisas* and *ta'zir*, outlining certain prescribed classic punishments such as cutting off the hands of thieves or stoning adulterers to death. The book offers a fresh and new interpretation of Islamic criminal in line with the idea of modern perspectives described earlier. Given well-publicized events in 2012 in Mali, where two women were stoned for adultery,[4] the chapter demonstrates ways in which it is possible to reform Islamic criminal law.

Lastly, the book revisits certain contemporary issues of debate in Islamic law. The authors have selectively chosen debates occurring not only in Western countries but also in many parts of the Muslim world. There are five issues: first, the banning of the burqa in some Western (and also Muslim) countries; second, building places for worship including discussion of cases such as the 'Ground Zero' mosque in New York and the minaret issue in Switzerland, and an overview of the recent events in Indonesia, Egypt and Australia; third, the debate on Sharia's compatibility with democracy, outlining three different approaches – traditionalist, secularist and what is described as 'the middle' way; fourth, *halal* food, including the issue of whether Islamic law can accept stunning before slaughtering or not with a Jewish comparison on the same issue; and fifth, the issue of apostasy in Malaysia, Egypt and the West. These debates are vehicles to demonstrate that contemporary issues are complex and plural, requiring understanding of Islam in line with principles of modern life, justice, human rights, democracy and the dignity of all humankind.

Throughout the book, the reader will find different terminologies or categories to describe the thought and ideas of individual scholars and groups of Muslims who align with a particular view on an issue or with an approach. The attempts to define, classify and identify differences amongst Muslims have been reflected in many scholarly works. Scholars in the contemporary era have used the terms 'modern' and 'traditional', 'conservative' and 'moderate' or 'fundamentalist' and 'liberal', or 'neo-modernism Islam', the last as a synthesis of modern and traditional scholarship. To this we could add the political dimensions imported into the concepts of 'Islamist', 'modernist' and 'secularist'. To some extent, the lines between these terms are often blurred and should be seen as such. One scholar may agree with a liberal approach in a case (for instance, to allow a woman to become the president of a Muslim nation), but he or she may strongly disagree with another liberal stance (for instance, that polygyny should be prohibited totally). In other words, two individuals might have some shared common visions, but when it comes to the details of each element of Islamic law, may take different positions. Categorizations tend to narrow the complexities and the dynamic of thought within any one group, making them not fully representative. Having said all this, although any categorization is far from perfect and can be contested, we have made an attempt in the book to define and justify the use of terms.

Muslims recognize that Islam and Islamic law contain a plurality of definitions, meanings and classifications. Different terms are used in Arabic, English and other languages to explain Islam, Sharia and Islamic law. In this book, terms have been defined in ways that reflect different Islamic religious and legal traditions: classical, contemporary, Middle Eastern, Southeast Asian and Western. In the West, and in English literature, references are made to terms such as 'traditionalist', 'fundamentalist', 'Islamist' or 'extremist' Muslims, and 'modernists'. Traditionalist Muslims can be considered those who live according to the strict teachings of traditional Islam. Fundamentalist Muslims can be understood as those calling for radical political change based on Islamic teachings. It is vital to note that extremist or Islamist movements are a subset of fundamentalist Islam, but not all fundamentalist Muslims are extremists. The term 'modernist' captures the political ideology of those who wish to reform Islam and place it at the centre of a 'modern' political entity. The approach taken in this book is to consider the majority of the world's more than 1 billion Muslims as 'mainstream Muslims'. They may well share aspirations of democracy and the rule of law and most certainly wish their children to live in a better world than the one they inhabit. However, they are not influenced by political or religious ideology to the extent of some other contemporary Muslim groups. The approaches of mainstream Muslims to Islam and the Islamic legal system are rich, pluralistic and evolving. They involve various cultural, philosophical, mystical and legal traditions.

Above all, this book is part of *ijtihad*: it is the interpretation of the authors. The Prophet said that '[w]hen a jurist or a judge exercises *ijtihad* and reaches a correct conclusion, they receive a double reward; but if the conclusion is incorrect, they will still receive a single reward'.[5] Drawing on the Prophet's words, we are encouraged to offer this book for the appreciation of all who read it.

NOTES

1. The Quran, Súra Zumar 39:17–18; Abdullah Yusuf Ali, *The Qur'an: Text, Translation and Commentary* (Tahrike Tarsile Qur'an, New York, 2005), 1241, with authors' amending translations.
2. Joseph Schacht, *An Introduction to Islamic Law* (Oxford University Press, New York, 1964), 5.
3. Allama Muhammad Iqbal, *The Reconstruction of Religious Thought in Islam*, 2nd edn (edited and annotated by M. Saeed Sheikh, Institute of Islamic Culture and Iqbal Academy Pakistan, Lahore, 1989), 99–116. There are many editions by many publishers in many languages.

4. Katarina Hoije, 'Islamists: Two Stoned to Death for Committing Adultery in Mali', *CNN News*, 3 August 2012.
5. Abu Dawud, *Sunan*, III, 1019, hadith No. 3585.

1. The nature of law, and its relationship with religion, in Islam

1. INTRODUCTION

Islamic law is one of the three major world legal systems after the common law and civil law systems. It is applicable, at least in part, in more than 55 Muslim countries and in a number of non-Muslim countries, such as India. The Islamic legal system originated in the Middle East in the late sixth century, and has developed mainly in that region. However the modern Islamic world, and hence potential applications of the Islamic legal system, extend well beyond the Middle East into Asia, Africa and Europe.

Similar to other legal systems,[1] the nature of Islamic law and its concept, meaning and sources are the subject of an extensive body of literature and contested views.[2] The nature of religion, and particularly the definition of 'Islam', is the subject of contested views as well, given the relationship between law and religion in Islam.

Most Muslims consider law to be divine and sacred. Legal principles revealed in the Quran and the Sunna (traditions of Prophet Mohammad) are immune from critical evaluation. Notwithstanding this fundamental characteristic of Islamic law, Muslim jurists have long extensively examined the application and interpretation of basic legal principles of Islamic law, and the nature of law in Islam. Just as the religion of Islam is not monolithic, neither is its legal system. Indeed the principles of Sharia are the subject of contested views throughout the history of Islam as well as in the contemporary world.

This chapter considers religion and law, the divine aspect of law, and the sacredness of law separately to highlight the fundamental importance of each aspect in understanding the legal system of Islam, and the implications of these characteristics of Islamic law for the development of rule of law-based systems in Muslim countries. Also, the relationship between religion and law in Islam is unique. While generally in Western literature scholarly work on law and religion is mainly concerned with the role of religion in the state and legal system,[3] in Islam law and religion are so closely related that it can be argued that one cannot be considered in isolation from the other. The divine aspects and sacredness of Islamic law are particularly important as these characteristics may prevent critical analysis of many traditional principles of Islamic law, and therefore may be obstacles in the development of a rule of law-based system in Muslim countries.

This chapter investigates the nature and meaning of 'law' in the Islamic legal system. In analysing the nature of law in Islam, the chapter will focus on the following selected characteristics of Islamic law: the relationship between law and Islam; the divine nature of Islamic law; sacredness of law in Islam; and sources of law in Islam. Finally the chapter will consider the opportunities and barriers these fundamental characteristics of Islamic law present for the development of rule of law-based systems in Muslim countries. The rule of law is an important modern concept that may be developed within the legal system of Islam, and could be considered to apply when law, instead of the state and powerful individuals, rules the society. There are elements within the Islamic legal system that can be used as foundations to develop a limited rule of law system in the legal system of Islam. The term 'rule of law' has varying and deeply contested meanings as the expression of an idea and as a doctrine.[4] The concepts of the rule of law in the Western legal tradition, and the nature of law more generally, are the subject of a wide variety of legal and philosophical theories.[5] This chapter does not propose to review in detail these debates.[6]

2. DEFINING TERMS

A number of terms in Islam and Islamic law that are used in English and other languages, particularly Arabic and Persian, have distinct meanings, which have been used interchangeably in English texts discussing Islamic law. It must be noted in particular that the four terms 'religion of Islam' (*din*), 'Islamic jurisprudence' (*fiqh*), 'Islamic law' and 'Sharia'[7] are not the same. There are differences between the concept of religion as commonly understood in the West, and the 'religion of Islam', which includes beliefs and rituals. There are also differences between Islamic jurisprudence (*fiqh*) and Sharia, which is commonly known as Islamic law in English literature. Furthermore, Sharia is more general than Islamic law as it includes non-legal principles.

Generally, Islam refers to the entire religion, including beliefs, rituals, morality and law.[8] *Fiqh* is the study of Islam to infer legal and religious principles. *Fiqh* is therefore not the same as 'Islamic jurisprudence' understood in terms of Western legal theory and philosophy. However, in

English literature the term *fiqh* is commonly translated to 'Islamic jurisprudence'. The term Sharia is similarly not exactly the same as Islamic law. Sharia is divided into the categories of transactions (*muamilat*), rituals (*ibadat*) and punishments (*uqubat*). Not all rituals are sanctioned by law, although some are.

Given that Sharia is a system of religious norms that includes many non-legal elements, there are diverse positions on the definition and nature of law in Islam that researchers interested in Islamic law need to consider carefully. The modern concept of Islamic law, which includes the various tribal and moral norms of different Muslim societies, is different from traditional or pure theoretical Sharia. Further, the definition of Islam may differ according to the various juristic schools of law. Nonetheless, a body of diverse legal principles originated with the advance of Islam, and became applicable in parts of various Muslim societies. The differences between Islamic schools (to be discussed later) and the variety of juristic interpretations and legal reasoning (*ijtihad*) may be branded as a divergence (*iktilaf*) that leads to a latitude in interpretation (*towsi'a*), which can be considered to demonstrate diversity within unity.[9]

In essence, Islamic jurisprudence (*fiqh*) means understanding of Sharia. The equivalent of what is called 'legal theory' in Western legal literature is, in Sharia, part of Islamic philosophy. Historically there has been conflict between philosophy and *fiqh* in Islamic scholarship.[10] This meant that *fiqh* was developed mainly as an area of Islamic scholarship that tried to understand Sharia without entering into the area of 'jurisprudence', or the philosophy of law in its Western conception. In order to infer principles of Sharia, a set of rules was developed in Islamic jurisprudence known as *usul al-fiqh*, which is translated in English as 'principles of jurisprudence'.[11] There are only a few works in English, and in Arabic, on proper legal theory,[12] as distinct from *fiqh*.

The closest area of scholarship to legal theory as understood in the West is that section of Islamic philosophy that discusses revelation (*wahy*) and sources of Sharia law. These subjects are also discussed in *usul al-fiqh*, but while *usul al-fiqh* does not generally raise questions about the fundamental principles and the nature of law, in Islamic philosophy, the purpose and nature of law and *wahy* (revelation) are discussed. Both Muslim scholars and jurists from the early stage of Islam[13] and Western scholars studying Islam have worked in this area.[14]

3. RELIGION AND LAW

The legal system of Islam is based on the religion of Islam. Islamic theology defines the principles of belief and the law of Islam. It prescribes what a person shall do or from what they shall refrain.[15] In practice, law in Islam is part of a religious system in which legal rules and rituals merge.[16] According to Seyyed Hossein Nasr, 'religion to a Muslim is essentially the Divine Law'.[17] Indeed this was the original concept of law in the early history of Islam. An important factor in understanding the concept and nature of Islamic law is that under Islam all acts are divided into five classes. These are obligatory (*wajib*), recommended (*mustahabb* or *mandoub*), permitted (*mubah*), disliked (*makruh*) and forbidden (*haram*).[18] One can be punished for omitting to perform acts in the first category. This means that even omissions of rituals considered *wajib* can be punished under an Islamic state. The second, third and fourth categories are more within the realm of religion and actions within these categories are rewarded or disapproved, but not sanctioned positively or negatively. Performing actions within the last category (*haram*) is punishable.[19] *Ta'zir* is a category of punishment for conduct where no specific punishment (*hadd*) has been provided by the Quran or Sunna and is defined as 'punishment imposed by the judge (*qadi*) or the state (*hakim*) for a crime or a sin where no punishment is provided by sharia'.[20] Failing to follow rituals such as praying (without legitimate cause) is a sin in Islam. In practice this was only applied by the Taliban government in Afghanistan. In certain areas of Saudi Arabia such as in Mecca and Medina, the religious police try to enforce proper religious rituals according to the state edict and prohibit any rituals inconsistent with Wahhabi teachings. According to Joseph Schacht, 'the central feature that makes Islamic religious law what it is, that guarantees its unity in all its diversity, is the assessing of all human acts and relationship, including those which we call legal, from the point of view of the concepts "obligatory/recommended/indifferent/reprehensible/forbidden"'.[21]

All human conduct is classified under one of the five categories. The general criteria for determining conduct types are subject to certain principles that Muslim jurists (*foqaha*) have developed called 'principles of jurisprudence' (*usul al-fiqh*). These principles are applied to infer the relevant principle (*hukm*) relating to each type of conduct.[22] If no principle can be found that requires or prohibits conduct within a specific jurisprudence then the conduct is considered as permitted (*mubah*), and deemed legally indifferent. Under this approach the omission of obligatory duties, whether ritualistic or not, and the commission of forbidden acts are sins and hence illegal and punishable by law.[23] All other activities, however, whether recommended, permitted or disliked are legally indifferent. This is the traditional and orthodox view of Islamic law.

Islamic jurists divide Sharia into two categories: rituals (*ibadat*) and transactions (*muamilat*), which cover the concepts of law proper.[24] Theoretically law and religion in Islam, to a great extent, overlap. A body of rules and regulations that apply to certain forms of conduct which are neither prohibited (*haram*) nor obligatory (*wajib*) has developed to deal with modern life. These more recent systems of rules in Muslim societies may not strictly be called Islamic law, but have nevertheless been adopted into the Islamic legal system. This body of law is not traditional Sharia or Islamic law but is a part of the legal system of modern Muslim societies. Indeed in almost all Muslim countries, including Saudi Arabia, the majority of rules applicable in the day-to-day relationships between individual Muslims are what can be labelled 'legally indifferent' under Sharia. The *haram* or *wajib* parts of the legal system, however, such as aspects of personal law (for example marriage, divorce and trusts)[25] and public law (government, constitution, law-making processes) are more influential in certain societies, such as Saudi Arabia.

In fact, the relationship between traditional Islamic law and modern, and mainly positivist, law has an unsettled status in contemporary Muslim societies. Islamic jurists and ordinary Muslims hold diverse opinions about how Sharia applies to certain aspects of a Muslim individual's life in the modern world. Some aspects, including marriage, divorce and the custody of children, are mainly regulated by what can be precisely labelled as Islamic law. Other aspects are subject to provisions that are not Islamic law, although they also may not necessarily contradict Islamic law. While principles of Islamic law govern family law, inheritance, trusts, contract, criminal law and certain other areas, modern regulations regulate matters such as corporations, broadcasting law, health law, food production, travel, immigration and the environment.[26]

While the relationship between law and religion in the Western world is more or less settled, it is not in the Islamic world. One important point with respect to the relationship between law and religion in Islam, and the establishment of the rule of law system in a Muslim country, is that religious authorities, that is to say, certain individuals, have a special status and may be beyond the law. This is one of the significant differences between the status of religion in the West, taken to mean Christianity, and in the Muslim world. More broadly, in Western history,

Christianity distanced itself, to some extent, from the Mosaic law.[27] Roman law, not Christian law, was the legal system of the Christian world, and canon law developed alongside the Roman law.[28] Common law in England developed based on Anglo-Saxon customary law and the orders of the kings.[29] Legal philosophy in the West developed the natural law theory to include basic Christian ideas. In the Islamic world, however, law, philosophy, legal theories and the idea of the state developed differently. Islam was a spiritual religion for only ten years as a faction of a major Arabian tribe (*Quraysh*) in the city of Mecca (610–620). Then it became a complete political, legal and military force in the first Muslim state of Medina (620 onwards). The Prophet of Islam was head of state, the chief justice, the commander of the Army, the mediator and the spiritual leader who was also the Messenger revealing the words and commands of God.

Later in the history of Islam the close relationship between religion and law was preserved in Muslim societies. Although in practice kings, caliphs and other rulers may not have observed the public and constitutional law of Islam, religious authorities enforced Sharia law, which regulated private relationships, and also Islamic criminal law, until the collapse of the Ottoman empire, when modern European codes were introduced in almost all the Muslim Middle Eastern countries except Saudi Arabia.

A. Law as Divine, and the Nature of Revelation

A fundamental feature of law in Islam, and one of the major challenges to law reform and the potential institution of a rule of law-based system in Muslim countries, is the divine character of Islamic law. Islam is the only religion whose followers believe that the Quran is the word of God, and therefore that Quranic laws are God's direct commands. According to Seyyed Hossein Nasr:

> [I]n the Islamic perspective, Divine Law is to be implemented to regulate society and the actions of its members rather than society dictating what laws should be. The injunctions of Divine Law are permanent, but the principles can also be applied to new circumstances as they arise. But the basic thesis is one of trying to make the human order conform to the Divine norm, not vice-versa … As in Judaism, for Islam Divine Law is more central than theological thought to the religious life … Even those who have sought to go beyond the formal level, through the tariqa to the absolute Truth, which transcends all forms, have never ceased to revere the sharia and to practice it. The greatest philosophers of Islam from Avicenna to Averroes practiced the sharia, so did the greatest saints and mystics.[30]

Professor Nasr presents an argument in relation to the depth and richness of Islam's spiritual and social values. He does not address how a legal and political system based on Sharia can evolve and operate without being debated and scrutinized at least within legal institutions, nor does he offer a practical model of an Islamic state based on Sharia, whether historical or modern.

According to Coulson, in Islam, 'law is the command of God, the acknowledged function of Muslim jurisprudence and from the beginning, was simply the discovery of the terms of that command'.[31] This is true in the sense that in Islam it has been accepted that the Quran is the word of God, and the Prophet Mohammad is directly associated with revelations from God. In traditional Islamic jurisprudence, God is 'the ultimate sovereign and possess[es] all the original rights and hence [is] the first source of law'.[32]

In spite of the fact that the majority of Muslim scholars accept that the Quran is the word of God revealed to the Prophet Mohammad,[33] and because of its divine source cannot be questioned, there have always been discussions about the interpretation of the Quran and the nature of revelation.[34] The earliest debate over the nature of the Quran occurred during reign of the Abbasid Caliph Mamun (813–833). At that time the view of the majority of Muslim jurists was that the Quran was eternal. A theological group, the *Mutazila*, argued that the Quran was created by God, but was not eternal.[35] The *Mutazila*'s rationalism was opposed, particularly by Ahmad Ibn Hanbal,[36] and their theology was not accepted by the majority of scholars (*ulama*), but was accepted by some influential Shia scholars. The rational theology of the *Mutazila* has led some Muslim commentators to label the *Mutazila* as liberals.[37]

In more recent times contemporary Muslim scholars have debated the nature of revelation and Prophethood and the Islamic legal principles from which these are derived. Notable scholars including Shah Waliallah,[38] Taha[39] and Iqbal[40] as well as a number of other Muslim scholars have expressed innovative views about revelation and the Quran. In addition, Abdullahi Ahmad An Na'im,[41] Nasr Hamid Abu Zayd[42] and Abdolkarim Soroush[43] are the best known contemporary Muslim scholars who have frequently commented on the nature of Quranic revelation. For example, Nasr Hamid Abu Zayd and Abdolkarim Soroush have recently argued that the words of God as revealed to the Prophet were expressed using the Prophet's own words.[44]

There are three main views of the nature of revelation (*wahy*) in the Muslim world. The official and most popular view is that the Quranic verses are the words of God revealed to the Prophet Mohammad and that the Prophet recited the exact words of God to the people.[45] The second view is that the content of the Quran was revealed to the Prophet by God, but that the Prophet used his own words to transfer the message of God to the people.[46] The third view holds that the Quran *is* the words of the Prophet, but because the Prophet of Islam has a divine personality his words are also the words of God.[47] In any case, under all of these perspectives, divine revelation guides what the Prophet of Islam said or did.

B. The Sovereignty of God

Public law principles in Islam are influenced by the doctrine of the sovereignty of God. Under theories of state in Islamic law God is the only sovereign, the only source of law and the source of authority.[48] Many Muslim scholars base their theories of the state and government on the principle that God is all-powerful, the ultimate owner of the heavens and earth, and the sole legislator.[49] This section will analyse the concept of the sovereignty of God and examine complications in its application to modern Muslim societies.

The sovereignty of God is expressed in contemporary statecraft including in Article 2 of the Iranian Constitution, which states that 'the Islamic Republic is a system based on belief in One God (there is no God but Allah), and the exclusive sovereignty of God, the acceptance of His rule, and the necessity of obeying His commands'.[50] Furthermore, Maudidi argues that in a Muslim society divine sovereignty requires that God's law, or Sharia, and not human-made law will govern.[51]

The concept of sovereignty of God is well established in Islamic theology and in particular in the area of Islamic jurisprudence known as *kalam*.[52] In terms of law it is commonly accepted that the basic principles of Islamic law are based on divine principles in the Quran and the Sunna, or are at least inspired by principles of the Quran and the Sunna. Islamic legal systems have blended access to divine legislation granted through the limited number of Quranic verses or Sunna on legal matters with the subjectivity and insight of human beings.[53] This blending can been observed in the Constitution of Iran, the only written constitution based on theocratic Islamic principles, and is manifested in article 56 of the Iranian Constitution, which states that: 'Absolute sovereignty over the world and man belongs to God, and it is He Who has made man master of his own social destiny. No one can deprive man of this divine right, nor subordinate it to the vested interests of a particular individual or group'.[54]

Although Muslims universally accept the principle of the sovereignty of God, there are substantial differences of opinion about how the will of

God can be applied in a Muslim society. These differences of opinion have been observed during and after the existence of a centralized Islamic state ruling over all, or the majority, of Muslim territory, which existed only for short periods of time in the history of Islam: during the Righteous Caliphates (632–661 AD), and during the very early stages of the Omayyad (661–750) and Abbasid (750–1258) Caliphates. After this period in time, different local and sectarian rulers governed the Muslim world.

Most Muslim rulers, states, governments and authorities during the last 15 centuries have claimed legitimacy on behalf of God. In some stages of Islamic history, around the twelfth and thirteenth centuries, for example, when a weak central caliphate existed in Baghdad, the Islamic world was ruled by numerous local and independent rulers who were mainly fighting with each other. Almost all of them claimed legitimacy on behalf of God. Unfortunately, history shows that states, rulers and powerful individuals throughout the history of Islam have exploited the idea of the sovereignty of God to oppress their people. Therefore, the notion of the sovereignty of God should be reconciled with human experience, intelligence and the will of people in order to avoid the misuse of power by states and rulers.

In reality, however, claiming that God is the sole legislator and that human-made law has no legitimacy cannot be sustained. People today do not have direct and clear access to the will of God, particularly after the cessation of the Revelation, which occurred after the death of the Prophet.[55] From an Islamic theology perspective, as human beings do not have perfect access to the will of God, they are not able to be the executor of the Divine Will without involving their subjectivity in the process.[56] According to a number of progressive Muslim jurists, the Prophet of Islam did not intend to apply a legal system over all Islamic territories for all time; rather he set out the general principles of law that Muslim societies can apply within the spirit of broader Islamic principles using their wisdom and human experience.[57]

As the above sections have demonstrated, the interpretations of the Quran and other sources of Sharia have always been the subject of contested views amongst Muslim scholars and theologians. In practice, while the majority of the principles underlying Sharia law are clearly not divine, Muslims consider certain basic principles that are expressly mentioned in the Quran to be divine. This may lead to these legal principles being considered sacred, and hence outside the limit of critical evaluation.

C. Sacredness of Law

As we have seen, the divine nature of law means that under traditional Sharia God makes the law, and God is the source of law-making through the Quran and the Prophet. In the history of Islam, however, apart from God, the Prophet and the Quran, many other institutions and beliefs have become 'sacred'. Islamic law in principle is a 'sacred legal system'.[58] This means that critical analysis of certain principles, including legal principles, may lead to blasphemy or apostasy.[59]

In recent years, and indeed in the last 200 years, some Islamic jurists have tried to limit the 'sacredness' of Sharia to areas of oneness of God (*towhid*), Islamic beliefs (*al aqayed*) and worship (*ibadat*) to find ways to examine the application of certain principles of Sharia.[60] Both governments in Muslim nations and Islamic jurists have tried to develop these limitations, as governments have abandoned the application of certain legal principles in traditional Sharia and jurists have tried to find certain methods to reform and adjust the traditional principles. As a result, some Islamic rules have been abandoned, although not rejected outright by Muslim societies. In other words, they are not practised although they may be prescribed in the form of written law.[61]

4. SOURCES OF LAW

Determining the sources of law is one of the most fundamental functions of any legal system. In two of the major modern legal systems of the world, civil law and common law, the legislature is the sovereign law-maker. There are other law-making institutions in both common and civil law systems, however, but other sources, such as case law in common law, are subordinate to the legislature's legislation.[62] In Islamic law there is a pyramid of sources with the Quran at the apex. The process of creating legal rules in the Islamic legal system, however, is far more complex than is commonly thought. In most Islamic law textbooks in English, as well as textbooks on Islamic jurisprudence in Arabic, the assumption is that there are four major sources of Islamic law: the Quran, the Sunna, analogical reasoning (*qiyas*) and consensus of opinion (*ijma*). During the life of the Prophet Mohammad, and for a few centuries after his time, those sources were the dominant sources of making legal rules in the Islamic legal system.[63] As the Islamic communities expanded beyond the Arabian Peninsula into Asia, Africa and Europe, these original sources did not provide broad enough legal principles for new situations. Islamic scholars (*ulama*) developed new methods of interpreting the original sources.

Those new methods are generally seen as three areas of scholarship: interpretation of the Quran (*tafsir*), understanding of Islamic jurisprudence (*fiqh*) and principles of Islamic jurisprudence (*usul al-fiqh*).[64] Therefore, the Quran is the most important source of law, but it is not the source of most law in Islam.

The Quran is a book about the relationship between God and people and consists of approximately 6600 verses[65] dealing predominantly with religion, prescriptions and other related issues such as the creation, the origin of human beings and, of course, rules (*ahkam*) and proper law.[66] Only about 10 per cent of Quranic verses are called in Arabic '*ayat al akham*' or verses relating to legal rules, but not all of these are analogous to the legal rules or proper law found in the modern world. The verses relating to rules also include those verses providing provisions for rituals such as daily prayer, pilgrimage (*hajj*) and fasting. Indeed verses relating to proper law such as governance, contractual law, criminal law and family law are limited to about 2 per cent of all Quranic verses. Similarly, the Sunna or prophetic reports which are what the Prophet of Islam said or did and consented to during his 23 years of prophesying cannot be considered as a complete code of law in the proper sense.[67] Only about 10 per cent of all sayings of the Prophet (*ahadith*; singular *hadith*) relate to proper law.

The third source is a consensus of Muslims (*ijma*), which may not even have a modern application, although it was for centuries an important source of law during the formation and development of Islamic law. In the modern world, the closest analogy to *ijma* may be the view of a majority of Muslim scholars, the practice of the majority of Muslim nations or the general principles of law practised and endorsed by Islamic societies.

In practice, Islamic scholars cite more than 12 sources of Islamic law.[68] These include the two primary sources (Quran and Sunna), and more than ten secondary sources. The secondary sources are: *ijma*,[69] *qiyas*,[70] the Islamic law version of equity (fairness) (*istihsan*),[71] consideration of public interests (*masaleh mursalah*),[72] custom and usage (*urf*),[73] presumption of continuity (*istishab*), blocking the means (*sadd al-dharai*) and personal reasoning of Muslim scholars (*ijtihad*).

It is notable that certain Islamic law principles relating to areas such as marriage and divorce, inheritance and criminal law are based on primary sources of Islamic law, particularly the text of the Quran.[74] Many other modern legal subjects, however, including corporate law, communications law, environmental and resources law, administrative law and immigration law, are regulated by modern law made by states and parliaments in Muslim countries.[75] Except in Saudi Arabia and Iran, in almost all the other Muslim countries the majority of legal rules are based on modern regulations. Iran and Saudi Arabia are the only countries whose legal system is claimed to be based on religious sources.[76]

Akin to any other legal system, over the last 15 centuries Islamic law has developed its own characteristics, specific sources, methodology and theories. Islamic law is not static, and has been developing over centuries through the works of jurists, judges, and states. The body of law known as Islamic jurisprudence (*fiqh*) and Sharia is, in effect, much more than the specific divine law as revealed to the Prophet Mohammad in the verses of the Quran.[77] Therefore, the proposition that Islamic law is purely divine law is not entirely accurate. Islamic law may have originated from divine sources as revealed in the revelations to the Prophet Mohammad, but most of its legal principles, as currently practised, were developed over centuries of time through the works of Muslim jurists and Muslim authorities. According to Hallaq, 'modern scholarship in the West as well as in the Muslim East, has drawn a line of separation between the legal pillars of religion and the rest of fiqh, regarding the former as "merely" ritualistic, pertaining to the "private sphere" of religious belief, and the latter as constituting the law "proper"'.[78] On this analysis, many Islamic legal principles may be, and indeed need to be, the subject of further critical evaluation without challenging the sacredness of law or the sovereignty of government.

5. THEORIES OF STATE IN ISLAMIC LAW

The rule of law requires the involvement of the state.[79] In the Western legal tradition, the rule of law holds the state accountable to its citizens. Islamic theories of state trend in the opposite direction: to bolster the power of the state and its leaders, rather than upholding the rights of its citizens. An understanding of the traditional theories of state, as well as their modern versions, will assist in the consideration of the conditions that will need to be met for the implementation of a rule of law system in Muslim countries.

Generally, in an Islamic state, God is considered as the sovereign law-maker,[80] as well as the ultimate legislator[81] and the final judge.[82] The application of Sharia, as the law made by God, the interpretation of its legal principles, the role of the rulers and the method of solving disputes between people in the absence of God's prophets, however, has been the subject of various legal and political theories. In the history of Islam both Sunni and Shia scholars have offered different theories of state and law. The two major theories are caliphate, the major Sunni jurisprudence theory of state and governance, and *Imamat*, the Shia jurisprudence theory of state and governance. Scholars from both theories have developed a variety of interpretations of state and governance ranging from strict, inflexible views on the state to interpretations that are more compatible with a limited democratic concept of the state.

A. Sunni Jurisprudence

The essential principle of an Islamic state is that the state is based on the sovereignty of God. The Sunni theory of state is based on the doctrine of caliphate. Under this theory Sharia law binds a caliph, but they still have extensive power in running the affairs of the society. According to some scholars the primary obligation of the caliph is to implement Divine law, and the leader is called 'the Deputy of God' (*Khalifat Allah*). The caliph rules the society based on the sovereignty of God, and hence is answerable to God only. Most Sunni Muslim scholars argue that a caliph is not able to be removed from power except in exceptional circumstances, such as neglecting one of the essentials of Islam. Most of pre-modern Islamic history is based on the Islamic caliphate system, such as the Righteous Caliphs, the Umayyad dynasty, the Abbasid Caliphates and the Ottoman and Safavid empires. Apart from the early Islamic caliphs (Righteous Caliphs), the majority of other caliphs ruled Islamic societies with absolute authoritarian power.

The theory of caliphate is articulated in two old texts on Islamic constitutional law, which are Abu Yusuf's book (*Kitab al-Kharaj*) and Mawardi's book (*al-Ahkam al-Sultaniyah*). Abu Yusuf (d. 798 AD) sought to lay down fundamental principles of Islamic taxation law and argued that caliphs are deputies of God on earth (*wolat al-amr fi ardhihi*).[83] The text of *Kitab al-Kharaj* considers, to a great extent, the authority of the caliph to be absolute.[84] Later, al-Mawardi (1058 AD) articulated the theory of the caliphate state in Islam, arguing that caliphs should have the required knowledge to interpret and apply the law of Islam.[85]

Although it can be said that the theory of the caliphate is the dominant theory of state under Sunni jurisprudence, it is not a unified concept. There are different sub-theories in relation to state and government in Islam, both in traditional and modern sources.[86]

Under the Sunni theory of the caliphate, the caliph, or the Islamic state, obtains its legitimacy from the divine law on behalf of God and his Prophet. According to the twelfth-century Sunni Hanbali scholar, Ibn Al-Jawzi, a leading Sunni scholar with a strict view on the nature of an Islamic state, 'the Caliph represents God as His deputy over the land and people and applies the laws and orders of God as they were performed by the Prophet'.[87] Under this theory the caliph has all the powers of making law (to the extent it is not inconsistent with the Quran and Sunna),[88] application of the law, and dispute settlements. In practice, all of the Islamic caliphs throughout history (Umayyad, Abbasid, Ottoman, Mughals, Persians, among others) have followed the path of holding absolute law-making, judicial and executive powers without being responsible to any other power.

Islamic law, however, is not a system produced or developed by the state. During the early stages of development of Islamic law during the lifetime of the Prophet Mohammad (610–633 AD), Islamic law was developed in a way that was very similar to common law, based upon either revelation or the decisions and sayings of the Prophet, in most cases in response to a specific legal question. After the Prophet, and particularly since the development of the major schools of Islamic law in the ninth century, Muslim scholars and jurists developed Islamic law.[89] Since the beginnings of Islam there have always been differences between theoretical developments in Islamic law by Muslim jurists, and the application of Islamic law by Islamic states.

Both traditional and modern Sunni scholars have provided the basis for more rational interpretations of the nature of an Islamic state. For example, according to Ibn Taymiyah (the famous traditional Hanbali jurist of the fourteenth century) the caliph does not have the authority of the Prophet and God in law-making or the application of Islamic law.[90] Other famous Sunni jurists have articulated ideas and principles that limit the role of the caliph and the Islamic state. Ghazali,[91] Mawardi,[92] Ibn Khaldun[93] and Shah Wali Allah[94] are among the famous Sunni jurists who have espoused rational political thoughts throughout the history of Islam.

B. Shia Jurisprudence

The theory of state under Shia jurisprudence is generally based on the doctrine of *Imamat*. Imam literally means 'the leader', but in Islamic jurisprudence '*Imamat*' is taken to mean the continuity of the rules of the Prophet based on the Sharia. There are a number of differences between the theory of *Imamat* under Shia jurisprudence and the theory of caliphate under Sunni jurisprudence. While both theories consider the imam or caliph to be the Deputy of the Prophet, ruling on behalf of God, a *shura* (council of Muslims) elects the caliph, whereas the Prophet himself appointed the imam. In the modern world the two theories are much closer.

In Shia Islamic jurisprudence, similar to Sunni, there are various theories about the nature and concept of the Islamic state.[95] One theory of the Islamic state is *Velayat Faghih*, which the Constitution of Iran has adopted.[96] In the nineteenth century Mulla Ahmad Naraghi first articulated the theory of *Velayat Faghih* in Islamic Shia jurisprudence.[97] Under this theory there must be a government that applies the divine law, and the head of state must be a learned Islamic scholar (*faqih*) and shall have certain personal characteristics, such as being just and pious.[98]

C. Islamic Theories of State in a Modern Context

There is no concept of the modern nation-state in Islamic jurisprudence. Traditionally, the state and government were considered within a single, unified political community of believers, known as 'the Muslim nation' or '*ummah*'. Like the legal theories of ancient Rome and medieval Christendom the Islamic concept of state was based on the 'theory of a universal state'.[99] In practice, however, apart from the unified Medina state, headed by the Prophet himself and the early stages of Umayyad and Abbasid dynasties, autonomous and later independent Islamic self-ruled entities and governments existed within the Muslim world. In any case, in the Islamic legal and jurisprudence texts the necessity of an Islamic state is emphasized and the state is endowed with great power. The rulers in both Sunni and Shia theories of state are empowered with extensive legal authority. For example, the founder of the Islamic Republic of Iran, Ayatollah Khomeini, on 7 January 1988 made a statement in which he asserted that the Islamic state enjoyed absolute power, similar to the power of the Prophet Mohammad, and was able to take all necessary measures, even to restrict certain 'pillars of Islam' such as prayer (*salat*), fasting and the *hajj* in special circumstances.[100]

None of the theories of states (*Imamat* in the Shia school, and caliphate in the Sunni school) are feasible in the modern world, with the international system of sovereign nation-states. As Majid Khadduri articulated, 'Islam was neither the first nor the last of the nations that sought to establish a world public order based on divine legislation'.[101] However, exclusive control of the whole, or a major part of the world, is not achievable, and given the nature of human societies, should not be contemplated. What may be achievable, and desirable, is that states and governments be subject to the rule of law.

6. ISLAMIC LAW PRINCIPLES DEVELOPED IN MEETING MODERN SOCIO-ECONOMIC CHALLENGES

Although Islamic law, in comparison with common law and modern civil law systems, may be underdeveloped, it is not frozen. As outlined earlier, the legal system of Islam has developed many extra-textual legal principles such as analogy (*qiyas*, analogical reasoning), equity or juristic preference (*istihsan*), public policy (*masaleh mursaleh*), presumptions of continuity (*istishab*), blocking the means (*sadd al-dharai*) and legal reasoning (*ijtihad*).

Various juristic schools have developed and diverse interpretations of law and religion have been promulgated throughout the history of Islam. While Islam provides certain fixed principles and limited sources of law, public policy and expediency played an important role during the time of the Prophet, Righteous Caliphs and other caliphates throughout the history of Islam.

In Muslim societies and countries today many legal principles are based on these considerations. The role of public policy and expediency is evident in the original sources of Islamic law, such as the Quran and the Sunna, as well as in some secondary sources of law, such as consideration of public interests (*masaleh mursalah*), custom (*urf*) and personal reasoning of learned Muslim scholars (*ijtihad*). According to Al-Ghazali, the objective of law is to protect five essential values: religion, life, intellect, lineage and property; and public policy consideration (*masaleh*) protects those values.[102] After the Prophet, the establishment of certain legal principles and institutions, such as imposing taxes on agricultural products, issuing currency and calendars, and establishing prisons, was based on *masaleh* and expediency. The majority of Muslim scholars consider that *masaleh* is a proper ground for legislation in an Islamic legal system.[103]

One important concept, which unfortunately has not been developed well in the Islamic legal system, is the doctrine of '*sadd al-dharai*'. This term literally means 'blocking the means'. The doctrine could potentially make Islamic law more flexible, by allowing the legislature in an Islamic state to prohibit certain acts that may facilitate evil. In other words, the state may provide precautionary regulations in order to avoid an evil or the commission of crime. Even certain lawful behaviours may be prescribed unlawful because they may lead to the commission of illegal acts. This doctrine, which traditionally placed limits on the law-making power of the state,[104] could be used to limit the power of the state in imposing harsh sets of rules on the society. Although in practice this doctrine can be used to expand the power of the state in imposing rigid rules upon a society, it gives flexibility to an Islamic legislature in the making and unmaking of legal rules. A practical example of the application of '*sadd al-dharai*' is the prohibition of private meetings (*khalwa*) between members of the opposite sex, in order to reduce the risk of sexual assault and *zinar*. Details of the doctrine are well discussed in Islamic jurisprudence textbooks, and are part of the principles of Islamic jurisprudence (*usul al-fiqh*).[105]

Although there has been strong emphasis on the divine aspects of an Islamic state, from the early history of Islam people have always had a role to play in an Islamic state. The Prophet of Islam always invited people to swear allegiance (*bay'a*) to him, and the first few caliphs of the earliest Islamic state came into power after people swore allegiance to them. In addition to *bay'a*, a number of key traditional Islamic concepts and institutions, such as consultation (*shura*) with people by the rulers, consensus (*ijma*) of Islamic scholars, reinterpretation (*ijtihad*) of religious rules and expediency (*maslahah*), may be used to establish Islamic forms of parliamentary democracy, representative elections and other civil society institutions.[106] Some modern reformers even argue that the caliphate system should be put aside in favour of other forms of government. According to Ali Abd al-Raziq:

> Muslims are free to demolish this worn-out system (of the caliphate) before which they have debased and humiliated themselves. They are free to establish the bases of their kingdom and the organization of their state according to more recent conceptions of the human spirit and according to the principles of government whose excellence and firmness have been consecrated by the experience of the nations.[107]

Fathi Osman has also observed that 'the head of a contemporary Muslim state can be elected directly by the people, or by the parliamentary representatives of the people, or can be nominated by those representatives as a candidate for or against whom the public then vote'.[108] For example, in the contemporary Muslim world, elements of democracy can be found in Indonesia, Malaysia and Turkey, among other countries. Potentially, Sharia law may accommodate many characteristics of a rule of law system. Given the discourse of the Muslim world on democracy, the rule of law and civil society, such a concept may be developed theoretically as well as in practice.

Ijtihad is one of the most important concepts in Islam and Islamic law. Its origin goes back to the earliest stage of Islam, when the Prophet

Mohammad sent one of his Companions (Maa'dh Ibn Jabal) to an area and asked him to make decisions on facts and disputes based on the Quran and the Sunna, and if he could not find the answer in either the Quran or the Sunna, to apply his own reasoning to determine the solution. After the death of the Prophet, Muslims were left with the Quran and the sayings of the Prophet, which took the form of oral statements for around 200 years after his death, before being written down. The first hadith book was written by Ahmad Ibn Hanbal (d. 855 AD), and was entitled *Al-Musnad*. The caliphs after the Prophet, and his Companions, cautiously employed *ijtihad*, which literally means 'seeking through hard work' or 'striving'; however, it is defined as exertion by *mujtahid* (learned scholars who employ *ijtihad*) in order to infer the rules of Sharia from its original textual sources (the Quran and the Sunna). According to Kamali, '*ijtihad* is a creative and comprehensive intellectual effort by qualified individuals and groups to derive the juridical ruling on a given issue from the sources of the Sharia in the context of the prevailing circumstances of society'.[109] The process of *ijtihad* after the death of the Prophet was exercised by the caliphs and, in a limited way, by the Companions of the Prophet. In Shia school, imams had a special status to interpret the Quran and state the rules of Sharia. When the Umayyad dynasty was overthrown by the Abbasids in the mid-eighth century, a space for Islamic scholarship developed within the conflict between the two dynasties. The dynastic rulers were no longer able to control the actions of their subjects as tightly, and Islamic scholarship flourished. Islamic scholars were able to use and develop *ijtihad* to create the body of Islamic jurisprudence (*fiqh*). During this period, four schools of Sunni *fiqh* and the Shia school of *fiqh* were developed. Four distinct Muslim jurists (Ahmad Ibn Hanbal, Malik Ibn Anas, Mohammad Ibn Idris Shafi'i and Abu Hanifah) of Sunni Islam developed the juristic schools of Hanbali, Maliki, Shafi'i and Hanafi. At the same time, Ja'afar Ibn Mohammad developed the Shia school of law, known as Ja'afari. For centuries, and indeed, until the present day, these major schools have dominated the areas of *fiqh* and Islamic law. These five jurists, known as 'imams', have dominated the Islamic jurisprudence as Plato and Aristotle dominated science and philosophy in the West, for centuries. However, it must be noted that, although they created schools of thought, and the caliphate institution tried to limit and confine development of Islamic law, within those schools, the gate of *ijtihad* was not really closed. Upon the death of those great jurists, their disciples employed *ijtihad* and contributed to the development of Islamic jurisprudence and law. For example, Mohammad Ibn Al-Khasan Al-Shaybani (d. 805 AD), was a pupil of Abu Hanifah and significantly employed *ijtihad* to produce his opus *Al-kharaj*. He contributed to the development of international relations and international law. Shaybani is known as the founder of international relations and law in the Muslim world.[110]

Great Muslim scholars used legal reasoning of *ijtihad* and contributed significantly to the development of Islamic jurisprudence (*fiqh*), Islamic philosophy, theology and theosophy, among many other areas of scholarship. These include Ghazali (philosopher, jurist and Sufi), al-Shawkani, Razi (Quranic scholar and philosopher), Ibn Rushd (Averroes; philosopher, theologian and jurist), Mawardi (public law scholar), Ibn Sina (Avicenna; Muslim philosopher and scholar), Rumi (philosopher and Sufi) and Ibn Taymiyah (*faqih*). More recently, Afghani, Abd al-Wahhab Khallaf, Mohammad Abduh, Mohammad Rashid Rida, Mohammad Iqbal and Hasbi Ash-Shiddieqy are among the notable Muslim scholars to have employed *ijtihad* in re-interpretations of Islamic teachings and law.

Ijtihad was developed as a method of finding solutions to contemporary issues based on the sources of Islamic jurisprudence, and the major goals and principles of Islam. It created an environment of discussion and exchange of ideas within various Islamic societies and schools of thought. The institution of *ijtihad* played an important role in the flourishing of the Islamic civilization which was pre-eminent in science and scholarship for centuries, in the Middle East, Asia and even Europe, until about 1500 AD. However from the sixteenth century the Islamic civilization weakened and Western civilization advanced, resulting in the increasing conservatism of Muslim societies and the consequent weakening of the institution of *ijtihad*.[111] From around the early seventeenth century, up to the early twentieth century, the Muslim world went through a dismal stage and the development of Islamic law froze. During the colonization of many parts of the Muslim world, the application of Islamic law was limited to Muslim personal law.

It can be said that *ijtihad* can be classified in three stages. The traditional *ijtihad*, which originated from the time of the Prophet Mohammad, flourished during the development of Sunni and Shia schools of jurisprudence (eighth to ninth centuries). The second stage started from around the ninth century and continued up to the early nineteenth century, during which time the four Sunni schools of law dominated the institution of *ijtihad*. The most recent stage, the new *ijtihad*, appeared in the late nineteenth to early twentieth centuries. The new *ijtihad* developed a methodology which is largely free of classical juristic interpretation.[112] Notable examples of *mujtahid*s who exercised new *ijtihad* are Shah Waliallah, Mohammad Taha and Mohammad Iqbal. Shah Waliallah argued that the Prophet of Islam never intended to universally apply a legal system that was designed for a specific society at a specific point in time (specifically, Arabia of the sixth century). Rather he established a system and urged Muslims to follow his principles in establishing their own system of rules within the general spirit of Islam.[113] Taha developed a methodology by which he argued that the Quran was revealed to the Prophet Mohammad in two stages: in Mecca and in Medina. The verses revealed to the Prophet in Mecca were the foundation of Islam and captured the spirit of Islam, and must be followed by all Muslims. The verses of the Quran that were later revealed when the Prophet had travelled to Medina, relating to legal matters, were revealed for the purpose of governing Medina. They applied to the particular facts and situations confronting the Prophet at that time and do not have universal application in all places and all times.[114] Iqbal articulated his legal reasoning around his area of expertise, philosophy. He argued that, by the completion of the religion of Islam, and the termination of the prophetic missions (Mohammad as the last Prophet), human beings had reached a stage of maturity and wisdom in which they could develop legal systems based on their reasoning and experience, including religious experience.[115] Several Muslim scholars (such as Abu Zeid and Soroush) employ *ijtihad* further, analysing the root of Islam, and interpreting the revelation (*wahy*). This was discussed above in this chapter.

Ijtihad, as a legal institution and a source of Islamic law, played an important role in the development of Islamic jurisprudence and law. It remains the most important mechanism for law reform under Islamic law.

7. HUMAN RIGHTS AND JUSTICE

Under the substantial theory of the rule of law, human rights and justice are important aspects of the rule of law system. Even proponents of the formal conception of the rule of law consider that there is a necessary relationship between human rights and the rule of law. According to Joseph Raz, 'civil rights' are an indispensable component of the rule of law system.[116] Ronald Dworkin considers the protection of moral rights to be part of the rule of law.[117] According to the United Nations' definition of the rule of law, it is expected that a legal system based on the rule of law should observe human rights principles and apply justice.[118]

The relationship between Islamic law and human rights and justice has been the subject of lengthy discussion during the last half-century. There is also an extensive literature both in European languages (for example, in English and French) and in Middle Eastern languages (Arabic, Persian,

Turkish) on human rights in Islam, and in particular, the intersection of human rights with Sharia law. Most of the available literature in Middle Eastern languages, and some of the works in European languages, emphasize the importance of human rights. They argue that principles of human rights are recognized in Islam and its legal system, and to an even greater extent than in the West.[119] In reality, the 15-century long history of Islam and the track record of more than 56 Muslim nations indicate serious inconsistencies with modern principles of human rights.

In order to understand the relationship between Islam, Islamic law and human rights, the definition of the principles of human rights and the specific version of Islam must be considered. Although there are a large number of legal principles for the protection of certain human rights that are applied in the laws of democratic countries and are universally recognized, 'the conceptual structure of human rights is not monolithic; nor human rights themselves hermetically sealed imperatives'.[120] Further, although international law sets out principles in a number of international human rights instruments, such as the Universal Declaration of Human Rights 1948,[121] there has been more emphasis on civil and political rights, rather than social and cultural rights. Concepts like cultural relativity, human responsibility and the universality or locality of human rights have been the subject of both scholarly and practical debate in recent years. Nonetheless, there are a large number of national and international legal principles concerning the protection of human rights, which are fairly universally recognized. Notable among these rights are: rights to life, liberty and security of person; equality before the law; protection from arbitrary arrest and detention; right to a fair and public hearing; freedom of opinion and expression; and gender equality.[122]

Under historical Sharia, or traditional Islam, human rights are not the central focus of the system. Sharia emphasizes religious and divine duties (*taklif*).[123] According to Mohsen Kadivar, true human rights in the traditional version of Islam are reduced to the religious duties of Muslims towards God and others.[124] Majid Khaddouri stated that 'human rights in Islam, as prescribed by the divine law, are the privilege only of the persons of full legal capacity. A person with full legal capacity is a living human being of mature age, free, and of Moslem [sic] faith'.[125] The term 'rights' in Arabic (and in Persian) is *haqq*, which literally means truth and reality. It has been said that *haqq* means 'duty as well as right, obligation as well as claim, law as well as justice'.[126] Under Islam human rights are observed only if directly related to the responsibilities that people have towards God.[127]

The issue of human rights and Islam is one of the most contentious areas of Islamic law, and is an important consideration in contemplating an Islamic rule of law system. As stated by some prominent Muslim and Western scholars, the fundamental principles underlying modern human rights in the West are substantially different to the notion of rights (*haqq*) and responsibility (*taklif*) in Islam.[128]

A rule of law system in the Muslim world requires an interpretation and approach to the law of Islam that is consistent with international human rights law. Principles of human rights, as adopted by international instruments, can be introduced in the Muslim world in two ways. One way is the introduction of human rights principles into the legal systems of Muslim countries, by introducing human rights principles into the constitutions of almost all Muslim countries or enacting legislation. In this way, international pressure and regular monitoring of the observation of human rights by the relevant agencies and institutions of the United Nations will be applied to ensure the implementation of international human rights rules.

A second way, and a better option, is for the Muslim world to adopt and institutionalize universal principles of human rights within the legal system of Islam. This will be feasible because of the potential rational approaches of Islamic law and because of the existence of diversity, both in the history of Muslim civilization and within contemporary Muslim societies. Nonetheless, Abdolkarim Soroush articulated that Muslim societies must change the nature of their culture to become societies where people know and demand their rights (*mohiq* people), rather than remaining in societies where people are only bound by obligations or responsibility (*mukallaf* people).[129]

8. CHANGES FROM WITHIN: THE IMPLEMENTATION OF A RULE OF LAW-BASED SYSTEM IN MUSLIM COUNTRIES

Sharia, the legal system of Islam, is a religious system, which is unique in its nature, in that Islam was never a purely spiritual religion. The law of Islam or Sharia from its early stage has gone through gradual change and has adopted a limited number of rational principles and methods of reasoning. The result of this has been that logic, philosophy and legal reasoning have entered into the study and development of law, within what is essentially a religious system. Can a modern rule of law system, as developed in the Western world, be effectively imported in Muslim countries? Or alternatively, could a rational legal system embedding a rule of law-based system be gradually developed within the general framework of the Islamic legal system? The sudden introduction of secular law into the Muslim world as happened after the collapse of the Ottoman Empire and during colonization may not be the answer.

Professor Seyed Hossein Nasr makes an interesting point that may generate valuable debate. He states that prior to the early twentieth century there was much harmony in Muslim countries between Sharia and non-divine law (*qanun*).[130] He then argues that the forced implementation of European legal systems in Muslim countries such as Egypt, Turkey and Iran created 'a tension between private religious life and the public domain and drew the majority of the population further away from their governments which they began to view as anti-Islamic'.[131] Nasr's argument suggests that if modern European legal principles had not been introduced into the legal systems of the Muslim world, the Islamic world would have attempted serious reforms on its own, and changed the Sharia legal system. The experience of Saudi Arabia, however, the only Muslim country where European legal principles were never introduced, does not support Professor Nasr's argument, because the tension there between the government and the people is similar to that in many other parts of the Muslim world. Furthermore, the introduction of Sharia in Pakistan in 1978 by General Mohammad Zia-ul-haq did nothing to reduce the gap between the moderate sub-continent nation and its mainly military government. Indeed, it fueled tensions that still continue today. Similarly, the introduction of a comprehensive Sharia system in Iran in 1979 did not reduce tensions in that Islamic state.[132]

There is no doubt that there have been sudden introductions of foreign legal systems into the Muslim world and that they have caused tensions. These tensions could be argued to be a factor in the rise of Islamic fundamentalism and calls for a 'pure' Sharia-based legal system, and the complete rejection of other modern legal influences. It is arguable that a rule of law system and a flexible pluralistic Sharia system may be able to co-exist, given the strengths and positive potential of Sharia legal system. These strengths include: Sharia's long tradition of pluralism in adopting other cultures' ideas; its elaboration of fundamental protective principles (including the limitations on arbitrary detention, and prevention of retrospective laws, among others); and its reflection of potential Sharia-derived human rights principles. It should be noted, however, that generally Islamic law emphasizes the obligations of individuals, rather than rights. Another challenge is that, in modern times, we do not have a practical example of such a system.

9. CONCLUSION

The meaning and the nature of law in the West are the subject of different legal theories developed over many centuries. Greek philosophers such as Plato and Aristotle and Christian scholars and legal jurists in the West have developed legal theories to define the 'law' and justify the validity and legitimacy of law. In the Western legal tradition all aspects of the law, particularly its sources and authorities, are subject to critical examination. While rule of law institutions such as an independent judiciary, legal profession and free press are strong in Europe, North America, Australia and many other countries, these institutions are weak or non-existent in the majority of Muslim countries, particularly in the Middle East.

In the Muslim world scholarly debates and legal theories were mainly concerned with interpretation of Islamic texts (particularly the Quran), but some examples of deep juristic debates on the nature of law and its philosophy do exist in the history of Islamic legal theory. The *Mutazila* debate of early Muslim history is the most important of the scholarly debates on the nature and philosophy of Islamic law. However, in more recent times the nature of law and the supremacy of law have entered Islamic jurisprudence and legal theory. Both Muslim and Western scholars have examined the nature of the Quran, the revelation and divine law, and other aspects of the nature of law in Islam in the twentieth century.

As this chapter has discussed, the legal system of Islam may be less developed in some areas and there are significant inconsistencies between Islamic law and many modern legal principles, particularly in relation to human rights. It is arguable, however, that Islamic law, given its strengths and positive potential, can be further developed and modernized to meet the new requirements of Muslim societies. These strengths include: Sharia's long tradition of pluralism in adopting other cultures' ideas and legal principles; its elaboration of fundamental protective principles (including the limitations on arbitrary detention, and prevention of retrospective laws, among others); and its reflection of potential Sharia-derived human rights principles. It should be noted, however, that generally, Islamic law emphasizes the obligations of individuals rather than rights. We also lack the demonstration value of a Sharia-informed rule of law system, as no such country exists at present.

The rule of law, as a vital aspect of stable and continuing democracies, is being adopted as an essential component of many countries' national and international policies, both in the West and among people who are struggling for democracy in the developing world. The rule of law could be implemented in the Middle East and the Muslim world using Islamic principles and modern and universal legal principles. While the exact nature of a rule of law system based on Islamic law principles may not be clear, it is arguable that, given the discourse of the Muslim world on democracy, civil rights and the rule of law, a rule of law concept may be developed in the Muslim world, both in theory and in practice in the future. This process must be gradual and may take decades and generations. A limited 'rule of law' system based on reformed and rationalized principles of Sharia may be established in the Middle Eastern and Muslim countries, but it must be developed from within and it will be slow and gradual.

NOTES

1. According to H.L.A. Hart, in Western jurisprudence and Western legal theories, the question, 'what is law' is indeed a puzzle. See H.L.A. Hart, *Essay In Jurisprudence and Philosophy* (Oxford University Press, Oxford, 1983), 5.
2. Literature on Islamic law is extensive in English, other European languages and in major Middle Eastern languages (Arabic, Persian and Turkish). Some of the best authorities on Islamic law in English, where the nature of law is discussed are: Noel Coulson, *A History of Islamic Law* (Edinburgh University Press, Edinburgh, 1964); Joseph Schacht, *An Introduction to Islamic Law* (Clarendon Press, Oxford, 1964): J.N.D. Anderson, *Islamic Law in the Modern World* (Greenwood Press, Westport, CT, 1959); Wael Hallaq, *Sharia: Theory, Practice, Transformation* (Cambridge University Press, Cambridge, 2009); Syed Ameer Ali, *The Spirit of Islam* (Kessinger Publishing, Whitefish, MT, first published 1891, 2003 edn); Asaf A.A. Fyzee, *Outlines of Mohammadan Law* (Tahir Mahmood (ed.), Oxford University Press, Oxford, 2008); Peri Bearman et al., *The Islamic School of Law* (Islamic Legal Studies Program, Harvard Law School, Boston, MA, 2005); Ignaz Goldziher, *Introduction to Islamic Theology and Law* (Andreas Hamari and Ruth Hamari (trans.), Princeton University Press, Princeton, NJ, 1981); Majid Khadduri, *War and Peace in the Law of Islam* (John Hopkins Unuiversity Press, Baltimore, MD, 1955); Bernard Weiss, *The Spirit of Islamic Law* (University of Georgia Press, Georgia, 1998); Sami Zubaida, *Law and Power in the Islamic World* (I.B. Tauris, London, 2003).
3. See for example, Peter Cane, Carloyn Evans and Zoe Robinson (eds), *Law and Religion in Theoretical Context* (Cambridge University Press, Cambridge, 2008).
4. On the definition of the 'rule of law' see Joseph Raz, 'The Rule of Law and its Virtue' (1977) 39 *Law Quarterly Review* 195; John Finnis, *Natural Law and Natural Rights* (Clarendon Press, Oxford, 1980), Chapter 10; Cheryl Saunders and Katherine Le Roy, 'Perspectives on the Rule of Law' in Cheryl Saunders and Katherine Le Roy (eds), *The Rule of Law* (Federation Press, Annandale, New South Wales, 2003); Matthew Kramer, 'On the Moral of the Rule of Law' (2004) 63 *Cambridge Law Journal*; Margaret Radin, 'Reconsidering the Rule of Law' (1989) 69 *Boston University Law Review* 781; Murray Gleeson, *The Rule of Law and the Constitution* (ABC Books, Sydney, 2000); Brian Tamanaha, *On the Rule of Law: History, Politics and Theory* (Cambridge University Press, Cambridge, 2004); David Clark, 'The Many Meanings of the Rule of Law' in Kanishka Jayasuriya (ed.), *Law,*

Capitalism and Power in Asia (Routledge, London, 1999), 28; and Richard Bellamy (ed.) *The Rule of Law and the Separation of Powers* (Ashgate, Aldershot, 2005).

5. On positivist theories of law see Jeremy Bentham, *Of Laws in General* (Athlone Press, London, 1970); John Austin, *The Province of Jurisprudence Determined and the Uses of the Study of Jurisprudence* (Westfield and Nicolson, London, 1954); James Harries, *Law and Legal Science* (Oxford University Press, Oxford, 1982); Hans Kelsen, *The Pure Theory of Law* (1967); Hans Kelsen, *General Theory of Law and State* (Univesity of California Press, Berkeley, CA, 1961). On natural law theory see Thomas Aquinas, *Summa Theologica* (Typographia Senatus, Rome, 1947); Thomas Hobbes, *Leviathan* (Penguin Books, Harmondsworth, 1651); John Locke, *Two Treatises of Government* (J.M. Dent, London, 1689–1690); Lon Fuller, *The Morality of Law* (Yale University Press, New Haven, CT, 1969); John Finnis, *Natural Law and Natural Rights* (Clarendon Press, Oxford, 1980); Robert George, *Natural Law: International Library of Essays in Law and Legal Theory* (Ashgate, Aldershot, 1991). On other modern theories of law see Evgeny Pashukanis, *Law and Marxism: A General Theory* (Transaction Publishers, Piscataway, NJ, 1978); H.L.A. Hart, 'Scandinavian Realism' (1959) 17(2) *Cambridge Law Journal* 233; Roscoe Pound, 'The Call for a Realist Jurisprudence' (1931) 44 *Harvard Law Review* 697; Katharine Bartlett, 'Feminist Legal Method' (1970) 103 *Harvard Law Review* 829; John Rawls, *A Theory of Justice* (Clarendon Press, Oxford, 1972).
6. For further discussion on the rule of law and its potential application in the Muslim world, see Hossein Esmaeili, 'The Nature and Development of Law in Islam and the Rule of Law Challenge in the Middle East and the Muslim World' (2011) 26(2) *Connecticut Journal of International Law* 329; and Hossein Esmaeili, 'On a Slow Boat Towards the Rule of Law: The Nature of Law in the Saudi Arabian Legal System' (2009) 26(1) *Arizona Journal of International and Comparative Law* 1.
7. The term 'Sharia' in Islamic literature is used in several different ways: in one sense, Sharia is used against '*tariqa*'. *Tariqa* refers to the mystical aspect of Islam and the practice of religious rituals. Sharia also refers to religious knowledge. Sharia may also be used in a general sense to refer to Islamic jurisprudence (*fiqh*), including all Islamic rules, rituals and law. In Western literature, it is specifically used to refer to the legal system of Islam. For an analysis of the meaning of Sharia, *fiq* and *tariqa* see Abdullah Saeed, *Islamic Thought: An Introduction* (Routledge, London, 2006), 43–5, Chapter 6.
8. While some Islamic scholars have argued that the nature of religion as revealed to the Prophet of Islam must be distinguished from the practice of Muslim societies, a more persuasive view is that 'Islam' in the contemporary world has come to mean the understanding and practice by Muslims of their religion. See Shirin Ebadi, 'Advancing the Consensus: 60 Years of the Universal Declaration of Human Rights: Keynote Address: Islam, Human Rights, and Iran' (2009) 23 *Emory International Law Review* 13, 17; Riffat Hassan, 'On Human Rights and the Qur'anic Perspectives' (1982) 19 *Journal of Economical Studies* 51; An'Naim, *Islam and the Secular State* (Harvard University Press, Cambridge, MA, 2008), 111.
9. See Noel Coulson, *A History of Islamic Law* (Edinburgh University Press, Edinburgh, 1964), 102; Wael Hallaq, *A History of Islamic Legal Theories* (Cambridge University Press, Cambridge, 1997), 202; Reza Afshari, 'An Essay on Islamic Cultural Relativism in Discourse of Human Rights' (1994) 16 *Human Rights Quarterly* 235, 271; Mohammad Hashim Kamali, *Principles of Islamic Jurisprudence*, 3rd edn (Islamic Texts Society, Cambridge, 2003), 229.
10. *Fiqh*, which is understanding of Sharia and the method of inferring legal and non-legal (such as moral and ethical) principles from Islamic textual and non-textual sources, is translated in English to 'Islamic jurisprudence'. Although not an accurate translation, it has been widely adopted in English Islamic legal literature.

There is some overlap between the concepts of *fiqh* and jurisprudence (legal theory); however, Islamic legal theory is more a subject of Islamic philosophy, which has been disliked by most Muslim jurists (*foqaha*).

11. For example, Kamali's book in English on 'Principles of Islamic Jurisprudence' has nothing to do with legal theory in the Western sense: Mohammad Hashim Kamali, *Principles of Islamic Jurisprudence*, 3rd edn (Islamic Texts Society, Cambridge, 2003).
12. See for example, Noel Coulson, *Conflict and Tension in Islamic Jurisprudence* (University of Chicago Press, Chicago, IL, 1969); Wael Hallaq, *Sharia: Theory, Practice, Transformation* (Cambridge University Press, Cambridge, 2009); Bernard Weiss, *The Spirit of Islamic Law* (University of Georgia Press, Georgia, 1998); Frank Griffel, 'The Harmony of Natural Law and Shari'a in Islamist Theology' in Abbas Amanat and Frank Griffel (eds), *Shari'a: Islamic Law in the Contemporary Context* (Stanford University Press, Palo Alto, CA, 2007), 38.
13. See below note 35.
14. See, for example, Ignaz Goldziher, *Introduction to Islamic Theology and Law* (Princeton University Press, Princeton, NJ, 1981); Theodor Nöldeke, *Das Leben Mohammeds* (1863); Noel Coulson, *Conflict and Tension in Islamic Jurisprudence* (University of Chicago, Chicago, IL, 1969); Joseph Schacht, *An Introduction to Islamic Law* (Clarendon Press, Oxford, 1964).
15. Duncan Macdonald, *Development of Muslim Theology, Jurisprudence and Constitutional Theory* (Russell & Russell, Kent, 1965), 66.
16. Abdulaziz Sachedina, 'Theology, Law and the Self-Governance of Religious Communities: Guidance or Governance? A Muslim Conception of "Two-Cities"' (2000) 68 *George Washington Law Review* 1079: 'Islam is a faith in the realm of the public. Sharia, the sacred law of Islam, regulates religious practice with a view to maintaining the individual's well-being through his or her social well-being. Hence, its comprehensive system deals with the obligations that humans perform as part of their relationship with the Divine Being and duties they perform as part of their interpersonal responsibility. Public order must be maintained in worship, in the market place, and all other arenas of human interaction'.
17. Seyyed Hossein Nasr, *Ideals and Realities of Islam* (Praeger, Westport, CT, 1966), 95. According to Imam Khomeini, the founder of the Islamic Republic of Iran, 'Islam has a system and a program for all the different affairs of society: the form of government and administration, the regulation of people's dealings with each other, the relations of state and people, relations with foreign states and all other political and economic matters. The mosque has always been the centre of leadership and command, of examination and analysis of social problems'. Hamid Algari, *Islam and Revolution: Writings and Declarations of Imam Khomeini* (Mizan Press, Berkeley, CA, 1981), 249–50.
18. Al-Amidi, *Al Amidi, Seif Al Din Abi Al Hassan Ali Ibn Abi Ali Ibn Mohammad, Al Ahkam Fi Usul Al Akham [The Principles of Islamic Rules]*, Vol. 1 (Dar Al-Kotob Al-limiyah, Beirut, 2005), 85.
19. Ibn Rushd, *Abu al Walid & Mohammad Ib Ahmed Ibn Mohammad Ibn Ahmed, Bedyat al Mujtahid wa Nihayat al Muqtasid [The Beginning of Jurisprudence]*, Vol. 1 (Dar Al-Kotob Al-limiyah, Beirut, 1988), 5; Duncan McDonald, *Development of Muslim Theology, Jurisprudence and Constitutional Theory* (Scribner, New York, 1965), 73; Wael Hallaq, *A History of Islamic Legal Theories* (Cambridge University Press, Cambridge, 1997); Reuben Levy, *The Social Structure of Islam* (Cambridge University Press, Cambridge, 1969), 202–3.
20. Seyeed al Sabiq, *Fiqh al Sunna [The Sunni Jurisprudence]*, Vol. 3 (Dar al-Fiker, Beirut, 1998), 393.

21. Joseph Schacht, *An Introduction to Islamic Law* (Clarendon Press, Oxford, 1964), 200.
22. Al-Amidi, *Al Amidi, Seif Al Din Abi Al Hassan Ali Ibn Abi Ali Ibn Mohammad, Al Ahkam Fi Usul Al Akham [The Principles of Islamic Rules]*, Vol. 1 (Dar Al-Kotob Al-limiyah, Beirut, 2005), 8.
23. Some scholars, such as Joseph Schacht and Abdulaziz Sachedina, have stated that courts under Sharia may not have jurisdiction in relation to personal acts unless matters of public welfare are involved or there is a claimant. Joseph Schacht, *An Introduction to Islamic Law* (Clarendon Press, Oxford, 1964), 189–90; and Abdulaziz Sachedina, 'Theology, Law and the Self-Governance of Religious Communities: Guidance or Governance? A Muslim Conception of "Two-Cities"' (2000) 68 *George Washington Law Review* 1079. Both Schacht and Sachedina failed to recognize the difference between the concept of crime under Sharia and the requirements of evidence and procedure in trials and sentencing. There is no doubt that, if personal and private acts are not brought to the attention of the court, then no action will be taken. However, the concept of law remains the same. Under Islam a sin is a crime and is punishable even if it is the most private act. According to Islamic jurisprudence (*fiqh*) any sin (*zanb*) for which there is no specific punishment in Sharia is punishable under *ta'zir*. Muslim jurists (*foqaha*) in jurisprudence texts state that *ta'zir* means '*al tadib ala zanben la hadd Fiheh wa la kaffareh*' (*ta'zir* is a punishment applicable to a sin for which there is no punishment or expiation): see Seyeed al Sabiq, *Fiqh al Sunna [The Sunni Jurisprudence]*, Vol. 3 (Dar al-Fiker, Beirut, 1998), 393.
24. Islamic teachings can be divided into four categories namely beliefs, moralities, rituals and non-ritual Sharia which is called jurisprudence of transactions (*fiq al muamilat*): Mohsen Kadivar 'Reconstruction of Wisdom: A Condition for Reconciling Religion and Human Rights', Paper presented at the *Human Rights Conference*, Mofid University, Qom, Iran, 16 May 2007, 6 (unpublished, a copy of the paper (in Persian) is filed with the author).
25. See generally Abdullah Ahmed An Na'im (ed.), *Islamic Family Law in a Changing World: A Global Resource Book* (Zed Books, London, 2002); and Jamal Nasir, *The Islamic Law of Personal Status*, 3rd edn (Brill, Leiden, 2002).
26. *Basic Law of Governance* (Saudi Arabia), Royal Order No. (A/91) 27 Shaban 1412H – 1 March 1992, article 48 states: 'The courts will apply the rules of the Islamic Shari'ah in the cases that are brought before them, in accordance with what is indicated in the Book and the Sunnah, and statutes decreed by the Ruler which do not contradict the Book or the Sunnah'. The text of the Basic Law of Governance is available in English: Kingdom of Saudi Arabia Minister of Foreign Affairs, *Basic Law of Governance*, accessed on 1 March 2012 at: http://www.mofa.gov.sa/Detail.asp?InNewsItemID=35297
27. Those 'who have not the law do by nature what the law requires' (Romans 2:14). However, there are many similarities between Talmudic law and Jewish history, and Islamic law and history. See Bernard Weiss, *The Spirit of Islamic Law* (University of Georgia Press, Georgia, 1998), 2–4.
28. George Mousourakis, *The Historical and Institutional Context of Roman Law* (University of Georgia Press, Georgia, 2003), 418–33.
29. On the history and development of English common law, see William S. Holdsworth, *A History of English Law* (Ashgate, Aldershot, 1922).
30. Seyyed Hossein Nasr, *The Heart of Islam, Enduring Values for Humanity* (Harper, San Francisco, CA, 2000), 117–19.
31. Noel Coulson, *A History of Islamic Law* (Edinburgh University Press, Edinburgh, 1964), 75.

32. Bernard Weiss, *The Spirit of Islamic Law* (University of Georgia Press, Georgia, 1998), 24.
33. See the Quran 26:192–4. See also, for example, Seyyed Hossein Nasr, *Islam: Religion, History and Civilisation* (Harper, San Francisco, CA, 2003), 37, who argues that 'The Quran is the central theophany of Islam, the verbatim Word of God revealed to the Prophet by the archangel Gabriel and transmitted by him in turn to his companions, who both memorized and recorded it'.
34. See Abdullah Saeed, *Islamic Thought: An Introduction* (Routledge, London, 2006), Chapter 2; and Fazlur Rahman, *Islam* (Weidenfeld & Nicolson, London, 1966), Chapter 2.
35. In the history of Islam, there were four theological theories about the nature of sin, God and the Quran. They were *Khavarej* [Kharijits], *Morjayoun* [Murjiites], the Mutazili and the Asharit. The Kharijits had a very extreme interpretation of religion, and their interpretation faded in its early stage. The more moderate position of the Murjiites rejected any relationship between being a Muslim and committing sins. The Mutazili emphasized reason and logic, and the use of rational deduction as tools in interpretation of the Quran. During the theological debate amongst different schools of philosophical thought, the Mutazili took the position that the Quran as the words of God should not be considered literally. In contrast, according to Asharits and scholars such as Ibn Hanbal, the words of the Quran were literal words of Allah and were eternal. See Fazlur Rahman, *Islam* (Weidenfeld & Nicolson, London, 1966), Chapter 5; Abdullah Saeed, *Islamic Thought: An Introduction* (Routledge, London, 2006), Chapter 5; George C. Anawati, 'Philosophy, Theology and Myticism' in Joseph Schacht and Clifford E. Bosworth (eds), *The Legacy of Islam* (Clarendon Press, Oxford, 1974), 350, 359–66. For further discussion of the *mutalizi*, see Nasr Hamid Abu Zayd, *Al-Ittijâh Al-'Aqlî fi al-Tafsîr: Dirâsa fî Qadiyat al-Majâz fi 'l-Qur'ân ind al-Mu'tazila [Rationalism in Interpretation: A Study of the Problem of Metaphor in the Writing of the Mutazilites]* (Al Markaz Al Tahaqafi Al Arabi, Berirut, 1996).
36. On Ahmad ibn Hanbal see Christopher Melchert, *Ahmad ibn Hanbal* (Oneworld, Oxford, 2006).
37. Asghar Ali Engineer, 'On Developing Liberation Theology in Islam' in Ali Engineer (ed.), *Islam and Revolution* (Anjanta Publications, Delhi, 1984), 13, 15.
38. On Shah Waliallah see Mohammad al-Ghazali (ed.), *The Socio-Political Thought of Shah Wali Allah* (International Institute of Islamic Thought and Islamic Research Institute, Islamabad, 2001).
39. Mahmoud Mohamed Taha, *The Second Message of Islam* (Syracuse University Press, Syracuse, NY, 1996).
40. See Allama Mohammad Iqbal, *The Reconstruction of Religious Thought in Islam* (M. Saeed Sheikh (ed.), Iqbal Academy Pakistan and Institute of Islamic Culture, Lahore, 1989).
41. See Abdullahi Ahmad An'Naim, 'Introduction' in Mahmoud Mohamed Taha, *The Second Message of Islam* (Syracuse University Press, Syracuse, NY, 1996).
42. Nasr Hamid Abu Zayd, *Naqd al-Khitâb al-Dînî [Critique of Islamic Discourse]*, 4th edn (Sina lil-Nashr, Cairo, 1998); Nasr Hamid Abu Zayd, *Rethinking the Qur'an: Towards a Humanistic Hermeneutics* (Humanistics University Press, Utrecht, 2004).
43. Abdolkarim Soroush, *Bast Tajrobeh Nabavi [The Expansion of Prophetic Experience]* (Serat, Tehran, 2006); Abdolkarim Soroush, *Bast Tajrobeh Nabavi [The Expansion of Prophetic Experience]* (Nilou Mobasser (ed.), Forough Jahanbakhsh (trans.), Brill, Leiden, 2009).
44. Nasr Hamid Abu Zayd, *Al-Ittijah al-'Aqli fi al-Tafsir: ditasa fi qadiyyat al-magaz fi'l Qur'an 'ind'l Mu'tazilah (The Rational Trend in Exegesis: a study of the problem of metaphor in the Qur'an by the Mu'tazilites)*, 4th edn (Al Markaz Al

Tahaqafi Al Arabi, Beirut,1998); Abdolkarim Soroush, *Bast Tajrobeh Nabavi [The Expansion of Prophetic Experience]* (Serat, Tehran, 2006); Abdolkarim Soroush, *Bast Tajrobeh Nabavi [The Expansion of Prophetic Experience]* (Nilou Mobasser (ed.), Forough Jahanbakhsh (trans.), Brill, Leiden, 2009).

45. Proponents of this approach cite several verses of the Quran in supporting their propositions: Quran, Súra Nisáa 4:82: 'Had it been from other than God, they surely would have found therein much discrepancy', Abdullah Yusuf Ali, *The Qur'an: Text, Translation and Commentary* (Tahrike Tarsile Qur'an, New York, 2005), 205; Quran 12:1: 'these are the words of revelation'; The Quran, Súra Yúsuf 12:2: 'We have sent it down as an Arabic Quran in order that ye may learn wisdom'. Abdullah Yusuf Ali, *The Qur'an: Text, Translation and Commentary* (Tahrike Tarsile Qur'an, New York, 2005), 550.
46. See Nasr Hamid Abu Zayd, *Mafhum al-Nass* (al-Hayah al-Misriyah al-Ammah lil-Kitab, Cairo, 1990).
47. For a discussion of different contemporary views on the revelation of the Quran and an informative discussion of 'revelation' in Islam, see Abdullah Saeed, *Islamic Thought: An Introduction* (Routledge, London, 2006), Chapter 3; see also Abdulla Saeed, 'Fazlur Rahman: A Framework for Interpreting the Ethico-Legal Content of the Quran' in Suha Taji Farouki (ed.) *Modern Muslim Intellectuals and the Quran* (Oxford University Press, The Ismaili Institute of Studies, Oxford, 2004), 37; Akbar Gangi, *Rowshanfekriy Faqihaneh [Jurisprudential Intellectualism]* (unpublished; a copy of the article, in Persian, is filed with the author).
48. 'It is He [God] Who has sent His Apostle with Guidance and the Religion of Truth to proclaim it over all religion' (Quran, Súra Fat-h 48:28). See also Noel Coulson, *A History of Islamic Law* (Edinburgh University Press, Edinburgh, 1964), 75; Seyyed Hossein Nasr, *The Heart of Islam, Enduring Values for Humanity* (Harper, San Francisco, CA, 2002), 1; Abdullah Saeed, *Islamic Thought: An Introduction* (Routledge, Abingdon, 2006), 43; Khaled Abou El Fadl, *Islam and the Challenge of Democracy* (Joshua Cohen and Deborah Chasman (eds), Princeton University Press, Princeton, NJ, 2004), 4.
49. 'Verily, this is My Way, leading straight: follow it: follow not (other) paths'; Quran, Súra An'ám 6:153. Abdullah Yusuf Ali, *The Qur'an: Text, Translation and Commentary* (Tahrike Tarsile Qur'an, New York, 2005), 336.
50. *Qanuni Assassi Jumhuri'I Isla'mai Iran [The Constitution of the Islamic Republic of Iran]* 1358 [1980] (amended 1989), Article 2(1), available at http://www.parstimes.com/law/Iran_law.html
51. Abou al-Ala Maudidi, *The Islamic Law and the Constitution* (Islamic Publications, New Jersey, 1980), 258.
52. An area of Islamic jurisprudence concerned with methodological discussions about words of God, the existence of God and dialectic Islamic philosophy. On *kalam* see Harry A. Wolfson, *The Philosophy of Kalam* (Harvard University Press, Cambridge, MA, 1976).
53. Khaled Abou El Fadl, *Islam and the Challenge of Democracy* (Joshua Cohen and Deborah Chasman (eds), Princeton University Press, Princeton, NJ, 2004), 4–71, 16.
54. *Qanuni Assassi Jumhuri'I Isla'mai Iran [The Constitution of the Islamic Republic of Iran]* 1358 [1980] (amended 1989), Article 56.
55. Khaled Abou El Fadl, 'Islam and the Challenge of Democratic Commitment' (2003–2004) 27(4) *Fordam International Law Journal* 4–71, 16.
56. Khaled Abou El Fadl, *Islam and the Challenge of Democracy* (Joshua Cohen and Deborah Chasman (eds), Princeton University Press, Princeton, NJ, 2004), 4–71, 16.
57. See below note 113.
58. This has been also noted by certain Western commentators, see for example, Joseph Schacht, *An Introduction to Islamic Law* (Clarendon Press, Oxford, 1964), 202.

59. According to Islamic Jurists (*foqaha*), rejecting or casting doubt on rules stated by the Quran or the Sunna in preference for modern positivist rules is considered an example of *kofr* (rejecting Islam by a Muslim) and is a crime under Islamic law as noted by a contemporary Muslim jurist: Seyeed al Sabiq, *Fiqh al Sunna [The Sunni Jurisprudence]*, Vol. 2 (Dar al-Fiker, Beirut, 1998), 304.
60. Iranian Philosopher Abdolkarim Soroush is a contemporary Muslim intellectual whose writing and thoughts are attracting attention in both the Muslim and non-Muslim world. He argues that, if religion plays any role in the public affairs of Muslim society, its legal principles should not be immune from critical evaluation because of the 'sacracy' of religion. See generally: John Cooper, 'The Limits of the Sacred: The Epistemology of Abdolkarim Soroush' in John Cooper et al. (eds), *Islam and Modernity, Muslim Intellectuals Respond* (I.B. Tauris, London, 2000), 38.
61. In the majority of Muslim countries, such as Egypt, Jordan, Kuwait, Bangladesh and Indonesia, only certain areas of Islamic law, such as marriage and divorce, form part of the legal system. In those few countries where Islamic law is the principal component of the legal system, such as Saudi Arabia and Iran, many Islamic rules prescribed in the Quran and the Sunna are not applied in practice. For example, the Iranian criminal code *Qanoo e Mujazit Islami* [Islamic Criminal Code] 1370 [1991] provides for hand amputation in case of theft (Article 201) (prescribed in the Quran 5:38), but over the past two decades the punishment has rarely been applied and never in the last few years. Also paying or taking *riba* (usury) is prohibited by the Quran (2:276), but Iranian banks pay and take one of the highest rates of interest in the world. Similarly in Saudi Arabia, Islamic rules relating to *jizya* (a special tax imposed on non-Muslims) prescribed by the Quran (9:29) is not practised. Although slavery has been abrogated in all Muslim countries since early in the twentieth century, sections on 'slavery' are still being taught in Islamic tertiary schools and jurisprudence centres in both Saudi Arabia and Iran, but are not practised in any Muslim country.
62. H.L.A. Hart, *The Concept of Law* (Oxford University Press, Oxford, 1961), 98.
63. See Mohammad al Khizry, *Tarikh al Tashria al Islami [History of Law Making in Islam]* (Dar Al-Kotab Al-Elmiyah, Beirut, 1994), in which the history of the law making process during the life of Prophet Mohammad, and up to the collapse of Abbasid Dynasty is reviewed.
64. See, for example, Abdullah Saeed, *Interpreting the Qur'an: Towards a Contemporary Approach* (Routledge, Oxford, 2005); Mohammad Hashim Kamali, *Principles of Islamic Jurisprudence*, 3rd edn (Islamic Texts Society, Cambridge, 2003); Abi Ishaq Ibrahim Bin Ali Al-Shirazi, *Al-Luma Fi Usul Al-Fiqh [The Foundations in Principles of Islamic Jurisprudence]* (Dar Ibn Kafith, Damascus, 2002); Imam Al-Harramain Abi Al-M'Ali Abd Al-Malik Ibn Abdullah Ibn Yusuf Al-Joveini, *Al-Burhan Fi Usul Al-Fiqh [Evidence in Principles of Islamic Jurisprudence]* (Dar Al-Kotab Al-Elmiyah, Beirut, 1997); Abol Hassan Mohammadi, *Mabani Estenbaht Huquq Islami [Principles of Inference of Islamic Law]* (Tehran University Press, Tehran, 2004).
65. There is no disagreement among Muslims on the text and content of the Quran, but some authors consider a paragraph as one verse while others may see it as two verses and hence the number of verses cited in the Quran may differ.
66. Muslim theologians consider the Quranic verses under five main headings namely preaching, polemics, stories, allusions and legislation: Shlomo D. Goitein, 'The Birth-Hour of Muslim Law? An Essay in Exegesis' in Wael B. Hallaq (ed.), *The Formation of Islamic Law* (Ashgate, Aldershot, 2004), 6970.
67. On Sunna as a source of law see Wael Hallaq, *Sharia: Theory, Practice, Transformation* (Cambridge University Press, Cambridge, 2009), 39–51; Mohammed Arkoun,

Rethinking Islam: Common Questions, Uncommon Answers (Robert D. Lee (ed. and trans.), Westview Press, Boulder, CO, 1994), Chapter 10.

68. See generally Mohammad Hashim Kamali, *Principles of Islamic Jurisprudence*, 3rd edn (Islamic Texts Society, Cambridge, 2003); Farooq Hassan, 'The Sources of Islamic Law' (1982) 76 *Proceedings of Annual Meeting – American Society Of International Law* 65; Kamil Musa, *Al Madkhal Ila al Tashria al Islami [The Genesis of Islamic Law Making]* (Mo'assahat Al-Risalah, Beirut, 1989) 196–222; Mohammad Hamidullah, 'Sources of Islamic Law – A New Approach' (1954) 1 *Islamic Law Quarterly* 205; Wael Hallaq, *The Origins and Evolution of Islamic Law* (Cambridge University Press, Cambridge, 2005); Burton Watson, *The Sources of Islamic Law: Islamic Theories of Abrogation* (Edinburgh University Press, Edinburgh, 1990).
69. Ahmad Hasan, *The Doctrine of Ijma in Islam – A Study of the Juridical Principle of Consensus*, 2nd edn (Kitab Bhavan, New Delhi, 2003); Sad ibn Nasir ibn Abd al-Aziz Shithri, *Qawadih al-istidlal bi-al-ijma: Al-itiradat al-waridah ala al-istidlal bi-al-dalil min al-ijma wa-al-jawab anha [The Procedures for the Use of Ijma Dar al-Muslim lil-Nashr wa-al-Tawzi]* (Dar al-Muslim lil-Nashr wa-al-Tawzi; al-Tabah, Ryadh, 1999).
70. Ahmad Hasan, *Analogical Reasoning in Islamic Jurisprudence: A Study of the Juridical Principle of Qiyas* (Islam Research Institute, Pakistan, 1986); Nadiyah Sharif Umari, *al-Qiyas fi al-tashri al-Islami: Dirasah usuliyah fi bayan makanatihi wa-atharihi fi al-jawanib al-tatbiqiyah [Qiyas in Islamic Lawmaking Process: Comparative Lectures Relating to the Position and Effects of Qiyas in Usul Fiqh Hajar]* (Dar al-Muslim lil-Nashr wa-al-Tawzi; al-Tabah, Ryadh, 1987).
71. Mohammad Hashim Kamali, *Istihsan and the Renewal of Islamic Law* (International Institute of Advanced Islamic Studies, Malaysia, 2004); Saim Kayadibi, 'Ijtihad by Ra'y, 'The Main Source of Inspiration behind Istihsan' (2007) 24(1) *The American Journal of Islamic Social Science* 73.
72. Abol Hassan Mohammadi, *Mabani Estenbaht Huquq Islami [Principles of Inference of Islamic Law]* (Tehran University Press, Tehran, 2004), 235–42.
73. Mohamed El Awa, 'The Place of Custom (Urf) in Islamic Legal Theory' (1973) 17 *Islamic Quarterly* 177; Hakim Imtiyaz Hussain, *Muslim Law and Customs: With a Special Reference to the Law as Applied in Jammu & Kashmir* (Srinagar Law Journal Publication, Srinagar, 1989); Andreas Haberbeck, 'Muslims, Custom and the Courts' (1982) 24 *The Journal of Indian Law Institute* 132; Chibli Mallat, *Introduction to Middle Eastern Law* (Oxford University Press, Oxford, 2007), 104–8.
74. For example, the Quran provides that Muslim men can marry women of their choice: two, three or four, if they can treat them justly (Quran 4:3). The law of polygamy has been practised for centuries in the Islamic world without any limitations. However, in the modern world, a few Muslim countries, such as Tunisia and Turkey, have banned the practice. Also, in most other Muslim countries, for example, Indonesia, Malaysia, Iran, Egypt, Pakistan and Bangladesh, there are limitations on polygamy. In a few countries, such as Saudi Arabia and Qatar, polygamy is practised in a traditional manner.
75. In Indonesia, for example, the legal system is based on a combination of several different legal systems, including *adat* law (traditional Indonesian customs), *syariah* (Islamic law), and colonial Dutch law. See Tim Lindsey, *Indonesia: Law and Society*, 2nd edn (Federation Press, Annandale, New South Wales, 2008), 3. In fact, the majority of legal principles, whether substantive or procedural, are based on the Dutch civil law system, except in a few areas, particularly personal law areas such as inheritance and family law. Even in these areas, traditional Islamic law has been significantly modified. See Michael B. Hooker, *Indonesian Islam: Social Change*

through Contemporary Fatāwa (Allen & Unwin and University of Hawai'i Press, Honolulu, Hawai'i, 2003); Michael B. Hooker, *Indonesian Syariah: Defining a National School of Islamic Law* (Institute of Southeast Asian Studies, Singapore, 2008); Tim Lindsey, *Indonesia: Law and Society*, 2nd edn (Federation Press, Annandale, New South Wales, 2008).

76. See Abbas Amanat, 'From Ijtihad to Wilayat-i-Faqih: The Evolutions of the Shi'ite Legal Authority to Political Power' in Abbas Amanat and Frank Griffel (eds), *Shari'a: Islamic Law in the Contemporary Context* (Stanford University Press, Palo Alto, CA, 2007), 120.
77. On the development of Islamic law see: Mohammad al Khizry, *Tarikh al Tashria al Islami [History of Law Making in Islam]* (Dar Al-Kotab Al-Elmiyah, Beirut, 1994); Kamil Musa, *Al Madkhal Ila al Tashria al Islami [The Genesis of Islamic Law Making]* (Mo'assahat Al-Risalah, Beirut, 1989); Wael Hallaq, *The Origins and Evolution of Islamic Law* (Cambridge University Press, Cambridge, 2005); Shaybani's Siyar and Herbert Liebesny (eds), *Law in the Middle East, Volume One: Origin and Development of Islamic Law* (AMS Press Inc., Brooklyn, NY, 1982); Chibli Mallat, 'From Islamic to Middle Eastern Law, A Restatement of the Field (Part I)' (2003) 51 *American Journal of Comparative Law* 699; Chibli Mallat, 'From Islamic to Middle Eastern Law, A Restatement of the Field (Part II)' (2004) 52 *American Journal of Comparative Law* 209; Norman Calder, *Studies in Early Muslim Jurisprudence* (Oxford University Press, Oxford, 1993); Abdullah Saeed, *Interpreting the Qur'an: Towards a Contemporary Approach* (Routledge, Oxford, 2005).
78. Wael Hallaq, *Sharia: Theory, Practice, Transformation* (Cambridge University Press, Cambridge, 2009), 229.
79. On the definition of the 'rule of law' see Joseph Raz, 'The Rule of Law and its Virtue', (1977) 39 *Law Quarterly Review* 195; John Finnis, *Natural Law and Natural Rights* (Clarendon Press, Oxford, 1980), Chapter 10; Cheryl Saunders and Katherine Le Roy, 'Perspectives on the Rule of Law' in Cheryl Saunders and Katherine Le Roy (eds), *The Rule of Law* (Federation Press, Annandale, New South Wales, 2003); Matthew Kramer, 'On the Moral of the Rule of Law' (2004) 63 *Cambridge Law Journal*; Margaret Radin, 'Reconsidering the Rule of Law' (1989) 69 *Boston University Law Review* 781; Murray Gleeson, *The Rule of Law and the Constitution* (ABC Books, Sydney, 2000); Brian Tamanaha, *On the Rule of Law: History, Politics and Theory* (Cambridge University Press, Cambridge, 2004); David Clark, 'The Many Meanings of the Rule of Law' in Kanishka Jayasuriya (ed.), *Law, Capitalism and Power in Asia* (Routledge, London, 1999), 28; and Richard Bellamy (ed.), *The Rule of Law and the Separation of Powers* (Ashgate, Aldershot, 2005).
80. 'Say: O God! Lord of Power (and Rule), Thou givest Power to whom Thou pleasest, and Thou strippest off Power from whom Thou pleasest: Thou enduest with honour whom Thou pleasest, and Thou bringest low whom Thou pleasest: in Thy hand is all Good. Verily, over all things Thou hast power' (Quran, Súra Ál-i-'Imrán 3:26; Abdullah Yusuf Ali, *The Qur'an: Text, Translation and Commentary* (Tahrike Tarsile Qur'an, New York, 2005), 128.
81. 'Then we put you on the (right) Way of Religion: so follow thou that (Way)' (Quran, Súra Játhiya 45:18); Abdullah Yusuf Ali, *The Qur'an: Text, Translation and Commentary* (Tahrike Tarsile Qur'an, New York, 2005), 1359.
82. 'Say O Messenger: And in whatever your people differ, the decision and the command is with Allah' (Quran, Súra Furqán 25:10).
83. Abu Yusuf and Ya'qub Ibn Ibrahim, *Kitab al-Kharaj* (Cairo, 1933), 71.
84. See Mohammad Qassim Zaman, 'The Caliphs, the "Ulama", and the Law: Defining the Role and Function of the Caliph in the Early "Abbasid Period"' in Wael Hallaq (ed.), *The Formation of Islamic Law* (Ashgate, Aldershot, 2004) 367, 380.

85. Al-Mawardi and Abu al-Hassan, *Kitab al-Akham al-Sultaniyyah [Book on the Principles of Government]*. The book is published by various publishers in many countries. On Mawardi and his book, see Ann K.S. Lambton, *State and Government in Medieval Islam* (Oxford University Press, Oxford, 1981); Haroon Khan Sherwani, *Muslim Political Thought and Administration*, 4th edn (Porcupine Press, Philadelphia, 1963), 99–112.
86. For English sources on concepts of the Islamic state see: Hamid Enayat, *Modern Islamic Political Thought* (Macmillan Press, London, 1982); Shad Saleem Faruqi, 'Concept of an Islamic State: Problems of Definition, Interpretation and Application in Southeast Asia', Paper presented at the *International Conference on Islam in South-East Asia*, Singapore, September 2001; Mohammad Hashim Kamali, 'Siyasah Shar'iyyah or the Policies of Islamic Government' (1989) 6 *American Journal of Islamic Social Science* 59; Noah Feldman, *The Fall and Rise of the Islamic State* (Princeton University Press, Princeton, NJ, 2008); Leonard Binder, 'Al-Ghazali's Theory of Islamic Government' (1955) 14 *The Muslim World* 229; Hamilton A.R. Gibb, 'Al-Mawardi's Theory of the Caliphate' in Hamilton A.R. Gibb, *Studies in the Civilization of Islam* (Routledge & Kegan Paul, London, 1962).
87. Abu'l-Faraj ibn al-Jawzi, *Al-Misbah al-Mudhi' li Dawlat al-Imam al-Mustadhi' [The Light …]* (Ibrahim Najiyya (ed.), Matba Al-Awqaf, Baghdad, 1979), 93.
88. In practice, this has never happened – Islamic caliphs, except the four early Righteous Caliphs, have always made laws and orders inconsistent with the original sources of Islamic law.
89. Noel Coulson, *A History of Islamic Law* (Edinburgh University Press, Edinburgh, 1964).
90. Qamar Al-Din Khan, *Ibn Taymiyah Wa Fikr Al Siyasi* (Maktabat Al-Fallah, Kuwait, 1973), 102–22.
91. Imam Mohammad Ghazali was a Persian theologian and Sufi who earned a place as one of the greatest Muslim scholars and had the title of the 'Renewer of Islam'. See generally William M. Watt, *Muslim Intellectual: A Study of al-Ghazali* (Aldine, Chicago, IL, 1963).
92. Mawardi was a famous political theory scholar of the eleventh century who laid down certain principles in relation to the function of the Islamic state and the Islamic caliphate. His famous book is *Al-Ahkam Al-Sultaniyeh. See further*: Hanna Mikhail, *Politics and Revelation: Mawardi and After (Islamic Surveys)* (Edinburgh University Press, Edinburgh, 1995).
93. Ibn Khaldun is a fourtheenth-century Muslim scholar, whose famous book is *Muqammah* [*The Introduction*]. He is a leading Muslim historian and sociologist who wrote on the nature of an Islamic state. See further Zaid Ahmad, *The Epistemology of Ibn Khaldūn* (RoutledgeCurzon, London, 2003), Part 16.
94. See below note 113.
95. See Mohsen Kadivar, *Nazariyehayeh Dowlat Dar Fiqh Shia [Theories of State in Shia Jurisprudence]*, 5th edn (Ney, Tehran, 2001), 30; Addulaziz Sachedina, *The Justice Ruler in Shi'ite Islam: The Comprehensive Theory of the Jurist in Imamite Jurisprudence* (Oxford University Press, Oxford, 1988); Hossein Modaressi 'The Just Ruler or the Guardian Jurist: An Attempt to Link Two Different Sh'ite Concepts' (1991) 3 *American Journal of Sociology* 111; Nikki Keddie, *The Roots of the Ulema's Power in Modern Iran* (Maisonneuve & Larose, Paris, 1964) 217.
96. Constitution of the Islamic Republic of Iran provides that (Article 5): 'During the Occultation of the Wali al-Asr (may God hasten his reappearance) [the last Shia imam believed to be hidden], the wilayah [custody] and leadership of the Ummah devolve upon the just (*'adil*) and pious (*muttaqi*) faqih [Muslim scholar], who is fully aware of the circumstances of his age; courageous, resourceful, and possessed of administrative ability, will assume the responsibilities of this office'.

97. Al-Mohaqeq Ahmad Naraghi, *A'vaayed al-Ayyam [Benefits of the Days]* (Chap Sanghi, Qom, 1408 AH, 1987), 185–206. The chapter on *velayat e-faqih* is published as an edited separate book in Tehran and Beirut. See Velayat al-faqih, *Bahthon Men Kitab A'vaayed al-Ayyam Lel Mowla al-Naraghi* (Sazman e-Tabliqat Islami, Tehran, 1410 AH, 1989).
98. Imam Ruhallah Khomeini, 'The Pillars of an Islamic State' in Mansoor Moaddel and Kamran Talattof (eds), *Contemporary Debates in Islam: An Anthology of Modernist and Fundamentalist Thought* (St Martin's Press, New York, 2000), 247, 248–50. See also: Hossein Seifzadeh, 'Ayatollah Khomeini's Concept of Rightful Government: The Velayat e-Faqih' in Mutalib and Taj ul-Islam Hashmi (eds), *Islam, Muslims and the Modern State: Case-Studies of Muslims in Thirteen Countries* (Macmillan Press, London, 1994), 197.
99. Majid Khadduri, 'Islam and the Modern Law of Nations' (1956) 50 *American Journal of International Law* 358.
100. Sahifeh Nour (a collection of Ayatollah (Emam) Khomeiny's speeches, letters, sermons, commands, etc.), Vol. 20, p. 170 (date of the letter is 7 December 1983). See also Mohsen Kadivar, *Nazariyehayeh Dowlat Dar Fiqh Shia [Theories of State in Shia Jurisprudence]*, 5th edn (Ney, Tehran, 2001), 108.
101. Majid Khadduri, *The Islamic Law of Nations: Shaybani's Siyar* (John Hopkins University Press, Baltimore, MD, 1966), xi.
102. Imam Abu Hamid Mohammed Ghazali, *al-Mustasfa min 'ilm al-usul [The Essentials of the Islamic Legal Theory]* (al-Matba'ah al-Amiriyyah, Cairo, 1913–1915), 139–40.
103. Mohammad Hashim Kamali, *Principles of Islamic Jurisprudence*, 3rd edn (Islamic Texts Society, Cambridge, 2003), 352.
104. Khaled Abou El Fadl, 'Islam and the Challenge of Democratic Commitment' (2003–2004) 27(4) *Fordham International Law Journal* 4, 29.
105. Mohammad Hashim Kamali, *Principles of Islamic Jurisprudence*, 3rd edn (Islamic Texts Society, Cambridge, 2003), Chapter 16.
106. John Esposito, 'Practice and Theory' in Khaled Abou El Fadl, *Islam and the Challenge of Democracy* (Joshua Cohen and Deborah Chasman (eds), Princeton University Press, Princeton, NJ, 2004) 93, 96.
107. Ali Abd al-Raziq, 'The Caliphate and the Bases of Power' in John Donohue and John Esposito (eds), *Islam in Transition: Muslim Perspectives* (Oxford University Press, Oxford, 2007), 24, 31.
108. Fathi Osman, 'Shura and Democracy' in John Donohue and John Esposito (eds), *Islam in Transition: Muslim Perspectives* (Oxford University Press, Oxford, 2007), 288, 289.
109. Mohammad Hashim Kamali, 'Shari'ah Law; An Introduction' (Oxford University Press, Oxford, 2008), 165.
110. See Majid Khadduri, *The Islamic Law of Nations: Shaybani's Siyar* (John Hopkins University Press, Baltimore, MD, 1966).
111. Mohammad Hashim Kamali, *Shari'ah Law; An Introduction* (OneWorld, Oxford, 2008), 169.
112. Wael Hallaq, *An Introduction to Islamic Law* (Cambridge University Press, Cambridge, 2009), 117.
113. See Mohammad al Ghazali, *The Socio-Political Thoughts of Shah Wali Allah* (Islamic Research Institude, Islamabad, 2001). Shah Waliallah's position on legal theory was followed by many Muslim jurists and philosophers such as Allama Mohammad Iqbal in his famous book: Allama Mohammad Iqbal, *The Reconstruction of Religious Thoughts in Islam* (Institute of Islamic Culture, Lahore, 1930). This book has been published and edited in various editions in different languages.

See for example, Mohammad Iqbal, *The Reconstruction of Religious Thoughts in Islam* (M. Saeed Sheikh (ed.), Institute of Islamic Culture, Lahore, 1996).

114. See Mahmoud Mohamed Taha, *The Second Message of Islam* (Syracuse University Press, Syracuse, NY, 1996).
115. Allama Muhammad Iqbal, *The Reconstruction of Religious Thought in Islam*, 2nd edn (edited and annotated by M. Saeed Sheikh, Iqbal Academy Pakistan and Institute of Islamic Culture, Lahore, 1989), 99–116.
116. Joseph Raz, *Ethics in the Public Domain, Essays in the Morality of Law and Politics* (Clarendon Press, Oxford, 1994), 360.
117. Ronald Dworkin, *A Matter of Principle* (Harvard University Press, Cambridge, MA, 1985), 11–12.
118. For the United Nations, the rule of law is 'a concept at the very heart of the Organization's mission. It refers to a principle of governance in which all persons, institutions and entities, public and private, including the state itself, are accountable to laws that are publicly promulgated, equally enforced and independently adjudicated, and which are consistent with international human rights norms and standards. It requires, as well, measures to ensure adherence to the principles of supremacy of law, equality before the law, accountability to the law, fairness in the application of the law, separation of powers, participation in decision-making, legal certainty, avoidance of arbitrariness and procedural and legal transparency'. 'Report of the Secretary-General on the Rule of Law and Transitional Justice in Conflict and Post-Conflict Societies', accessed on 15 December 2010 at: http://daccess-dds-ny.un.org/doc/UNDOC/GEN/N04/395/29/PDF/N0439529.pdf?OpenElement. See further United Nations Unites, 'Rule of Law Coordination and Resources Group, Joint Strategic Plan 2009-2011', accessed on 15 December 2010 at: http://www.unrol.org/files/RoLCRG%20Joint%20Strategic%20Plan.pdf
119. See, for example, Tahir Mahmood, 'Islamic Law on Human Rights' (1984) 4 *Islamic and Comparative Law Quarterly* 32; Sayyid Abu al-Ala Mawdudi, *Human Rights in Islam* (Khurshid Ahmad and Ahmad Said Khan (trans.), Islamic Foundation, Markfield, 1976); Riffat Hassan, 'On Human Rights and the Quranic Perspectives' (1982) 19 *Journal of Ecumenical Studies* 51; Mohammad Talat al-Ghunaimi, 'Justice and Human Rights in Islam' in Gerald E. Lampe (ed.), *Justice and Human Rights in Islamic Law* (International Law Institute, Washington, DC, 1997), 1.
120. David Kinley, 'Human Rights, Globalization and the Rule of Law: Friends, Foes or Family?' (2003) 7 *UCLA Journal of International and Foreign Affairs* 239, 254.
121. *Universal Declaration on Human Rights*, GA Res 217A (III), UN GAOR, 3rd sess., 183rd plen. mtg, UN Doc A/810 (10 December 1948), http://www.unhcr.org/refworld/docid/3ae6b3712c.html
122. The literature on international human rights is extensive. A few good sources are Henry Steiner et al., *International Human Rights in Context* (Oxford University Press, Oxford, 2007); Robert McCorquodale (ed.), *Human Rights* (Ashgate, Aldershot, 2003); Philip Alston, *The United Nations and Human Rights* (Oxford University Press, Oxford, 1992).
123. Abdulkarim Soroush, *Wisdom, Intellectualism and Religious Conviction* (Serat, Tehran, 2005), 135.
124. Mohsen Kadivar, *Human Rights and Intellectualism in New Directions in Islamic Thought: Exploring Reform and Muslim Tradition* (Kari Vogt, Lena Larsen and Christian Moe (eds), I.B. Tauris, London, 2009), 47, 50.
125. Majid Khaddouri, 'Human Rights in Islam' (1946) 243 *Annals of the American Academy of Political and Social Science* 79.
126. Seyyed Hossein Nasr, *The Heart of Islam, Enduring Values for Humanity* (Harper, San Francisco, CA, 2002), 281.

127. Ibid., 282.
128. See Abdulkarim Soroush, *Wisdom, Intellectualism and Religious Conviction* (Serat, Tehran, 2005), 135; Mohsen Kadivar, *Reconstruction of Wisdom: A Condition for Reconciling Religion and Human Rights* (unpublished, a copy of the paper (in Persian) is filed with the author), 6. This paper was presented at the *Human Rights Conference*, Mofid University, Qom, Iran, 16 May 2007; Abdullah An'Naim, *Islam and the Secular State: Negotiating the Future of Sharia* (Harvard University Press, Cambridge, MA, 2008); Abdullah An'Naim (ed.), *Human Rights in Cross-cultural Perspectives: A Quest for Consensus* (University of Pennsylvania Press, Philadelphia, PA, 1995); Abdullah An'Naim, *Toward an Islamic Reformation: Civil Liberties, Human Rights and International Law* (Syracuse University Press, Syracuse, NY, 1990); Khaled Abu El Fadl, 'The Human Rights Commitment in Modern Islam' in Joseph Runzo et al. (eds), *Human Rights and Responsibilities in the World Religions* (Oneworld, Oxford, 2002), 331; Khaled Abu El Fadl, *Speaking in God's Name: Islamic Law, Authority, and Women* (Oxford University Press, Oxford, 2003); Charles Kurzman (ed.), *Liberal Islam: A Sourcebook* (Oxford University Press, Oxford, 1998).
129. Abdolkarim Soroush, *Bast Tajrobeh Nabavi [The Expansion of Prophetic Experience]* (Serat, Tehran, 2006), 292.
130. Seyyed Hossein Nasr, *The Heart of Islam, Enduring Values for Humanity* (Harper, San Francisco, CA, 2000).
131. Ibid., 122.
132. On the Islamization of Iranian law see Said Amir Arjomand, *The Turban for the Crown: The Islamic Revolution in Iran* (Oxford University Press, Oxford, 1988); Roy P. Mottahedeh, *The Mantle of the Prophet: Religion and Politics in Iran* (Oneworld, Oxford, 1985).

2. Islamic law and institutions

1. INTRODUCTION

As is commonly understood, Islamic law or Sharia is practised by individual Muslims, and encompasses the practices of ritual as well as social interaction. Islam teaches that, in the hereafter, every Muslim will be held responsible for their own deeds: if they follow Allah and the Prophet's guidance then they will enter paradise; otherwise they will be sent to hell. It must be understood that Sharia applies first in the daily life of individual Muslims. However, this does not mean that Islamic law has not been institutionalized into different forms ranging from state administration to Islamic non-governmental organizations. Islamic law, therefore, operates at both private and public levels. Islamic law is a dynamic force in both public and private spheres, but outsiders most often observe its dynamic nature in Islamic institutions, rather than from the actions of individual Muslims. A pertinent example of the strength of Islamic institutions can be seen in the Western media's misapplication of concepts associated with the Taliban or al-Qaeda, which has led some people in the West to think that their actions are truly representative of Islam.

This chapter focuses on Islamic legal institutions or other institutions where Islamic law is being taught or used as a core guiding principle. The purpose of this chapter is to examine and evaluate how those institutions contribute to the development of Islamic law in public life. First, it will discuss ways of understanding Islamic government, followed by a brief discussion of Islamic councils (*shura*) and judiciary (*qada*). Second, it will consider the status and role of those who issue Islamic guidance in the form of fatwas (*dar al-ifta*). Third, it will review the role of the mosque (*masjid*) and Islamic schools (*madrasa*). Finally, it will discuss the role of other major Islamic institutions, namely, Islamic organizations, political parties and *halal* certifiers.

2. UNDERSTANDING THE ISLAMIC STATE AND ISLAMIC POLITICAL LEADERS

The question of whether Sharia established a certain form of government remains controversial. Taqiyuddin al-Nabhani opines that the caliphate (*khilafa*) is the valid form of Islamic government contemplated under Sharia.[1] His views are supported by classic Muslim thinkers such as al-Mawardi (974–1058), who took the view that the establishment of the Islamic state (*al-Imama* or *khilafa*)[2] is obligatory, since it is intended to act as the enacter of the prophecy, in upholding the Muslim faith and managing the affairs of the world (*al-imama mawdu'ah li khilafa al-nubuwwa fi hirasat al-din wa siyasa al-dunya*).[3] Muslims had never been without a caliph until Mustapha Kemal abolished the *khilafa* system in 1924.[4] Since then, the idea of a non-caliphate structure of government has been introduced. The imposition of non-caliphate governments by colonizers could be considered proof that other forms of government are concepts that are alien to the Muslim tradition.[5] For instance, Ahmad Husayn Ya'qub clearly states that the system of political Islam is not a system of democracy (*al-nizam al-siyasi al-Islami laysa nizaman dimuqratiyyan*).[6] Since the Islamic state is eponymous with the *khilafa*, when a caliph is present the Islamic state exists. Therefore, it cannot be said that there is a genuine Islamic state in existence today. Many Islamic movements such as *Hizbut Tahrir* are attempting to re-establish the caliphate, and for this reason they refuse to imitate the Western concept of government.

The fall of the Ottoman Caliphate in 1924 led to the notion of nation-states in Muslim communities. Since the early twentieth century, the concepts of nationalism, along with democracy, republicanism and the rule of law, have been incorporated into the political and legal discourses of Muslim scholars. They began to ask: is the caliphate the only true form of Islamic government? Did the practices of the caliphate from Abu Bakar (the first caliph) until the Ottomans have the same form? They went further, by returning to the primary sources of Islam (the Quran and the Sunna) in order to define the structure of Islamic government.

Scholars who took a substantive approach to Sharia, such as Muhammad Abduh, Ali Abdur Raziq and M. Husayn Haykal, came to the conclusion that the universality of Islam lies not in its political structure, but in its faith and religious guidance. Abduh believed that 'political organization is not a matter determined by Islamic doctrine but is rather determined from time to time according to circumstances, by general consultation within the community'.[7] Similarly, Raziq argued that the caliphate was the product of history, an institution of human, rather than divine, origin, a temporary convenience, and therefore a purely political office with no religious meaning or function. The strict rules which the Prophet set down concerned only such things as prayer and fasting; and they were in fact rules appropriate for his particular culture, and for people in a simple state with a natural government.[8] According to Haykal, there is no standard system of government in Islam. The Islamic community is free to follow any governing system that ensures equality among its citizens (both in rights and responsibilities) and in the sight of the law, and manages affairs of state based on consultation, by adhering to Islam's moral and ethical values.[9] It is worth noting that both the Quran and the Sunna literature do not prefer a definite political system; in contrast, both of these primary sources of Islamic law have laid down a set of principles, or ethical values and political morals, to be followed by Muslims in developing life within a state. Therefore, the claim that the *khilafa* is the only valid type of Islamic government is questionable.

The administrations of Islamic states from the first caliph until the fall of the Ottoman Empire have shown great variations in practice. For centuries, there were several caliphates or dynasties (Buyids, Saljuks and Fatimid) operating at the same time in different locations; thus, the claim of there being a single caliph for all Muslims has not been entirely true. In fact, since the Umayyad era (661), the institution of the caliphate resembled a monarchy where the caliph was replaced by his heirs, not through *shura* (consultation) with Muslim communities.[10] Such practices are against the tradition of the first four guided caliphs (*alKhulafa al-Rashidun*).

Islamic legal tradition justifies the elements or the principles of constitutionalism, and consequently, the idea of upholding the rule of law is not an alien concept for Muslims.[11] Abd al-Wahhab Khallaf states that the Islamic government is a constitutional, as opposed to a tyrannical, government (*al-hukuma al-islamiya dusturiya*).[12] In other words, based on his understanding of the Sharia, government in Islam is not based on the charisma of the person. He also asserts that Islam guarantees individual rights (*huquq al-afrad*) and separates power into *al-sulta al-tashri'iya*, *al-sulta al-qada'iya*, *al-sulta al-tanfidhiya*, which could easily be classified as the legislative, judiciary, and executive powers, respectively.[13] Khallaf's views can be justified on the grounds that the Quran provided the basic principles for a constitutional democracy without providing the details of a specific system. Muslims were to interpret these basic principles in the light of their customs and the demands of their historical consciousness.

The pre-conditions to becoming a Islamic political leader (caliph, imam or sultan) have been discussed widely by Muslim political thinkers. Al-Mawardi, for instance, argued that there are seven conditions for eligibility for supreme leadership. He stressed that, among other things, a caliph should be of Arab nationality, in particular, of the notable Qurayshite descent. A caliph needed sound hearing, vision and speech, physical fitness and freedom from handicaps to movement or agility of action.[14] Al-Ghazali went further by outlining 10 conditions which have to be met: a candidate must be an adult, of healthy mind, free and not a slave, a male, of Quraysh descent, healthy of hearing and vision, have real power, possess guidance, possess knowledge and be observant of religious obligations.[15] From these conditions, it is interesting to note that only two are mentioned in the Sunna: of Quraysh descent and of the male gender. Literally speaking, the other conditions are not found in either the Quran nor the Sunna. They are based on al-Ghazali's and al-Mawardi's own judgment. Even so, these two conditions for leadership (Quraysh descent and male gender) are open for discussion.

The need for the leader to be of Quraysh descent was qualified by Ibn Khaldun (1332–1406), who attempted to re-interpret the saying of the Prophet, 'the leader comes from the tribe of the Quraysh'.[16] According to Khaldun, the word 'Quraysh' does not mean Quraysh literally, but should be read as requiring the leader to possess the characteristics of the Quraysh, such as strength, intelligence and capability. At the time of Ibn Khaldun, it was necessary to re-interpret the Sunna to take account of the current political reality, because Islam had spread far beyond the Middle East and it was practically impossible for political leaders to trace their lineage to the Quraysh tribe. In arguing for a broader interpretation of the Sunna, Ibn Khaldun opposed those jurists who continued to maintain that Qurayshite descent still formed a condition of the caliphate, even if the prospective Qurayshite candidate was incapable of meeting their obligations towards the Muslim community.[17]

The presence of female leaders throughout history contradicts the interpretation that an Islamic political leader must be male. In her book, *Forgotten Queens of Islam*, Mernissi investigates Islamic women who have risen to power, how they accomplished the feat and under which social constructs and limitations they operated. Many women who came to power, or had great influence over men in power, are profiled, along with their ascent and descent. Mernissi covers accounts of women from pre-Islamic times such as Balqis, Queen of Sheba, to 'A'isyah and Benazir Bhutto, and also Megawati Soekarnoputri in Indonesia (2001–2004). She argues that, throughout the history of Islam, a small number of women have seized power in both political and military spheres in

Muslim lands just as in the West. However, since the very thought of a woman ruler is so outrageous to Islamic historians, many of these women are downplayed in some historical accounts.[18]

Of the one billion Muslims living in predominantly Muslim countries,[19] 28 per cent live in 10 countries that, according to their constitutions, declare themselves to be Islamic states.[20] There are an additional 12 predominantly Muslim countries that have chosen to declare Islam as the official state religion without any constitutional declaration that they are Islamic states.[21] By contrast, the constitutions of 11 predominantly Muslim countries proclaim the state to be secular.[22] These countries account for nearly 140 million Muslims, or 13.5 per cent of the Muslims living in predominantly Muslim countries. Finally, the 11 remaining predominantly Muslim countries have not made any constitutional declaration concerning the Islamic or secular nature of the state, and have not made Islam the official state religion. This group of countries, which includes Indonesia, the world's most populous Muslim country, accounts for over 250 million Muslims.[23] Again, this informs us that there is no single model of state–religion relationship in the Muslim world. It also should be noted that approximately 300 million Muslims live in countries that are not predominantly Muslim, such China, India and Russia.

In Islamic tradition, the world was split into two divisions: the territory of Islam (*dar al-Islam*), comprising Islamic and non-Islamic communities that accepted Islamic sovereignty, and the rest of the world, called the territory of war (*dar al-harb*).[24] More precisely, if Muslims live in a country or area that prohibits them from practising their faith or that officially declares war on Muslims, such an area is called *dar al-harb*. Muslims have two options, either to migrate to other areas such as *dar al-Islam* or *dar al-amn* (see below), or to fight against the oppression.

As has been noted above, approximately 300 million Muslims live in countries that are not predominantly Muslim, such China, India and Russia, so can we say that those 300 million Muslims live in the *dar al-harb*? Some Muslim scholars maintain and believe that the labelling of a country or place as being a part of *dar al-Islam* revolves around the question of religious security. This means that, if a Muslim practises Islam freely in his place of abode despite their place of residence being secular or un-Islamic, then they will be considered to live in the *dar al-Islam*. *Dar al-Islam* is also known and referred to as *dar al-salam*, or house/territory of peace. The term appears in the Quran (10:25 and 6:127) as one name of the Paradises. Other scholars have proposed a third category of territory, such as *dar al-amn* (territory of safety), *dar al-da'wa* (territory of invitation) or *dar al-'ahd* (territory of truce). Basically they are all terminologies proposed to describe the status of

Muslims either in the West or in other non-Muslim societies where Muslims have the right to practise their religion despite the fact that Sharia is not established or governed in that area or country. The issue will be discussed further in Chapter 3.

3. THE ROLE OF THE *SHURA* IN ISLAMIC GOVERNANCE

One of the key concepts of Islamic governmental system is *shura*, a consultation process with the people (particularly with members of the *shura* council) in matters related to public affairs. Although there is a direct reference to the term *shura* in two verses of the Quran (3:159 and 42:38) it is an essentially contested concept, as the Quran does not set out detailed provisions on the technical aspects of the *shura*.

The requirements of *shura* were first examined during the reign of the second caliph, ‘Umar b. Khattab, who did not want to follow the method used by Abu Bakr when the latter appointed him. Instead, ‘Umar appointed six people and asked them to select the next caliph. It seems that ‘Umar was the first caliph to institutionalize the *shura*, although in its first form it had been left solely to the discretion of the caliph as to whom he should consult. This explains why in al-Mawardi’s book the main task of *shura* council is to appoint the caliph and the *shura* council itself is appointed by the previous caliph.[25]

Others have interpreted the role of the *shura* as advice provision, wherein the ruler merely asks religious leaders, tribal leaders or influential people for advice. Such an interpretation was practised by Mu’awiya, who governed from 661 to 680.[26] The implication of this practice is that the ruler does not have any obligation to follow or implement the advice. Abul A’la Maududi, for instance, takes the view that the head of state is not obliged to follow the opinion of the *shura* council, which is the opinion supported by the majority of votes of the *shura*. He can also follow the opinion supported by a minority group, and he can even completely neglect the majority or minority opinion of the *shura* council.[27]

Fazlur Rahman rejects this kind of *shura*, on the grounds that this totally alters its original foundation. The role of the *shura* should be to provide ‘mutual advice, through mutual discussions, on an equal footing’.[28] A *shura* council has an equal position to the government. Therefore, the outcome of the *shura* should be legally binding on both the ruler and the community. Hasan al-Turabi provides a solid justification for this, when he recalls that ‘the Prophet used to consult his companions and take their views on almost every issue related to public affairs, and sometimes even related to his private life, though he was the Prophet of God and supported by divine revelation.'[29]

According to Rahman, the phrase 'the affairs of the Muslims are run on the basis of their consultation' (*amruhum shura baynahum*) in the Quran 42:38 refers to the community as a whole, not an elite nor any specific group.[30] Rahman's interpretation is opposed by Maududi[31] and 'Abd al-Wahab Khallaf,[32] who express the view that those participating in *shura* must be a well-specified group of people (that is to say, Muslim scholars, *ulama*).[33] One of the consequences of Rahman's interpretation of the *shura* membership being open to the community as a whole is that it is the community that chooses its representatives (*shura* council), not the head of state. Given the practice of the *shura* in Islamic history, allowing the community to choose who makes up the *shura* will radically change the face of Islamic government. For instance, this would inevitably change the governance of Saudi Arabia, which is currently a monarchy, without elected representative institutions or political parties. At present, the Consultative Council (*Majlis al-Shura*) consists of 150 members appointed by the king, rather than chosen by the broader community.[34]

How then could members of the *shura* council be elected? Once again, neither the Quran nor the classic works of Muslim scholars cover this topic. This provides wide room for the application of reasoning based on the principles of Islam (*ijtihad*) in the modern era. Even a fundamentalist thinker, like Sayyid Qutb, does not insist on a particular form of *shura*. According to Qutb, let the Muslim community decide its own methods to facilitate the *shura*, having regard to the community's environment, social circumstances and particular requirements.[35] Therefore, Muslims have the ability to choose an electoral system, and to determine the best system for casting and counting votes, with regard to the situation in the country concerned, such as its geography, ethnic composition, demography, political format, legal system and so on. According to Gamil Mohammed El-Gindy, the flexibility of the *shura* makes it compatible with a modern electoral system.[36]

Apart from appointing the caliph, other functions of the *shura* representatives (*ahl alikhtiyar*) were not determined by classic Muslim scholars. Major questions remain, such as what are the other functions of the *shura*? Has the parliament the right to legislate? This has been a major question, since legislation in Islam is a crucial matter. The bottom line is that the parliament cannot produce legislation or regulation that contradicts the Sharia. However, what the words 'contradiction' and 'Sharia' mean remain a subject for debate, particularly in the 'grey' areas where the Quran and the hadith did not mention or discuss the issues.

4. THE ROLE OF THE JUDICIARY IN ISLAMIC GOVERNANCE

The role and definition of the judiciary (*qada*) has been discussed widely in Islamic law literature. It is claimed that the independence of the judiciary is 'a cardinal principle of Islam'.[37] This claim is supported by a number of arguments. Firstly, Muhammad Idris alShafi'i takes the view that a judge must be a Muslim scholar (*mujtahid*), because mastery of the religious sciences and integrity of character are required to perform reasoning based on the principles of Islam (*ijtihad*).[38] Khallaf shows similar views when he states that 'persons who are in charge at the court are *mujtahid*' (*fakana rijal al-qada' min almujtahidin*).[39] In the context of judicial independence, such views are significant, on the grounds that not only must judges possess the same knowledge as Muslim scholars (*mujtahid*), but also their decisions must be based on their independent judgment of religious problems.

The theory of *ijtihad* requires judges to be independent in the exercise of personal reasoning. 'Umar, the second caliph, is considered to have been the first person to guarantee judicial independence.[40] Judicial independence was guaranteed by the practices of the first four right guided caliphs (*al-Khulafa al-Rashidun*), who respected the judges' decisions. For instance, Kamali provides examples that 'Umar (the second caliph) and 'Ali (the fourth caliph) appeared before judges as parties to litigation, and both made clear statements that the judge should not give them any special treatment.[41] Another example of caliphs respecting the independence of judges occurred when 'Usman, the third caliph, appeared personally before the court to get back a suit of armour from a Jew. However, 'Usman's claim was dismissed, since the only witnesses who supported his claim were his slave and his son; both were not competent witnesses under Islamic law.[42]

The third argument supporting the claim to judicial independence in Islam is the existence of the process 'the redress of wrongs' (*wilaya al-mazalim*). This process is the embryo of the administrative tribunal, or constitutional court, in the modern sense. Mawardi has outlined ten areas that can be reported to this tribunal, including oppression and maltreatment of the public by government officials, and the implementation of sentences when judges are too weak to enforce them, owing to the sentenced person's power or social standing.[43]

These arguments in support of judicial independence throughout the history of Islam demonstrate that the judiciary (*qada*) played a vital role in the administration of the state and the life of the community and also in the transmission of Islamic traditions. However, this claim should be examined critically. There was, from early times, reluctance on the part of the pious to accept office as judges from the caliph, for fear of jeopardizing their integrity. For instance, Yazid ibn ‘Amr, Governor of Iraq, proposed Abu Hanifah, the imam of the Hanafi school, as a judge for the law-court of Kufah. He refused the appointment. Following his refusal, at the command of Yazid, he was given a whipping, 110 blows to the head. His face and head swelled. Abu Hanifah was not alone; other pious scholars like Zufar (Abu Hanifah's disciple), ‘Abd Allah b. Faruq (a scholar-jurist at Qairawan) and Aban b. Isa b. Dinnar (a Muslim scholar in Spain) refused to serve as judges, owing to executive interference with the judiciary.[44] However, it should be noted that Abu Yusuf (d. 798 AD), the chief disciple of Imam Abu Hanifah, was the Chief Justice (*qadi alqudat*) under the Harun al-Rasyid regime.[45]

Irit Abramski-Bligh observes that, during the Umayyad and early Abbasid periods, judges were assigned non-judicial functions as tax collectors, tribal administrators, governors and chiefs of police. He cites that, under Mu'awiyah regime, Fadala b. ‘Ubayd al-Ansari was in charge of the *qada* and military raiding, and ‘Abida b. Qays al-Salmani served as both judge and part of the military staff.[46] This suggests that the independence of the judiciary in the early Islamic periods was dependent on the personal attitude of both caliph and judge, since the *qada* was not as yet institutionalized and formalized as a clearly religious–judicial post, separate from governmental–administrative work. This explains why the topic of the independence of the judiciary in Islamic history is a controversial one. One can point to a certain period of time, or to certain persons, to prove either the independence or the subordination of the judiciary in Islam. For instance, one of the unstated conditions of becoming a judge in Nasrid kingdom of Granada (629/1232 to 897/1492) was loyalty to the sultans. The political elite used removal from office as a mechanism for control of the judiciary.[47] However, in Cordoba (fifth/eleventh century), unlike other officials, the judges' jurisdictional authority could be terminated only by dismissal; it could not be temporarily interrupted by the interference of the ruler in a particular case.[48] This controversy is understandable since the notion of judicial independence is a modern one, and it is difficult to judge periods in history against more recent experience.

However, in modern time, most (if not all) Muslim countries claim to guarantee judicial independence. In Saudi Arabia, for instance, the Basic Law provides for an independent judiciary (Article 46). In Egypt under the Hosni Mubarak regime, the Constitution provided for the independence and immunity of judges, and forbade interference by other authorities in the exercise of their judicial function. Judges were appointed for life, with mandatory retirement at age 64.[49] In Iran, according to Article 164 of its Constitution, a judge cannot be removed, whether temporarily or permanently, from the post he occupies, except by trial and proof of his guilt, or in consequence of a violation justifying his dismissal. All these three Muslim countries are in favour of judicial independence, at least as written in their constitutions.

5. THE ROLE OF THE *DAR AL-IFTA* IN ISLAMIC GOVERNANCE

Apart from the government, parliament and judiciary, there is also another legal institution that plays a significant role in Muslim societies: *dar al-ifta* (literally, the house of fatwas). In Egypt, for instance, the *dar al-ifta* is a government agency, established in 1895, charged with issuing Islamic legal opinions on any question to Muslims who ask for fatwas. The agency issues around 5000 fatwas a week, including both official fatwas that the Egyptian Mufti Sheikh Ali Gomaa (b. 1951) crafts on important issues and more routine fatwas handled via phone and Internet by a dozen or so subordinate muftis.[50] Sheikh Ali Gomaa is one of the internationally most respected Islamic jurists and considered as a highly promoted champion of moderate Islam and gender equality, while at the same time he is an object of hatred among Islamists or fundamentalists. In 2012 he visited Jerusalem and sparked criticism in Cairo.

In Saudi Arabia, in 1971 King Faisal established the Permanent Committee for Islamic Research and Fatwas (*al-Lajnah ad-Da'imah li al-Buhuth al-'Ilmiyyah wal-Ifta*) whose task is to issue fatwas. Currently, its Chair is Sheikh 'Abd al-Aziz (b. 1940). He is labelled the Grand Mufti of Saudi Arabia.[51] At the international level, there is a Fiqh Academy (*Majma' al-Fiqh al-Islamiy*) that was created at the decision of the second summit of the then Organisation of the Islamic Cooperation (OIC), 1974, and inaugurated in February 1988. It consists of all sheikhs and scholars from 57 state members of OIC. The Fiqh Academy is based in Jedda, Saudi Arabia, and headed by Sheikh Ahmad Khalid Babakr (b. 1940).[52] Fatwas will be considered in more detail in Chapter 4.

6. THE ROLE OF THE MOSQUE (*MASJID*) IN THE ISLAMIC COMMUNITY

Unlike in the Catholic Church, there is no hierarchy of mosques in Islam that defines the order or structure of the ministry. Literally, the mosque (*masjid*) is a place of worship. It is recommended for Muslims to prayer together in the mosque. However, Muslims can also pray in their homes or anywhere else. The imam leads the prayers in mosques or wherever Muslims pray as a group. In the large mosques there are usually official imams who lead the prayer. Large mosques sometimes play a political role as well. In many Muslim countries, political subjects are preached by imams at Friday congregations on a regular basis. In other Islamic countries, imams are banned from mentioning political issues. The mosque is also a place for learning Islamic knowledge. Children learn how to recite the Quran in the mosques. Many mosques also have libraries with Islamic texts. Outside of prayer times, many Muslim scholars teach their students sitting together in a study circle. This informal teaching can be observed when one visits mosques in Mecca, Medina, Cairo or other cities in Muslim countries. In other words, the mosque also has a function as a centre for information and education. Mosques can also be used for dispute settlement, involving the imam as an arbiter or mediator for family issues.[53] In Western countries, Muslim migrants have built and use mosques as a means of building their community. The mosque becomes a place for social gathering and celebration such as the feast at the end of Ramadan.[54]

The acceptance of female leadership in mosques is a significant change from much historical practice, signalling the mainstream acceptance of some form of female Islamic authority in many places. Muslim women have established themselves in a variety of religious leadership roles ranging from instructors of mosque to (re)interpreters of texts, leaders of prayer and even heads of women-only mosques. These women base their claims to authority on the knowledge acquired through at least some formal religious training, and supplemented by experience as a religious instructor or volunteer. Other factors that can feature in their claims to authority include a pious reputation, a charismatic style, family ties to religious leadership or education, and demonstrated commitment to religious outreach work.[55] It is worth noting that in 2004 Muslim author and feminist Asra Nomani proposed the Islamic Bill of Rights for Women in the Mosque. It lists 10 rights that women should be granted in regard to their participation at the mosque, such as entering the mosque through the main entry door, and not being required to only enter through the back, and to have full access to the mosque without separation by artificial barriers designed to segregate women from men. The list goes on to grant women the right to freely address the members of the congregation whether they be men or women and to hold leadership positions as well as to receive equal treatment to men.[56]

Muslims face towards the Ka'ba in Mecca when they pray. This direction is known as the *qibla*. The Ka'ba is located at the centre of a holy mosque in Mecca (the *masjid alharam*)[57]. Most mosques contain a wall niche (*mihrab*) that indicates the *qibla*. The fact that Muslims all pray towards the same point has traditionally been considered to symbolize the unity of all Muslims worldwide under the Law of God. In Islamic law, the *qibla* has an importance beyond community prayers (*salah*) and plays a part in various ceremonies. For instance, the head of an animal that is slaughtered using *halal* methods is aligned with the *qibla*. After death, Muslims are buried with their heads in the direction of the *qibla*.

The mosque is the outward and most visible symbol of Islam. The earliest mosques were built without minarets, as the call to prayer was performed elsewhere. It was reported that the Muslim community of Medina gave the call to prayer from the roof of the house of Mohammad, which doubled as a place for prayer. Around 80 years after Mohammad's death the first known minarets appeared.[58] The main function of the minaret is to provide a vantage point from which the call to prayer is made. The call to prayer is issued five times each day: dawn, noon, mid-afternoon, sunset and night. Minarets also function as air-conditioning mechanisms: as the sun heats the dome, air is drawn in through open windows then up and out of the minaret, thereby providing natural ventilation.

There have been several controversies regarding mosques in the West in the first decade of the twenty-first century. These issues will be discussed in Chapter 10, but it is worth noting in this chapter that Switzerland held a referendum in November 2009 that led to a constitutional amendment banning the construction of new minarets. The amendment was approved by 57.5 per cent of the participating voters.[59] In New York, a media controversy erupted after it was announced that a community planned to construct an Islamic community centre in the near vicinity of the World Trade Center Site. Park51 (originally named Cordoba House) was described as a 13 storey Islamic community centre in Lower Manhattan. The majority of the centre was planned to be open to the general public and its proponents said that the centre would promote interfaith dialogue. Plans for the centre included a Muslim prayer space which, owing to its location two blocks from the World Trade Center site, was labelled by some media commentators and politicians as the 'Ground Zero mosque', although numerous commentators argued that it was neither a mosque nor at Ground Zero.[60]

7. THE ROLE OF THE *MADRASA* AND ISLAMIC UNIVERSITY IN ISLAMIC COMMUNITY

In Islamic tradition, a *madrasa* is a college of Islamic law.[61] The *madrasa* was an educational institution in which Islamic law was taught according to one or more schools of thought: Maliki, Shafi'i, Hanafi, Hanbali or Ja'fari. There is no consensus on the origin of the *madrasa*. Various scholars have tried to show that it was inspired by Buddhist monasteries in Central Asia, or that it was the outgrowth of the function of the *masjid* (where Islamic law was also taught), or that it arose from inns (*khans*) that were built near mosques. In the latter case, these inns served as residences for the students.[62] The mosque–inn complex thus represented the transition to the *madrasa*. According to Gary Leiser, the Western college could have originated from the *madrasa*.[63]

In the Shia Muslim world, there are two significant seminary centres: Najaf (Iraq) and Qom (Iran). The Najaf seminary has hundreds of years of tradition of Islamic scholarship, particularly in *fiqh*.

In South Asia, after the 9/11 terrorist attack, *madrasa* were portrayed as Islamic schools that taught terrorism. They were suspected to foster anti-Western, traditionalist or even fundamentalist views and to train al-Qaeda fighters. This broader description arose owing to several *madrasa* being related to a number of suicide bombers.[64] For instance, in Pakistan, the 2007 siege by government forces of Islamabad's Red Mosque and its *madrasa* complex, whose imam and students staged an armed resistance against the state for its support of the 'war on terror', reinforced concerns about *madrasas*' role in regional and global jihad. By 2006 *madrasas* registered with Pakistan's five regulatory boards for religious schools were enrolling over 1 million male and 200,000 female students.[65]

In Indonesia, another form of Islamic school is an Islamic boarding school (*pesantren*). There are approximately 6000 *pesantren*, but again, after the 9/11 terrorist attack, owing to the broader conclusions drawn by commentators referring to a single *pesantren* led by Abu Bakar Baasyir, the image of the *pesantren* as a school of terror has emerged in Western media. The *pesantren* actually can be described as a non-formal institution, consistent with a social educational system. Its educational programme is formulated internally and it is, in general, free from formal stipulations, containing formal, non-formal and informal processes running day and night, where students (*santri*) live and learn classic Arabic texts under the tutelage of a *kiai* (the head of *pesantren*, and a respectful Javanese term for a spiritual leader). Accordingly, the *pesantren* is not only a place of study, but a paradigm of the process of life itself. It is supported by a set of continually developing values such as, first, the viewing of life as the observance of religious duty, both religious ritual per se and the desire to do social service; second, the demonstration of a profound love and respect for the observance of religious duty and community service; and, finally, the willingness to sacrifice all for the well-being of the community.[66]

While the *madrasa* in modern society provides Islamic education up to high school level, their students continue their studies in Islamic universities. The oldest university in the Muslim world is al-Azhar University in Cairo, founded in 970. As a comparison, the oldest continually operating university in the Western world, the University of Bologna in Italy, was built in 1088. Al-Azhar University mainly focuses on Islamic subjects, but since 1961 non-religious subjects have been added to its curriculum. Students who want to learn Islamic law will enrol in the Faculty of Sharia. During the early part of the twentieth century, Al-Azhar became the locus for reformist views of Islam, mainly under the influence of Muhammad Abduh (1849–1905), and many future international religious leaders and teachers received their training there. During the 1990s, there were approximately 6000 international students enrolled at Al-Azhar, and they represented 75 countries.[67] The current Grand Sheikh of al-Azhar is Mohamed Ahmed el-Tayeb (b. 1946). The position is a respectable prestigious Sunni Islam title and a prominent official title in Egypt, and is considered by many Muslims to be the highest authority in Sunni Islamic thought and Islamic jurisprudence. It is worth noting that Sheikh Ahmed el-Tayeb earned his PhD from Sorbonne University and he emphasizes interfaith dialogue and is known for his relatively progressive fatwas.

Another notable Islamic university is Umm al-Qura University, which is a public university in Mecca, Saudi Arabia, and was established as the College of Sharia in 1949 before being joined by new colleges and renamed Umm al-Qura by King Abdul Azis's royal decree in 1981. Umm al-Qura University is primarily an Islamic university that offers degrees in Islamic Law and Arabic language studies. However, it offers degrees in medicine as well as some applied sciences. It has student exchange programmes with Purdue University, Tufts University and Kings College London.

8. ISLAMIC ORGANIZATIONS AND POLITICAL PARTIES

While Muslims still associate with a particular school of thought (*madhhab*) in practising Islamic law, the role of Islamic organizations in modern time cannot be ignored. Different organizations have been formed inspired by socio-cultural, religious and economic issues as well as political ideology. On the one hand, organizations have developed to pursue a real agenda for society that differs from government policies; on the other hand, organizations have become an effective tool for maintaining solidarity and unity among their followers. This part of the chapter will review the Islamic organizations of the influential Muslim countries, Indonesia and Egypt, as well as international Islamic organizations.

Generally it can be said that there are two groups of Indonesian Muslims: the traditionalists and the modernists. The traditionalists are mainly concerned with pure religion (*din* or *ibadat*). Islam is, for them, mostly in the form of Islamic jurisprudence (*fiqh*). They recognize *taqlid* (the obligation to follow the *ulama*'s opinion without reserve). In other words, they tend to restrict the role of *ijtihad* in preference to, and out of deference for, the established opinions of the masters of the schools of Islamic jurisprudence. Traditionalist Muslims in Indonesia are represented by the Nahdlatul Ulama. At the moment, the Nahdlatul Ulama is the biggest Islamic organization in Indonesia, numbering 30 million supporters.[68]

Indonesian modernists are concerned with the nature of Islam in general. To them Islam is compatible with the demands of time and circumstance. They recognize the Quran and hadith as the basic sources of their ideas and thought. Furthermore, they maintain that 'the gate of *ijtihad*' is still open and they reject the idea of *taqlid* (blind following). Muhammadiyah is the organization that represents modernist Muslims. It has 28 million supporters in Indonesia and has built many schools, universities and hospitals. Moreover, it re-interprets Islam within the modern context.[69]

In Egypt, the most important Islamic organization is the Muslim Brotherhood (*alIkhwan al-Muslimun*). It is considered to be one of the largest Islamic movements in the world, and is the largest political opposition organization in many Arab states. Founded in 1928 by Hasan al-Banna, it has an estimated 2 million members. Its ideas have gained it supporters throughout the Arab world and influenced other Islamist groups with its model of political activism combined with Islamic charity work. The Muslim Brotherhood originated as a religious social organization, preaching Islam, teaching the illiterate, setting up hospitals and even launching commercial enterprises.[70] The Muslim Brotherhood was a banned political group in Egypt until the 2011 revolution and Mubarak's fall.

On 29 June 2011, as the Brotherhood's political power became more apparent and solidified following the 2011 Egyptian revolution, the

United States announced that it would reopen formal diplomatic channels with the group, with whom it had suspended communication as a result of suspected terrorist activity. There was much speculation as to whether the Muslim Brotherhood would dominate the new Egyptian political landscape. In the 2012 general elections the Muslim Brotherhood's political party, Freedom and Justice, gained more than 40 per cent of the seats in parliament. On 24 June 2012, the election commission announced that Mohamed Morsi, Chair and also a Freedom and Justice candidate, had won Egypt's presidential runoff against Ahmed Shafiq, the last prime minister under deposed leader Hosni Mubarak. According to official results, Morsi took 51.7 per cent of the vote while Shafiq received 48.3 per cent.[71] A Morsi spokesman announced that the president-elect would appoint a Christian and a female as vice-presidents.[72] However, the Supreme Constitutional Court of Egypt dissolved the parliament based on the recent elections.[73] As the largest, most popular and most effective opposition group in Egypt, the Muslim Brotherhood would undoubtedly seek a role in creating a new government, but the consequences of this new role, particularly with regard to the relationship of Islam, democracy and the rule of law, were uncertain, particularly when the Muslim Brotherhood must deal with the role and power of the Supreme Council of the Armed Forces.

There is substance to the fear that democracy in the lands where Islam is the majority religion will produce Islamic theocracy. In 1992 the Islamic Salvation Front (Front Islamique du Salute) won a majority in Algeria and in 2006 Hamas won elections for the Palestinian Legislative Council. These democratically elected organizations had pledged their support for an Islamic theocracy. However, Indonesia is somewhat different from the experiences of 'Islamic democracy' in the Muslim world. The outcome of general elections and constitutional reform in Indonesia showed how the call for the inclusion of Sharia in Article 29 of the Constitution was rejected through democracy. According to the 1998–2002 amendments to the Constitution, Indonesia remains a republic, with a presidential system and three branches of government.[74] While democracy opens the opportunity for the establishment of Islamic political parties, in the elections of 1999, 2004 and 2009, Islamic political parties failed to win a majority of seats. The Indonesian experience demonstrates that Islamic political parties have assigned religious meanings to national institutions and have tended to more readily endorse the state's policies and practices, whereas, interestingly 'secular' political parties have adopted Islamic issues in their political strategy. The support for democracy and the rule of law by religious organizations, including the two main Islamic organizations (Nahdlatul Ulama and Muhammadiyah), is important for maintaining the social capital of democracy. Since democracy requires political engagement and political participation, participation in religious organizations leads the community to be more open towards the complexities of social life.[75] In this sense, it does require a reinterpretation of religious ideas that are conducive to embracing democratic values. By engaging in this reinterpretation, religious groups can play a central role in the development and consolidation of democracy.

At the international level, an important Islamic organization is the OIC, which is the second largest inter-governmental organization after the United Nations and has a membership of 57 states spread over four continents. The OIC is the collective voice of the Muslim world and works to safeguard and protect the interests of the Muslim world in the spirit of promoting international peace and harmony among various people of the world. The Organization was established by a decision of a summit which took place in Rabat, Kingdom of Morocco on 12th Rajab 1389 Hijra (25 September 1969).[76]

Another influential international Islamic organization is the European Council for Fatwa and Research (ECFR), a Dublin-based private foundation, which was founded in London on 29–30 March 1997 on the initiative of the Federation of Islamic Organisations in Europe. The ECFR is a largely self-selected body, composed of Islamic clerics and scholars, presided over by Sheikh Yusuf al-Qaradawi (b. 1926).[77] It should be noted that some of al-Qaradawi's views have been controversial in the West (particularly with regard to the Israeli–Palestinian conflict): he was refused an entry visa to the United Kingdom in 2008, and barred from entering France in 2012. One of the aims of ECFR is to issue collective fatwas that meet the needs of Muslims in Europe, solve their problems and regulate their interaction with the European communities. The ECFR only refers to Sharia as a framework for one's personal life, and they are not advocates of replacing the current legal system with Sharia law.

9. *HALAL* CERTIFIERS IN MUSLIM SOCIETY

The last institution that will be discussed in this chapter is *halal* certifiers. *Halal* is a Quranic word meaning lawful or permitted. In reference to food, it is the dietary standard, as prescribed in the Quran. The Quran regulates Muslims on this matter with the beautiful phrase '*halalan thayyiban*' (Qur'an 2:168). *Halal*, as discussed above, means permissible based on Islamic law. *Thayyib* means good, in reference to good quality, healthy, environmentally friendly and respecting of human values. *Halal* and *Thayyib* together build the harmony of life, the balance of universe. General Quranic guidance dictates that all foods are *halal* except those that are specifically mentioned as *haram* (unlawful or prohibited). Not only are blood, pork and the meat of dead animals *haram*, but it is also required that the *halal* animals be slaughtered while pronouncing the name of Allah at the time of slaughter.

Halal certificates are becoming a global symbol for quality assurance, both for individual Muslims and for companies involved in global trade. It is no longer a simple matter of *halal–haram* in a traditional sense. Johan Fischer, for instance, examines the ways in which Malay immigrants create spaces for *halal* consumption in London, thereby elucidating the complex social, economic, cultural and political interrelation between Malay individuals, their host country and their country of origin.[78] London is home to a substantial number of Malays and Malaysian political and religious organizations. Muslim immigrants seek to find *halal* food, but how, where and what they can eat depends on many things: Islamic authorities who issue *halal* certificates, food suppliers, information on *halal* butchers and shops, and so on.

The development of new technology in food processing, cosmetics and medicine, to name a few areas, along with the potential market for *halal* products of several trillion dollars, creates some challenges for Muslim scholars and leaders. All parties must come to a common understanding followed by cooperation. The parties involved in the *halal* industry are Muslim scholars and leaders on one side, and scientists investigating and auditing the products, together with companies and business certifiers, including related government officers, on the other side of the spectrum. All parties must reach agreement to ensure that *halal* products/ingredients are prepared and stored separately from non-*halal* food items, and there must be a clear means of distinguishing between *halal* and non-*halal* foods. Cross-contamination between the equipment/utensils used for *halal* and non-*halal* food, which may occur during food collection, washing or storage, should be avoided.

Owing to the different schools of thought in Islam, as well as different techniques of audit and investigation among scientists, and competing business interests, there may be some difficulty in maintaining consistency of *halal* certification. To illustrate this issue further, take the example of gelatine. The use of gelatine is very common in food products. The source of gelatine is not required to be identified by the United States Food and Drug Administration on product labels.[79] When the source is not known, it can be from either *halal* or *haram* sources, hence gelatine is a questionable food product for Muslims. Muslims avoid products containing gelatine unless they are certified *halal*. Common sources of gelatine are pigskin, cattle hides, cattle bones and, to a smaller extent, fish skins. *Halal* products use gelatine from cattle that have been slaughtered in an Islamic manner or from fish.

In the Islamic legal tradition, the Hanafi school proposed the widespread use of the method 'change of state' (*istihalah*) to classify food.[80] The *istihalah* method recognizes that wine is *haram*; however, if the same wine turns to vinegar it becomes *halal*, which is based on the hadith of the prophet.[81] The use of the vinegar derived from wine is *halal* as long as no wine remains in it.[82] From these examples, it becomes clear that, if an unlawful food item changes state, then the original ruling also changes. Can we apply this concept to gelatine from pigskin? The Hanafi school might support this assertion and say that gelatine from pigskin is *halal*. However, the Shafi'i school takes the view that, if *istihalah* is conducted through a normal and natural process, the changed product will be considered *halal*. If, however, the product is engineered via chemical or mechanical means, it will not be considered *halal*.[83] Different rulings applying the reasoning of the various schools of Islam will have different outcomes. One could imagine one *halal* certifier following the Hanafi school could issue a *halal* certificate, whereas another *halal* certifier might refuse to issue a *halal* certificate for a particular product using gelatine from pigskin following the Shafi'i school. Other products raising a similar issue include the use of alcohol in medicine and cosmetic products, or rennet and other animal-based enzymes in cheese-making processes.

The use of *halal* certification has become relatively common, even in countries that do not have a Muslim majority. In South Africa, most chicken products have a *halal* stamp. The South African National Halal Authority issues certificates and products bearing this logo range from water and snacks to meat-free products (which may contain non-*halal* ingredients).[84] The South African National Halal Authority also licenses the use of the *halal* logo in restaurants where the food is *halal* and no alcohol or pork products are served.[85] In the UK, China, Malaysia or Singapore, *halal* fried chicken restaurants that have thousands of outlets serve *halal* foods, such as the ChicKing Fried Chicken, Kentucky Fried Chicken, Brown's Chicken and Crown Fried Chicken companies. As of February 2009, Kentucky Fried Chicken restaurants in the UK began to sell *halal* meals in a number of restaurants.[86] In New York City there are numerous *halal* food carts in business that serve kebabs, chicken platters and other *halal* fast foods, whereas in Europe, there are many Muslim-owned (and therefore *halal*) doner kebab shops. An Ohio county passed a law in 2005 that bans the sale, distribution or production of food mislabelled *halal* when county authorities determine that the food does not meet Islamic dietary standards.[87]

In 2011, the Halal Products Certification Institute was established in California and became the first worldwide corporation to certify *halal* consumer products such as cosmetics, personal care products and perfumes and fragrances. The Institute was established by Islamic intellectual scholars and Muslim scientists to assure the dissemination of *halal* consumer products.[88] In China, *halal* restaurants run by Hui Chinese provide typical Chinese food, except that they do not serve pork, and it is known as Chinese Islamic cuisine.[89] In Australia, there are around 15 *halal* certifiers that issue *halal* certificate for both domestic and export products.

In Indonesia, the Indonesian Council of Ulama established the Assessment Institute for Foods, Drugs and Cosmetics on 6 January 1989. The Assessment Institute brings together Muslim scientists and auditors with a Fatwa Committee consisting of experts and scholars on Islamic studies to issue *halal* certificates. The scientists, who have backgrounds in chemistry, food science, biochemistry, agro industry, biology, physics and veterinary science conduct the investigations, checking the ingredients in their laboratories, while the Muslim scholars examine the report from the scientists using classic and modern *fiqh* literature before issuing a *halal* certificate. It has been estimated that the trade value of *halal* products in the global market has reached more than $US600 billion and the trade will keep increasing at 20–30 per cent annually. The potential market for *halal* products is the world's Islamic population, which is of the order of 1600 million people.

10. CONCLUSION

This chapter has discussed how Islamic law operates in societies, particularly in the context of legal institutions. Islamic law has many different faces in a practical sense. A number of rules in Islamic law, such as praying or giving to charity, can be practised without the involvement of any legal institution, but more and more legal institutions have been set up to encourage Muslims to practise their religion with the communities. In fact, in Islam the good faith of communities takes priority over that of individuals. The Quran was revealed over a 23-year period in piecemeal fashion in response to the various questions and problems facing the evolving Muslim community. As the religion spread and the borders of Muslim lands expanded, all of the different civilizations, each with their own codes of law, traditions and cultures, had to be incorporated into the *ummah*. The adaptation of Islamic law according to time and circumstance is necessitated by changes in society, and the influx of various cultures and material conditions. In short, Islamic teachings regulate both social and individual behaviour.

NOTES

1. See Taqiyuddin al-Nabhani, *Nizam al-Islam*, available at http://www.hizb-ut-tahrir.org/PDF/EN/en_books_pdf/system_of_islam.pdf
2. He did not distinguish the technical meanings of *al-imama* and *al-khilafa*. Both terms have the same general meaning.
3. Abu Hasan al-Mawardi, *al-Ahkam al-Sultaniyya* (Dar al-Fikr, Beirut, 1983), 5.
4. On the historical view of the abolition of the caliphate in 1924, see Hamid Enayat, *Modern Islamic Political Thought* (Macmillan, London, 1982), 52–68.
5. It is worth noting that Ottoman Empire for several hundred years was not a unified form of state ruling the Muslim world. Indeed, by the later stages of the Abbasid Caliphate there were different types of Islamic states in many parts of the Muslim world. For example, during the later stage of the Ottoman Empire, there were Safavid ruling in Persia, Moguls, India and other small Muslim states in other parts of the Muslim world. None of those states, including kings of Persia and Afghanistan, and Mogul emperors, had authority from the Ottoman caliphs to rule. Therefore, Muslims had other types or forms of government that were not necessarily the Islamic caliphate. Nonetheless, theoretically and based on classical Islamic teaching (and in Islamic jurisprudence), the caliphate was the only form of government recognized in Islam. More information on the history of Islamic government can be read in Ann K.S. Lambton, *State and Government in Medieval Islam* (Oxford University Press, New York, 1991); Munawir Syadzali, *Islam and Governmental System: Teachings, History, and Reflections* (INIS, Jakarta, 1991); Ahmad Syalabi, *al-Hukumah wa al-Dawlah fi al-Islam* (Maktabah al-Nahdah al-Misriyah, Cairo, 1958).
6. Ahmad Husayn Ya'qub, *al-Nizam al-Siyasi fi al-Islam: ra'y al-sunna, ra'y al-shi'a, hukm al-shar'* (Mu'assasah Ansariyan, Iran, 1312 A.H.), 250.
7. See Malcolm H. Kerr, *Islamic Reform: The Political and Legal Theories of Muhammad 'Abduh and Rashid Rida* (University of California Press, Berkeley, CA, 1966), 148.
8. See Hamid Enayat, *Modern Islamic Political Thought* (Macmillan, London, 1982), 62–8.
9. See Musdah Mulia, *Negara Islam: Pemikiran Politik Husain Haikal* (Paramadina, Jakarta, 2001).
10. For a full account see Antony Black, *The History of Islamic Political Thought: From the Prophet to the Present* (Edinburgh University Press, Edinburgh, 2001), 18–31.
11. See numerous articles in Eugene Cotran and Adel Omar Sherif (eds), *Democracy, the Rule of Law and Islam* (Kluwer Law International, London, 1999).
12. Abd al-Wahhab Khallaf, *Al-Siyasa al-Shar'iyya* (Salafiyah, Cairo, 1350 A.H.), 25.
13. Ibid., 57–8.
14. Abu Hasan al-Mawardi, *al-Ahkam al-Sultaniyya* (Dar al-Fikr, Beirut, 1983), 6.
15. Munawir Syadzali, *Islam and Governmental System: Teachings, History, and Reflections* (INIS, Jakarta, 1991), 55.

16. Ahmad bin Hanbal, *Musnad Ahmad*, hadith No. 11859.
17. Ibn Khaldun, *Muqaddimah* (Dar al-Bazi, Mecca, 1978), 194–6; see also Muhammad Mahmoud Rabi', *The Political Theory of Ibn Khaldun* (Brill, Leiden, 1967), 122–4.
18. See Fatima Mernissi, *The Forgotten Queens of Islam* (University of Minnesota Press, Minneapolis, 1993).
19. The data here is taken from Tad Stahnke and Robert C. Blitt, 'The Religion–State Relationship and the Right to Freedom of Religion or Belief: A Comparative Textual Analysis of the Constitutions of Predominantly Muslim Countries' (2005) 36 *Georgetown Journal of International Law*.
20. These states are Afghanistan, Bahrain, Brunei, Iran, Maldives, Mauritania, Pakistan, Oman, Saudi Arabia and Yemen.
21. They are Algeria, Bangladesh, Egypt, Iraq, Jordan, Kuwait, Libya, Malaysia, Morocco, Qatar, Tunisia and UAE.
22. The secular Muslim states are Burkina Faso, Chad, Guinea, Mali, Niger, Senegal, Azerbaijan, Kyrgyzstan, Tajikistan, Turkey and Turkmenistan.
23. Albania, Lebanon, Syria, Indonesia, Comoros, Djibouti, Gambia, Sierra Leone, Somalia, Sudan and Uzbekistan have no constitutional declaration regarding either an Islamic or secular state.
24. For a full account see Patricia Crone, *Medieval Islamic Political Thought* (Edinburgh University Press, Edinburgh, 2004), 358–92.
25. Abu Hasan al-Mawardi, *al-Ahkam al-Sultaniyya* (Dar al-Fikr, Beirut, 1983), 22.
26. More information on the basic concept of Shura, see Ahmad Al-Raysuni, *Al-Shura: The Qur'anic Principle of Consultation* (IIIT, Richmond, 2011).
27. Abul A'la Maududi, *Political Theory of Islam* (Islamic Publications, Lahore, 1985).
28. Fazlur Rahman, 'The Principle of Shura and the Role of the Ummah in Islam' in Mumtaz Ahmad (ed.), *State, Politics, and Islam* (American Trust Publications, Indianapolis, IN, 1986), 90–91.
29. Mishal Fahm al-Sulami, *The West and Islam* (RoutledgeCurzon, London, 2003), 123.
30. Fazlur Rahman, 'The Principle of Shura and the Role of the Ummah in Islam' in Mumtaz Ahmad (ed.), *State, Politics, and Islam* (American Trust Publications, Indianapolis, IN, 1986), 95.
31. Maududi believes that only the *ulama* can legislate on matters not covered by the Holy Texts. Abul A'la Maududi, *First Principles of the Islamic State* (Islamic Publications, Lahore, 1983), 30–31.
32. Khallaf proposes that they should consist of Muslim scholars (*al-mujtahidun wa ahl al-futya*). Abd al-Wahhab Khallaf, *Al-Siyasa al-Shar'iyya* (Salafiyah, Cairo, 1350 A.H.), 42.
33. See Fazlur Rahman, 'A Recent Controversy Over the Interpretation of Shura' (1981) 20 *History of Religions* 291–301.
34. See generally, Hossein Esmaeili, 'On a Slow Boat Towards the Rule of Law: The Nature of Law in the Saudi Arabian Legal System' (2009) 26(1) *Arizona Journal of International and Comparative Law* 1–47.
35. See Sayed Khatab, 'The Concept of Jahiliyyah in the Thought of Sayyid Quthb', Ph.D. Thesis, University of Melbourne (September 2002), 245.
36. Gamil Mohammed El-Gindy, 'The Shura and Human Rights in Islamic Law: The Relevance of Democracy' in Eugene Cotran and Mai Yamani (eds), *The Rule of Law in the Middle East and the Islamic World* (I.B. Tauris, London, 2000), 166; see also Ibrahim Hosen, 'Fiqh Siyasah dalam Tradisi Pemikiran Islam Klasik', (1993) 2(4) *Jurnal Ulumul Qur'an* 58–66.
37. Shad Saleem Faruqi, 'Constitutional Law, the Rule of Law and Systems of Governance in Islam' (Paper presented in for conference entitled 'Islamic Law and the West: Can Secular Laws and Syari'ah Co-Exist?', Asian Law Centre, University of Melbourne, 19 September 2002), 3.

38. Ibn Rusyd, *Bidayah al-Mujtahid*, Vol. 2 (Dar al-Fikr, Beirut, 1980), 377.
39. Abd al-Wahhab Khallaf, *Al-Siyasa al-Shar'iyya* (Salafiyah, Cairo, 1350 A.H.), 47.
40. Muhammad al-Zuhayli, *Tarikh al-Qada' fi al-Islam* (Dar al-Fikr al-Mu'assir, Beirut, 1995), 91.
41. Mohammad Hashim Kamali, 'Appellate Review and Judicial Independence in Islamic Law' in Chibli Mallat (ed.), *Islam and Public Law* (Graham and Trotman, London, 1993), 53.
42. C.G. Weeramantry, *Islamic Jurisprudence* (Macmillan, Basingstoke, 1988), 80.
43. Abu Hasan al-Mawardi, *al-Ahkam al-Sultaniyya* (Dar al-Fikr, Beirut, 1983), 80–92.
44. More information on the refusal of appointment of judges in the early centuries of Islam can be found in Noel J. Coulson, 'Doctrine and Practice in Islamic Law' (1956) 18 *Bulletin of the School of Oriental and African Studies* 2, 211–26.
45. See Al-Haj Mahomed Ullah Ibn S. Jung, *The Administration of Justice of Muslim Law* (Idarah-I Adabiyat-I Delhi, Delhi, 1977).
46. Irit Abramski-Blig, 'The Judiciary (Qadis) as a Governmental-Administrative Tool in Early Islam' in Wael Hallaq (ed.), *The Formation of Islamic Law* (Ashgate, Burlington, VA, 2004).
47. See M. Isabel Calero Secall, 'Rulers and Qadis: Their Relationship During the Na'rid Kingdom' (2000) 7(2) *Islamic Law and Society* 235.
48. See Christian Muller, 'Judging with God's Law on Earth: Judicial Powers of the Qadi al-Jama'a of Cordoba in the Fifth/Eleventh Century' (2000) 7(2) *Islamic Law and Society* 159.
49. See Articles 163–173 of the 1971 Egyptian Constitution (amended in 2007).
50. The official website of *dar al-ifta* of Egypt is http://www.dar-alifta.org/Module.aspx?Name=aboutdar&LangID=2
51. Their website (also available in English) is http://alifta.net/
52. Its website is only in Arabic, at http://www.fiqhacademy.org.sa/
53. Please see Chapter 6.
54. See Martin Frishman and Hasan-Uddin Khan (eds), *The Mosque: History, Architectural Development & Regional Diversity* (Thames & Hudson, New York, 2002).
55. More information can be found in Masooda Bano and Hilary Kalmbach (eds), *Women, Leadership, and Mosques* (Brill, Leiden, 2011).
56. See the list at: http://www.beliefnet.com/Faiths/Islam/2005/06/The-Islamic-Bill-Of-Rights-For-Women-In-Mosques.aspx
57. Two other holy mosques in Islam are *masjid al-nabawi* (*the Prophet's mosque*) in Medina and *masjid al-aqsa* in Jerusalem.
58. Paul Johnson, *Civilizations of the Holy Land* (Weidenfeld and Nicolson, London, 1979), 173.
59. Girma Yohannes Iyassu Menelik, *Europe: The Future Battleground of Islamic Terrorism* (GRIN Verlag, Munich, 2010).
60. See Imam Feisal Abdul Rauf, *Moving the Mountain: Beyond Ground Zero to a New Vision of Islam in America* (Free Press, New York, 2012).
61. See George Makdisi, *The Rise of the Colleges: Institutions of Learning in Islam and the West* (Edinburgh University Press, Edinburgh, 1981).
62. A useful study of the traditional roles of a *madrasa* in Islamic societies is Gary Leiser (1986), 'Notes on the Madrasa in Medieval Islamic Society' 76(1) *The Muslim World* 16–23.
63. Gary Leiser, 'Madrasa' in Josef W. Meri (ed.), *Medieval Islamic Civilization: An Encyclopedia* (Routledge, London, 2006), 457.
64. Jamal Malik (ed.), *Madrasas in South Asia: Teaching Terror?* (Routledge, London, 2007).
65. Masooda Bano, *The Rational Believer: Choices and Decisions in the Madrasas of Pakistan* (Cornell University Press, Ithaca, NY, 2012).

66. Nashihin Hasan, 'Character and Function of Pesantren' in Manfred Oepen and Wolfgang Karcher (eds), *The Impact of Pesantren in Education and Community Development in Indonesia* (P3M, Jakarta, 1987), 83–5.
67. Azim Nanji, 'Al-Azhar' in Josef W. Meri (ed.), *Medieval Islamic Civilization: An Encyclopedia* (Routledge, London, 2006), 85.
68. More information can be found in Greg Barton and Greg Fealy (eds), *Nahdlatul Ulama: Traditionalist Islam and Modernity in Indonesia* (Monash Asia Institute, Clayton, 1996); see also Nadirsyah Hosen, 'Collective Ijtihad and Nahdlatul Ulama' (2004) 6(1) *New Zealand Journal of Asian Studies* 5–26.
69. More information can be found in M. Sirajuddin Syamsuddin, 'Religion and Politics in Islam: The Case of Muhammadiyah in Indonesia's New Order,' Ph.D. Thesis, University of California Los Angeles (1991); see also Nadirsyah Hosen, 'Revelation in a Modern Nation State: Muhammadiyah and Islamic Legal Reasoning in Indonesia' (2002) 4(3) *Australian Journal of Asian Law* 232–58.
70. Barry Rubin, *The Muslim Brotherhood: The Organization and Policies of a Global Islamist Movement* (Palgrave Macmillan, Basingstoke, 2010).
71. As reported in 'Muslim Brotherhood's Mursi Declared Egypt President', BBC Online, available at http://www.bbc.co.uk/news/world-18571580
72. Sarah Mourad, 'Egypt to see First Female, Coptic Vice-presidents: Morsi Team', *Ahram*, 26 June 2012.
73. David D. Kirkpatrick, 'Blow to Transition as Court Dissolves Egypt's Parliament', *The New York Times*, 14 June 2012.
74. See Nadirsyah Hosen, 'Indonesia: A Presidential System with Checks and Balances' in T. Röder and R. Grote (eds), *Constitutionalism in Islamic Countries: Between Upheaval and Continuity* (Oxford University Press, Oxford, 2012).
75. Saiful Mujani, 'Religious Democrats: Democratic Culture and Muslim Political Participation in Post-Suharto Indonesia', Ph.D. Thesis, Ohio State University (2004).
76. Noor Ahmad Baba, *Organisation of Islamic Conference: Theory and Practice of Pan-Islamic Cooperation* (Oxford University Press, Oxford, 1994).
77. See their website at: http://www.e-cfr.org/
78. See Johan Fischer, *The Halal Frontier Muslim Consumers in a Globalized Market* (Palgrave Macmillan, New York, 2011).
79. See their official website at http://www.fda.gov/default.htm
80. Ibn Abidin, *Hasyiyah Radd Al-Muhtar 'ala al-Durr al-Mukhtar*, Vol. 1 (Dar al-Alam al-Kutub, Riyadh, 2003), 314.
81. Muslim, *Sahih Muslim* (Dar al-Qalam, Beirut, 1987), hadith no. 2051.
82. See Ibn Rushyd, *Bidayah al-Mujtahid*, Vol. 1 (Dar al-Fikr, Beirut, 1980), 461.
83. Wahbah al-Zuhayli, *al-Fiqh al-Islamy wa Adillatuhu*, Vol. 7 (Dar al-Fikr, Beirut, 1997), 5265.
84. See their website at: http://www.sanha.co.za/a/index.php
85. See Peter Shaw-Smith, 'South Africa: The *Halal* Kingdom', *Gulf Business*, 30 July 2012.
86. Debra Killalea, 'Fast Food Chain KFC Converts Eight London Restaurants to *halal*-only Menu', *Daily Mail*, 6 May 2009.
87. Joel Kurth, 'Wayne County Law Fines for Fake Islamic Diet Ads', *The Detroit News*, 5 August 2005.
88. See their website at: http://www.hpcia.com/welcome
89. More information can be found in Morris Rossabi, *Governing China's Multiethnic Frontiers* (University of Washington Press, Seattle, WA, 2005); and Dru C. Gladney, *Dislocating China: Reflections on Muslims, Minorities, and Other Subaltern Subjects* (University of Chicago Press, Chicago, IL, 2004).

3. Seeing a Western nation through Muslim eyes: Citizenship and the Sharia in modern nation-states

1. INTRODUCTION

The significant increase in the number of Muslims, either born in Western countries or migrating to these countries, has raised questions about Muslims and citizenship in the Western world. Nearly one-third of the total population of Muslims in the world are living in non-Muslims states.[1] Citizenship in non-Muslim countries, which involves respecting and applying secular legal systems and participating in social and public life, are some of the issues that Muslims may face in Europe, North America and Australia.

Modern national and international legal concepts, such as the state, citizenship and certain individual rights, are different from the traditional Islamic concepts, such as *ummah* (the Muslim nation), *kofr* (unbelief versus belief in Islam) and *dhimmah* (the status of non-Muslims living in an Islamic state).

Under traditional Islamic law the term *ummah* was used to describe the community of Muslims, which extended beyond geographical political borders and therefore was not compatible with today's dominant doctrine in international relations, which places great emphasis on states limited by geographical borders. Nevertheless, in both traditional Islam and in modern Muslim countries, the notions of states and citizens (or nationals) have, in general, been well accepted, and this will be demonstrated in this chapter. However, tensions between the traditional doctrines of Islam and the modern concept of nation-state do exist. These potentially inconsistent understandings may not pose a significant problem for Muslim states in how they conduct their relations with the rest of the world. Instead they may feed a conflicted mentality of some However, individual Muslims within Muslim or non-Muslim states may experience some conflict arising from inconsistencies which may lead to tensions between them and their communities.

The position of this chapter will be that Muslims in the West are able and willing to live in harmony with Islam and maintain their Muslim culture while participating in their respective Western societies as fellow citizens. This has been articulated by Tariq Ramadan:

> We are currently living through a veritable silent revolution in Muslim communities in the West: more and more young people and intellectuals are actively looking for a way to live in harmony with their faith while participating in the societies that are their societies, whether they like it or not. French, English, German, Canadian, and American Muslims, women as well as men, are constructing a 'Muslim personality' that will soon surprise many of their fellow citizens … They are drawing the shape of European and American Islam: faithful to principle of Islam, dressed in European and American cultures, and definitively rooted in Western societies.[2]

Given that many Muslim citizens in modern Western countries continue to practise some principles of Sharia applicable to their personal lives and relationships, inconsistencies may arise between the application of personal Sharia law and the responsibilities and obligations of Muslim individuals within their respective legal systems. (This is discusssed in Chapter 5 on Islamic family law.) Historically, Muslims have been members of different societies and have taken up the responsibilities and obligations of modern citizenship. However, a small minority of Muslims in the West draw on certain traditional notions of Islamic law that will be explored in this chapter, which have the potential to generate tension and discordance by contradicting some of values embedded in modern Western legal systems.

This chapter will first briefly discuss the doctrines of nationality and citizenship in modern legal systems. Next, it will analyse the concepts of *ummah* and the associated notions and citizenship in Sharia. Finally, it will discuss contemporary aspects of citizenship for Muslims and the application of Sharia within modern states.

2. NATION-STATE, CITIZENSHIP AND NATIONALITY

There are different meanings for the term 'state'.[3] The concept of a nation-state originated in the Europe during the Middle Ages and developed through the Renaissance, and is today recognized in modern international law. Before the advent of the doctrine of 'nation-states', there were major imperial powers, tribes and local entities but no nation-states.[4]

Citizenship, which defines membership of a common society, is a political enterprise.[5] It is an important institution of modern societies that is related to national identity.[6] The history and concept of citizenship are concerned with political and legal theories related to the independence and status of individuals, and the recognition of independent sovereign nation-states. While concepts of sovereignty developed during the Middle Ages in Europe and are rooted in Western political and philosophical tradition, the doctrine of sovereignty was not confined to a specific territory or geographical border, but was associated with the unity of God in a *Respublica Christiana* and was considered to be universal.[7] The Roman Catholic figure of the sovereignty of God takes the form of the Pope on Earth.[8] The doctrine of a universal *Respublica Christiana* was gradually replaced by the concept of the sovereign and an independent nation-state, which emerged in Europe from the mid seventeenth century. The concept of individual sovereign states steadily became more widely accepted, so that by the nineteenth century it formed the basis of various international conventions. Moreover, by the twentieth century the primacy of nation-states was well recognized by the League of Nations (1919) and the Charter of the United Nations (1945).

A 'state' is defined in legal theory and in international law as having a population inhabiting a defined territory with a form of ordered government, a legal system, a degree of independence and a capacity to enter relations with other states.[9]

Nationality is another modern concept that is connected to the concept of the nation-state. This term describes the legal connection between an individual and the state.[10] The International Court of Justice in the *Nottebohm* case defined nationality as:

> [a] legal bond having as its basis a social fact of attachment, a genuine connection of existence, interests and sentiments, together with the existence of reciprocal rights and duties. It may be said to constitute the juridical expression of the fact that the individual upon whom it is conferred, either directly by the law or as the result of an act of the authorities, is in fact more closely connected with the population of the State conferring nationality than with that of any other State.[11]

Citizenship, which is used more in a domestic law context, refers to the connection of an individual to a political and geographical entity. In the Western legal tradition the notion of citizenship originated in the Athenian city-state and had a narrow interpretation, only confined to free men who owned property.[12] Modern citizenship is part of a new nation-state doctrine that establishes a reciprocal relationship between the state and citizens. Citizenship is a bundle of rights and duties relating to a person's social role in society.[13] The rights and duties of individuals, as well as those of states, are regulated by the legal system. The legal system may be based on the principles of democracy, which derive from people's decisions through voting, or it could be imposed by unelected sovereigns. This means that citizenship derives from both international law and domestic law. International law recognizes state sovereignty and national laws determine an individual's nationality and citizenship. Recent globalization has forced some changes to the strict concept of political boundaries of nationality and citizenship in some regions of the world, such as the European Union. International immigration and the significant movement of people across borders have also caused some issues with respect to traditional concepts of loyalty and citizenship. For example, in 2011, 24.6 per cent of Australia's population was born overseas.[14]

Muslims are not only citizens of many non-Muslim countries, but the concept of citizenship is also now present in all Muslim countries. This means that, although all Muslims follow the same religion, an Arab Muslim of Iraq is only recognized as a citizen of Iraq and not of other Arab Islamic states in the region.[15]

3. SHARIA IN A MODERN NATION

Historically, in Islam the political community of believers (*ummah*) with its leader (the Prophet, an imam or a caliph) had no territorial border but individual Muslims were members of the *ummah* regardless of the territory in which they lived.[16] As Khadduri explained: 'Islamic law, like all ancient law, had a personal rather than a territorial character and was obligatory upon the Muslims, as individuals or as a group, regardless of the territory they reside in'.[17]

Under Islam there is no separation of religion and law. The dominant approach of the majority of Muslims, including those residing in the West, is that in the Islamic tradition, law and religion are considered to be the same, or to predominantly overlap. In most other societies and nations, notably those based on Christianity, Buddhism or Hinduism, law and religion are regarded as being largely separate; however, for many Muslims and historically in Muslim societies, law and religion have been, and still are, inextricably entwined.[18] Islam has its own unique system of law with distinctive features, such as its divine origin and the sacredness of certain legal principles, as discussed in Chapter 1.[19] Western literature on Islamic law and the writings of most Muslim scholars make clear that in Islam religion and law are the same,[20] although the boundaries of religion extend beyond legal principles.

Under Islam, as reviewed in Chapter 1, the experiences of life are divided into five classes (obligatory (*wajib*), *mandoub*, *mubah*, *makruh* and prohibited (*haram*)). Only two categories, obligatory (*wajib*) and prohibited (*haram*),[21] are the subject of proper Islamic law. The other three categories are traditionally concerned with the boundaries of ethics and morality. It is not intended here to discuss in detail the nature of law and religion in Islam,[22] but adopting the presumption that law and religion overlap allows the implications of this overlap for Western Muslim to be considered.

Different Arabic and English terms are used to explain Islamic concepts. As outlined further in Chapter 1, it is very important to understand that the terms 'Islam', 'Sharia' and 'Islamic law' have different meanings and classifications. The term 'Islam', and hence the religion of Islam, has various interpretations. Islam can be divided into scriptural Islam (based on the Quran), the understanding by Muslims of Islam (*fiqh*) and historical Islam (understood in terms of the development of Muslim civilization). Furthermore, the understanding and interpretation of Islam (*fiqh*) can be divided into different interpretations such as fundamentalist, traditional Islam and modernist Islam. Apart from these classifications, Islam can be divided into another series of overlapping categories: Sharia-orientated Islam (known simply as Sharia); philosophical Islam (*hikmat*); mystical Islam (Sufism or *irfan*); and theological Islam (*kalam*). To these sub-classifications, one may also add secular Muslims or secular Islam to denote an approach to religion that limits it to a personal relationship between God and the individual.[23] Terms such as 'fundamentalist', 'traditionalist' and 'modernist' are contemporary terms used predominantly in the last few decades since the 1970s. Conservative views on Islam presented by scholars such as Seyyed Qutb are labelled in English literature as 'fundamentalist'. However, in mainstream Western media, 'fundamentalism' also refers to Islamic scholars and Muslim political parties and organizations which support the establishment of Islamic states. These groups present Islam as a political ideology. 'Traditional' Islam, emphasized by scholars such as Seyyed Hossein Nasr, refers to Islam as the main force guiding individuals' lives, but does not imply a political ideology or goal. 'Modernist' Islam refers to an approach that proposes re-interpretations of Islam and Sharia to accommodate modern circumstances and conditions.

However, there are other categorizations of Islam. 'Sharia-oriented' Islam or *Islam fiqhahati* refers to the approach to Islam that emphasizes the behaviour-regulating function of Islam, known as Sharia. A majority of Islamic *foqaha* (plural of *faqih*) works are concerned with Sharia and the rules of conduct under Islam. It should be noted that *foqaha* may also discuss other aspects of Islam, such as Islamic philosophy (*hikmat*) and Islamic theosophy (*irfan*), but with less emphasis than in Sharia. Philosophical Islam refers to an approach where scholars see a broader picture of Islamic principles and emphasize the messages of Islam. As with Western philosophy, *hikmat* scholars seek to answer the 'big' questions about life: why we are here, the nature of life and death, and the meaning of 'oneness of God' (*towhid*). Avicenna (Ibn Sina), Omar Khayam and Averroes (Ibn Rushd) were Islamic scholars who wrote on Islamic philosophy. Mystical Islam (Sufism or *irfan*) refers to an approach to Islam that dominated some parts of the Muslim world, or influenced Islamic scholarship for centuries, up to the mid-twentieth century. Sufism was, indeed, a reaction to the rigidity of Sharia as applied by Omayyed and Abbasid caliphs for centuries. The most significant scholars of Sufi Islam were Ghazali (d. 1111) and Ibn Arabi (d. 1240). Ghazali, who was a Chief Justice of Baghdad before reaching the age of 40 during the Abbasid period, left legal scholarship for Sufism and *irfan*: in other words, he became a follower of mysticism order (*tariqah*). Ghazali's liberal views dominated Muslim scholarship up to the mid-twentieth century, when more conservative views started to become prevalent. Ibn Arabi, like many other followers of Sufism, had an approach and interpretation of the Quran and hadith based on the centrality of love (*ishgh*) in religion. In his view, the love offered in *tariqah* can be found in the mosque, the church or the synagogue.[24] Theological Islam (*kalam*) refers to an approach to religion based on a study of theology (*kalam*).

4. VERSIONS OF ISLAM IN THE WEST

When referring to Islam, whether in the West or elsewhere, each of those categories may be relevant, but for the purpose of this paper the focus will be on Sharia-orientated Islam and its relevance in the West. Sharia will be discussed within the framework of three phases of Islamic history: traditional Islam, historical Islam and the modern Muslim world (as distinct from modernist Islam).[25]

The first phase, which can be called traditional Islam, started with the advent of Islam and continued during and beyond the Righteous Caliphate (632–661) for almost half a century. This period was superseded by the independent juristic work of great Muslim scholars in the mid eighth century and coincided with the end of the Umayyad dynasty and the start of the Abbasid Caliphate. Therefore, reference to traditional Islam in this chapter indicates Sharia that developed at the time of the Prophet and the

Righteous Caliphate, and through the juristic works of Muslim scholars in the eighth and ninth centuries. The theoretical basis of traditional Sharia is the Quran, the Sunna and the original development of Islamic jurisprudence, while the practical basis for Sharia as implemented in Muslim societies developed early in the Islamic caliphate.

Historical Islam describes the period from the mid seventh century (the time of the Prophet) to the final collapse of the Ottoman Empire in the early 1900s. The modern era of Sharia began at the time of the collapse of the Ottoman Empire, and encompasses the emergence of modern nation-states in the Muslim world, and the introduction of modern European legal codes in Muslim territories, as well as the movement of Muslims, and thus the Sharia, into non-Muslim lands.

5. TERMS

Instead of using terms such as 'fundamentalist', 'puritan' and 'extremist', on the one hand, and 'modernist' on the other, this chapter uses different terms in the context of Muslims living in modern nation-states, including Western countries. It is proposed here that the term 'marginal' might be used to refer to a minority group in the Muslim societies of modern Western democratic states while the term 'mainstream' best describes the majority of Muslims. Other terms, such as 'violent', 'terrorist' and 'honour killers' that are sometimes associated with Muslims in Western societies are more closely related to the subject-matter of criminal law and are not relevant to this discussion because behaviour such as gang rape, violence, murder and the brutal treatment of women is not associated with Islam as a religion. Although a very small minority of individuals may justify these acts with reference to religion, the perpetration of crimes such as the ones mentioned is more closely associated with other factors. Apart from problems with the terms 'fundamentalist' and 'extremist' on the one hand, the terms 'modernist' and 'progressive' are similarly inapplicable to the everyday experiences of Muslims in the West. These terms resonate for political parties, groups or intellectuals, and do not resonate with the lives and experiences of ordinary Muslims. Terms such as 'mainstream' are more appropriate to describe the majority of people of a certain ethnic or religion background, in this case Muslims.

6. THE MUSLIM NATION (*UMMAH*) IN THE MODERN ERA

Under traditional and historical Islam the concept of the nation-state was subsumed under the concept of the Muslim nation (*ummah*). The term *ummah* is also known as Allah's commonwealth.[26] In traditional Islam the ideal world included the equivalent of one nation (the *ummah*), one state (the caliphate) and one legal system (Sharia). The basic principle of the political structure of the *ummah* was the association of individuals bonding with each other based on their religion.[27]

The doctrine of *ummah* is referred in both the Quran and the hadith. According to the Quran, Muslims are the best of all communities and are bound by common belief and obligations to God; they are required to assist people to be good.[28] The first treaty of Islam was drafted by the Prophet Mohammad and constituted a formal agreement between Mohammad and all the tribes and families of Medina, including Jews, Muslims, Christians and pagans. In it the Muslim community was defined as 'an *ummah* in distinction from the rest of the people'.[29] While the term *ummah* once referred to a community of Muslim believers, in recent times it has come to be seen by many Muslims as a vast multicultural collective with well-defined cultural features. Riaz Hassan found that the notion of *ummah* consciousness among Muslims in Muslim countries such as Indonesia, Malaysia, Pakistan, Egypt, Kazakhstan, Iran and Turkey was strong in comparison to that of modern Muslims living elsewhere.[30] Hassan concluded:

> The empirical evidence and my observations have led me to the conclusion that strong religious piety is reinforcing the traditionalistic self-image of Islam in Muslim countries. This is producing a kind of cultural conditioning that is not conductive to the pursuit of rational, objective and critical scholarship because of the ideological control imposed by the traditionalistic self-image of Islam.[31]

The original *ummah* was established in Medina (622 AD) when an agreement was concluded between the people of Medina, then known as Yathrib,[32] Jews of Medina and the Prophet Mohammad and his followers, who had migrated from Mecca as a result of persecution by their own people. The agreement is known as the Charter of Medina. Although the agreement was within the boundaries of the city, it included various tribes of Medina, Mecca and Jews. Later, the Jews and pagans were excluded from the original *ummah*, which was the result of several breaches of treaties that existed between Muslims and Jews. However,

Jews, as well as Christians, were granted the status of People of the Book and their life, property and practice of religion (with some limitations) were recognized and protected within the *ummah*. According to Bernard Lewis:

> From the start, the Islamic *umma* had a dual character. On the one hand it was a political society – a chieftaincy which swiftly grew into a state and then an empire; on the other it was a religious community, founded by a Prophet and ruled by his deputy. In its origins, it followed the only acceptable political model, that of the Arabian tribe or tribal confederacy.[33]

The life of the city-state of Medina, and later Mecca, was just over 10 years. Afterwards, the Islamic state expanded into other parts of the Middle East, Africa and Asia. However, the practice of the Prophet in the state of Medina, as well as the practice of his companions and followers, is significant in shaping the concept of Islamic *ummah*. The caliphate and the *ummah*, as practised and developed in the very early stage of Islamic history, steadily weakened over the centuries, so that by the tenth century the once-united community had disintegrated into numerous smaller autonomous Muslim entities, and collapsed formally in 1918. According to Majid Khadduri, the city-state of Medina became imperial from 632 AD to 750 AD and then universal for about two centuries, up until 900 AD, when it became decentralized and fragmented.[34]

The decentralization and fragmentation of the Islamic state (caliphate) and the formation of national states occurred for both internal and external reasons. The internal reasons were the conflicts that existed within the Islamic *ummah* from the earliest stage of Islam, when civil wars took place and different schools of thought and sects emerged. The external reasons included the rise of national identity within the expanded world of Islam and the formation of modern nation-states in the nineteenth century.

There are now over 57 independent Muslim countries that are sovereign, independent members of the United Nations. The concept of *ummah* in the contemporary world seems to be of more religious than legal significance. The Islamic *ummah* means that Muslim individuals are bound together because of their religion. Under international law, as well as domestic law, there are no significant legal consequences attached to being a member of the *ummah*. Nevertheless, in international relations, or in interpersonal relations, the *ummah* may be relevant. There are a number of international and regional multilateral legal institutions that are associated with Islam and Muslims, such as the Organisation of Islamic Cooperation and the Islamic Development Bank.[35] In the domestic law of some Muslim countries, such as Saudi Arabia, Iran and Malaysia, Islam is either the principal source of law or *a* source of law and, therefore, being a Muslim has significant legal consequences under these domestic legal systems. In the West, it is the idea of citizenship and individual rights that has substantial legal consequences. However, religious groups in the West, including Muslims, have religious agencies, schools, mosques and other Islamic institutions that may accommodate aspects of Islamic principles and laws.

The closest concept to *ummah* in the Western countries, such as Australia, France and the UK, is the Muslim community. However, a better way to describe Muslims in Western countries is to use the term 'Muslim communities', owing to the intra-communal diversity of Muslims who have different interpretations of Islam and diverse and distinctive cultural and ethnic backgrounds. Ideally, Muslim communities in the West (the *ummah*) should be moral and vibrant communities that practise Islam within the boundaries of domestic law in the country where they live.

7. *DHIMMAH*

The concept of *ummah* is also associated with the concept of *dhimmah*, held in traditional Islam to be a status given to certain non-Muslims (Christians, Jews and, according to some schools, Zoroastrians), which guaranteed security of their life and property, and freedom to practise their religion, but which did not accord full citizenship.[36] Traditionally, non-Muslims could practise their own law and religion in return for payment of a special tax (*jizya*) to the Islamic state. Under this system, religious minorities could only enjoy partial citizenship rights. The *dhimmah* system was significant, as religious minorities could regulate their personal law according to their own religious law. Consequently, Muslim judges were obliged to enforce their religious law when both parties followed a particular minority religion. This is reflected in the Iranian Constitution, which provides that: 'Iranian Zoroastrians, Jews, and Christians are the only recognized religious minorities that are free to practise their religion (within the boundaries of the law) and to practise their personal law [marriage, divorce, inheritance and wills] according to their religion'.[37]

The *dhimmah* system was developed to determine political allegiance on the basis of religious affiliation, and it is in contrast to the modern doctrine of allegiance based on a territory.[38] These traditional Islamic doctrines of *ummah* and *dhimmah* are related to the principle of Islamic international relations (*siyar*) known as the territorial division of the world into the Muslim territory (*dar al-Islam*) and non-Muslim territory (*dar al-harb*). The former refers to the territory under Muslim rule at the time of the Abbasid Empire, and the latter (which literally translates from Arabic as 'territory of war') consists of all the states and communities outside the world of Islam.[39]

Historically, the boundary of the *dar al-Islam* was within the borders of the Islamic caliphate. As the caliphate became decentralized from 900AD, the concept of territorial division of the world became less significant, particularly while different Islamic states were in a state of war with each other. Furthermore, Muslim jurists developed a third division called *dar al-sulh* (territory of peace), also known as *dar al-hayad* (neutral territory).[40] This applied to almost all territories that were not in war with the Islamic state.

The *dhimmah* system has been replaced with the modern international system of territorial states in almost all Muslim countries. Nevertheless, there is some limited application of the *dhimmah* in a few Muslim countries, such as Saudi Arabia and Iran. In Iran, the legal status of Christians, Jews and Zoroastrians is recognized by the Constitution and members of these religious communities can practise their religion, although, Baha'is are not recognized as an official religious minority and cannot have their own places of worship or practise their religion publicly. The transformation was instituted by modern international influences, in some cases by European colonialism, but Muslim societies have voluntarily sustained the state-based citizenship system.[41] However, conflicts between the modern concept of citizenship and certain traditional Islamic doctrines, such as *dhimmah* and its original values, still emerge sporadically in Islam and in Muslim societies.[42]

In the modern era, certain Muslim groups and Islamic scholars have tried to revive this notion of Islamic public law.[43] This means establishing the Islamic caliphate or a strict Islamic state where non-Muslims are treated as *dhimmi*s if they are Christians or Jews.

8. MUSLIMS, CITIZENSHIP AND SHARIA

For many Muslims, belonging to the community of Muslims is very important. For some, belonging to the Muslim community is more important than their sense of nationality. For some Muslims, the payment of Islamic taxes, such as *zakat*, is more important than paying conventional taxes. Many Muslims marry and divorce according to Islamic law and are more concerned about the consequences of religious law than the domestic legal system of the country in which they live.

The question to be addressed in this chapter is: do Muslims, who adhere to certain principles of Sharia (that is, mainly to Islamic beliefs, rituals and Muslim personal law) challenge notions linked to citizenship, such as Australian, British, French or other national identities and sovereignty? For example, the national identity of modern nation-states, such as Australia, has many diverse components and complexities.[44] Important facets of the national identity of modern democracies are adherence to the rule of law, human rights and the equality of men and women. These particular aspects of the Western democratic national identity may pose challenges for some Muslims who adhere faithfully to certain principles of Sharia, which they are concerned may conflict with these modern principles.

There are opinions in many Western countries that the continued practice of Sharia by Muslims in the West may threaten certain core values of these democracies. Supporters of the view that Muslim immigration poses a threat to modern national identities cite traditional public law doctrines of Islamic law, such as the concept of *ummah* and the territorial divisions of the territory of Islam (*dar al-Islam*) and the territory of war (*dar al-harb*) in support of an argument that Muslim migrants cannot integrate into Western societies.[45] They argue that Muslims consider themselves as part of the *ummah* and view non-Muslim territories as the land of war and hence do not accept the notion of belonging to other modern non-Muslim societies, which is a key element of upholding citizenship in Western societies.[46] This is an extreme view held by only a very small minority of Muslim individuals and does not reflect the views and practices of the overwhelming majority of Muslims living in non-Muslims countries.

The traditional concepts of Islam, such as the *ummah*, have been modified and now have more moral than legal significance. The doctrines of *ummah* and the territorial division of the world into *dar al-Islam* and *dar al-harb* were the traditional, fundamental principles of international relations in Islam for many centuries. At the time, these doctrines were progressive compared with the pre-existing rules. However, over the last few centuries, these principles have been changed and modified. The practical non-adherence to a strict version of *ummah* and *dar al-Islam* can be seen in the actions of the three dominant Muslim states of the last few centuries (the Ottomans, the Persian Empire and the Mughal Empire). These empires entered into varieties of bilateral and unilateral treaties with other nations and practically recognized geographical and political boundaries. In all three empires, there were sizeable communities of non-Muslims. Under the Muslim Mughal Empire, the overwhelming majority of the population was Hindu, not Muslim.

Nevertheless, in recent times segments of Muslim communities in modern democratic societies, such as the UK and Australia, have begun to elaborate an approach to certain principles of Sharia and how these should apply in such societies. Some immigrants to the West have encountered difficulties in understanding and participating in the complex nature of democratic societies and have found a stronger bond with certain public aspects of Islam in a superficial approach. Members of this segment are predominately unemployed and so have turned to extremist views, to crime and to other anti-social behaviours. They are intolerant of others and of the legal norms of modern societies and are susceptible to sectarian and extremist beliefs. While they are a very small minority, unfortunately they are sometimes influential in the Muslim communities since they may be in charge of Muslim institutes and centres.

The approach of this minority uses certain specific principles of Sharia that were articulated by Muslim jurists in defined circumstances and periods, such as the doctrines of *ummah*, jihad (warfare),[47] the territorial division of the world, the concept of *dhimmah*, and the status of unbelievers (*kofr*). These principles were developed by Muslim jurists during the expanded periods of the Islamic caliphates (632AD–900AD). However, sources of Islamic law, including the Quran, Islamic jurisprudence (*fiqh*) and Sharia embody a large number of principles that emphasize pluralism within societies, freedom of religion and respect for treaties and covenants. Obviously, Muslims who migrate and live in non-Muslim countries enter into agreements and covenants by obtaining visas and citizenship, which bind them to the domestic law of the state in which they live. For example, the Quran, the Sunna and the history of Islam emphasize the strict obligations of Muslims to observe their agreements, contracts and duties. According to the Quran: 'it is not the symbol of righteousness that you turn your faces towards the east or the west (praying), but through righteousness is to believe in Allah … and to fulfil your agreements'.[48] The message of Islam not only promotes pluralism, respect for the law, treaties and covenants, and rights of individuals and communities; the content of Islamic jurisprudence and certain principles of Sharia, discussed elsewhere in this book, endorse respect for legal systems where Muslims live.

A. 'Marginal' Interpretations of the Quran: Interpreting *kofr*

'Marginal' Muslims in the West, or conservative scholars in the Muslim world, have sometimes interpreted Quranic principles using a literal and inflexible method. One clear example of this interpretation of the Quran is the way that some Muslims understand the term 'unbeliever' (*kofr*). The Quran uses the term *kofr* in many verses, but its exact meaning, particularly in legal terms, is not clear.[49] The literal meaning of *kofr* is 'covering' and is taken to mean denying the truth. In legal terms it means the rejection of Islam, in terms of denying the existence of God or the prophetic mission of the Prophet of Islam. A number of verses in the Quran, revealed during the conflict with non-believers in Medina (613–623 AD), ordered Muslims not to socialize and enter into friendships with non-believers of Mecca.[50]

The legal principles set out in the Quran were revealed, developed and applied in special circumstance in the early history of Muslim societies. It is crucial to understand that they have been reformed and adopted by subsequent Muslim societies and Muslim jurists. Many of the principles elucidated in the Quran may no longer apply or may apply in a substantially different way. Most of the legal principles of Islam developed from the sixth century onwards – after the time of the Prophet – and are mainly the product of human knowledge and the experience of Muslim individuals, state and scholars. Therefore, a superficial approach to the principles of Sharia, using only the words of the Quran without also considering the development in understanding of those words and concepts over the centuries, breeds a negative view about a society, which can limit the ability of Muslims to freely and happily enjoy their lives.

Using such an interpretation of *kofr* may result in Muslims not fully engaging in the societies where they live and being concerned about socializing and forming friendships with non-Muslims. According to the Quran, 'Allah does not forbid you establishing relationship and to do justice to those who have not fought you because of your religion and have not driven you out of your homeland, verily Allah likes those who consider justice towards other people'.[51] Obviously, Muslims who are citizens of Western countries by virtue of their citizenship have been granted protection and rights similar to Western nationals and according to the Quran must be involved in relationships with others in their adopted countries. This means that they have to embrace and observe their rights and duties as citizens of any nation.

B. Using a Negative Interpretation of the Quran, Súra Nisáa 4:141

Religions, including Islam, may be interpreted in different ways. In particular, the content of the Quran can be interpreted differently according to context. Sometimes, certain Quranic principles may be approached negatively. For example a verse of the Quran (Súra Nisáa 4:141) provides:

> (These are) the ones who wait and watch about you: if ye do gain a victory from God, they say: 'Were we not with you?' But if the Unbelievers gain a success, they say (to them): 'Did we not gain an advantage over you, and did we not guard you from the Believers?' but God will judge betwixt you on the Day of Judgment. And never will God grant to the Unbelievers a way (to triumph) [authority] over the Believers.[52]

Based on the last part of this verse ('[a]nd never will God grant to the Unbelievers a way (to triumph) [authority] over the Believers'), some Muslim jurists have developed a legal principle, known as the rule of *nafy sabil*,[53] which implies that Muslim states and authorities should avoid certain relations with non-Muslim states and that authority by unbelievers over believers is not allowed by the Quran. This could mean that Muslim public authorities must maintain their independence in their international relations from non-Muslims. One interpretation of this injunction leads to the conclusion that it is un-Islamic for Muslims to abide by the laws of non-Muslim authorities. However, this presumption can be historically, logically and practically challenged. This verse of the Quran was specifically revealed to denounce those members of the Medina community who did not have loyalty to the Islamic state of Medina while they demanded their share of the spoils. However, at the same time they would ask the unbelievers of Medina for their share. The Quran states that there would be no triumph over the believers by non-believers of Mecca. Indeed, Muslims triumphed over non-Muslims in both Medina and later in Mecca. Therefore, this statement cannot be interpreted as a universal principle; rather it referred to a specific situation concerned with the hypocrites (*monafiqin*) in Medina and their expectation of obtaining a share from the triumph of the unbelievers over Muslims in Medina. It does not suggest that Muslims shall not follow the law of a country they reside in if that country is not ruled by Sharia. Indeed there are only a few Muslim states that claim authority from Sharia in their law-making procedures. Ironically, many Muslims recently migrating to Europe, Australia and North America are those who have escaped those states.[54] A practical consequence of such an interpretation would result in a lack of respect for the law in almost all countries as well as a delay in establishing effective legal systems in the Muslim world.

A more general interpretation of the last part of the Quranic verse 4:141 can be seen in the development of legal principles in Islamic jurisprudence (*fiqh*). For example, according to Muslim jurists,[55] one rationale for the prohibition of marriage of a Muslim woman with a non-Muslim man is to avoid the authority and triumph of non-Muslims over believers. Obviously, the nature of marriage and the marriage relationship in the modern world, including in Muslim countries, has changed significantly. This is particularly relevant in modern democratic nations, such as Australia and the UK, where marriage is a union between two equal persons and no party has authority over the other.[56]

C. The 'Mainstream' Muslim Majority

The history of Muslim societies, as well the history of Muslim communities resident in non-Muslim countries (such as India and Africa), demonstrates that the majority of Muslims, like people everywhere, are for the most part law-abiding citizens of their respective community. Their approach to religion is also nonextremist, traditional and customary.

Despite the focus within some sectors of the media and community in Western countries on the war-like characteristics of Islam, often referred to as 'jihad', Muslims are no more war-like than any other people. In fact, the assumption that the history of Islamic societies and Muslim communities, whether as a majority or minority, is a history of war, conflict and discrimination is not factually correct. Some societies and nations *were* ruled by Muslim rulers for centuries, but the majority of people in those nations were non-Muslims and this can be seen in the history of such countries as India, Spain, Lebanon, Armenia and Georgia. In addition, Muslim communities, as minority groups, peacefully co-existed with non-Muslim majorities for centuries and have been loyal citizens and law-abiding members of their community. Examples include Muslim communities in India, the Balkans, Thailand, the Philippines, Fiji, and many African countries.[57] Muslim immigration to the West, including to Europe, North America and Australia, is a recent phenomenon. Between 2001 and 2007 the Gallup organization conducted a comprehensive series of interviews (totalling 50,000 hours) with nationals of more than 40 Muslim nations, concluding that 'about 9 in 10 Muslims are moderates'.[58]

Muslim communities in modern democratic countries endeavour to harmonize their religious beliefs with the principles that exist within a modern nation-state, such as a modern conception of citizenship, being law-abiding and loyal citizens. There are challenges to a complete synergy between Islam and the experience of life in the West, but given the diversity and cultural wealth of Muslim communities and the nature of democratic legal systems and cultures, it is highly likely that the Muslim communities will prosper along with other ethnic and religious groups within Western societies.

Islamic law generally binds individuals and many Muslims observe Sharia personal law even if they happen to be in non-Muslim territories or in a country that is secular. Observance of certain principles of Sharia by Muslims in a non-Muslim society may not be contradictory to state law as long it is reasonably consistent with the legal boundaries of that state. Muslims have generally adjusted their religion to the realities of contemporary society. Indeed Sharia has developed mainly free of state interference, largely through independent legal consultation (*fatwa*) and by independent Muslim jurists (*foqaha*) in the form of Islamic jurisprudence (*fiqh*). The understanding of Islam can be adjusted readily and can be applied in various societies comprising different cultures and social practices but within the legal system of the host country.

The majority of Muslim communities in democratic societies such as Australia adhere to the dominant and practical version of Islam with an emphasis on the essence of Islam, which is a belief in one God, rituals and the humanitarian message of Islam and Muslim personal law, which will help Muslim communities to prosper as members and citizens of democratic societies.

9. CONCLUSION

The concepts of citizenship and nationality are inventions of Western legal and political traditions and modern international law, and are associated with the development of the modern nation-state. The corresponding concept in traditional Islamic law is the doctrine of *ummah* or the Muslim community of believers. This doctrine and its associated notions, such as the caliphate and *dhimmah*, have been transformed in the Muslim world to encompass the modern concepts of citizenship and the nation-state. Furthermore, these public law aspects of Sharia are more the concern of political parties, states and legal scholars and are not of much immediate interest to ordinary Muslims living in non-Muslim countries.

For the majority of Muslims living in non-Muslim countries, Islam and Sharia both refer, in broad terms, to a belief in God, the humanitarian message of Islam, rituals and Islamic personal law. The majority of Muslims in Western countries are concerned with acknowledgement of their identities, the practice of their faith and the preservation of their tradition and their family life and values. This approach to Islam is compatible with modern democratic legal systems and with values such as the rule of law, human rights and the equality of people. However, it must be acknowledged that a very small proportion of Muslims may still feel tension between traditional concepts of Islamic law and modern international norms relating to the nation-state and the national concept of citizenship, and its rights and responsibilities.

The history of Muslim societies, whether as the dominant population or as a minority, reveals that Muslims have been members of their particular community and that they discharge the responsibilities and obligations that come with contemporary citizenship. The overwhelming majority of Muslims living in modern democratic states, like most members of other religious or ethnic groups, are law-abiding, hard-working men and women who wish to live in harmony with their community. As John Esposito has pointed out, 'despite problems, however, Muslims long regarded as "other" are now part of the fabric of our society, as neighbours, co-workers, citizens, and believers'.[59] Nevertheless, certain traditional notions of Islam, if not dealt with rationally and wisely, may generate tension and apprehension and can motivate a marginal minority to ignore the fundamental legal values of modern legal systems. This may lead to the isolation and marginalization of parts of the wider Muslim community in modern democratic nations. It is therefore vital that those with the skills and understanding within the Muslim communities of Western countries pursue all avenues to ensure that Islam, as applied and understood in their community, encompasses the true richness and depth of one of the world's great religions.

NOTES

1. Muhammad Anwar, 'Muslims in Western States: The British Experience and the Way Forward' (2008) 28(1) *Journal of Muslim Minority Affairs* 125.
2. Tariq Ramadan, *Western Muslims and the Future of Islam* (Oxford University Press, Oxford, 2004), 4.
3. D.P. O'Connell, *International Law*, Vol. 1 (Stevens & Sons, London, 1970), 283.
4. Walther Hug, 'History of Comparative Law' (1932) 45 *Harvard Law Review* 1027, 1034.
5. J.M. Barbalet, *Citizenship* (Open University Press, Milton Keynes, 1988), 1.
6. Stephen Castles and Alastair Davidson, *Citizenship and Migration: Globalization and Politics of Belonging* (Macmillan, Basingstoke, 2000), 10.
7. Harold Laski, *The Foundations of Sovereignty and Other Essays* (Allen & Unwin, London, 1921), 2.
8. Ronald A. Brand, 'Sovereignty: The State, the Individual, and the International Legal System in the Twenty First Century' (2002) 25 *Hastings Journal of International & Comparative Law* 279, 281.

9. H.L.A. Hart, *The Concept of Law* (Oxford University Press, Oxford, 1961), 216. See also the 1933 Montevideo Convention on Rights and Duties of States, Article 1.
10. D.P. O'Connell, *International Law*, Vol. 2, 2nd edn (Stevens & Sons, London, 1970), 670.
11. *Nottebohm (Liechtenstein v Guatemala)* ICJ Rep (1995) 4, 23.
12. On the historical background of citizenship see D. Heater, *Citizenship: The Civic Ideal in World History, Politics and Education* (Longman, New York, 2004); and T.L. Dynneson, *Civism, Cultivating Citizenship in European History* (Peter Lang, New York, 2001).
13. Jose V. Ciprut, 'Citizenship: Mere Contract, or Construct for Conduct?' in Jose V. Ciprut, *The Future of Citizenship* (The MIT Press, Cambridge, MA, 2008), 1, 17.
14. 'Key facts from the 2011 Census', *The Australian* (21 June 2012), available at http://www.theaustralian.com.au/national-affairs/key-facts-from-the-2011-census/story-fn59niix-1226404283130
15. For some further discussion on citizenship and Muslims, see Tariq Modood, Anna Triandafyllidou and Rocard Zapata-Barrero, *Multiculturalism, Muslims and Citizenship, A European Approach* (Routledge, London, 2006).
16. See Majid Khadduri (translated with an introduction, notes and appendices) *The Islamic Law of Nations, Shaybani's Siyar* (John Hopkins University Press, Baltimore, MD, 1966).
17. Majid Khadduri, *War and Peace in the Law of Islam* (John Hopkins University Press, Baltimore, MD, 1955), 45.
18. In the view of Professor Nasr: '[R]eligion to a Muslim is essentially the Divine Law': Seyyed Hossein Nasr, *Ideals and Realities of Islam*, 2nd edn (Praeger, Westport, CT, 1975), 95.
19. See Chapter 1.
20. Abdulaziz Sachedina, 'Theology, Law and the Self-Governance of Religious Communities: Guidance or Governance? A Muslim Conception of "Two-Cities"' (2000) 68 *George Washington Law Review* 1079. See also Seyyed Hossein Nasr, *Ideals and Realities of Islam* (Praeger, Westport, CT, 1966), 95.
21. Al-Amidi, *Seif al-din Abi al_Hassan Ali ibn Abi Ali ibn Mohammad, Al-akhan Fi Usul al-ahkam* [The Principles of Islamic Rules], Vol. 1 (Dar Al-Kotob Al-limiyah, Beirut, 2005), 85.
22. For a scholarly discussion of the 'nature' of law in Islam, see Bernard G. Weiss, *The Spirit of Islamic Law* (University of Georgia Press, Georgia, 2006).
23. Mehdi Bazargan (1906–1994), the first Prime Minister of Iran after the 1979 Islamic Revolution, who strove for the establishment of an Islamic state for over half a century, changed his position in the latest stage of his life. He published a book entitled *Hereafter and God: the Mission of the Prophets* and argued that human experience and rationales as well as some principles of religion must be employed to manage human's affairs. See, Mehdi Bazargan, *Akherat wa Khoda, Hadaf Besat Anbia [Hereafter and God: the Mission of the Prophets]* (Khadamat Farhangi Rasa, Tehran, 1998), 79–80.
24. Yahya Kabir, *Irfan wa ma'rifat ghodi* [Theosophy and knowledge of the Divine] (Matbouat Dini, Qom, 2006), 370.
25. For a sound discussion of different categories of Islam, see generally the writings of contemporary Muslim scholars, such as Khaled Abou El Fadl, *The Great Theft, Wrestling Islam from Extremists* (Harper, San Francisco, CA, 2005); Abdullahi Ahmed An-Na'im, *Islam and the Secular State: Negotiating the Future of Shari'a* (Harvard University Press, Cambridge, MA, 2008); Allama Muhammad Iqbal, *The Reconstruction of Religious Thought in Islam* (Iqbal Academy Pakistan and Institute of Islamic Culture, Lahore, 1989); Abdolkarim Soroush, *Bast-e Tajrobeh-yi Nabavi [The Expansion of Prophetic Experience]* (Serat, Tehran, 2006). See also the English

translation: *The Expansion of Prophetic Experience*, translated by Nilou Mobasser and edited with Analytical Introduction by Forough Jahanbakhsh (Brill, Leiden, 2009).

26. F.E. Peters, *Islam, A Guide for Jews and Christians* (Princeton University Press, Princeton, NJ, 2003) 127.
27. A.K.S. Lambton, 'Islamic Political Thought' in Joseph Schact and C.E. Bosworth (eds), *The Legacy of Islam*, 2nd edn (Clarendon Press, Oxford, 1974) 404, 405.
28. The Quran 3:104 and 110.
29. For a translation of the text of this treaty see Majid Khadduri, *War and Peace in the Law of Islam* (John Hopkins Press, Baltimore, MD, 1955), 206–9.
30. Riaz Hassan, *Inside Muslim Minds* (Melbourne University Press, Melbourne, 2010), 232.
31. Ibid., 232–3.
32. The Quran 33:13. The name of Medina was, before Islam, Yathrib. After the arrival of the Prophet, the city was named Medina Al Nabi, which means 'City of the Prophet'. Medina in Arabic means 'civilization' and 'establishment': see Abdulaziz Ben Ibrahim Al Omari, *Rasoullollah wa Khatam Al nabiein, Din wa Doulat [The Messenger of Allah, and the Seal of the Prophets, Religion and State]*, Vol. 2 (Bisan, Beirut, 2011), 482.
33. Bernard Lewis, 'Politics and War' in Joseph Schact and C.E. Bosworth (eds), *The Legacy of Islam*, 2nd edn (Clarendon Press, Oxford, 1974), 156, 157.
34. Majid Khadduri (translated with an introduction, notes and appendices) *The Islamic Law of Nations, Shaybani's Siyar* (John Hopkins University Press, Baltimore, MD, 1966), 20.
35. See generally, *Organisation of Islamic Cooperation* (24 June 2012), http://www.oic-oci.org/home.asp; Islamic Development Bank, *Islamic Development Bank: Twenty-Six Years in the Service of the Ummah, 1935H-1420H (1975-2000G)* (2000).
36. Majid Khadduri (translated with an introduction, notes and appendices), *The Islamic Law of Nations, Shaybani's Siyar* (John Hopkins University Press, Baltimore, MD, 1966), 177.
37. The Constitution of the Islamic Republic of Iran 1980, as amended in 1990, Article 13.
38. Abdullahi Ahmed An-Na'im, *Islam and the Secular State: Negotiating the Future of Shari'a* (Harvard University Press, Cambridge, MA, 2008), 129.
39. Majid Khadduri (translated with an introduction, notes and appendices), *The Islamic Law of Nations, Shaybani's Siyar* (John Hopkins University Press, Baltimore, MD, 1966), 53.
40. Khadduri, *supra* note 16, 12; Mohammad Reza Ziaei Bigdeli, *Islam Wa Hoghough Bein Al Melal [Islam and International Law]* (Sherkat Sahami Enteshar, Tehran, 1989), 64–5.
41. Abdullahi Ahmed An-Na'im, *Islam and the Secular State: Negotiating the Future of Shari'a* (Harvard University Press, Cambridge, MA, 2008), 134.
42. Ibid.
43. See, for example, the writings of Sayyid Qutb: Sayyid Qutb, *Ma'alim fi al-Tariq [Milestones]* (Dar al-Sharuq, Cairo, 1964), for the English translation see Sayyid Qutb, *Milestones* (Kazi, Chicago, IL, 2007); and Seyed Abul 'Ala Maudoodi, *Towards Understanding Islam* (Khurshid Ahmad (trans. and ed.), American Trust Publications, Indianapolis, IN, 1977).
44. Brian Galligan and Winsome Roberts, 'Multiculturalism, National Identity, and Pluralist Democracy, The Australian Variant' in Geoffrey Brahm Lever (ed.), *Political Theory and Australian Multiculturalism* (Berghahn Books, New York, 2008), 209, 216.

45. John Stone, 'The Muslim Problem and What to Do About It' (2006) 9 *Quadrant* 11; Paul Stenhouse, 'Islam's Trojan Horse?' (2007) 12 *Quadrant* 11; for a more international discussion of citizenship and multiculturalism see Irene Bloemraad et al., 'Citizenship and Immigration: Multiculturalism, Assimilation, and Challenges to the Nation-State' (2008) 34 *The Annual Review of Sociology* 153.
46. John Stone, 'The Muslim Problem and What to Do About It' (2006) 9 *Quadrant* 11, 30. The history of Australian immigration shows that migrants from many other backgrounds (Irish Catholics, Italians and Greeks, Asians, etc.) were treated similarly to how Muslims are treated now. Ironically, John Stone, who in 'The Muslim Problem and What to Do About It' (2006) 9 *Quadrant* 11 stated 'I do not believe that this latest body of newcomers [Muslims] amongst us will emulate the examples of their predecessors from Italy, Greece, Poland, the Baltic states, or more recently Vietnam, Hong Kong and China', while having previously stated that 'Asian immigration has to be slowed. It's no use dancing around the bushes': Peter Mares, *Borderline: Australia's Response to Refugees and Asylum Seekers in the Wake of Tampa* (University of New South Wales Press, Sydney, 2002), 113.
47. See this chapter at page 122.
48. Quran 2:177. See also Quran 2:40, 3:76, 8:27, 8:60, 8:72, 6:152, 9:4, 9:5, 9:7, 9:12, 9:13, 23:1–8, 70:32.
49. Abdullahi Ahmed An-Na'im, *Islam and the Secular State, Negotiating the Future of Sharia* (Harvard University Press, Cambridge, MA, 2008), 120.
50. See for example, Quran 4:143; 8:72; 9:28.
51. Quran 60:8
52. Abdullah Yusuf Ali, *The Qur'an: Text, Translation and Commentary* (Tahrike Tarsile Qur'an, New York, 2005), 225. I have inserted the word 'authority' in translation of the Arabic word '*Sabila*' which is translated by Yusuf Ali as 'a way (to triumphs)'.
53. For a discussion of this principle in Islamic jurisprudence (in Arabic) see Mirza Hassan Bojnourdi, *Al-Qavaeid Al-fiqhiyajh [The Rules of Islamic Jurisprudence]* (Nashr Alhadi, Qom, 1969), Vol. 1, 157–67.
54. For example, the majority of Afghan refugees fled the rule of the Taliban (1996–2001) or the insurgency (2004 to present [2012]).
55. See for example, Al-Sayyed Al-Sabiq, *Fiqh al-Sunnah [Sunni Jurisprudence]*, Vol. 2, 73.
56. For the nature of marriage in Australia, see generally Patrick Parkinson, *Australian Family Law in Context: Commentary and Materials*, 4th edn (Thomson Reuters Professional Australia, Pyrmont, New South Wales, 2012).
57. This is not to say that there have never been instances of strife or ethnic tension in these countries, merely that the presence of Muslim communities has not led to conflict.
58. The result was published in a book in 2008. See John Esposito and Dalia Mogahed, *Who Speaks for Islam? What a Billion Muslims Really Think* (Gallup Press, New York, 2008), 97.
59. John Esposito, *What Everyone Needs to Know About Islam* (Oxford University Press, New York, 2002), 174.

4. Fatwa and muftis[1]

1. INTRODUCTION

A fatwa (plural in Arabic is fatawa, in English fatwas) is a legal opinion issued by an Islamic law specialist on a specific issue. The task of issuing fatwas (*ifta*) is one entrusted to leading Islamic scholars or jurists as the ruling or opinion must be arrived at through a deep understanding of Islamic law using the correct Islamic methodology (*fiqh*) as outlined in Chapter 1. As Islam has no centralized, international priestly hierarchy, there is no uniform determinant as to who can issue a valid fatwa; nor is there one definitive academic qualification or admission process. By tradition these highly respected jurists are adult, Muslim, males (although this is now being challenged by modernist scholars, as discussed later), who are trusted, reliable, free of the causes of sin and defects of character, firm in thought and upright in conduct. They are known as *ulama* (singular *alim*). In the Shia tradition jurists are also known as *foqaha* (singular *faqih*). Some are given the specialist task of issuing fatwas and are given the revered title of 'mufti' in the Sunni schools, or 'ayatollah' in the Shia tradition. As an *alim* one may engage in collective reasoning based on the principles of Islam (*ijtihad*) and become a member of scholarly body, such as a council of *ulama*. One North African mufti has stated simply that anyone who is learned and whose religious sentiments are recognized by others may issue a fatwa.[2] Today the important requisites for *ifta* are recognition by a significant number of followers or appointment to a position of mufti by a Muslim ruler or government.

In Muslim nations the role for fatwas is well established and valued. While many non-Muslims know the word 'fatwa', it is fair to say that few in the West understand what a fatwa actually is, or appreciate the contribution made by fatwas to Islamic jurisprudence and their role in the everyday lives of Muslims. The fatwas Western media organizations choose to report are typically those that are sensational, amusing or concerning, and that highlight a cultural clash with Western values and practices. Reports of the banning of yoga and beauty pageants in

Malaysia,[3] the destruction of the Bamiyan Buddhist statutes in Afghanistan,[4] a prohibition on women studying at tertiary institutions,[5] or the Saudi fatwa that prohibits women driving cars in the Kingdom[6] make the concept of fatwas concerning to non-Muslims. The many condemnatory fatwas that followed the 2006 publication of cartoons satirizing the Prophet Mohammad in the Danish newspaper, *Jyllands-Posten*, were regarded as inflaming the violent response seen in Muslim countries. The most significant fatwa on this was a collective one issued under the name of the World Islamic Scholars,[7] in which 38 prominent Islamic muftis, jurists and scholars opined that the publication was an 'entirely unacceptable crime of aggression that has violated the highest sanctities of the Muslim people',[8] and called on the Danish government and Danes to apologize, condemn and bring an end to this attack. The fatwa also called on Muslims to exercise self-restraint and not engage in violent retribution, a point missed by Western media.[9] However, the fatwa that has most shaped Western perceptions of fatwas was the 1989 ruling of Ayatollah Khomeini in which he condemned Salman Rushdie's book *Satanic Verses* for its 'opposition to Islam, the Prophet, and the Qur'an' and called on 'all zealous Muslims to execute them [Rushdie and the publishers] quickly … so that no one will dare insult the Islamic sanctities'.[10] Although Khomeini's fatwa was denounced as invalid by many Muslim scholars, it attracted much media attention and has continued to be a focus of public discourse on core human rights, and in particular the perceived dichotomy of freedom of speech or defence of religion.[11] For many in the West, Khomeini's fatwa defined their understanding of the fatwa and made the term inextricably linked with a sentence of death or with an anti-Western sentiment. The mental association between 'fatwa' and death sentence has not lessened in the decades since Khomeini's pronouncement and may have been reinforced by the publicity given to Ayatollah Khamenei's reaffirmation in 2005 of the continuing validity of his predecessor's original 1989 fatwa denouncing Rushdie. Although fatwas containing an execution decree are extremely rare, the fallout from the Ayatollah's ruling in the West has been a tainting of the word 'fatwa' itself in the mind of many non-Muslims.

For Muslims, however, fatwas are a positive and integral component of Islamic law and inform all aspects of life. Since the time of the Prophet, fatwas have been the vehicle by which Muslims can seek legal direction on matters of concern, whether profound or mundane. In giving guidance on what is permitted (*halal*) and what is forbidden (*haram*), a fatwa facilitates compliance with Islamic law and adherence to one's faith. This chapter sets out the role for fatwas by explaining their distinctive place in Islamic law and their significance in its development and application in contemporary times. A brief explanation of fatwas in both historical and doctrinal contexts is provided before examining the practice of issuing fatwas in the Muslim world. To highlight the different approaches, the chapter will consider *ifta* in several contexts, including the role played by a state mufti as in Saudi Arabia, the Indonesian model of collective *ijtihad* and transnational models based on on-line fatwas. The second half of the chapter will go beyond Muslim countries to consider the important role of fatwas in non-Muslim countries, particularly in the West, where Muslims strive to accommodate Islamic religious requirements within the framework of secular societies. It will be shown how fatwas act as beacons of guidance through the challenge of adhering to two sets of laws: those of Islam and the enacted national laws. Fatwas in the West fulfill an important role in social and cultural transformations amongst Muslim communities; such a role is limited to a personal, individual and private level and as such does not negate the primacy of national law in the lives of Muslim citizens.

2. WHAT IS A FATWA?

As noted at the outset, a fatwa is generally a non-binding legal opinion or ruling given by a recognized Islamic legal specialist. In the Shia tradition of Islam, the legal specialists (*mujtahid*) who issue fatwas are their Ayotallahs and Grand Ayatollahs (*Ayatollah-e Ozme*). These men are recognized as the leading Islamic religious and legal scholars of their time and their knowledge and ability are such that they are held in highest esteem by their fellow Shia clerics. In the Sunni schools (*madhhabs*) of Islam fatwas traditionally are issued by acclaimed jurists (*muftis*) or by an authoritative specialist body of Islamic scholars (*ulama*). A fatwa will be issued in answer to a question pertaining to Islamic law as asked by an individual inquirer (*mustafti*), a judge (*qadi*), a government authority, a corporate entity, an institution or an organization. Although the fatwa will be given in response to a submitted question, it may also be published or disseminated in some form to the wider Islamic community. In this way, a fatwa gives guidance to the individual questioner while its dissemination educates, informs and guides others. Although by tradition a fatwa is not binding, a small number of countries do give fatwas legal force, either by the government granting legal status to fatwas issued by state muftis, as occurs in Saudi Arabia, or by sanctioning the enforcement of fatwas that are published and gazetted, as happens in Malaysia. In the majority of Islamic countries, as in the non-Muslim ones, compliance with a fatwa is voluntary. Many Muslim countries try to ensure standards by making the issue of an unauthorized fatwa a criminal offence.[12] Fatwas are often compiled and categorized into collections, and important fatwa collections have been established by leadings jurists and at major centres of Islamic scholarship, notably Al-Azhar University in Egypt and the Council of Fiqh in Mecca. These collections remain important reference points in contemporary Islamic jurisprudence.

3. THE EMERGENCE OF *IFTA* AND ITS DEVELOPMENT THROUGH THE CENTURIES: HISTORICAL AND DOCTRINAL INSIGHTS

> [when] [t]hey ask thy instruction … [S]ay: God doth instruct you. (Súra Nisáa 4:126)[13]

The origin of *ifta* (the issuing of fatwas) lies in the practice of the earliest Muslims asking questions and receiving answers directly from the Prophet Mohammad during his lifetime. Following the Prophet's death, this role was entrusted to his companions in keeping with the Quranic direction that 'if ye realise this not, ask of those who possess the Message'.[14] So it was the men and women[15] who had best known the Prophet who became, in effect, the first muftis, providing fatwas when questions arose requiring direction and guidance for members of the fledgling Muslim community on the Arabian Peninsula. These early fatwas were issued on a wide variety of subjects, both sacred and practical, and collections of fatwas started to develop. Most prolific was Ibn 'Abbas, whose fatwas were compiled in 20 volumes.[16] The result was that the process of issuing fatwas became the entrenched mechanism for providing accurate guidance on Islamic law. It was to the legal specialist that the judges turned when difficult cases or novel points of law arose with a resulting bifurcation between those entrusted with applying the law, the judges, and those entrusted with interpreting and developing the law, the legal specialist or jurist. This was a well-entrenched practical division by the eighth century, that is, the second century of the Islamic calendar.[17]

In Umayyad times (661–750), muftis served not only as legal consultants for judges and individuals, but also issued fatwas at the request of provincial governors. By the late Umayyad period, fatwa-giving had also become an important instrument of political criticism. It is reported, for example, that in the year 714 Sa'id bin Jubayr produced a fatwa criticizing the tyrannical behaviour of al-Hajjaj,[18] the political ruler or governor of Iraq. In Andalusia (711–1609) the jurists were indeed powerful; they were part of the *shura* council of the amirs and caliphs. In the Ottoman and Mughal political systems the chief mufti was designated as Syaikh al-Islam. The fatwas of the life-appointed Syaikh al-Islam had great influence in the courts across the empire and it became an established practice for litigants to request a fatwa prior to their hearing in order to strengthen their case in court.[19] He had political power, being the designated head of the *ulama*, and thus appointed the judges and other muftis for the vast Ottoman Empire. Those mufti were also appointed to various other positions, including market inspectors, guardians of public morals and advisors to governments on religious affairs.[20]

The significance of the fatwa in the pedagogy of Islamic law coupled with the mufti's undisputed command of the law was such that throughout Islamic history the mufti was often a powerful figure. For example, in the mid-twentieth-century the Lebanese mufti of the republic was actually an important political leader. Brinkley Messick points out that some grand muftis, appointed in various states over the past century, wielded considerable political influence through their official fatwas.[21] In 1804 Uthman ibn Fudi issued his fatwa to declare jihad in West Africa. In 1857, the *ulama* of Delhi issued a fatwa of jihad against British rule. In 1907, the *ulama* of Marrakesh issued a fatwa deposing the Sultan of Morocco.[22] It is well known that, in 1964, the transfer of power to King Faisal was made possible by a fatwa of the Saudi *ulama*.[23] In Indonesia, K.H. Hasyim Asy'ari of Nahdlatul Ulama issued a fatwa on the religious necessity of defending Indonesian independence (1945) and waging jihad against the Dutch Army, which was trying to reestablish its power in Indonesia.[24] A recent instance of influential political fatwas can be found in post-Baathist Iraq, where Ayatollah Ali Al-Sistani's fatwas have given guidance throughout the troubled period of American and allied entry and occupation of Iraq. In addition to his reported 2003 fatwa directing Iraqis not to resist the entry of Western forces, al-Sistani issued fatwas encouraging Shia to participate in the elections and in the democratic constitutional processes in Iraq.[25] Muqtada Al-Sadr has also issued fatwas that at times have been at variance with those of the more moderate al-Sistani; however, both are illustrative of the contemporary role fatwas are playing in the political, as well as religious, outcomes in Iraq.

Throughout history, the theory of private fatwa-giving held that fatwas should be given for free; however, gifts and various forms of pious support were common. Official muftis, however, were salaried or received set fees from their questioners, and many grew wealthy in their position.[26] Jacques Waardenburg explains that, although most were private scholars, some muftis were appointed to official positions, notably in Mamaluk Egypt and in the Ottoman Empire. Today, while some have been appointed mufti of the state, others provide consensus as part of advisory councils of religious scholars or constitutional assemblies of scholars.[27]

While the establishment of the Egyptian Grand Mufti dates to the late nineteenth century, state muftis were not appointed until after the middle of this century in a number of other nations, including Saudi Arabia (1953), Lebanon (1955), Malaysia (1955) and Yemen (1962). As state-appointed muftis are salaried government employees who are generally also in control of the nation's religious administration, there are perceptions that their role may be compromised to ensure religious legitimacy for particular government, or its policies, especially in authoritarian regimes. Although most Arab nations have a state mufti, there is considerable variation in the Arab world in their appointment, tenure, background and training, formal relationship with the ruler or government, the scope of the fatwas issued and their dissemination, and whether the mufti represents the government internationally on religious and other issues. A comparative typological analysis by Skovgaard-Petersen of the state muftis of Lebanon, Syria and Egypt highlights this variation.[28] In addition to the institutionalization of muftis within government, another significant modern organizational development is the appearance of specialized committees charged with collective fatwa giving. Institutions with titles such as '*Dar al-Ifta*' (literally house of guidance) have appeared in many Muslim countries[29] and also in Western countries where Muslim minorities are equally seeking guidance in aspects of Islamic law and faith. The *Ifta* Department of the Canadian Council of Muslim Theologians is but one example.

In both political and scholarly communities, doctrinal struggles between opposed states or competing instructional centres have been played out in 'fatwa wars'. Accordingly, to the extent that fatwas are contestable, a dissatisfied questioner might approach another mufti for a second opinion, while opponents might seek out different mufti to vindicate their respective positions.

4. CONTEMPORARY *IFTA*

Fatwas also have a long-standing role in the legitimization of new social and economic practices. The topics in the Quran did not include modern issues such as insurance, corneal transplant, banking and family planning, to name but a few, and Muslim scholars have to issue fatwas, by analysing the core values of the Quran and the Sunna, in order to deal with modern problems. For example, in the Ottoman Empire, a fatwa was issued in 1727 authorizing the printing of non-religious books; vaccination was declared legitimate in an 1845 fatwa; and several fatwas were used to legitimize low interest rates, selling on credit, and the practice of establishing cash endowments (*waqf*).[30] Banking and Western modes of financing have been a rich field for fatwas throughout the last century as legal scholars guide their followers on which banking transactions are acceptable in Islam and avoid the charging of interest (*riba*). Contemporary fatwas consider social and economic practices that challenge boundaries in the twenty-first century, including the legitimacy of genetically modified crops and foods, organ donation, stem-cell research, cloning and surrogacy.

Fatwas can also deal with spiritual and devotional issues and religious rituals, and each collection of fatwas will have a large compendium dealing with these issues. Fatwas also cover a vast array of worldly (*al-dunya*) issues, from the trivial to ones dealing with matters of life and death. A government might ask for a fatwa about the permissibility of setting up a water recycling programme or whether a particular birth control method or organ donation should be endorsed in government clinics. Non-governmental organizations such as the International Red Cross might ask for a fatwa on whether it is permissible for cornea transplants to be performed, as occurred in Indonesia in 1979. Individuals ask questions that range from the everyday – is it permissible (*halal*) to drink coca-cola, to wear fingernail polish when praying, to have botox injections or to send a Christmas card to a Christian? – to finding out what is permissible for significant life issues – is it permissible (*halal*) to work as a computer analyst in a firm that sells insurance, to undergo in vitro fertilization, to have a blood transfusion or to refuse military service?

A. Case Example – Permissibility of Post-mortems

Insight into the structure and methodology traditionally employed in *ifta* can be seen by considering a fatwa on whether post-mortems are permissible in Islam. It was issued by Hasanayn Muhammad Makhluf, Grand Mufti of Egypt (1945–1990) and translated and analysed by Rispler-Chiam.[31] Like most fatwas, it commences with a question: 'According to the Sharia, is it permitted to perform a post-mortem examination for scientific purposes or in criminal cases?'

At the time this was an important question as post-mortems necessarily involve postponement of burial, transfer of the body to different locations and violation or desecration of the human body, all of which are prohibited under Islamic ethics and law. In responding to the question, this mufti commenced with a discussion of medicine in general and the high regard in which it is held in Islamic law. This was confirmed by references to the two most authoritative sources of law in Islam, the Quran, which is the direct word of God, and the Sunna, which are legal rules derived from the recorded and verified practices of the Prophet. In his fatwa, the mufti highlights the medically related practices of the Prophet to show how he sought cures and remedies whenever he, or a member of his family, was ill. A hadith recorded and verified by al-Bukhari recounts his edict: 'Cure yourselves, because God did not create an illness without a remedy' (al-Bukhari 1928, 71: 582). The fatwa also draws on the word of God from the Quran, Súra Baqarah 2:184–5 and Súra Baqarah 2:196, which allow concessions from certain religious obligations for people who are ill. One of these is that an ill person can break his or her fast (fasting during the month of Ramadan being one of the five obligatory pillars of Islam) if it would enable vital or life-saving medical treatment to be given or avoid the illness worsening.[32] Having established the basis for his ruling in the two primary sources of law, the Quran and Sunna, the mufti determined that the practice of medicine is so essential in Islam that its provision amounts to a religious duty for Muslim communities.

Grand Mufti Hasanayn Muhammad Makhluf then proceeded in his fatwa to employ secondary sources of law. These are the juristic techniques and scholarly methods sanctioned by Islamic jurisprudence (*fiqh*). He employed analogy (*qiyas*) to demonstrate how the duty to practise medicine cannot be fulfilled unless a doctor has knowledge of the internal components of the human body and that this level of knowledge can only be attained through dissection. Therefore if post-mortems are essential for medical knowledge to progress, they must be an essential part of medical education, in the analogous way that ablution is necessary for the obligation of prayer. His ruling on the first part of the question was that post-mortems were permissible for legitimate scientific purposes.[33]

The Grand Mufti then addressed the second part of the question on the use of post-mortems for solving criminal cases. He held that these were also permissible on the basis of ensuring justice: they lead to the discovery of truth in criminal cases so that 'no innocent person is oppressed and no convicted criminal escapes punishment'.[34] He supported this statement by employing the legal method of public benefit (*maslaha*) to show that the positive outcome of doing justice, which is of benefit to all, outweighs the damage done through violating the human body. He held that '[w]henever the benefit outweighs the harm permission is granted, whenever the harm outweighs the benefit, a prohibition is issued'.[35] The Grand Mufti drew additional support from an earlier fatwa by Sheykh Yusuf al-Dajawi, which also legitimized post-mortems by balancing the good over the bad in accordance with the spirit of Islamic law. Al-Dajawi drew a parallel with the permitted practice of opening the stomach of a dead person to extract a sum of money if it was known to have been swallowed before death. The Grand Mufti's fatwa concluded that, while post-mortems are permissible, they must be performed only when necessary and not too often. Doctors should be God fearing and should 'know that God is All-seeing, Almighty and All-guiding'.[36]

The Grand Mufti's fatwa on post-mortems demonstrates the process by which Islamic scholars give considered responses to questions. Typically a fatwa will commence with the primary sources, then extend these by applying appropriate juristic techniques such as consensus, analogy and public benefit, together with analysis of previous juristic opinions. Many fatwas are shorter than the post-mortem fatwa discussed, and are quite succinct, especially if they consider a question relating to an already established topic. As the product of *ijtihad*, a fatwa is guidance which a Muslim, whether the questioner or not, can follow secure in the knowledge that it is the opinion of a great jurist or group of jurists. However, as noted above, there can be other fatwas that use the same methodology but arrive at a different conclusion. The Grand Ayatollah of Iraq, Al-Sistani, prohibited post-mortems for Muslims whether for educational or investigative reasons, although permitted them for non-Muslims.[37] In a fatwa from the Saudi Arabian Permanent Committee of Fatwas, the scholars came to the same position on criminal autopsies, but to a different conclusion on post-mortems for scientific educational purposes. The Council relied on hadith that the dignity of a Muslim while dead is the same as when alive,[38] to deem that dissection of inviolable Muslims (that is, persons not subject to capital punishment) should not occur for educational purposes but be limited to 'corpses of persons subject to capital punishment'.[39] Whilst the preponderance of fatwas do give religious support to post-mortems, albeit with some qualifications and reservations, their voluntary nature means that for some devout Muslims this reassurance of legitimacy will be accepted while for others it will be insufficient to overcome concerns about the sanctity of the human body and delay in burial.[40]

B. Distinction between Fatwas and *Qada* (Cases)

It is a point of distinction with the common law that in Islam it is the jurist, whether Ayatollah, mufti or religious scholar (*alim*), not the judge (*qadi*), who is the one contributing to the development of the law. The *qadi* is solely an adjudicator and 'neither contributes to the development of the law nor stands among the most learned in it'.[41] Patrick Glenn finds close parallels between the mufti and the Roman jurist or the modern European law professor as each possesses knowledge of immense amounts of law and has great analytical abilities that are used to provide legal opinions to the courts.[42] Today the fatwa of a mufti or other Islamic scholar or council of scholars is still frequently filed in Sharia courts as a means of informing the judge on the applicable law for the case in hand. Frank Vogel has analysed the features of fatwa that distinguish it from the judgment (*qada*) of the *qadi*, issued in response to a case before in him.[43] First, the fatwa potentially has universal application to a class of persons to whom the ruling applies, whereas a judgment has a unique application to the parties and the event judged. Also the fatwa is not obligatory but is advisory to the person requesting it, but a *qada* is compulsory and will be enforced by the state. While the mufti leaves the truth of facts to be determined by the requestor, the judge tests the facts through examination and employment of evidentiary procedures. In addition, Muhammad Khalid Masud notes that, as copies of court judgments were kept in the Sharia court records with no wider distribution through publication or referencing, there could be no application of the concept of precedent. In contrast, important fatwas were published, distributed and frequently collected in book form to 'be cited across space and time'.[44] A final point of distinction is that *qadi* gives *qada* with respect to disputes that entail interests of this world (*al-dunya*), whereas a mufti can also deal with the 'hereafter' and with matters of ritual law and spirituality that are outside the domain of the judge.[45]

C. Diversity within Muslim Nations for *Ifta*

Although the place for fatwas in Muslim nations is evident, the sources entrusted with supreme religious authority for *ifta* vary, as does their nexus with state political authority. Two contrasting positions are Saudi Arabia and Indonesia. In Saudi Arabia, official fatwas are enforced by the police and by the courts. A case in point is the prohibition on women driving. This is not contained in legislation or Royal Decree but in a 1990 fatwa of the Grand Mufti[46] Abdallah Bin Baz, in which he opines that a woman driving a car is a 'source of undeniable vice' that could lead her to commit a *haram* act, such as abandoning her veil (*hijab*) or meeting with a man (*khilwa*). A court case was commenced in 2012 by two female Muslims activists against the Interior Ministry for refusal to issue them with driving licences. One of the grounds in the case was the status of a 20-year-old fatwa in the absence of enacted legislation.[47] Courts too will seek fatwas when matters of legal uncertainty arise in cases before them. By contrast, in Indonesia, the world's largest Muslim nation, there is no equivalent of an official fatwa, nor a government appointed mufti or *ifta* authority. In Indonesia, the voluntary nature of fatwas is its defining feature, with fatwas just as important for Indonesian Muslims who 'esteem their ulama principally as religious patrons, whose advice and exemplary lives are to be followed'.[48]

i. The Kingdom of Saudi Arabia

In Saudi Arabia the official source for *ifta* is the Grand Mufti and the Council of *Ulama*, of which the mufti is the chairman, and they operate within the government department of Scholarly Research, *Ifta* and Guidance. Perhaps in a move to deflect questioners and Muslims away from other Saudi and Middle Eastern scholars 'issuing … fatwas that clash with the official line of the Saudi religious establishment led by the Council of Senior Ulema', the government in 2007 set up a fatwa website so that official fatwas could be quickly accessed and the official view given. The number of fatwas provided is in the tens of thousands and the issues covered are extensive but reflect a local orientation. For example, among the ten 'most popular' fatwas are questions on 'the best way to teach non-Arabic speaking Muslims about Islam', whether it is *haram* to break traffic rules when it does not harm others and the permissibility of a range of activities undertaken in Saudi internet cafes. The legal opinions expressed in the fatwas reflect the conservative outlook of the Hanbali school with a Salafi stance.[49] The opinions of the highly influential theologian Shaykh Muhammad ibn Abdul-Wahhab are frequently cited in the rulings. In keeping with this traditional approach, Wahhab advocated literal interpretations of the holy texts and the avoidance of innovations.[50] The collections of official Saudi fatwas draw on the primary sources of law, namely the Quran, and contain extensive and detailed citing of hadith, rather than any of the more flexible methodologies possible through the approaches to legal questions known as *maslaha* or *qiyas*.[51] On the website, there is also the major 30 volume collection of fatwas from the previous Grand Mufti, Ibn Baz[52]. Some recent fatwas issued by the current Grand Mufti and his Council of *Ulama* have been contested and refuted by other Muslim scholars, including the controversial 2012 fatwa issued in response to a question from a Kuwaiti parliamentarian on whether a ban should be imposed on building new churches in Arab countries. The fatwa called for the destruction of all Christian churches on the Arabian Peninsula, stating that the region is the 'sacrosanct base of Islam which no disbeliever is allowed to violate', citing numerous hadith, including one in which the Prophet said that the region must have only one religion, Islam. It concludes it is an 'Islamic duty to forbid disbelief because it entails the worship of other than Allah and contradicts the Shari'ah'.[53] Fatwas in Saudi Arabia are powerful controlling forces on the lives of individuals, institutions and the government.

ii. The Republic of Indonesia

Although Indonesia does not have an appointed state mufti, the role of *ifta* flourishes in an environment where pluralism abounds. Questioners, whether individuals, communities, organizations or the government, can choose the *alim* or *ulama* in whom they have respect and confidence. The three dominant *ifta* organizations are the Nahdlatul Ulama, established in 1926, Muhammadiyah, established in 1912, and Majelis Ulama Indonesia, established in 1975. In all three, there are female members on the Fatwas Committees, with MUI having the highest female representation.

Lay Indonesian Muslims can procure the fatwa they want simply by choosing the right *ulama* to ask. Indonesia does not have an appointed state mufti, but as the largest Muslim country in the world, benefits from many Islamic organizations such as the NU, the Muhammadiyah and the MUI, each of which consists of separate branches in more than 20 provinces. It is possible that a fatwa from one organization may differ from those of other organizations. It can also happen that a fatwa issued from the national organization is different from one given by the provincial organization. Again, a fatwa from one provincial branch may be at variance with a fatwa from another province, even though both belong to the same organization. Therefore, it is possible to have many fatwas in Indonesia covering one case.[54] Before issuing fatwas, each organization holds a meeting attended by their *ulama* and, if necessary, other scholars. They discuss the subject and, if consensus is reached, a fatwa is issued at the conclusion of the meeting.

It is worth considering that both the MUI and the NU state that each fatwa has equal status and cannot cancel out others. This is matched with the norm of Islamic law, '*ijtihad* is not reversible' (*ijtihad la yunqad*).[55] This means that the ruling of one scholar arrived at by means of *ijtihad* is not reversed by the ruling of another scholar also reached through *ijtihad*, in the absence of a clear text from the Quran or hadith to determine the issue, and provided that neither decision violates any of the rules governing the propriety of *ijtihad*. Thus, the two decisions have equal authority. This legal maxim is important, because there are sometimes many fatwas covering the same case, including some issued by the national and provincial branches of the same organization. Thus, a fatwa from the national organization cannot cancel one from a provincial branch. This indicates the element of democracy and tolerance towards other opinions.

Indonesian *ulama* have also responded to everyday issues. Fatwas on medical science regarding matters such as vasectomy and tubectomy, cornea transplant, euthanasia and pills for prevention of menstruation have been issued. Furthermore, *ulama* have also considered economic issues such as banking and insurance. The environment is also covered by an Indonesian fatwa, as is the lawfulness of the mechanical slaughtering of animals. This chapter will discuss three examples. First, the MUI issued a fatwa on cornea transplants in June 1979. This was requested by the Red Cross, and the MUI ruled that cornea donation was lawful, provided it was agreed to and witnessed by close relatives and that the removal of the cornea was carried out by qualified surgeons.[56] Second, the NU issued a fatwa on the environment in 1994. This fatwa said that poisoning the environment, whether water, air or earth, is *haram* and is categorized as criminal.[57] This fatwa is stronger than the statement of the MUI in 1983 that every Muslim is obligated (*wajib*) to keep the environment clean and to prevent the poisoning of it.[58] The MUI did not mention that failure to do so was criminal. The background to these fatwas was that a number of industrial companies had degraded the environment, the effect of which was to cause diseases in people. Third, in the mid-1970s, the public was concerned that beef sold in the market in Jakarta was not *halal*, because the slaughtering of the cattle was carried out by a mechanized method rather than the traditional system. In response to this concern, the MUI on 18 October 1976 issued a fatwa stating that the meat produced by the mechanized slaughtering system was *halal*. It is interesting to note that the fatwa further stated that such a system was more in line with the teachings of the Prophet than the traditional system, in so far as the suffering of the animals slaughtered was minimized. The idea behind the fatwa was very clear, namely, to try to meet the challenges of a modern economy.[59]

5. FATWAS IN NON-MUSLIM COUNTRIES

Fatwas are an instrument that allows Islamic law to respond to modern developments and to new challenges. This makes them an indispensable tool for Muslims in secular Western countries. A fatwa can be used to examine not only whether certain beliefs or practices amongst their Muslim community are congruent with the principles of Islamic law, but also how local practices and values can be accommodated with scripturalist ideals. In other words, a fatwa is a viable tool through which a community can adjust itself to internal and external social, political and economic change. It is essential to note that fatwas in the West are not intended to compete with or to replace national laws and regulations. Fatwas operate at personal, individual and private levels and their operation amongst the Muslim community does not contradict the spirit of a secular state. Borrowing from the concept of legal pluralism outlined in the writings of Masaji Chiba, fatwas in Europe, Australia and North America come under the 'unofficial law' banner. According to Chiba, apart from official law, there is another level of law that transcends the legal, and yet needs to be counted into the equation because it influences the operation of legal systems in more substantial ways. Such 'law' is not officially authorized by the official authorities, but is authorized in practice by the general consensus of a certain circle of people and by having a distinctive influence upon the effectiveness of the official law. This scenario is offered by Chiba partly as a means of balancing the general presentation of legal pluralism as one of a harmonious working together of the different levels of law.[60]

In the absence of a state institution in Western countries, authority for *ifta* is socially conferred, so that the request for a legal opinion and in turn its acceptance rest solely on the esteem with which the individual or the organization is held in the eyes of a questioner. Authority cannot be proclaimed; it must be attained. This plurality enables new discourses on authority to emerge that are contemporary and resonate within a Western context. This could include the issuing of fatwas by female Islamic scholars, in keeping with the role fulfilled by A'isha, the Prophet's wife (after his death) and which has been accepted by some progressive Muslim scholars,[61] and recently by the Makkah International Conference on Fatwa and Its Regulations.[62] It may also lead to the emergence of a distinctively Western *fiqh*, one in which the compatibility of being Muslim within a national framework supersedes former ethnic and theological divides. Scholars in Britain sense the emergence of a contextually relevant form of Islamic law labelled 'English Sharia' (*angrezi shariat*) in which the Sharia has been mediated by the English socio-legal context.[63] In Europe, *fiqh* of minorities (*fiqh al-aqalliyyat*) has also been so identified with Europe-centred fatwas fuelling its development. The role of the European Council of Fatwa and Research has made a significant contribution to this. Established in 1997 to bring together Islamic scholars based in Europe, the first goal of the Council was to unify 'the jurisprudence views between them in regards with the main Fiqh' issues'.[64] This unification pertains only to the jurisprudence of the four Sunni schools of law. Each year the Council issues a significant number of fatwas through collective *ijtihad* that they declare are designed to 'meet the needs of Muslims in Europe, solve their problems and regulate their interaction with the European communities, all within the regulations and objectives of Sharia'.[65] Membership is not limited to European Scholars and at least half of its members are from parts of the Middle East, including the Council's President since inception, Professor Yusuf Al-Qaradawi, an internationally renowned scholar and prolific issuer of fatwas. The agreed *fiqh* methodology of Council is to commence with the Quran, Sunna, consensus and analogy and then, where necessary, employ secondary sources, notably *maslaha*, *durara* and *istihsan*.[66]

A. Case Study: Fatwa in Australia

The Australian Islamic community is diverse: Muslims have come from over 70 countries, belong to 50 different ethnic or cultural groups, and speak a variety of different languages and dialects.[67] All the schools of law are represented and there is a broad spectrum of interpretative views from liberal and progressive at one end through to moderate and to conservative and literalist (or fundamentalist) at the other end. Given the voluntary nature of *ifta* and this multicultural context, it is not surprising that there is no dominant fatwa-issuing authority. Muslims from Saudi Arabia are likely to seek a conservative Wahhabi perspective,[68] whereas immigrants from another Muslim nation may seek a modernist view. Muslims who have been in Australia for several generations, together with recent converts, may seek views that are quite attuned to Australian life and local practice. New arrivals and converts have been found to be significant users of fatwas, but expert scholarly advice is required by Muslim minorities everywhere as they respond to the challenges of life in a secular Western society. For these reasons, *ifta* in Australia, like Indonesia, is undertaken by a range of organizations and individuals. The main organizations are the Australian National Imams Council (ANIC),[69] Australian Federation of Islamic Council (AFIC),[70] both of which have affiliated state councils, and the Darulfatwa Islamic High Council.[71] A limitation of fatwa in Australia is the absence of a record or collection of fatwas issued by either ANIC or AFIC. Only Darulfatwa provides a ready mechanism for requesting a fatwa, with their 'Ask the Mufti' web page, which enables questioners requiring a fatwa to submit it on-line. In keeping with the collective approach, the fatwas are not issued by one scholar, with the website listing the names of five sheikhs who it states are 'qualified and holding different degrees and from universities such as Al Azhar'.[72] The categories of questions submitted range from matters of adherence to Islamic ritual, belief and practices to ones directly centred on the adaptation of Islamic norms and practices to the Australian context. They show the role fatwas play in responding to the social and cultural challenges of migration and minority status of Muslim communities.

Darulfatwa has published around 40 fatwas on their website. The questions deal with many spiritual matters, such as guidance on the integrals of prayer, dealing with temptation and repentance, and the timing of prayers, as well as fatwas seeking help with the practical realities of life in a secular country, including acceptable ways under Islam to buy a house or obtain Sharia-compliant financing, and whether certain foods and drinks are *halal*. In addition, individual scholars, usually imams with scholarly training, provide guidance at the local mosque community level. While there is a Grand Mufti of Australia, the position has been linked always to one of the national Muslim organizations. At first the title was bestowed by AFIC's former executive body, and more recently by ANIC. Each of the holders of the title of Grand Mufti has been controversial, for different reasons, and the difficulty is that each has been seen as a spokesman for one sector, rather than for all Muslims in Australia. The diversity amongst Australian Muslims, however, does make it difficult to have a single mufti who can be accepted and recognized by all. The result is that Muslims in Australia are free to select the organization or individual that best suits his or her religious, cultural and ideological needs. In addition to the institutions described above, there are many imams and sheikhs issuing 'private' fatwas to their Australian mosque congregations. Given that there is no hierarchy in Islam, each Muslim is free to seek guidance from any scholar in whom he or she has confidence and to accept or reject their ruling. This means that Australian Muslims can request fatwas from overseas muftis and scholars and many choose to do so. The internet has facilitated this process and the *ulama* across the globe have been innovative in employing the new technology for giving fatwas and for disseminating key information on Islam.[73]

6. THE ON-LINE FATWA PHENOMENON

On-line fatwas are one aspect of the burgeoning cyber Islamic environment that enables Muslims to enter into dialogue with others, and to access and distribute Islamic information globally. E-fatwas have provided Muslim across the globe with an array of alternative Islamic opinions and interpretations. The process of searching Islamic websites for suitable religious opinions can be called 'fatwa shopping', or surfing on the ‘inter-madhab net’.[74] Potentially, it opens all sorts of new and alternative interpretations of Islam alongside the more traditional versions. It can open the eyes of Muslims who are entrenched in their own local brand of Islam to the diversity of their religion in its global form.

Many national fatwa-issuing organizations such as Majlis Ugama Islam Singapura, Majelis Ulama Indonesia, Jabatan Kemajuan Islam Malaysia, the European Council for Fatwa and Research and the Fiqh Council of North America provide an on-line fatwa service. The nature of the internet, which permits anonymity, gives questioners the chance to pose private and controversial questions without fear of being identified. Another feature is that on-line fatwas potentially have a much broader application to all those users who find themselves in a similar position to the questioner, whereas a face-to-face fatwa has a unique application to the parties concerned. This suggests that on-line fatwas will be cited across space and time. The diversity of opinion found on the internet could help push reform within Islam, particularly in reducing its dependence on the old methodology, which was a product of the sociological structure of classical and medieval Muslim societies. On-line fatwas can be seen not only as a tool for Muslims to examine whether certain beliefs or practices within the Muslim community are congruent with the principles of Islamic law or not, but also as viable tool through which a society can adjust itself to internal and external social, political and economic change.

In the context of authority, now almost anyone can set themselves up as an authority on Islam and issue legal opinions. This might be seen as democratic, although providing widely divergent views on what is permitted (*halal*) and what is forbidden (*haram*) could lead to information anarchy. In other words, a consequence of letting anyone and everyone issue a fatwa on the internet is that quality assurance is minimal. Some fatwa givers will take the time to check their references; others may not. Things become even more complex as bloggers and open forums, comment threads and other mechanisms in the internet arrive with a mix of news, hoaxes and speculation from unreliable sources. What is credible and what is baseless becomes increasingly difficult to discern. With the absence of a formal framework for deciding who may become a mufti on the internet, it has become very hard to stop people from declaring themselves muftis. This media-mufti phenomenon has flourished in the cyber environment.[75]

A visit to sites such as Islam On-line,[76] Islamtoday,[77] Ask the Imam,[78] Islam Q&A[79] and Fatwa on-line[80] show that such sites receive a large numbers of questioners, and that Muslims from non-Muslim countries like Australia are strongly represented as questioners. The domain report of Islam Q&A[81] shows that, of the 128 countries from which requests had been received, the UK, France, the Netherlands, the United States and Australia were amongst the largest users (after Saudi Arabia). It was instructive to see that there had been well over 1 million requests for fatwas from the domain .au (Australia) when Australia has a population of only 500,000 Muslims. This supports the contention of Alexandre Caerio that the demand for fatwas in the Western world appears greater than that in Islamic countries.[82] He argues this because there is a discontinuation in the transmission of Islamic knowledge that propels young people to find ways adapt Islamic law to their Western context. In addition, there is a need, in particular for women, to 'elaborate strategies of survival and to navigate skillfully between different normative orders'.[83]

However, the practice of asking foreign Islamic websites in preference to ones based in the country where the individual Muslim resides could be problematic as foreign Muslim scholars who answer the questions may not understand life in that nation, or in the West generally. This fact could be disadvantageous, particularly when a foreign-based Islamic website is trying to answer questions closely related to life and social interaction in secular societies, like Australia or the United States. Since many on-line mufti do not live in the West, their answers might not be suitable for a Muslim living in a Western country like Australia. For instance, a mufti not living in a Western country might misunderstand the cultural context when considering whether it is permissible for a Muslim to say 'Merry Christmas'. In the West, this greeting should be seen as a cultural practice, rather than identified as a symbol of a theological battle between Islam and Christianity, but one Indonesian website, Syariah Online,[84] strongly forbids it, as does Mufti Ikram ul Haq of the Fatwa Center of America.[85]

7. CONCLUSION

This chapter has aimed to demonstrate that fatwas in Islam should be seen as part of mechanism for growth and change in Islamic law, which makes Islamic law adaptable to social change. Wael Hallaq correctly points out that:

> our enquiry suggests that the juridical genre of the fatwa was chiefly responsible for the growth and change of legal doctrine in the schools, and that our current perception of Islamic law as a jurists' law must now be further defined as a Muftis' law. Any enquiry into the historical evolution and

later development of substantive legal doctrine must take account of the Mufti and his fatwa.[86]

Unlike the Quran, the fatwa emerges as only an intellectual activity that could be right in a certain time and place and be wrong in another time and place. A fatwa can be revised by the same mufti, either because it is contrary to the Quran, the Sunna or consensus (*ijma*) or because there is a social change that influences the validity of the original fatwa. This would suggest that a fatwa is not a sacred thing. Fatwas are adaptable to social change, particularly where previous rulings have proven no longer suitable to the situation.

Collective *ijtihad* is also considered an apt solution for the crisis of thought in the Muslim world, since it allows modern, contemporary and complex problems to be resolved, and tends to reduce any fanaticism in the schools of Islamic law. One of the reasons for its moderating effect is that a number of Muslim scholars from different schools of law and various disciplines of science have to sit together to perform *ijtihad* collectively. The aim is to reach consensus. This procedure is advocated by Muslim scholars who appreciate and apprehend that problems in the modern era are far more complex than they were at the time of the Prophet 15 centuries ago. Accordingly, Muslim communities in the twenty-first century expect Muslim scholars to provide broad answers to their problems, not only from the viewpoint of Islamic law, but also from other perspectives. The *ijtihad* that is needed in this era is *al-ijtihad al-jama'i*[87] – *ijtihad* as collective reasoning of the community.

In the West, *ulama* should reduce their dependence on the old methodology, which was a product of the sociological structure of classical and medieval Muslim societies.[88] The *ulama* should start to offer new concepts, or a reformulated methodology for Islamic law, in order to deal with modern phenomena in the twenty-first century. In other words, they need to develop new interpretations of original sources while studying the interpretations of the past, both to learn from their insights and to understand them as products of their historical environment. This may also mean that Muslim women, in the tradition of A'isha, will be a part of this process to ensure that fatwas are always responsive to the issues and challenges facing Muslims today. From the media one can get the impression that the Sharia is locked in a static medieval vault of Taliban construction, but it can be a living, evolving and dynamic force. As this chapter has demonstrated, fatwas are a mechanism for growth and adaptability inherent in Islam that can be valued by Muslim and non-Muslims alike.

NOTES

1. This chapter develops concepts and material first published in *Griffith Law Review* in 2009. See: Ann Black and Nadirsyah Hosen, 'Fatwas: The Role in Contemporary Secular Australia' (2009) 18(1) *Griffith Law Review*, 405–27. We thank *Griffith Law Review* for giving permission for us to republish some parts of the original article in this chapter.
2. Muhammad Khalid Masud, Brinkley Messick and David S. Powers, 'Muftis, Fatwas and Islamic Legal Interpretation' in *Islamic Legal Interpretation* (Harvard University Press, Cambridge, MA, 1996), 8, 18.
3. Robin Brant, 'Malaysia Clerics Issue Yoga Fatwa', *BBC World News*, 22 November 2008: http://news.bbc.co.uk/2/hi/7743312.stm. See Roger Mitton, 'A Compulsory Course and a Beauty Contest Ban Worry non-Muslims', *Asiaweek*, 18 July, 1997: http://www.asiaweek.com/asiaweek/97/0718/nat4.html
4. Mullah Umar's fatwa, issued 26 February 2001, called for all idols of worship to be destroyed. Note also there were fatwas issued from muftis in other countries, including Egypt, Iran and Morocco, condemning the destruction of the Buddhas.
5. Trudy Harris, 'Anti-West Fatwas Hit Australia', *The Australian*, 21 July 2005, 11.
6. Fatwas issued by Sheikh Abdul Aziz bin Baz, Grand Mufti of Saudi Arabia, 'Saudi Arabia launches official fatwa site', AFP, 6 October 2007: http://afp.google.com/article/ALeqM5ieknl8SALh4EU3aNHjNXbx43bX0A
7. 'Declaration of Fatwa by World Islamic Scholars about Danish Cartoons', issued in *Tabsir*: 20 February 2006, http://www.tabsir.net/?p=132
8. Ibid.
9. Ibid.
10. For the translated text of the fatwa and the text of the confirmation of the execution order see Daniel Pipes, *The Rushdie Affair: The Novel, the Ayatollah and the West* (Transaction, New Brunswick, NJ, 1990) 27, 30. Also, James Crossley and Christian Karner, *Writing History, Constructing Religion* (Ashgate, Aldershot, 2005) 85–7.
11. M. Slaughter, 'The Salman Rushdie Affair: Apostasy, Honor and Freedom of Speech' (1993) 79 *Virginia Law Review* 153; Elizabeth Mayer, 'Islam and the State' (1991) 12 *Cardozo Law Review* 1047; Shoaib Qureshi and Javed Khan, *The Politics of Satanic Verses: Unmasking Western Attitudes* (Muslim Community Studies Institute, Leicester, 1989); Steve MacDonogh (ed.), *The Rushdie Letters: Freedom to Speak, Freedom to Write* (Brandon, Kerry, 1993); M. Ashan and A.R. Kidwai, *Sacrilege Versus Civility: Muslim Perspectives on the Satanic Verses Affair* (Islamic Foundation, Markfield, 1993).
12. Brunei and Bangladesh.
13. Abdullah Yusuf Ali, *The Qur'an: Text, Translation and Commentary* (Tahrike Tarsile Qur'an, New York, 2005), 220.
14. Súra Nahl 16:43, in Abdullah Yusuf Ali, *The Qur'an: Text, Translation and Commentary* (Tahrike Tarsile Qur'an, New York, 2005), 667.
15. These included the Prophet's secretary Zayd b. Thabit and his wives, in particular A'isha. This fact becomes important in the contemporary debate as to whether women can issue fatwas.
16. Muhammad Khalid Masud, Brinkley Messick and David S. Powers, 'Muftis, Fatwas and Islamic Legal Interpretation' in *Islamic Legal Interpretation* (Harvard University Press, Cambridge, MA, 1996), 8, 18.
17. Wael B. Hallaq, *The Origins and Evolution of Islamic Law* (Cambridge University Press, Cambridge, 2005), 89.

18. Muhammad Khalid Masud, Brinkley Messick and David S. Powers, 'Muftis, Fatwas and Islamic Legal Interpretation' in *Islamic Legal Interpretation* (Harvard University Press, Cambridge, MA, 1996), 8, 9.
19. Yvonne Yazbeck Haddad and Barbara Stowasser, *Islamic Law and the Challenges of Modernity* (Rowman & Littlefield, Lanham, MD, 2004), 83.
20. See Muhammad Khalid Masud, *Islamic Legal Philosophy: A Study of Abu Ishaq al-Shatibi's Life and Thought* (Islamic Research Institute, Islamabad, 1977).
21. Brinkley Messick, 'Fatwa: Process and Function' in John L. Esposito (ed.), *The Oxford Encyclopedia of the Modern Islamic World*, Vol. 3 (Oxford University Press, Oxford, 1995), 12.
22. A.S. Dallal, 'Fatwa: Modern Usage' in John L. Esposito (ed.), *The Oxford Encyclopedia of the Modern Islamic World*, Vol. 3 (Oxford University Press, Oxford, 1995), 15–16.
23. James P. Pistacori, 'The Role of Islam in Saudi Arabia's Political Development' in John L. Esposito (ed.) *Islam and Development: Religion and Sociopolitical Change* (Syracuse University Press, Syracuse, NY, 1980), 128.
24. See Amiq, 'Two Fatwas on Jihad against the Dutch Colonization in Indonesia: A Prosopographical Approach to the Study of Fatwa' (1998) 5 *Studia Islamika* 87. See also Nadirsyah Hosen, 'Fatwa and Politics in Indonesia' in Arskal Salim and Azyumardi Azra (eds), *Sharia and Politics in Modern Indonesia* (Institute of Southeast Asia Studies, Singapore, 2003).
25. Office of the Grand Ayatollah Sistani Website at: http://www.sistani.org/html/eng/; Charles Kursman, 'Pro-US Fatwas' (2003) 10 *Middle East Policy* 155–67.
26. Brinkley Messick, 'Fatwa: Process and Function' in John L. Esposito (ed.), *The Oxford Encyclopedia of the Modern Islamic World*, Vol. 3 (Oxford University Press, Oxford, 1995).
27. Jacques Waardenburg, 'Mufti' in John L. Esposito (ed.) *Islam and Development: Religion and Sociopolitical Change* (Syracuse University Press, Syracuse, NY, 1980), 151.
28. Jakob Skovgaard-Petersen, 'A Typology of State Muftis' in Yvonne Yazbeck Haddad and Barbara Stowasser, *Islamic Law and the Challenge of Modernity* (Alta Mira Press, Walnut Creek, 2004), 81–97.
29. Muhammad Khalid Masud, Brinkley Messick and David S, Powers, *Islamic Legal Interpretation* (Harvard University Press, Cambridge, MA, 1996), 27–8.
30. A.S. Dallal, 'Fatwa: Modern Usage' in John L. Esposito (ed.), *The Oxford Encyclopedia of the Modern Islamic World*, Vol. 3 (Oxford University Press, Oxford, 1995), 15–16.
31. The original fatwa in Arabic has been translated in English and analysed in terms of structure and content by Rispler-Chiam; see Vardit Rispler-Chiam, 'Postmortem Examinations in Egypt' in Muhammad Khalid Masud, Brinkley Messick and David S. Powers (eds), *Islamic Legal Interpretation* (Harvard University Press, Cambridge, MA, 1996), 278–85.
32. See the Quran, Súrah Baqarah 2:185: 'Ramadhán is the (month) in which was sent down the Qur'an, as a guide to mankind, also clear (Signs) for guidance and judgement (between right and wrong). So every one of you who is present (at his home) during that month should spend it in fasting, but if any one is ill, on a journey, the prescribed period (should be made up) by days later. God intends every facility for you; He does not want to put you to difficulties. (He wants you) to complete the prescribed period, and to glorify Him in that He has guided you; and perchance ye shall be thankful'. Abdullah Yusuf Ali, *The Qur'an: Text, Translation and Commentary* (Tahrike Tarsile Qur'an, New York, 2005), 73.

33. Vardit Rispler-Chiam, 'Postmortem Examinations in Egypt' in Muhammad Khalid Masud, Brinkley Messick and David S. Powers (eds), *Islamic Legal Interpretation* (Harvard University Press, Cambridge, MA, 1996), 278.
34. Ibid., 281.
35. Ibid.
36. Ibid., 282.
37. Dariusch Atighetchi, *Islamic Bioethics: Problems and Perspectives* (Springer, Dordrecht, 2007), 117–19.
38. Hadith related by Ahmad, Abu Dawud and Ibn Majah on the authority of A'isha that the Prophet said: 'Breaking a deceased person's bone is akin to breaking it when alive'.
39. The Council of Senior Scholars, Saudi Arabia, decree no. 47 dated 20 August 1396 A.H. on autopsy, located on-line at http://www.alifta.com/Fatawa/FatawaChapters
40. For example it is documented that Pakistani families in the UK are reluctant to allow post-mortems; see A. Sheikh, A.R. Gatrad and S. Dhami, 'Culturally Sensitive Care for the Dying is a Basic Human Right' (1999) 319 *British Medical Journal* 1073.
41. Patrick Glenn, *Legal Traditions of the World*, 2nd edn (Oxford University Press, New York, 2004), 178.
42. Ibid.
43. Frank Vogel, 'The Complementarity of *Ifta* and *Qada*: Three Saudi Fatwas on Divorce' in Muhammad Khalid Masud, Brinkley Messick and David S. Powers, *Islamic Legal Interpretation* (Harvard University Press, Cambridge, MA, 1996), 266. There are countries such as Indonesia where there are female judges in Sharia courts, but in the majority of Muslim countries, including Saudi Arabia (where Vogel undertook his research), the role remains the preserve of men.
44. Muhammad Khalid Masud, Brinkley Messick and David S. Powers, 'Muftis, Fatwas and Islamic Legal Interpretation' in *Islamic Legal Interpretation* (Harvard University Press, Cambridge, MA, 1996), 8, 19.
45. Ibid.
46. Fatwa on Women's Driving of Automobiles Shaikh Abdel Aziz Bin Abdallah Bin Baz 1990.
47. '*Continued* Call for the Repeal of Saudi Arabia's Fatwa on Women Driving', *Equality Now*, accessed on February 2012 at: http://www.equalitynow.org/take_action/discrimination_in_law_action_0
48. Nadirsyah Hosen, 'Behind the Scenes: Fatwas of Majelis Ulama Indonesia (1975–1998)' (2004) 15(2) *Journal of Islamic Studies* 147, 148.
49. Salafis take the practice of the earliest Muslims (salaf) as the purest model for all Muslim societies.
50. For example, the fatwa issued which prohibits any celebration of the Prophet's birthday (*mawlid*) or any person's birthday on the ground that it is 'an innovation' introduced by deviant Muslims that mimics Christian practices and festivals and must be rejected. Fatwa no. 2362 and Fatwa no. 4091, Part 3: Fatwas of the Permanent Committee, Group 1, Vol. 3, 'Aqidah (3), Al-Mawlid.
51. See discussion of these terms in Chapter 1.
52. His Eminence Shaykh 'Abdul-'Aziz ibn 'Abdullah ibn 'Abdul-Rahman ibn Muhammad ibn 'Abdullah Al Baz.
53. Fatwa no. 21413: Fatwa of the Permanent Committee, Group 2, Vol. 1, 'Aqidah, Acts commensurate with Kufr, ruling on building temples in the Arabian Peninsula.
54. More information on Indonesian fatwas can be found in Nadirsyah Hosen, 'Collective *Ijtihad* and Nahdlatul Ulama' (2004) 6 *New Zealand Journal of Asian Studies* 5–26; Nadirsyah Hosen, 'Behind the Scenes: Fatwas of Majelis Ulama Indonesia (1975–1998)' (2004) 15 *Journal of Islamic Studies* 147–79; see also Nadirsyah

Hosen, 'Revelation in a Modern Nation State: Muhammadiyah and Islamic Legal Reasoning in Indonesia' (2002) 4 *Australian Journal of Asian Law* 232–58.

55. Muhyi al-Hilal Sarhan, *al-Qawa'id al-Fiqhiyah* (Jami'ah Baghdad, Baghdad, 1987), 64.
56. Majelis Ulama Indonesia, *Himpunan Keputusan dan Fatwa Majelis Ulama Indonesia* (Sekretariat MUI, Jakarta, 1995), 165.
57. K.H. Azis Masyhuri (ed.), *Masalah Keagamaan Hasil Muktamar dan Munas Ulama Nahdlatul Ulama 1926–1994* (PP RMI and Dinamika Press, Surabaya, 1997), 401.
58. Majelis Ulama Indonesia, *Himpunan Keputusan dan Fatwa Majelis Ulama Indonesia* (Sekretariat MUI, Jakarta, 1995) 102–103.
59. Mohamad Atho Mudzhar, 'Fatwas of the Council of Indonesian Ulama: A Study of Islamic Legal Thought in Indonesia 1975–1988', Ph.D. Dissertation, UCLA (1990), 205.
60. See Masaji Chiba's works: *Asian Indigenous Law in Interaction with Received Law* (1986); *Legal Pluralism. Toward a General Theory through Japanese Legal Culture* (Tokai University Press, Tokai, 1989); 'Other Phases of Legal Pluralism in the Contemporary World' (1998) 11(3) *Ratio Juris* 228–45; and *Legal Cultures in Human Society* (Shinzansha International, Tokyo, 2002).
61. Islamic scholar Soad Saleh has an Egyptian satellite TV show, *Women's Fatwa* see Sharon Otterman, 'Fatwas and Feminism: Women, Religious Authority, and Islamic TV', accessed on 11 April 2009 at: http://www.tbsjournal.com/Otterman.html
62. Abdul Rahman Shaheen, 'Women may issue Fatwas', *Gulf News* 27 January 2009, accessed on 11 April 2009 at: http://www.gulfnews.com/News/Gulf/saudi_arabia/10279429.html
63. Ihsan Yilmaz, *Muslim Laws, Politics and Society in Modern Nation States* (Ashgate, Aldershot, 2005), 66.
64. See http://www.euro-muslim.com/en_u_foundation_details.aspx?news_id=343
65. See http://www.euro-muslim.com/en_u_foundation_details.aspx?news_id=343
66. See discussion of these methodologies in Chapter 1.
67. For background on the Australian Muslim community see Abdullah Saeed, *Islam in Australia* (Allen and Unwin, Sydney, 2003); Abdullah Saeed and Shahram Akbarzadeh (eds), *Muslim Communities in Australia* (University of New South Wales Press, Sydney, 2001); Jamila Hussain, *Islam: Its law and Society*, 2nd edn (Federation Press, Leichhardt, 2004).
68. 'Revealed: the Saudi Paymaster in Australia', *The Sydney Morning Herald*, 10 September 2005. See generally on Wahabism or Wahhabiyah: Hamid Algar, *Wahhabism: A Critical Essay* (Islamic Publications International, Oneonta, 2002) and David Commins, *The Wahhabi Mission and Saudi Arabia* (I.B. Tauris, London, 2006).
69. ANIC claims to be 'the sole national organization of Imams and Islamic Scholars with broad community representation', elected a Council of Fatwa, consisting of seven imams, and also now appoints the mufti of Australia.
70. AFIC is the umbrella organization for state Islamic Councils.
71. Darulfatwa's stated goal is 'to announce and disseminate Islamic judgments (fatwa) which Muslims need in their daily lives' by employing a collective approach and supporting views of moderation.
72. http://www.askthemufti.com/
73. See Gary R. Bunt, *Islam in the Digital Age: E-Jihad, Online Fatwas and Cyber Islamic Environments* (Pluto Press, London, 2003).
74. Ihsan Yilmaz, *Muslim Laws, Politics and Society in Modern Nation States* (Ashgate, Aldershot, 2005), 39.
75. Bettina Graf, 'Sheikh Yusuf Al-Qaradawi in Cyberspace' (2007) 47 *Die Welt des Islams* 403–21.

76. Based in Doha, Qatar with fatwas issued by a committee of scholars headed by Dr Yusuf Qardawi, accessed 26 October 2008 at: http://www.islamonline.net/livefatwa/english/select.asp
77. Based in Saudi Arabia with fatwas issued by committee of scholars supervised by Sheikh Salman bin Fahd al-Oadah, accessed 26 October 2008 at: http://www.islamtoday.com/fatwa_archive_main.cfm
78. South African site with fatwas issued by Mufti Ebrahim Desai, accessed 26 October 2008 at: http://islam.tc/ask-imam/index.php
79. Saudi Arabian site with fatwas issued under supervision of Shaykh Muhammad Saalih al-Munajjid, accessed 26 October 2008 at: http://63.175.194.25/index.php?ln=eng
80. Saudi Arabian site designed to give English speaking Muslims access to translations of officially published Arabic fatwas, accessed 26 October 2008 at: http://www.fatwa-online.com/
81. Accessed 12 September 2005 at: http://63.175.194.25/
82. Alexandre Caeiro, 'Transnational "Ulama", European Fatwas, and Islamic Authority: A Case Study of the European Council for Fatwa and Research' in Stefano Allievi and Martin van Bruinessen M (eds), *Production and Dissemination of Islamic Knowledge in Western Europe* (Routledge, Abingdon, 2010), 37.
83. Ibid.
84. http://www.syariahonline.com/new_index.php/id/1/cn/24458
85. http://www.askamufti.com/Answers/ViewQuestion.aspx?QuestionId=947
86. Wael Hallaq, 'From "*Fatawa* to *Furu*": Growth and Change in Islamic Substantive Law' (1994) 1 *Islamic Law and Society* 65.
87. Yusuf Al-Qaradawi, 'al-Ijtihad wa al-Tajdid baina al-Dawabit al-Syar'iyyah wa al-Hajat al-Mu'asirah', interview in *al-'Ummah* (Qatar, 31 May 1984), 48.
88. More information on Islamic legal theory can be read in Wahbah Al-Zuhayli, *Usul al-Fiqh al-Islamiy* (Dar al-Fikr, Beirut, 1986); Muhammad Salam Madkur, *Manahij al-Ijtihad fi al-Islam* (Matba'at Jami'ah, Kuwait, 1974); Mohammad Hashim Kamali, *Principles of Islamic Jurisprudence* (Islamic Texts Society, Cambridge, 1991); Taha Jabir Al-Alwani, *Source of Methodology in Islamic Jurisprudence* (International Institute of Islamic Thought, Herndon, 1993).

5. Islamic family law

1. INTRODUCTION

Whether living in a traditional Muslim nation or in the secular West, family law or 'personal status law',[1] has special significance for Muslims. There are several reasons why. The first is that the Quran has many verses (*ayat*) setting out legal principles and rules for marriage, divorce and family relationships. This means there has always been a clear foundation for Islamic family law, emanating directly from the revelations from God to the Prophet Mohammad. The reformist nature of many of these verses indicates that family law was an important dimension of God's message for Muslims. Many of these reforms either abolished or reconstructed practices that were detrimental to women and children,[2] making them ground-breaking in feminist terms with Muslim women given legal entitlements that were not attained in the West for a thousand or more years. In addition, the example of the Prophet as a married family man cemented the importance of the family in every Muslim society, and the many hadiths (*ahadith*) on family matters, together with the expansion of laws by the jurists, enabled family law to develop into a comprehensive legal compendium. The second reason is cultural and sociological. Poulter has argued that family law embodies the 'quintessential culture of a distinctive group … which cannot be discarded lightly'.[3] It goes directly to individual identity within a shared identity of the family and extends to a shared belonging to the worldwide community of Muslims (*ummah*). While Western models have superseded many other aspects of Islamic law, notably in the commercial and criminal spheres, family law, according to Poulter, has become more 'precious and worthy of preservation worldwide'.[4] Family laws were generally not abolished by colonial powers but retained, although often codified and modified.[5] Family law therefore remained central to Muslim identity in colonized Muslim lands, both at an individual and at a community level. An-Na'im argues that, as governments in Muslim states continued the colonial approach of leaving family law in the private not the public realm, control over it remained in the hands of the religious scholars (*ulama*) rather than the state.[6] While modernizing forces within the ruling elites of many Muslim nations secularized and reformed other areas of law, An-Na'im argues that for reasons of political expediency, governments conceded control over family law to the *ulama*. This allowed conservative and literalist interpretations to survive into the twenty-first century. However, as 'the most developed area of Sharia, over which the *ulama* have had the highest monopoly',[7] family law remains 'a highly symbolic location of the struggle between the forces of traditionalism and modernism',[8] or in the words of Abdul Rahman, the forces of 'dynamism versus ossification'.[9]

Family law therefore remains a source of contestation between conservative or traditionalist Islamic views and modernist egalitarian ones. Modernists allow revisiting of the primary sources of law in Islam to permit revitalized interpretations to emerge, ones which favour autonomy and greater gender equality. Modern interpretations also prioritize the egalitarian message and spirit in the Quran over the understanding of jurists (*fiqh*). As *fiqh* is a product of human reasoning of the Divine message, undertaken in a context that resonated in the tribal societies of past centuries; the question is whether it should unquestioningly continue to bind Muslims in modern times. The historical, authoritative, political and practical reasons for adhering to traditional interpretations of Islamic family law have been challenged by modernist forces bolstered by the interconnectedness brought by globalization; the growth of international norms and standards, many of which demand equalities of gender, legal status, race and religion, and sexual orientation unheard of a few centuries ago in any nation or society; increasing educational and economic standards across the Muslim world; greater participation of women in the workforce, public life and academia; and acknowledgement of religious and ethnic pluralism.

As noted above, the sociological 'identity' aspects of family law are central to the Muslim psyche, but 'identity' of this type is important to other communities as well, including ones where political and ideological 'battles' were fought in previous centuries to separate church and state, and to attain equal franchise in law for women, whether in Christian Europe or in Muslim Turkey. Now the fight in many countries is being waged for same-sex equality. In these countries, points of tension or friction can arise between the largely laissez-faire approach to regulating relationships between consenting adults, and the approach of Islamic family law that by comparison is categorized as 'regressive', 'medieval' or 'discriminatory'. It appears that Islamic family law is in a contest on two fronts: the first within Islamic family law, between traditionalist and modernist Islamic perspectives; and the second between Islamic law as an entity and the secularists of Western liberal thought.

Related to the internal struggle between modernism and traditionalism within Islamic jurisprudence, there is the practical question of how a religion-based system of law can respond to the encroachment of secularism. Islamic family law is promoted frequently as a bastion against secular society. Governments in Muslim nations, and Muslim minorities in the West, advocate that perhaps the best way to defend their families from 'corrupting' Western influences and impermissible (*haram*) practices (such as prostitution, alcohol and drug use, pornography, child abuse, marital breakdown, extra-marital affairs, illegitimate children, same-sex relationships or neglect of the elderly) is to adhere to Islamic family law. By operating within this system of values, families can be more secure, and nations will not have to deal with the economic, political and social ramifications of family dysfunction in Western societies.

The survival, reform and in some cases revival of Islamic family law as a state-endorsed system in the twenty-first century is proof of its resilience and relevance for over 1400 years. All Muslim majority nations, with a few exceptions, notably Turkey, adhere to a form of Islamic family law, with many more nations, including India, Singapore, Israel, Thailand and the Philippines, enacting statutes to allow for the separate administration of Islamic family law for their Muslim citizens and for a separate system of Islamic courts. Singapore, for example, has legislation, namely the *Administration of Muslim Law Act 1966*, mandating Islamic family law for Singapore's Muslim minority with separate government-funded Sharia courts and an administrative body, the Islamic Religious Council. The significant migration of Muslims to Western nations over the last few decades has seen representatives of Muslim minorities in Europe, North America and Australia put forward arguments in favour of similar grants of Muslim autonomy over personal status matters. The challenge this brings to Western secular legal systems will be discussed later in this chapter, but it is worth noting at this point that many Muslims in Western nations continue to live in accordance with Islamic family laws and values. These have not had to be abandoned, as for the most part, such laws are either compatible with the liberal family law regimes in Western nations or can operate alongside, in 'the shadow of' the state-based family law regime.[10]

So while Islamic family law may have more currency than most other areas of Islamic law, notably criminal law,[11] its application today is far from identical or uniform. Divergence makes Islamic family law the perfect vehicle by which to appreciate the role of interpretation through *ijtihad* and the juristic variance made possible by incorporating views of the different schools of law or the distinctive and entrenched customary practices that Islam encountered as it spread beyond Arabia. Custom shaped past practices. It continues to influence present ones. The customary and regulatory practices of *adat* in Southeast Asia, for example, inform family life in ways that depart from the tribal and kin-based patriarchal practices of the Arabs. In Southeast Asia more egalitarian relationships between husband and wife exist and women's integrated role both in the community and in economic production contrast with the seclusion and segregation in traditional Arab lands. Variance in family law highlights the inherent adaptability of Islamic law to respond to cultural, political and social realities. One of these realities is the growth of nation-states. Compliance derived from religious commitment has shifted to one of state enforcement, with the subtleties of *fiqh* replaced by rigidity of codification. An-Na'im argues that in this way Islamic family law has been transformed. Today the majority of Muslim nations have Islamic family law in statutory form that represents the 'will of the State', which is adjudicated and enforced by the 'apparatus of the State'.[12] Adaptation of Islamic family law is also evident in the response to the increasing reach of modern international law, including human rights instruments such as the Convention on the Elimination of All Forms of Discrimination against Women. Muslim countries have addressed these factors of modernity in different ways, with responses tailored to suit the exigencies of national development as well as religious, cultural or political forces. Menski believes that Muslim societies will 'inevitably negotiate and create different types of Islamic law', whether this occurs officially or unofficially, or happens within or outside a Muslim state.[13] The laws of Muslim societies will always be culture-specific because, he argues, they are 'lived systems managed and manipulated by real people'.[14]

To explore modern perspectives on Islamic family law, this chapter will provide an overview and analysis of the key components of Islamic family law, marriage, divorce and custody, noting points of juristic agreement in addition to key interpretative differences, particularly where modernist perspectives have informed debate and reforms. Some reflections are also provided on the challenge for Muslims in Western countries where Islamic family law is also adhered to, but without state endorsement or support. Designed to remove hardship and injustice, Islamic family laws were inherently reformist and modifications and assimilations occurred to embody the needs of society as Islam spread and evolved.

2. MARRIAGE (*NIKKAH*)

> And among His Signs is this, that He created for you mates from among yourselves, that ye may dwell in tranquillity with them, and He has put love and mercy between your (hearts): verily in that are Signs for those who reflect. (Quran, Súra Rúm 30:21)[15]

As this Quranic verse shows, marriage was ordained by God as part of divine guidance for all people. It is not obligatory,[16] but highly recommended (*mustahabb*) with the Prophet exhorting, 'marriage is my tradition and anyone who avoids it is not part of my ummah'.[17] The Prophet Mohammad was a married man, and his personal example highlights marriage as a bedrock institution in all Muslim societies. Unlike some Christian and Buddhist orders where celibacy is the greatest manifestation of devotion to God, the converse is true in Islam: 'No house has been built in Islam more beloved in the sight of Allah than through marriage.'[18] A contract of marriage is necessary for any sexual relations to be lawful. In many parts of the Middle East virginity is not just a cultural expectation, but also a legal one.[19] Violation of this law, having a sexual relationship outside of marriage, may be subject to the *hadd* offence of *zina.* This is discussed in Chapter 10. Owing to the high evidentiary requirements, convictions for *zina* are rare in the few conservative Muslim countries that employ Sharia criminal law, but Islam's unequivocal position that sexual relations must take place within marriage sits at odds with the West's acquiescence for couples 'living together', single women having children and the recent promotion of concepts such 'friends with benefits'. Although these arrangements are contrary to the teachings of the Christian church, today's secular states legally recognize adult autonomy, which gives rise to full sexual freedom. In Islam, marriage is also necessary to establish the paternity of children. A child being born to a married woman gives rise to a presumption of paternity[20] from which come rights to inheritance and maintenance. In addition, marriage gives mutual rights and obligation to the husband and wife, which are discussed later, but which include the husband's obligation of maintenance and a wife's duty of obedience together with their mutual rights of inheritance and to sexual fulfilment within their marriage.

A. Features of Marriage

In Islam, marriage is held to be not a sacrament,[21] but a legal contract (*nikkah*) between two parties with legal capacity to contract. Although it is a contract and thus in the realm of transactions (*mu'amilat*), in spirit it crosses into the realm of the spiritual and religious (*ibadat*).[22] Marriage can only be between a man and a woman. Same-sex marriages are not legally possible and same-sex relations are unlawful. In some countries, notably Iran, homosexual acts constitute the serious criminal offence of *liwat*, which, if proven, attracts the death penalty.[23] In other countries, *liwat* is criminalized with fines, corporal punishments or the imposition of prison terms, while still others do not prohibit homosexual acts by law.[24] In addition there is juristic agreement that there are three permanent legal impediments to a valid Muslim marriage. Their derivation lies in the Quran, Súra Nisáa 4:23.[25] The first of these permanent impediments is concerned with consanguinity, that is, prohibited family relationships with a descendant or ascendant. A man is prohibited from marrying his mother, grandmother, daughter, granddaughter, sister, niece or aunt, and a woman from marrying a man with the comparable family relationship. Unlike Western law, there is no prohibition or discouragement of marriage between cousins, which continues as a common practice in many Muslim nations. The second prohibition relates to affinity relationships. A man is prohibited from marrying his mother-in-law or his stepmother and any of their descendants, or his daughter-in-law or stepdaughter. Nor can a man be married to two sisters at the same time. The third prohibition had more currency in earlier times when the practice of 'wet-nursing' was quite common, and prohibits a person of either sex from marrying another if they were breastfed by the same woman,[26] as this is akin to a foster relationship. These conditions are permanent and the relationship creates a status known as '*mahram*', which has other legal consequences as discussed later in this chapter.

i. Religious requirements

In order to preserve Islam and Muslim practices within the family, Islamic law imposes religious (*din*) adherence requirements for marriage validity. Similar rules also apply in other faith traditions, such as Judaism, Orthodox Christianity and Roman Catholicism. In Islam, there is scholarly consensus that a Muslim woman is prohibited from marrying a man who is not Muslim.[27] If he converts to Islam then the marriage will be valid. This is why it is classified as a temporary not permanent prohibition. The basis for it is the Quran, Súra Baqarah 2:221: 'Nor marry (your girls) to unbelievers until they believe'.[28] Although the same verse (2:221) tells men: 'Don't marry unbelieving women (idolaters), until they believe', the position for a Muslim man is more complicated as a later verse in the Quran, Súra Máida 5:5 says: '(lawful unto you in marriage) are (not only) chaste women who are believers, but chaste women among the People of the Book, revealed before your time'.[29] Following this revelation, the Prophet married a Jewish and then a Christian woman. Most schools, but only a handful of nations today,[30] allow a Muslim man to marry a 'woman of the book' (*kittabiyah*), which includes Christian and Jewish women. Some Shia jurists also include Zoroastrians within this classification. Although *kittabiyah* believe in one God and share similar scripture (teachings in the Abrahamic tradition), such interfaith marriages are seen as socially and religiously undesirable. As Islam holds that the children of an inter-faith marriage will be Muslims, a non-Muslim mother is seen as not equipped to fully raise them in accordance with Islam. Perhaps for this reason, some scholars have acknowledged the *kittabiyah* exception, but argue that this ruling applies only to women whose families were Christian or Jewish at the time of the revelation. Unless the family lineage can be traced back to that time, a *kittabiyah* marriage remains unlawful for Muslim men. This narrower interpretation makes inter-faith marriages practically impossible and has led many countries, including Malaysia, Brunei and Singapore, to pass laws disallowing the exception altogether.[31] The result in these countries is that non-Muslims of either gender will be required to convert to Islam for a valid Islamic marriage. In these multi-religious and multi-ethnic nations of Southeast Asia, Muslim–non-Muslim marriages remain a divisive issue[32] closely linked to conversions to, or from, Islam, and the contentious matter of apostasy. The religious requirements also mean that, if the woman converts to Islam, her existing marriage to a non-Muslim becomes void. Similarly a conversion out of Islam by either party will result in dissolution of the marriage on the ground of apostasy. In Western nations, where religion no longer plays a part in marriage validity under state law, this is a concerning and sensitive issue for Muslims. In plural communities arguments have been made for a re-reading of the Quranic verses (Quran 2:221; 5:5; 60:10) so that the category of 'believers' is not confined to Muslims, but interpreted to include all who believe in God, particularly Christians and Jews,[33] which would significantly reduce the non-believer category. Conversely, Azizah al-Hibri makes an argument that, in the West, the Islamic prohibition must extend to male as well as female Muslims, because the reality in the Western context is that a Muslim father could lose custody/guardianship of his children, and so could not fulfil the Islamic obligation to raise them as Muslims if his wife was non-Muslim.[34] Inter-religious marriages occur in Western nations through civil ceremonies, but Muslim imams or celebrants will rarely officiate. Inter-faith marriages come with social stigma and can lead to estrangement with the Muslim's family and ostracism from their Muslim community.

Another temporary prohibition in Islamic law is that a woman who is married cannot marry another man until her marriage to her husband has terminated either through lawful divorce or through his death; nor can she marry until the period of her *iddah* has passed. The *iddah* period after divorce is set out in the Quran, Súra Baqarah 2:228: 'Divorced women shall wait concerning themselves for three monthly periods',[35] and after death, in the Quran, Súra Baqarah 2: 234, widows must wait 'four months and ten days'.[36] The practical rationale for *iddah* is that it provides a time frame within which a woman will know if she is pregnant.

The majority of scholars agree that a person cannot marry while in the state of purity for undertaking the *hajj* pilgrimage or the *umrah* pilgrimage (*ihram*). Sexual relations are forbidden during *ihram*, although there are some conflicting hadith in regard to the *umrah* pilgrimage with the Shia and Hanafi schools allowing this while the other three Sunni schools do not.

B. The Marriage Contract

While there is a religious dimension to marriage, with the Prophet reported as saying that those who marry fulfil half their religion, an Islamic marriage is first and foremost a legally binding contract.[37] As such, if there are no impediments to marriage, as outlined above, the marriage contract (*nikkah*) requires an offer and acceptance (*ijab and qabul*) made by two persons with the legal capacity to enter a contract, which is witnessed and the dower (*mahr*) specified. In addition there is consensus that legal conditions can be stipulated in the contract, of which a breach may terminate the marriage. Each of these legal requirements will be considered in this chapter; however, it should be noted that they need to be understood in a social context in which local customs and practices are drawn on to make the marriage ceremony and accompanying ritual culturally distinctive. Muslim marriages today draw on past customary traditions as well as on modern, Western practices. Religious rituals, such as the recitation of the opening verse of the Quran (the *fatiha*), are interwoven into the marriage ceremony. What the bride and groom wear, the bridal preparations, the days and format of the festivities, the symbolism within the marriage contact,[38] as well as the format of the ceremony, and whether the celebrations are gender-segregated, will vary considerably across the Muslim world.

Although a customary practice, rather than a legal requirement, betrothals of some form are common in most Muslim countries. Because it is a time when gifts are given and money spent on wedding preparations, rules have developed from customary practices, in regard to the return or retention of gifts and wedding expenditure during a betrothal period, should one party decide not to proceed with the marriage. In the Shafi'i school, for example, the return of gifts will turn on whether there is a valid reason for the party not to proceed, and if there is none, the person in default is liable to return betrothal gifts and cover any wedding expenditures.[39]

i. Offer and acceptance (*ijab* and *qabul*)

Although marriage can be instigated by either party, an offer (*ijab*) and a statement of acceptance in response (*qabul*) are required. Usually the offer comes from the man, but it is possible for a woman to make the offer, and so it was that Khadija, the first wife of the Prophet, instigated their marriage. Usually the local custom is that the families of the prospective husband and wife negotiate the marriage contract. The actual words vary according to custom and practice and some contracts are written or stated in the past tense to ensure certainty, for example, 'I have accepted this marriage'. The legal requirement for acceptance also varies, with some schools (Hanbali, Maliki, Shafi'I and Shia) holding that consent to a marriage can be withheld by a bride's male legal guardian (*wali*), who is usually her father, otherwise the nearest paternal male blood relative – ascendant or descendant. Shia and the Hanafi school allow an adult woman to give her own consent to a marriage; however, a marriage guardian is required for a minor female or minor male. When the minor reaches the age of puberty, however, they can veto the marriage. The legal basis for requiring the permission of a *wali* lies in hadiths, and not the Quran. The result is that, without the consent of her *wali*, any marriage is invalid (*batil*) and dissolved. The *wali* also participates on the bride's behalf in the exchange of words that makes the marriage contract. In many countries the bride will not be present at the *nikkah* ceremony. While the role of the *wali* is recognized in contemporary legislation, several Muslim countries[40] have instigated reforms to allow a Sharia Court judge (*qadi*) to assume the role of *wali* should one of the parties believe that a *wali* has unreasonably refused his consent, or in cases where a women has no one to act as a *wali*, or he cannot be found.[41] The *Iranian Civil Code* (1928) section 1043 provides that 'marriage for a virgin girl is subject to permission from her father or grandfather. If they withhold consent without justified reasons, the daughter can obtain permission from the Family Court and enter into a marriage with the person whom she has specified before the court'. Legislative provisions like this empowers a court to make enquires to determine whether permission for marriage should be given or withheld. One of the key inquiries is into the groom's suitability (*kafa'a*). There is considerable juristic debate about what is required of a suitable prospective husband. Traditionally, lineage, morality, occupation and religious adherence were crucial to this determination as the aim was to ensure that one's daughter was not married to a person of poor character or of a lesser social, financial or religious standing than her family. These criteria were not obligatory but were recommended. They were not applied to men, who could marry a wife of 'lesser standing'. However, the 'equality' principle (*kafa'a*) has been questioned in modern times as contrary to the Quran, Súra Hujurát 49:13: 'Verily the most honoured of you in the sight of God is (He Who is) the most righteous of you'.[42]

Although the institution of the *wali* developed, in part, to ensure that women, especially those of a young age, made wise marriage decisions, the practice has been criticized in contemporary times as unnecessary and paternalistic. Women today are as likely to be as well-educated, informed and as devout as men. Hence, the modernist interpretation is that consent of the woman is all that should be required and the role of *wali* should be consigned to history. The *wali*'s role could lose its legal status and become symbolic, similar to the now symbolic practice in Christian weddings of the father 'giving away' his daughter to the groom. The continuance of the male guardian's power to give consent to a marriage is seen as the main contributor to forced marriages, and particularly the forced marriage of minors. Forced marriages are distinguished from facilitated and arranged marriages, where, in the case of the latter, the bride has consented to her family finding her a suitable husband and approves of the choice made. In an arranged marriage, therefore, the bride consents to the marriage. In general, while an explicit statement of consent to be married is preferred, there is orthodox jurisprudence, developed from hadith, that in the case of a young (virgin) girl, her silence can be taken as acquiescence amounting to consent.[43] The derivation of this construct is said to arise from female modesty,[44] but it is one of several contributors to cases of forced marriages, which are discussed later in the chapter.

ii. Legal capacity

A person who marries must have the capacity to understand the legal consequences and the significance of the act. Both of these forms of capacity are linked to age and intellectual competency. A person who is mentally ill or who has a severe intellectual impairment lacks the capacity to consent. As a specific minimum age for marriage was not laid down in the Quran, the jurists developed the position that one becomes an adult, capable of giving consent to and of consummating a marriage, at puberty. Marriage of girls, and boys, below the age of puberty cannot take full legal effect until it is consummated, so there can be a delay of several years. Puberty is established by the traditional physical signs of maturity. In early times the marriage of young girls was frequent, even if these were not consummated until the girl reached puberty, and the practice has continued in some parts of the Muslim world, including Saudi Arabia, Yemen, Palestine and South Asia. However, while some nations, including Brunei, have not specified an age for marriage, many others have introduced a minimum age, which varies according to the country. As noted earlier, most Muslims countries allow minors to marry with the consent of their marriage guardian (*wali*), or with court approval. In Iran, under section 1041 of the *Civil Code* 1928, the minimum age for a girl is 13, and for a boy is 15, although this same section provides that a guardian may seek permission from the court to marry a minor before they have reach the required age if the marriage is in the best interests of the minor. In Libya the minimum age is 20 years for men and women,[45] but many nations have a gender differentiation. In Algeria, the age is 21 years for men and 18 for women,[46] while in Jordan the minimum age is 16 years for men and 15 for women.[47] Pakistan's set minimum is 18 years for boys and 16 years for girls, with penal sanctions for contracting child marriages.[48] However, as marriages between minors are not invalid according to the Quran, these proliferate in rural parts of the country in accordance with traditional local practices. Research in Egypt found that rural areas supported young marriages for religious reasons (to prevent moral wrongdoing); for economic reasons (so that the wife's labour can assist her husband's family, particularly her mother-in-law in the home and in the fields); and for cultural reasons (to prevent spinsterhood).[49] In the West, some Muslim migrants continue the practice of underage marriages both as part of their cultural tradition and also to ensure the virginity of their daughter in a social milieu where female sexualization and promiscuity are apparent.

iii. Dower (*mahr*)

An obligatory requirement of every marriage contract is the specification of the dower (*mahr*, also called marriage gift or portion), which some equate with consideration, while others argue that it is no more than a 'sign of respect'.[50] It is sometimes called *faridah* or *sadaq*, importing the notion of friendship, or *mas kahwin*, in Southeast Asia. If *mahr* were construed as consideration, it would imply that marriage was akin to a contract of sale whereas, in effect, *mahr* is property or a financial entitlement that accrues to the wife for her exclusive use. Once given, a wife can also voluntarily remit the *mahr* back to her husband. *Mahr* can be promptly settled, in which case it is paid at the time of the marriage, or deferred, which is when it becomes an obligation or debt a husband owes to his wife to which she is entitled should the marriage terminate by death or in some divorce situations. *Mahr* can be a combination of both 'prompt' and 'deferred', and it can be paid in instalments. Custom influences the payment of *mahr*. Wynn reports that in Saudi Arabia the tradition is for *mahr* to be paid at the time of the wedding ceremony while in other Arab countries a deferred portion is more usual.[51] In Malaysia, the *mas kahwin* is paid at the time of the marriage ceremony. To defer it in the Malaysian context would be embarrassing for both the groom and the bride, as it would imply that the groom could not afford to pay.[52] The *mahr* is an integral part of the Islamic marriage contract, and is the traditional means by which a wife can support herself should the marriage terminate through divorce where there is no fault on her part, or through the death of her husband. In the latter situation, any remaining *mahr* will be in addition to her share of her husband's estate. *Mahr* can involve significant sums of money, property and objects of value, as well as items of symbolic significance. The Quran did not lay down a formula for determining the *mahr*, but there is a benchmark from what the Prophet set down for his daughter Fatima, which is known as *mahr el Fatima* and was quite a modest sum. However, families wanting the best for their daughters can negotiate large sums and there have been fatwas calling for restraint in *mahr* negotiation so as not to unfairly financially burden a husband and his family. There is great variation on how *mahr* is formulated, not just between schools and nations, but also within nations. Practices in rural areas many markedly differ from those in urban ones.

As the entitlement of the wife, *mahr* is negotiated prior to the marriage. Traditionally a bride's *wali* would negotiate her *mahr* on her behalf. In contemporary times, it may be the case that the bride-to-be is also involved in such negotiations, but cultural factors can still be relevant, as a prospective wife may not want to be seen as mercenary, or focusing on the possibility of divorce at the outset of the marriage. It also is interesting that the provision of *mahr* has not diminished even as modernity has resulted in Muslim women participating in business, working for governments and entering professions such as medicine, law and teaching – all with salaries equal to those of men. The religious and also cultural imperative to provide a generous *mahr* in money or property remains strong. Just as it is the wife's right to use the *mahr* as she wishes, she also has an exclusive right to use any salary or other income she herself earns or receives and need not contribute any of it to the household expenses. Financial realism means that couples, particularly in the West, jointly contribute to the household and family expenses, but this could never be required of a wife under Islamic law. In cases of divorce, *mahr* can be highly contentious, and may require judicial determination. The need for recourse to the courts applies especially when *mahr* becomes a bargaining tool in certain divorce avenues, notably *khul'* (discussed later in this chapter). Where there is dispute about the *mahr* or it is evident that the price or value specified in the contract was too low, a court may calculate an equivalent dower, taking into account the circumstances of the couple or the practice of the local community. As there are no formal Sharia courts in the West, disputes involving *mahr* may not be able to be adequately settled, highlighting a legal lacuna for Muslim couples living in the West.

iv. Witnesses

There is juristic agreement that a *nikkah* should be witnessed, which is derived from a hadith that there can be no marriage without witnesses. Consistent with the witness requirements for all contracts, including commercial ones, two male Muslim witnesses are preferred but two female witnesses in place of one male witness may be accepted. This is in accordance with the general rule laid down in the Quran, Súra Baqarah 2:282. While there is jurisprudential debate on the validity of a marriage without witnesses, or with female or non-Muslim witnesses, in practical terms the issue is less important today as many countries have standard marriage contract forms that have a witness section. This is so in Iran, where Shia by tradition did not hold witnessing to be a necessary requirement for a valid marriage, although two witnesses are required for a divorce.[53]

v. Conditions (*shurut*)

As marriage is a contract, either party can include conditions as part of their marriage (as long as these conditions are not against Sharia or not against the core purpose of marriage), which when breached can have certain legal consequences, including providing a ground for divorce or prescribing a penalty for non-compliance. Standard clauses deal with monogamy, location of the marital home, the right of a wife to continue her studies or to work, the amount of the maintenance a wife is to receive and guarantees for visits with her family members. These conditions are a sanctioned means to ensure rights and benefits for married women. Men too can insert stipulations,[54] but as they have the power to divorce unilaterally, there is less need for this. Most conditions are for the benefit of the wife. While the schools vary as to the validity they accord to the various types of contractual stipulations,[55] most nations now have standardized clauses (*taliq*) attached to the marriage contract form. This means that it is unusual for a *wali* or for the wife-to-be to draft their own conditions. Nik Norani Nik Badli Shah has criticized the trend towards standardization of conditions. In Malaysia, she argues, standardization has greatly limited the parties' freedom to make their own stipulations and has also weakened the bargaining position of women.[56] Some nations, such as Iran, include an 'other conditions' component on the standard form that allows tailor-made stipulations to be added. As is discussed later, some contracts stipulate that the wife has the irrevocable power of attorney on behalf of her husband to divorce whenever she wishes. This practically makes women equal to men in terms of divorce rights. Currently, in Iran, there are over 25 standard conditions, one of which is that any property obtained during the course of marriage should be divided between the couple equally in the event of separation or divorce. The conditions included in a marriage contract should reflect the individual expectations of the couple about to embark on married life, but they also reflect changes and aspirations within Muslim societies. In Saudi Arabia, Wynn reports, brides today are specifying that they will not live with their husband's family (the traditional Arabian practice) but in a nuclear household, a trend described as turning 'away from viripatrilocal to neolocal residence'.[57] Also in Saudi Arabia, the right to work or study and to have a personal driver are common conditions that reflect the restrictions on women in the Kingdom, where women cannot drive and where segregation prevails. The marriage contract has become a means by which women in Saudi Arabia can gain greater personal autonomy. In Egypt, research by Essam Fawzy on Egypt's personal status laws found that stipulations varied significantly between rural and urban women. For example, the right to work and the right to be free from insults and physical punishment were stressed by urban women, but were rarely included by women from rural areas.[58]

However, although conditions in the marriage contract have been designed to protect women, their enforceability in Islamic courts even today can be variable. The Hanbali school allows the greatest scope for enforcement, but judges in all Sharia courts have to first determine whether the condition in question is valid or void.[59] A condition that is contrary to a Quranic text, or one that undermines the nature of marriage itself, may be held to be void, such as a condition that a wife will not engage in intercourse with her husband, or that he must divorce an existing co-wife. In the Shafi'i school such a condition could invalidate the entire marriage contract, but in the Hanbali school only the condition would be rendered void. One of the more common conditions is that a husband is bound to be monogamous. Scholars in the Shafi'i and Maliki traditions may hold this condition to be void, as it contravenes the right of polygyny given to a husband in the Quran (Súra Nisáa 4:3), while finding the marriage contract otherwise valid. In the Hanbali tradition, while a monogamy clause is valid, it does not prevent a husband from marrying a second wife, but enables the first wife to ask the court for a divorce. Another condition that can have important ramifications and is supported by contemporary reformers is for the marriage contract to stipulate a delegated right of divorce (*talaq*) to the wife, which is essentially a right for the wife to divorce herself on the husband's behalf. By delegating his right to *talaq* to her, the wife in effect is pronouncing divorce on his behalf. There are differences of opinion about whether the delegated right of divorce (*talaq al-tafwid*) is a conditional or unconditional right of divorce,[60] and whether it may be an under-utilized option in contemporary times. This is discussed later in the chapter.

C. Other Forms of Marriage

i. Polygyny[61]

Traditionally Islamic law has allowed a husband to have up to four wives at the same time. The basis for this is the Quran and also the tradition of the Prophet. Although the Prophet had been monogamous for 24 years while married to his first wife Khadija, after her death he entered into a series of polygynous marriages. The Quran specifies that polygyny is acceptable on condition that the husband does justice to each wife. The Quran (Súra Nisáa 4:3) says, 'marry women of your choice, two, or three, or four; but if ye fear that ye shall not be able to deal justly (with them), [t]hen only one … will be more suitable, to prevent you from doing injustice'.[62] Overall, the Quran recommends monogamy, as at Súra Nisáa 4:129 there is a warning that '[y]e are never able to be fair and just as between women, even if it is your ardent desire'.[63] Modern interpretations emphasize the statement recommending monogamy at 4:129 and argue that either stringent conditions should be imposed to ensure enforcement of the Quran's justice and equality requirements or that polygyny be prohibited altogether. This view has been legislated in Tunisia and Turkey, which have criminalized polygyny, and any such marriage is not recognized as lawful. Other nations have taken a 'safeguards' approach to polygyny, implementing judicial oversight to ensure adherence to the justice and equality requirements. Safeguards include obtaining the permission of or consulting with an existing wife or wives,[64] establishing a court to scrutinize the husband's financial ability to provide for, and separately house, another wife and future children, requiring an explanation of how a husband will be able to treat wives equally, examining whether an existing wife or wives and children will be disadvantaged, or inquiring into the reasons for a husband needing another wife. Reasons for needing another wife that a court or arbitration council[65] may accept include a wife's infertility, sexual incapability or unfitness for conjugal relations, illness or a physical or mental impairment. As a husband could readily divorce an infertile or ill wife under Islamic law, the polygyny provision allows her to continue as his wife and be provided and cared for by him, which may, it is argued, be kinder and fairer than a divorce. It is also felt that many women are better off economically in a polygynous marriage than as a divorcee.

Nations vary on what is required for lawful polygyny and many now set this out in statutory form. Even so, as is seen in Malaysia, there can be tensions between courts, parliaments and religious scholars on this issue. In 1980, several of the Malaysian states reformed their law on polygyny by adopting strict requirements for a husband to satisfy in order for the Sharia court to approve a polygynous marriage, making it among 'the most enlightened in the world'.[66] However, as Zainah Anwar explains, men who wanted to bypass this court approval process (probably because they would not succeed in satisfying the court's requirements) would 'forum shop', by going to another jurisdiction, such as the Philippines or a state like Terengganu with easier standards, to contract their polygnist marriage there and subsequently have it registered in their home state. Alternatively, they could marry without approval and pay a fine, and some men even risked the possibility of a jail term if convicted for marrying without court approval.[67] Religious scholars and Islamist groups objected to the reforms, and in particular to the requirement that a husband had to prove that his existing wife and children would not suffer a reduction in their standard of living. The basis of the scholars' objection was that it was inevitable that an additional marriage would impact on the existing family's standard of living, making it too onerous a requirement.[68] As a result of the objections to the court approval process, the law was amended in 1994 to delete the relevant provision. This amendment was part of a broader trend across Malaysia that has taken away the protections ascribed in law in favour of giving judges wider discretion to approve polygynous marriages.

The traditionalist view of polygyny is that something permitted by God and endorsed by the Prophet in his own life can never be prohibited. Traditionalists highlight that the Quranic limitation of four wives was a significant reform to the practices of pre-Islamic Arabia, and although the Quranic equality provision is acknowledged, it is seen in purely financial terms, eschewing broader notions of justice. Traditionalists also argue that polygyny has social benefits as it reduces the likelihood of extramarital relationships and sexually transmitted diseases, as well as keeping families intact rather than breaking them by divorce. For traditionalists, polygyny is an article of faith, making it an issue between a man and his God, which does not warrant the intrusion of the state either through the court or through legislation. Several states in the Middle East, including Saudi Arabia, Oman, Kuwait and Jordan, retain the orthodox *fiqh* on this. The modernist view is that it is practically impossible for husbands to treat co-wives equally and justly, making the second Quranic verse on doing justice between wives tantamount to an injunction against polygyny. Such divergence of views highlights that the issue of polygyny remains contentious, and is at the fracture line of the modernist/traditionalist divide. The trend across most Muslim nations is away from polygyny, but its link with traditional Islam means that it stays in the spotlight. Prohibition of polygyny is rare, although as noted above, many Muslim nations now restrict the practice, making polygyny a conditional, not absolute, right of the husband. Turkey abolished the practice in 1926,[69] followed 30 years later by Tunisia (in 1956). Interestingly, the 1956 Tunisian decision was cited with approval by the Supreme Court of Bangladesh in the case of *Jesmin Sultana v Mohammad Elias*.[70] The court noted that the Bangladeshi law that allowed for a co-wife with the approval of the Arbitration Council was contrary to the Tunisian interpretation of the Quran and the court recommended the current law be repealed by Parliament and replaced with a section prohibiting polygamy (including polygyny) altogether. No amendment was made. In 2011 the new government in Tunisia stated that polygyny is likely to be re-instated as lawful as the new state wishes to better align itself with Islam.[71] In addition, there is evidence in both Turkey and Tunisia that, although the prohibition on polygyny significantly reduced its practice, it was not eradicated altogether but went 'underground',[72] with these wives having no rights under the civil law.

Just as polygyny is not widely practised in Muslim nations, it is not common amongst the Muslim diaspora in the West. In reflecting on the realities of polygyny in Canada and North America, Clarke and Cross write that today 'polygamous marriage is ultimately damaging to the Muslim community'.[73] This is because the standards of traditional law cannot be replicated in modern Western contexts. Husbands with several wives are unlikely to provide equal support or time for each of their wives and the expense incurred in educating children and managing more than one household on one income means that the children are inevitably disadvantaged. Western legal systems may recognize polygyny in certain situations. Australia and England legally recognize polygamist marriages lawfully contracted in an overseas country, provided that neither party was domiciled in Australia or the UK at the time. The co-wives are recognized as lawful wives, which equally entitles them and their children to government welfare benefits. However, if either party was domiciled in the Australia or the UK at the time of a marriage ceremony,[74] a polygamist marriage could not lawfully have taken place. In addition, it would constitute the criminal offence of bigamy.

ii. Temporary (*mutah*) and ambulant (*misyar*) marriages

In some parts of the Muslim world, there are additional forms of marriage that attract both juristic support and condemnation. It is reported anecdotally that the numbers of such marriages are increasing, and this trend includes Muslims living in the West.[75] Both *mutah* and *misyar* marriages are tolerated, but most jurists are critical and disapprove of the practice. The role of these forms of marriage is to legalize any sexual intercourse that takes place, so the offence of *zina* is avoided, to protect the legal status and legitimacy of any children born from the union, and to ensure that women involved in these marriages receive some legal and social protection.

Temporary marriage (*mutah*, sometimes 'marriage of enjoyment'[76]) is an established Shia, especially Jafari school, practice. All Sunni schools reject the validity of *mutah*. Although the Caliph Umar prohibited it, the Shia position is that one cannot forbid something the Prophet allowed.[77] *Mutah* allows for a fixed term of marriage, with the date of expiry stipulated in the marriage contract. When the term expires the marriage ends, but can be renewed through a new contract. The duration can be for a short or long period, although marriages of a day or less are seen as undesirable, as are *mutah* marriages with a virgin girl. However, when the date expires the woman cannot marry another man until her *iddah* period has passed. Any children of a *mutah* marriage are legitimate and are entitled to inherit from both parents; however, there are no inheritance rights between husband and wife. A *mutah* marriage requires a contract where *mahr* is specified, and can also have conditions. Although a *mutah* wife is not entitled to maintenance, a sum to fulfil that function could be specified as a condition in the contract. Unlike permanent marriages, there is no numerical limit on *mutah* wives.[78]

Ambulant or itinerant marriage (*misyar*) is a practice that developed in the Sunni heartlands of Saudi Arabia. As with *mutah*, the requirements of a contract, witnesses and some form of *mahr* are present, but the marriage is not registered, nor is there a wedding ceremony. Arguably, *misyar* marriages violate the normal rights and duties of marriage, as the couple do not reside together, but the husband comes to visit the wife on occasions at her parents' home. The word *misyar* comes from the Arab root 'to march' as the husband marches or travels to the wife's residence for short periods.[79] A *misyar* husband is not required to maintain his wife, nor fulfil any of the requisite marital duties. *Misyar* is sometimes used to obtain a travelling marriage, as a *misyar* wife will accompany her husband when he goes abroard. A fatwa issued by the Grand Mufti of Saudi Arabia in 1996 legalized *misyar* marriages on the basis that they fulfilled the formal conditions of a valid marriage contract.[80]

D. Rights and Duties within Marriage

> And women shall have rights similar to the rights against them, according to what is equitable; but men have [a] degree (of advantage) over them. (Quran, Súra Nisáa 2:228)[81]

In Islamic law, marriage creates reciprocal rights and duties between husband and wife. This is not the same as a commonality of resources in the marriage, nor as Mir-Hosseini explains a parity of rights and obligations between spouses.[82] There is consensus of the jurists in all schools that maintaining one's wife (*nafaqah*) is the first duty of a husband. Food, clothing, housing and medical care are the minimum standards of *nafaqah*. There is no prohibition on the wife contributing to any of these expenses, but it is not her duty to do so. Even if a wife has her own income gained through employment, business or inheritance that results in her income exceeding her husband's, it remains his legal obligation to support her. There is some difference of opinion as to whether this level of financial support is determined solely by the husband's income and ability to pay, which is the Shafii approach, or by the wife's background and how she lived prior to the marriage, which is the Hanafi approach, or by their joint financial circumstances, which is the Hanbali view.[83] However, the Quran makes it clear that people should live within their means, as shown at Súra Talaq 65:7: 'Let the man of means spend according to his means: and the man whose resources are restricted, let him spend according to what God has given him. God puts no burden on any person beyond what He has given him. After a difficulty, God will soon grant relief'.[84]

There is also agreement that the husband's responsibility to provide financial support for his wife continues for as long as the marriage endures. In the case of a revocable divorce, the maintenance continues for her *iddah*, or if she is pregnant until the child is born, in accordance with the Quran (Súra Talaq 65:4),[85] but after that time the traditional opinion is that the husband's responsibility ends. If the wife's own resources and *mahr* are insufficient, the expectation is that the wife will return to her family for support. Where the husband divorces the wife with no fault on her part, there exists a practice of providing her with an additional sum of money, described as a 'consolatory gift' (*mutah*). This is set out in the Quran (Súra Baqarah 2:236): 'There is no blame on you if ye divorce women before consummation or the fixation of their dower; but bestow on them (a suitable gift), the wealthy according to his means, and the poor according to his means; – a gift of a reasonable amount is due from those who wish to do the right things'.[86] The requirement to provide *mutah* has been variously interpreted as obligatory (by the Shafi'i school) or as optional (by the Hanafi school), but today legislation in many nations empowers Sharia courts to determine the amount of *mutah*. In Brunei Darussalam, a wife can apply to the Sharia Court for a *mutah* assessment and the husband can be ordered to pay a sum the Court considers fair and just in accordance with Islamic law.[87] Modernists challenge the traditional view that maintenance ends once a divorce becomes irrevocable. They interpret the Quran (Súra Baqarah 2:241), 'For divorced women maintenance (should be provided) on a reasonable (scale). This is a duty on the righteous',[88] as not closing the door to financial support at the end of the *iddah*, but as allowing for fair and reasonable support to continue, either for as long as it is needed, or until the divorced wife remarries.

In return for their husband's maintenance, there are obligations a wife must fulfil. One of these is the requirement to be faithful and obey the wishes of her husband, otherwise this will be considered as disobedience (*nusyuz*). *Nusyuz* is described in legislation in Brunei as 'an act by a wife against her husband which is considered unfaithful' or when she 'unreasonably refuses to obey the lawful wishes or commands of her husband'.[89] If either occurs, a husband is legally relieved of his duty to maintain and support her. This issue of obedience has been discussed and analysed perhaps more than any other, particularly in modernist discourse. Its legal derivation is the Quran, Súra Nisáa 4:34:

> Men are the protectors and maintainers of women, because God has given the one more (strength) than the other, and because they support them from their means. Therefore the righteous women are devoutly obedient, and guard in (the husband's) absence what God would have them guard. As to those women on whose part ye fear disloyalty and ill conduct, admonish them (first), (next), refuse to share their beds, (and last) beat them (lightly); but if they return to obedience, seek not against them means (of annoyance): for God is Most High, great (above you all).[90]

The traditionalist analysis of this verse has three components. First, the analysis states that the Quran explicitly differentiates in gender terms, making women subordinate to men. It is the husband who is the stronger, and thus superior, and men are required to protect and maintain women.

Second, 'righteous women' are obedient, which equates religiosity with compliance. Third, the traditionalist analysis lays down the concept of disobedience and ill-conduct (*nusyuz*), and puts in place a three-stage process for a husband to follow, including 'beating (lightly)' if the wife refuses to be obedient. Traditionalist jurists have outlined a series of acts and omissions that will establish a wife's disobedience (*nusyuz*). These include a wife who without a valid reason refuses to live with or to socialize with her husband, leaves the house without his permission, refuses to move with him to another home or place, or refuses to engage in sexual relations with him. Courts can intervene to determine whether a wife has been *nusyuz*, which if accepted by the court, can have significant legal consequences. A husband whose wife is *nusyuz* is relieved of his duty of maintenance. A husband can also raise disobedience in divorce proceedings, which may act as a defence. *Nusyuz* can serve to reduce or negate *mahr* and *mutah* payments. *Nusyuz* is also a relevant factor in determining custody of children. In addition, it can constitute a criminal offence in its own right.[91]

Modernist scholars argue that these aspects of the traditional interpretation of verse 4:34 are inaccurate as the verse needs to be read in conjunction with other verses in the Quran, including ones relating to equality of gender, notably Súra Ahzáb 33:35, where the concept of equality between men and women is repeated nine times. Engineer argues that the concept of superiority assumed when men are called the 'protectors and maintainers of women' is not present in the Arabic word used, *quwwamuna*, from which the English translation is taken. Instead verse 4:34 sets out the husband's obligation 'to take full care of women'.[92] Also, he notes that the verse should be considered in its sociological context, in which it was unusual for women to earn an income and it was the norm that women and children were fully dependent on men.[93] Other scholars, including Maulana Azad hold that the 'disobedience' in the verse does not specify to whom it is directed, so it should be read as disobedience to God and his commands, and not just to one's husband, or that 'disobedience' is of both kinds, in that there is a spectrum of disobedience: to God on the one hand and to one's husband on the other.[94] Some jurists, including Engineer, distance themselves from traditional views of *nusyuz* by limiting it to 'rebellion' and 'sinfulness' on the part of the wife. This means it only arises in cases of improper sexual conduct with another person, physical and mental cruelty and persistent ill will towards one's husband.[95] It also is argued that a husband too can engage in similar conduct and so the *nusyuz* concept applies to both genders.

E. Contemporary Issues

i. Registration of Islamic marriage

To ensure compliance with the marriage law of a country, many countries have increased their oversight of marriage through registration. Not adhering to registration requirements for Muslim marriage has had consequences in both Muslim and secular countries.

Marriage is described as customary (*urfi*) when it takes place in a Muslim country where registration of the marriage is required by law, but the marriage remains unregistered. As Islamic law by tradition did not require state registration or notarization and the key ingredients of the marriage are still present, most jurists regard *urfi* marriages to be valid marriages. In countries like Egypt that require marriage registration, *urfi* marriages have legal implications for the husband, wife and children. Without registration the courts lack jurisdiction to hear claims for maintenance and *mahr* enforcement.[96] In Egypt, Fawzy writes that *urfi* is the most popular means of circumventing Egyptian state family law, which a woman may do in order to keep her entitlement to a former husband's pension, or which a widow may pursue to have her son exempted from national service.[97] The *urfi* union is religiously valid but falls outside state law. Turkey's *Civil Code* 1926 (revised 2002) requires a civil ceremony for a valid marriage, which means that marriages performed by imams in accordance with traditional Turkish marriage ceremonies are not recognized by law. A religious marriage (imam *nikkah*) can only be performed after the couple are already officially married.[98] However, religious marriage without a civil registration ceremony continues, particularly in rural areas. To deal with this, the Turkish government has passed a series of amnesties whereby the legitimacy of these *urfi* unions is recognized.[99]

Muslim couples in Western countries are able to marry under the state's family law, which gives rise to a registered or official marriage, and they may also marry in accordance with the relevant Islamic laws. Marriage in the West can therefore be two events, as occurs in some European countries, or it can be the same event as in England, Spain and Australia. In Australia, the *Marriage Act 1961* (Cth) allows Islamic marriage ceremonies to be performed and registered by a recognized marriage celebrant or minister of religion, which for Muslims will usually be an Imam from their mosque. Muslim marriages can therefore be simultaneously valid under Islamic law and Australian law. Despite the ease of holding a valid marriage under both Islamic and national law, a number of Muslims in these countries will just have a *nikkah* to make their union a lawful marriage in Muslim terms but will not have their marriage registered. The exact figures are not known; however, it is estimated in England that one-third to one-half of Muslim marriages for persons domiciled in England fall into this category.[100] There are several possible reasons for this. First, the person selected by the couple to perform the ceremony is not qualified or registered by the government to conduct marriages.[101] Second, the marriage does not meet state requirements for a lawful marriage as one or both parties may be under the lawful age for marriage, which in Australia is 18 years,[102] or the marriage is polygynous, which is unlawful and a criminal offence,[103] or could be seen as a 'forced' or 'servile' marriage.[104] Third, the married couple might not recognize or might even reject the authority and legitimacy of secular law. A religious wedding is highly linked to identity and tradition. In this way, marrying according to Islam is a reassertion of one's religious and cultural identity.[105] Alternatively the invalidity of the marriage according to the state's family laws may not be a conscious decision but simply owing to a lack of knowledge about the law of the land. Fourth, not registering a religious marriage allows a husband a quick and easy divorce (*talaq* by pronouncement) should he want to keep this option at the ready. Fifth, there are few legal or social consequences from not having a registered marriage as de facto entitlements in most Western countries mimic what accrues to formal marriage anyway.

ii. Forced marriage

Perhaps one of the areas of greatest criticism and controversy in Islamic family law is the persistence of the practice of forced marriages in some Muslim countries,[106] and the fact that forced marriage has been imported by Muslim immigrants into Western countries. Forced marriage is the term given when parents use duress (usually coercion through threat, actual violence or inducements) to ensure a marriage takes place against the will of their child. As noted earlier, it is the factor of duress or coercion that distinguishes a forced marriage from an arranged or facilitated marriage where the bride or groom willingly agrees to marry the person chosen by their family. The courts in England have considered the difference between arranged and forced marriage. Justice Munby described an arranged marriage as perfectly lawful and to be 'respected', noting that it is a conventional concept in many societies.[107] Forced marriages are not confined to Muslim societies, as Coptic and other Christian, Hindu and 'traveller' families also engage in the practice. The German government's report in 2011 found that 83 per cent of such marriages in Germany were from Muslim families.[108] Forced marriage does not only affect young girls, as there are cases of women over 18 years and also of boys who are forced to marry, although it is most prevalent for families with daughters below marriageable age. The German research showed that in Germany the largest proportion of victims were from Turkey (23 per cent) followed by Serbia, Kosovo, Montenegro, Iraq and Afghanistan, with 44 per cent of persons who were threatened or subjected to forced marriages being holders of German passports.[109] The demography of forced marriage is different in the UK as forced marriage primarily affects women from the Indian subcontinent, although cases from Afghanistan, Turkey, Iran, Sudan and other parts of northern Africa were reported.[110]

In Islamic law, consent is necessary for a lawful marriage. In addition, Muslims are obliged to adhere to state law, which will ordinarily specify that consent must be freely and voluntarily given. How is it, then, that forced marriages can be officiated by Muslim clerics? Their rationale lies in the classical Islamic jurisprudence that granted contractual powers to the *wali*, including the authority as guardian to marry off minor or prepubescent children, known as *ijbar* or *ilzam*.[111] The condition was, that on attaining puberty the child must accept or reject the marriage. If the marriage was accepted at puberty, this amounted to consent, and hence the *nikkah* was valid.[112] Rejection of the marriage meant that the *nikkah* was invalidated. A son unhappy with the marriage could unilaterally divorce his wife at that stage, but for the daughter it was always more difficult, even though coercion was an established ground for annulment (see below). The power that devolved to the *wali* over many centuries is open to abuse. The age of the children married under such authority meant they were, and are still, unlikely to be unaware of their rights under Islamic or national law. Also open to misuse was the traditional juristic view that a woman's consent could be given through 'acquiescence, silence, laughter or silent crying'.[113] When consent does not have to be articulated or the signature of the wife given on the marriage document a grey area opens up. This is true too in other legal systems where the concept of consent also poses challenges and leads to controversial cases. It has been argued by Anitha and Gill that 'consent and coercion in relation to marriage can be better understood as two ends of a continuum, between which lies degrees of socio-cultural expectation, control, persuasion, pressure, threat and force'.[114] In the Scottish case of *Mahmud v Mahmud*, Prosser J stated that, 'if under pressure – and perhaps considerable pressure – a party does change his or her mind and consents to a marriage, with however ill grace and however resentfully, then the marriage is in my opinion valid'.[115]

How governments respond to documented cases of forced marriage is a matter of debate in Muslim and Western nations. The practice of forced marriage is rarely condoned, but nevertheless is allowed to continue. Some sections of immigrant communities in Western countries engage in wilful blindness when accepting the misguided belief of the parents, or the father, that they are 'protecting their child, helping to build stronger families, or preserving cultural or religious traditions'.[116] European nations have responded to the incidence of forced marriage in a variety of ways. Norway uses criminal sanctions to prohibit forcing a person to enter into marriage (through violence, threats, undue pressure or depriving a person of their freedom), inciting a person to marry in another country or agreeing to a marriage on behalf of a minor. All of these activities carry a penalty of up to six years' imprisonment.[117] Aiding and abetting these activities is also an offence that carries the same penalty as applies to primary offenders.[118] Belgium, Germany and Denmark have also criminalized forced marriage activities, although with lesser imprisonment and fine regimes. In 2007, the UK took a civil, not criminal, law route with its *Forced Marriages (Civil Protection) Act* 2007. Their rationale was that, by using civil rather than criminal provisions, victims will be encouraged to seek protection because it does not involve reporting family members and risking their imprisonment. Once a potential forced marriage is reported, either the victim or a third-party individual or organization can make an application to the court for an order to prevent it. In addition, the UK established a Forced Marriage Unit, which provides a range of support, counselling and legal services to victims, including a 24 hour helpline.[119] However, in mid-2012, with forced marriages not abating, England and Wales followed Scotland in introducing laws with criminal sanctions,[120] including imprisonment for parents who, a court finds, forced their child to marry against their will. There was bi-partisan support for criminalization. Home Secretary, Theresa May, argued that criminalizing such marriages would send 'a strong message that it will not be tolerated'[121] with the Prime Minister describing the practice as 'completely wrong' and 'little more than slavery'.[122] In 2011, the Australian government undertook a consultative process in order to determine whether criminal sanctions, civil orders or other community-based measures such as counselling and access to information should be adopted to address the practice of forced marriage in Australia. The Minister for the Status of Women, Kate Ellis, has indicated that a separate offence of 'forced marriage' will be enacted in 2012.[123]

3. DIVORCE

> In the sight of Allah, the worst of all permissible acts is divorce (*talaq*). (Hadith reported by Ibn Umar)

The Quran permits divorce, but it is a disliked outcome, one that, if possible, should be avoided. Yet the message in the Quran is also clear that couples need not stay in an unhappy or destructive marriage, but instead should part 'with kindness'.[124] So although divorce is permissible, options for reconciliation and mediation[125] are integral to divorce proceedings and are discussed in Chapter 7. Persuasion and strong pressure may be brought to reconcile a couple so they stay married, and imams warn their congregations of the undesirability of divorce. The Islamic law on divorce is quite complex as there are different legal processes for men and women, as well as variation between schools and nations. The relative ease with which a husband can divorce in comparison to his wife has been criticized by modern scholars like Mir-Hosseini as tilting the balance of power in a marriage in favour of the husband and resulting in the disempowerment of women.[126] Addressing this inequality is the task embraced by reformers, and modern perspectives in the law of divorce are emerging.

A. Divorce by the Husband

A husband-initiated divorce is straightforward in all schools of law as men have the power to divorce extra-judicially through unilateral pronouncement of divorce known as *talaq*. *Talaq* literally means 'breaking' the bond of marriage. There is a recommended Sunna process to follow. The husband in person, or his representative, should make a pronouncement that he is divorcing his wife in clear and unequivocal words, orally or in writing. Words such as 'I divorce you' are clear, whereas 'we can't live together' are equivocal. *Talaq* must take place at a time when the wife is not menstruating. Jurists have developed circumstances that may be considered by a court as invalidating a pronouncement of *talaq*, for example, if it was said in anger, or in jest, or while the husband was mentally ill or intoxicated, or if it was conditional, for example a threat of divorce were a certain act to happen or unless a behaviour changed. The circumstances of each case are scrutinized to determine whether, even in these circumstances, the husband actually intended to divorce his wife. Contemporary jurisprudence also considers how the pronouncement can be made, given the availability of telephones, text messaging and email. The consensus from cases in Malaysia, Saudi Arabia and the United Emirates is that, provided the wording is clear, these new media can be used. A husband does not have to have a reason for wanting a divorce, although jurists categorize divorce without a reason as ethically reprehensible (*makruh*). Nor, in classic jurisprudence, did the wife need to be present or know of the pronouncement, as *talaq* was a unilateral action and, provided the pronouncement itself was clear and heard or witnessed by others, it was valid. Again there is considerable jurisprudence on this point especially in the Sunni schools, but this issue has been largely resolved by most Muslim countries enacting legislative provisions requiring official notice and registration of the *talaq* with the Sharia court or other registering body.

After the pronouncement of *talaq*, a husband must wait three months[127] (the wife's *iddah* period) before the divorce becomes final. Once final, the husband can remarry unless his wife is pregnant, in which case the divorce becomes final only after the birth of the child. If the couple reconcile during the three-month waiting period their marriage continues. During the three-month period the husband provides for his wife and children. The decision to reconcile (*ruju*) is for the husband and does not require the wife's consent, which means that during the *ruju* period she cannot refuse to continue with the marriage. What amounts to an act of reconciliation[128] and whether an express declaration is needed is the subject of juristic divergence, but it is recommended that the act or declaration be sufficiently explicit and that there are witnesses to it, 'so a wife can't be deceived'[129] about resumption of the marriage. Again, modern states will have legislation dealing with this, which will require the husband to advise the court of a resumption of their conjugal relationship. The divorce application is thereby judicially dismissed.

To ensure that a wife is not left in an uncertain position about her marriage, the Quran set a limit on the number of times a husband can make a divorce pronouncement and then reconcile: 'A divorce is only permissible twice: after that, the parties should either hold together on equitable terms, or separate with kindness' (Quran, Súra Baqarah 2:229).[130] Therefore, regardless of the time that has passed, a third *talaq* means that the divorce is irrevocable and final (*talaq ba'in*). The former husband and wife can no longer live together, nor is he required to maintain her, although any remaining *mahr* must be paid. The couple cannot remarry, unless the wife marries another man and they divorce, which then allows her to undertake a new *nikkah*. The act of a triple *talaq* where a husband makes three pronouncements in immediate succession has been the subject of considerable juristic opinion and difference. A triple *talaq*, colloquially known as a 'quickie divorce', is done to circumvent the three-month *iddah* and reconciliation period. As this is contrary to the spirit and intent of the law on divorce, the practice is controversial, but the majority Sunni view seems to be that, while the divorce is valid, it is morally reprehensible, even sinful. Shia jurists reject a triple *talaq* and some Sunni scholars, including Ibn Taymiyah, have ruled that triple divorce pronouncements are, in law, equal to just one.

According the Shia school, divorcing a wife three times in one session (pronouncing *talaq* three times) is not considered as three separate divorces. However, if a man has divorced his wife for the third time after three sequential and separate marriages, this then requires the wife to marry another and consummate the marriage before the husband can remarry her.

B. Divorce by the Wife

Islamic law gave wives the right to divorce their husbands in certain circumstances. From the passages on divorce in the Quran, together with hadith providing circumstances in which the Prophet allowed women to divorce, Islamic jurists developed a range of processes that a wife could utilize to have her marriage dissolved. The simplest way was for a wife to ask, or persuade, her husband to pronounce *talaq* for them both or for them to come to a mutual agreement (*mubarat*) that they want the marriage to end with neither at fault, or both equally at fault. In *mubarat* the spousal dislike of the marriage is mutual and the amount of compensation is agreed upon, but will not usually exceed the value of the *mahr*. Otherwise, a wife will need to go to court for a legal pronouncement of divorce. There are several options available to her, including divorce (*ta'liq*) by breach of a marriage condition, also a delegated divorce (*talaq-i-tafwid*); annulment or fault divorce (*faskh*); no-fault divorce where a wife dislikes her husband (*kuhl'*); dissolution because of the husband's cruelty (*dharar*); and divorce by conversion. There are also several rarely used processes that are still found in the law of uncodified *fiqh*-based nations, and in codified form in many Muslim nations with legislation governing divorce. Each will be briefly considered before the chapter analyses the trends and modern directions in the law of divorce.

i. Divorce by redemption

Although a wife does not have the unilateral right to *talaq,* she can divorce her husband without any legal ground of complaint against him. This is divorce by renunciation or redemption of the wife (*kuhl'*, or *cerai tebus talaq*). Zulficar sees *khul'* as the balance to the male right to *talaq.*[131] The origins of *khul'* lie in the Quran, Súra Baqarah 2:229:

> It is not lawful for you, (men), to take back any of your gifts (from your wives), except when both parties fear that they would be unable to keep the limits ordained by God. If ye (judges) do indeed fear that they would be unable to keep the limits ordained by God, there is no blame on either of them *if she gives something for her freedom.*[132]

This verse is complimented by several hadith,[133] one of which recounts that the Prophet allowed a wife to return the garden her husband gave her when they married (her *mahr*) in return for her divorce from him. In *khul'* the wife requests divorce and in return provides her husband with compensation, which is usually the return of part or all of her *mahr*, or if her *mahr* was deferred, foregoes her rights to it, along with rights to maintenance during her *iddah.* The *khul'* divorce is irrevocable. If the husband agrees, he will pronounce *talaq* on those terms, or a court will order him to do so once the court has settled the amount of the compensation payable by the wife. There is debate on the matter of whether the husband must agree to this and whether his lack of consent negates *khul'*. Jurisprudence developed over many centuries in which the dominant position was that a grant of *khul'* was contingent upon the husband's consent. However, in recent times when this issue has been revisited, this fetter has often been removed, especially in cases where arbitration failed to bring about agreement. Egypt, Bangladesh and Pakistan, for example, allow a woman to unilaterally apply to a registrar or a court who can grant *khul*' without the husband's consent.[134] In some countries the husband's consent is required, for example in Algeria[135] and Singapore.[136] The courts in Libya will intervene to determine the amount of compensation where the wife claims that hardship will result if the full *mahr* is returned.[137] In Malaysia, it is possible for *khul*' to occur without the husband's consent, but it is a lengthy process involving the court, a conciliation process and two rounds of arbitration.[138]

ii. Fault divorce

A wife can also seek a judicial dissolution or annulment of her marriage (*faskh*, also *tatliq* or *tafriq*) citing valid legal grounds for a court to make such a decree. In traditional *fiqh* there was considerable variation between the schools on the availability of *faskh*, which ranged 'from being non-existent in the Hanafi school … to extensive in the Maliki school … with Shafi'i and Hanbali schools falling in the middle of the spectrum'.[139] The typical matters that could be covered by *faskh* are desertion by a husband (the time period considered to be desertion varies from 90 days to one year), impotence of the husband, failure to consummate the marriage after a certain period has lapsed (there are varying views on whether this has to be wilful refusal), detention or imprisonment of the husband (time period varies), the husband's failure to support his wife (time period varies), the husband suffering from insanity (which Brunei has broadened to include AIDS, HIV or venereal disease in a communicable form),[140] and in the Maliki school, abuse or harm (*dharar*) including physical, verbal and emotional abuse. Although, in some of the Gulf countries where family law is not codified, the provisions of the different schools are applied following the classical manuals, the trend elsewhere in recent divorce legislation is to adopt the more extensive Maliki schools grounds rather than the restricted ones of other schools. This is seen in Malaysia's *Family Law (Federal Territories) Act* 1984 (Act 303) where 12 grounds of *faskh* are now specified. Rather than following traditional Shafi'i law, the drafters of the legislation used public interest (*maslaha*) to adopt the Maliki approach.[141] However, as a court process is required, the wife has to be able to prove her allegations, some of which may require medical or other expert testimony. With some conditions, a court may order a stay of proceedings to ensure that the pleaded affliction is permanent, not temporary. Shah writes that, although the wife retains her *mahr*, *faskh* divorces remain difficult to obtain.[142] *Faskh*, as annulment, can be used to rectify an impediment to lawful marriage, for example if the couple are *mahram* to each other, or there is a religious impediment arising from a conversion after the *nikkah*. *Dharar*, as physical abuse or psychological harm, is identified as a separate form of divorce in some countries, including Jordan, Kuwait and Egypt. *Dharar* divorce entitles a wife to her full *mahr* entitlement. The *Iranian Civil Code* in articles 1121–1132 provides a number of conditions whereby the marriage can be subject to *faskh* divorce. These include certain inabilities in the man, such as being incapable of having sexual intercourse or being insane, or certain inabilities in the woman, such as certain incurable diseases. These conditions can lead to *faskh* divorce only if the parties did not know of the conditions before marriage (Article 1126).

iii. Divorce by breach of a condition

The third avenue open to a wife arises when her husband breaches a valid condition of their marriage, as set out in their contract. As discussed above,[143] these conditions allow a wife, usually through her *wali*, to stipulate matters of importance to her to which if not adhered to by her husband can become a ground for dissolution of the marriage. Freedom to impose conditions is specifically recognized in legislation in Jordan, Morocco, Syria and Tunisia. In some cases divorce based on a breach of condition of the marriage contract can be straightforward, but in many parts of the world this type of divorce (*tal'iq* or a *cerai taklik* in Southeast Asia) can be difficult to obtain for several reasons. First, some conditions may be deemed void by the judge, for example a condition requiring monogamy, which means that the marriage contract remains valid. Second, as the breach must be proved in court, a husband can dispute the facts presented by his wife. Where proof is difficult, this enables a court to decide in favour of saving a marriage, rather than ending it. If the husband wants the marriage to continue, the court may delay the determination to see if the issue can be resolved between them over a period of time. In such situations, arbitration to bring about reconciliation may be ordered. Third, a husband may raise the defence of his wife's disobedience (*nusyuz*), which will require the wife to prove she was not disobedient before there can be divorce by *tal'iq*.[144] Where the contract specifies that the husband grants to his wife the power to divorce herself according to her wishes (*tafwid*), it is in effect a delegation to her of his authority to pronounce *talaq*. It is *talaq-i-tafwid*, or in Egypt *'isma* – 'the right to divorce herself whenever she wants' – provided it is a term of the marriage contract.

The authority for the delegation of *talaq* lies in the Quran, Súra Ahzáb 33:29–30, where the Prophet told his wives they were at liberty to live with him or to choose to separate from him, in effect to end their marriage. Although the Prophet's wives chose to stay married to him, this verse is the foundation for the lawfulness of a delegation of *talaq* to a wife, either as a condition in the *nikkah* or given later post-nuptially. Most frequently, the delegation is conditional, that is, it is linked to another stipulation, the most common of which is the husband taking a second wife without the first wife's consent. However, the delegation of *talaq* need not be constrained in any way, and provided the terms are clear and unrestricted, a wife can pronounce *talaq* at her discretion.[145] There are different views of when and how the delegation of authority can be revoked or whether a delegated *talaq* once pronounced is revocable by the husband or irrevocable (*ba'in*) with immediate and final effect.[146] It is a matter of how the delegation was worded, so if the contract states, 'she [the bride] will have full power to leave me for ever, to give three *talaqs* (irrevocable divorce) to herself and to take another husband',[147] the right for the wife to exercise *talaq* is clear and final. A wife exercising *talaq-i-tafwid* is 'not *talaq*-ing her husband, she is *talaq*-ing herself on behalf of her husband'.[148] In a situation where a husband can pronounce *talaq* extra-judically, this right also accrues to the wife, so *tafwid* 'effectively equalizes the access of spouses to extra-judicial divorce'.[149] In Egypt, for example, the inclusion of *'isma* in a marriage contract gives the wife the legal authority to divorce herself before the registrar, and a court hearing is not required. Nor does it prejudice the husband's right of *talaq*. The legal effect is to confirm equal right of termination for both husband and the wife. It is interesting to observe that, while most Sunni scholars accept *talaq-i-tafwid* as legitimate, it is not widely utilized. The reasons for this are largely cultural and lie in the patriarchal ethos embedded in cultural practices that in turn have imbued Islamic law. This highlights what Mir-Hosseini describes as 'a tension, between what the Shari'a in theory grants women and what happens in practice' with 'Shari'a ideals, and the spirit of its legal rules, … often modified, by-passed or even negated when they are translated into a legal code or when they are interpreted and applied in courts'.[150] Some of the cultural factors covered by Mir-Hosseini's description are the role of the *wali* and the fact that, by tradition, the terms of the marriage contract are negotiated for women by their fathers or by their families. This in effect excludes women from having an active say in the terms that will govern their marriage. The male religious functionaries who officiate at a wedding and the drawing up of the marriage contract reflect a reluctance to give women equal access to divorce.[151] Sonbol notes that in Egypt a husband who allows his wife to hold *isma* is belittled and the practice is rarely used as it is considered unacceptable and demeaning to men.[152] It also can be seen as problematic for a wife to be so focused on marital breakdown at the outset.

C. Other Forms of Divorce

Brief mention will be made of several of the other legal avenues to terminate a marriage. Divorce by way of *li'an* is laid down in the Quran, Súra Núr 24:6–9. Divorce by *li'an* occurs when a husband takes an oath in which he swears four times before God that his wife has committed adultery. The wife in turn will under each of her oaths deny the allegations. On the fifth swearing of the oath, when the husband invokes the wrath of God should he be lying, the judge will accept this as true and the couple are divorced. Unlike the criminal offence of adultery (*zina*), the husband does not need to offer witnesses or any proof of the adulterous act. In this way, *li'an* circumvents any criminal consequences. A husband using the oath cannot be charged with false accusations of adultery (the offence of *qazf*), nor can his wife be charged with adultery (*zina*). *Li'an* is used to defeat the presumption of paternity, that is, that the child of a marriage is legally presumed to be the child of the husband. Divorce by *li'an* means the child has no legal father, just a mother, and all rights and duties of a paternity dissipate.

Divorce by oath is rarely used today, nor are two other modes of divorce – *ila* and *zihar.* Both are regulated in the Quran, and are thought to be pre-Islamic practices that were continued by early Muslim communities. The basis for *ila* is Quran, Súra Baqarah 2:226–7, which requires a husband to take an oath to abstain from sexual intercourse for four months or more; after that time the court can order him to have sexual intercourse, or to divorce his wife.[153] If he refuses, then the court will terminate the marriage. *Zihar*, set out in the Quran, Mujadila 58:2–4 (also mentioned at Súra Ahzáb 33:4), similarly occurs when there is a statement made by the husband in which he foreswears sexual relations with his wife, but can atone for this by charitable acts.[154]

D. Contemporary Issues in Divorce

i. Western and secular nations

One of the recurring issues in most secular countries is that the lack of a formal Sharia court system to manage divorce cases has imposed difficulties on Muslim women initiating divorce, and in seeking *mahr* and *mutah* entitlements. In the ad hoc secular system, a Muslim wife has to find 'someone' or some organization she believes can effect a religious divorce, which in England maybe be a Sharia Council or in Australia, an imam or sheik whose religious authority is informally recognized by the others. This has led to inconsistency and unaccountability in family law proceedings, as individuals or groups can simply put themselves forward as sufficiently scholarly, pious or authoritative to make family law determinations, especially for the ethnic community with which they are aligned. These men may look to contemporary interpretations on matters such as polygyny, *talaq* divorce or custody, or adhere to patriarchal and conservative interpretations. When conservative interpretations prevail, women may find it difficult to obtain a religious divorce, as for example a *khul'* divorce may be refused unless the husband agrees to it. Similarly a husband's statement of facts may be accepted in preference to a wife's in cases where she seeks a fault divorce. In the absence of court resources, proving a breach of a marriage contract condition can be nearly impossible. The result of the ad hoc approach to Muslim family law in the West leaves some Muslim women disadvantaged, even vulnerable, especially recent migrants who may have little knowledge of the local language or of avenues available outside their immediate family or mosque. It gives rise to phenomenon known as 'limping' marriages, where a wife can obtain a secular divorce, but a religious one is denied. This is well documented in Australia[155] and also in the UK[156] and in secular Muslim Turkey.[157] How a Western secular court will treat *mahr* is equally problematic as there is no equivalent in the common law or in European law generally and so a range of responses are possible. *Mahr* has been categorized as a term of the contract to be independently enforced under contract law; or as one factor to take into consideration when determining ancillary relief and property settlement post-divorce; or as irrelevant to any such determinations. Fournier analysed court decisions on *mahr* in several Western jurisdictions and found inconsistent and unpredictable results.[158]

4. CHILDREN, CUSTODY AND MAINTENANCE

'Your child has rights over you' (hadith reported in Sahih Muslim)

Children are considered a trust from Allah (*amanah*) and are not to be seen as possessions but as blessings from God to be cherished.[159] Although only Fatima survived him, the Prophet was father to six children, and much of Islam's original guidance on children is contained in hadith. As his own father Abdullah died before Mohammad was born and his mother Amina died when he was five or six, the Prophet was orphaned at a young age and raised by his grandfather and then his great uncle, Abu Talib. Throughout the Quran there are passages with references to 'orphans'.[160] Arshad writes that the word 'orphan' is not as narrowly construed as it is in the West (meaning both parents are deceased) and instead refers to a child who lacks the support and care of his or her parents, which may arise from circumstances other than death.[161] The Prophet is known to have been compassionate and kind towards children. As set out in the hadith, children have rights over their parents, and in turn the Quran, Súra Ahqaf 46:15 requires children to be kind to their parents.[162] Children have the right to know their parents and for this reason adoption traditionally was not allowed. In fact the Quran condemned the practice of adoption.[163] However, fostering (*kafalah*) was encouraged, a practice that enables a child to be maintained, cared for and educated in the same manner as would be provided by a parent, but without alienating the child from his or her living relatives, or removing the child's inheritance rights from his or her birth family, and without changing the child's name. By adding these modifications a Sharia-compliant form of Islamic adoption has emerged in several Muslim nations,[164] and guardianship through *kafalah* is a recognized alternative process to adoption in some non-Muslim countries, notably Spain and the UK.[165]

Children have the right to be loved, cared for and treated with kindness. Both parents share in raising their child, but just as Islam requires a husband to maintain his wife, he too is the one legally responsible for the financial maintenance (*nafaqah*) of each of his children. Again the father's financial responsibility is according to his means. As the father is financially responsible for raising the children, he is their legal guardian. Islam distinguishes between guardianship and custody, with the mother considered the custodian of the child, generally until the child reaches a certain age. The age varies according to the circumstances and the school of law. Matters of custody, financial support and guardianship mainly become relevant when parents divorce or one parent dies. The general formula is that, where the mother would have custody of the child, it devolves to the maternal female relatives, for example, maternal grandmother or aunt, and then to the female side on the paternal line. Similarly, legal guardianship of the father devolves to males in his paternal lineage.

The first legal presumption of custody (*hadhanah*) is that babies and young children should be with their mother. On this there is agreement between the schools, and breastfeeding is recommended for children up to the age of two years. If the couple divorce during these early years, it is a father's financial obligation to provide spousal and child maintenance. After the child has reached the age of two years, there is juristic variance in who should gain custody. The Maliki stance is that the mother has custody of a son until he attains puberty and custody of a daughter until she marries. The Hanbali approach is that a child of either sex should be with its mother (or related female custodian) until the age of seven, after which time he or she can express a preference and transfer of custody to the father can take place. In the Shia tradition, the mother has the right of custody of young children, for a boy until the age of two years and for girls until the age of seven years. However, recent changes to the *Civil Code of Iran* have made a modification. Article 1169 of the Code now states that, 'in cases of divorce or separation the custody of a child is the right of the mother until the child reaches seven years of old and thereafter the father has priority'. In cases of disputes between parents over the custody of the child, the court will determine this based on the best interest of child.[166] Shafi'i and Hanafi schools and Shia also take into account the wishes of children at certain ages when they are considered capable of making a decision about custody,[167] but this is only one factor as the custodian must also be morally and physically fit for the role. Custody of a Muslim child should be undertaken by a Muslim, although a *kittabiyah* mother may be allowed custody in Hanafi and Maliki schools. A woman can lose her presumptive right to custody of a young child if she is of bad conduct, prevents the father from seeing his child, becomes an apostate, neglects or abuses the child, or importantly, if she remarries. An exception in Sunni jurisprudence is if the new husband is a relative of the child close enough to be within the prohibited degrees of marriage.[168] If a woman loses her right to custody in the circumstances outlined it passes to the father.

When marriages dissolve there can be considerable angst about who will have the custody of children. In a Muslim nation the rules on guardianship and custody are well established and understood. Concepts of 'joint custody' and 'shared parenting orders' do not apply. In modern common law countries, reforms to this area of family law have meant that the mother and father, whether married or not, are equally entitled to apply for the custody of a child, which is determined by a court applying the 'best interests of the child test'. Courts look at a range of factors[169] and the role of culture and religion in the upbringing of the child is considered amongst many other factors. For Muslims, this approach can be concerning as outcomes may not reflect Islamic priorities and a judge in a secular court will not defer to what the Islamic law is at the point where this countermands the best interests of the child. Parents may opt for Islamic mediation through the intervention of imams, or Sharia tribunals and counsellors to resolve custody in accordance with Islamic law. When a common law court has made a parenting order involving a Muslim child, particularly if one parent has left the jurisdiction, a dissatisfied party has on occasions defied the parenting order and abducted the child. Although there is international law governing such cases through the 2008 *Hague Convention on the Civil Aspects of International Child Abduction*, few Muslim countries are signatories to this Convention.

5. CONCLUSION

> Like all aspects of the legal system of each country, family law is really based on the political will of the state, and not the will of God. (Abdullahi A An-Na'im[170])

This chapter has shown that Islamic family law in the twenty-first century is eclectic. Traditionalist perspectives compete and at times co-exist with modernist perspectives. Several trends are evident. First, a century or more of colonial input has seen uncodified *fiqh* replaced by statutes that cover the field of Islamic family law in most, but not all, Muslim nations.[171] Second, state control and regulation of marriage and divorce has seen courts assume greater oversight of family matters. Now, in many jurisdictions, Islamic marriages and *talaq* divorce requires court registration, and judicial approval is needed for polygynous unions. Third, adherence to one school of law has been replaced by the hybrid approach of *takhayyur* that endorses the picking and choosing of legal rules from a variety of sources and schools. The adoption of the more expansive Maliki grounds for *faskh* divorce in several Hanafi and Shafi'i school countries, such as Malaysia, is a case in point. Fourth, acknowledgement of international norms has meant that principles of equality and nondiscrimination inform family law reforms in many countries. In Tunisia, radical reforms were introduced in the 1950s to prohibit polygyny and to give women more or less the same access to divorce as men. Fifth, the jurist's monopoly over knowledge of Islamic law has been challenged by an educated new breed of scholars, including many women and Muslims residing outside the Middle East. These scholars do not depend on classical *fiqh* texts and treatises but engage directly with the source of their faith and the law, the Quran and Sunna. In this process, once unassailable traditionalist doctrines have been reappraised so new solutions to contemporary issues can emerge. Finally, there has been a democratization of knowledge, as improved literacy across the world, together with the proliferation of information and opinion via the Internet and other electronic mediums, enable Muslims everywhere to obtain guidance on Islam from sources other than the Imam of their mosque or the state-appointed mufti.

The aim of modernist interpretations is to recapture the spirit of egalitarianism and justice that were the hallmark of Islamic family law at its inception. The aim is to employ *ijtihad* to re-evaluate accretions, particularly ones supporting patriarchal dominance. The proliferation of modernist views of Islamic family law is resulting in significant law reform, as this chapter has shown. The authority of the *wali* has been checked in some jurisdictions by allowing *qadis* to review and overturn their decisions. Scholars have articulated that there is scope for further reduction in the *wali*'s role in light of changed social conditions in which the educational and financial status of women is equal to that of their male counterparts in many Muslim societies. Another area of reform has been marriageable age. Most countries have now legislated to set a minimum age for marriage and, while the minimum age may not yet be fully adhered to, the legislation sets a clear standard. There has also been a re-appraisal of the Quranic and juristic basis for polygyny with the trend being towards court approval for a polygynous marriage which requires the husband to satisfy pre-conditions. Similarly, modernist perspectives have questioned the inequalities in divorce proceedings between men and women, which have resulted in a range of legal reforms. These include the need for official registration of or court approval for *talaq*, disallowing triple *talaq*, increasing the range of faults to support fault-based divorce claims (*faskh*), including physical or psychological harm as ground for divorce, awarding *khul'* divorces regardless of a husband's consent, and expanding *tal'iq*. Not yet fully endorsed or widely utilized, except in India, is the option of delegating *talaq* to the wife. This would ensure that wives had the same access to divorce as their husbands and has the potential to be 'the most potent weapon in the hands of a Muslim wife to obtain her freedom (from an unhappy marriage) and without the intervention of any court'.[172] Zulficar notes that this direction is a reflection of the contractual nature of the Islamic marriage contract. She argues that, if a contract is concluded based on mutual consent, it is natural to require termination by mutual consent or by providing 'each with a unilateral right of termination'.[173] In addition there has been expansion of assistance in the post-divorce period, with maintenance post-*iddah* being legislatively and judicially allowed.

However, modernist approaches have not gone without strident criticism, having been labelled 'un-Islamic' and as unsound aberrations.[174] An-Na'im believes that in the early part of the twentieth century modernists had the upper hand, but by its end, the 'fundamentalists' had the stronger political platform, preferring to reverse advances made for women's autonomy. Krivenko asserts that the desire of governments and religious elites to preserve and protect Islam from outside forces meant that a conservative vision of women and their role in the family and society had to be maintained. Keeping women in a legally inferior position became proof of the Islamic credentials of the power-holders,[175] and many women have supported this stance as the only authentic Islamic way. Although modernist voices are more frequently lauded in the West, they are not always heard in Muslim states, and when they are, there can be a political or religious backlash, as seen in the winding back of the once progressive family law reforms in Malaysia. Even in secular modern Singapore, its Sharia Court with mandatory jurisdiction over Muslim marriage and divorce repeatedly demonstrates a traditionalism which scholars such as Abdul Rahman believe has impeded the 'progress of genuine legal reform' for Singapore's Malays.[176] Time will tell how other flag bearers for modernist perspectives of Islamic family law, like Tunisia, fare in the twenty-first century and conversely whether conservative states, like Saudi Arabia, embrace reform.

NOTES

1. Personal status law includes inheritance (*mirath*) and religious trusts (*waqf*) as well as family law, as in the *Syrian Law of Personal Status* (1953).
2. For example, the prevalent practice of infanticide of baby girls in pre-Islamic Arabia was abolished after the revelation condemning it: see Quran, Súra Takwir, 81:8–9. A

modified practice was limiting polygamous marriages to four wives at the same time and placing conditions on the practice.

3. Sebastian Poulter, 'The Claim to a Separate Islamic System of Personal Law for British Muslims' in Chibli Mallat and Jane Connors (eds), *Islamic Family Law* (Graham & Trotman, London, 1990), 147.
4. Ibid.
5. See for example Ann Black, '"The Stronger Rule of the More Enlightened European": The Consequences of Colonialism on Dispute Resolution in the Sultanate of Brunei' (2009) 13(1) *Legal History* 93–122. Also Noor Aisah Abdul Rahman, 'Muslim Personal Law with the Singapore Legal System: History, Prospects and Challenges' (2009) *Journal of Muslim Minority Affairs* 109, 112.
6. Abdullahi A. An-Na'im (ed.), *Islamic Family Law in a Changing World* (Zed Books, London, 2002), 17.
7. Ibid.
8. Ibid., 18.
9. Noor Aisha Abdul Rahman, 'Muslim Personal Law with the Singapore Legal System: History, Prospects and Challenges' (2009) *Journal of Muslim Minority Affairs* 109, 113.
10. Ann Black, 'In the Shadow of our Legal System: Shari'a in Australia' in Rex Ahdar and Nicholas Aroney (eds), *Shari'a in the West* (Oxford University Press, Oxford, 2010), 240–54.
11. See Chapter 10.
12. Abdullahi A. An-Na'im (ed.), *Islamic Family Law in a Changing World* (Zed Books, London, 2002), 18.
13. Werner Menski, *Comparative Law in a Global Context: The Legal Systems of Asia and Africa* (Cambridge University Press, New York, 2006), 353.
14. Ibid.
15. The Quran, Súra Rúm 30:21, in Abdullah Yusuf Ali, *The Qur'an: Text, Translation and Commentary* (Tahrike Tarsile Qur'an, New York, 2005), 1056. The Libyan law reflects this in its definition of marriage as 'lawful pact which is based on a foundation of love, compassion and tranquillity which makes lawful the relationship between a man and a woman neither of whom is forbidden in marriage to the other'. Law No. 10, *Law of Personal Status, 1984,* Libya.
16. There is a view that marriage becomes obligatory if a Muslim is likely to sin if he or she remains unmarried. Some famous religious scholars including Ibn Taymiyah did not marry.
17. Hadith of the Prophet narrated from Ayesha (Sunan Ibn Majeh, 1846): http://www.imamu.edu.sa/DContent/BOOKS/arabic_ibook11/page_2629.pdf; also see hadith of the Prophet (Wasaelush Shia, Vol. 14, 25) cited at: http://www.al-islam.org/marriage-handbook/3.htm#_ftn4
18. Hadith of the Prophet (Wasaelush Shia, Vol. 14, 3) cited at: http://www.al-islam.org/marriage-handbook/3.htm#_ftn4
19. Abdullahi A. An-Na'im (ed.), *Islamic Family Law in a Changing World* (Zed Books, London, 2002), 96. The marriage contract, *'aqd-al-nikah*, means, in Arabic, the contract of coitus.
20. Presumption of paternity can only be rebutted by a special oath, known as *li'an*: Quran Súra Núr, 24:6–9.
21. Sacrament is a visible sign instituted by Christ to give grace, so marriage, the union of a man and a woman, is regarded as a sign of the union of Christ and the church. If a couple makes a contract regarding their marriage, the most common example being a premarital agreement, it is something quite different from the marriage itself. For a comparison see Charles Donahue Jr, 'The Western Canon Law of

Marriage' in Asifa Quraishi and Frank E. Vogel (eds), *The Islamic Marriage Contract* (Harvard University Press, Cambridge, MA, 2008), 46–56.

22. Ziba Mir-Hosseini, 'A Woman's Right to Terminate the Marriage Contract: The Case of Iran' in Asifa Quraishi and Frank E. Vogel (eds), *The Islamic Marriage Contract* (Harvard University Press, Cambridge, MA, 2008), 215.
23. See the *Iranian Islamic Punishment Act*, 1991, Iran, sections 108–26.
24. Homosexual conduct is not illegal in the Muslim majority states of Indonesia, Turkey or Albania; however same-sex marriage remains illegal.
25. See Abdullah Yusuf Ali, *The Qur'an: Text, Translation and Commentary* (Tahrike Tarsile Qur'an, New York, 2005), 186.
26. *Islamic Family Law Order 1999*, Brunei Darussalam, section 9 (3). A man or woman cannot marry a person connected through *sesusuan*, defined in section 2 as a child below the age of two years being breastfed on at least five occasions by a woman who was not his or her natural mother.
27. This has been codified in legislation in the law of many countries, such as Syria (*Personal Status Laws* 1953, Article 48-2), Kuwait (Law No. 51/1894, Article 18-2), Yemen (*Personal Status Code* No. 20/1992, Article 29), and Iran (*Civil Code* 1928, Article 1059).
28. Abdullah Yusuf Ali, *The Qur'an: Text, Translation and Commentary* (Tahrike Tarsile Qur'an, New York, 2005), 87.
29. Ibid., 241–2.
30. Lebanon discourages inter-faith marriages but will register and recognize them if validly contracted outside Lebanon.
31. The book referring to lawgivers in the Abrahamic Tradition. See generally Maznah Mohamad, 'Islam and Family Legal Contests in Malaysia: Hegemonizing Ethnic over Gender and Civil Rights', Asia Research Institute Working Paper series No. 109, National University of Singapore, 8.
32. Gavin Jones, Chee Heng Leng and Maznah Mohamad (eds), *Muslim-non-Muslim Marriage: Political and Cultural Contestations in Southeast Asia* (Institute of Southeast Asian Studies, Singapore, 2009).
33. L. Clarke and P. Cross, *Muslim and Canadian Family Laws: A Comparative Primer* (Canadian Council of Muslim Women, Ontario, 2006), 22.
34. Azizah al-Hibri, 'An Introduction to Muslim Women's Rights' in Gisela Webb (ed.), *Windows of Faith: Muslim Woman Scholar-activists in North America* (Syracuse University Press, Syracuse, NY, 2000), 69.
35. Abdullah Yusuf Ali, *The Qur'an: Text, Translation and Commentary* (Tahrike Tarsile Qur'an, New York, 2005), 92.
36. Ibid., 94.
37. See the *Personal Status Law of Algeria*, Law 84, (1984) which defines marriage as a 'contract that takes place between a man and a woman according to Islamic law'. Under Kuwaiti law marriage is a 'contract between a man and a woman who is lawfully permitted to him, the aim of which is cohabitation, chastity and national strength': *Kuwait Personal Status Law* No. 51 (1984).
38. For example, within the Shia marriage contract, in some cases the *mahr* will typically specify symbolic items including a mirror, candlesticks or candelabras, and a Quran. The mirror and candlesticks draw on the pre-Islamic Zoroastrian symbols of light and fire, with the Quran representing the importance of Islam in their marriage.
39. *Islamic Family Law Order*, 1999, Brunei Darussalam, section 14.
40. Ibid., section 12 states that a marriage will be void and not registered unless the consent of the *wali* of the woman in accordance with Islamic law is given (section 12 (a)), or if the *wali* cannot be found, or refuses to give his consent without

reasonable grounds, the Sharia judge can act as a *wali Hakim* and make inquiries as determine whether consent should be given to the marriage (section 12 (b)).

41. The *Iranian Civil Code* 1928, section 1043 provides 'marriage for a virgin girl is subject to permission from her father or grandfather. If they withhold consent without justified reasons, then the daughter can get permission from the family court and enter into a marriage with the person who she has specified before the court'.
42. Abdullah Yusuf Ali, *The Qur'an: Text, Translation and Commentary* (Tahrike Tarsile Qur'an, New York, 2005), 1407. See Laleh Bakhtiar, *Encyclopedia of Islamic Law: A Compendium of the Views of the Major Schools* (ABC International Group, USA, 1996), 428.
43. A'isha recounted that the Prophet said a virgin feels shy, so her silence means consent. Sahih Bukari and Brinkley Messick, 'A Marriage Case from Imamic Yemen', in Asifa Quraishi and Frank E. Vogel (eds), *The Islamic Marriage Contract* (Harvard University Press, Cambridge, MA, 2008), 165; Kecia Ali, 'Marriage in Classical Islamic Jurisprudence', in Asifa Quraishi and Frank E. Vogel (eds), *The Islamic Marriage Contract* (Harvard University Press, Cambridge, MA, 2008), 19.
44. Raffia Arshad, *Islamic Family Law* (Sweet & Maxwell, London, 2010), 47. Brinkley Messick, 'A Marriage Case from Imamic Yemen', in Asifa Quraishi and Frank E. Vogel (eds), *The Islamic Marriage Contract* (Harvard University Press, Cambridge, MA, 2008), 165.
45. Abdullahi A. An-Na'im (ed.), *Islamic Family Law in the Changing World* (Zed Books, London, 2002), 176.
46. Ibid., 165.
47. Ibid., 120.
48. *Child Marriage Restraint Act* 1929 (Pakistan).
49. Lynn Welchman (ed.), *Women's Rights and Islamic Family Law: Perspectives on Reform* (Zed Books, New York, 2004), 47–8.
50. Robyn Emerton (ed.), *Women's Human Rights: Leading International and National Cases* (Cavendish, London, 2005), 254–5.
51. Lisa Wynn, 'Marriage Contracts and Women's Rights in Saudi Arabia' in Asifa Quraishi and Frank E. Vogel (eds), *The Islamic Marriage Contract* (Harvard University Press, Cambridge, MA, 2008), 205.
52. Nik Noriani Nik Badli Shah, 'Legislative Provisions and Judicial Mechanisms for the Enforcement and Termination of the Islamic Marriage Contract', in Asifa Quraishi and Frank E. Vogel (eds), *The Islamic Marriage Contract* (Harvard University Press, Cambridge, MA, 2008), 199.
53. *Iranian Civil Code* 1928, section 1134 (divorce *khotbeh* must be performed before two male and just witnesses).
54. Conditions from Egypt include that the wife look after the house, be obedient and treat her husband well: Amira El-Azhary Sonbol, 'A History of Marriage Contracts in Egypt', in Asifa Quraishi and Frank E. Vogel (eds), *The Islamic Marriage Contract* (Harvard University Press, Cambridge, MA, 2008), 96.
55. Kecia Ali, 'Marriages in Classical Islamic Jurisprudence', in Asifa Quraishi and Frank E. Vogel (eds), *The Islamic Marriage Contract* (Harvard University Press, Cambridge, MA, 2008), 12.
56. Nik Noriani Nik Badli Shah, 'The Islamic Marriage Contract in Malaysia', in Asifa Quraishi and Frank E. Vogel (eds), *The Islamic Marriage Contract* (Harvard University Press, Cambridge, MA, 2008), 187.
57. Lisa Wynn, 'Marriage Contracts and Women's Rights in Saudi Arabia' in Asifa Quraishi and Frank E. Vogel (eds), *The Islamic Marriage Contract* (Harvard University Press, Cambridge, MA, 2008), 208.

58. Essam Fawzy, 'Muslim Personal Status Law in Egypt', in Lynn Welchman (ed.), *Women's Rights and Islamic Family Law* (Zed Books, New York, 2004), 85.
59. See, Nik Noriani Nik Badli Shah, 'Legislative Provisions and Judicial Mechanisms for the Enforcement and Termination of the Islamic Marriage Contract', in Asifa Quraishi and Frank E. Vogel (eds), *The Islamic Marriage Contract* (Harvard University Press, Cambridge, MA, 2008), 189–90.
60. Muhammad Munir, 'Stipulations in a Muslim Marriage Contract with Special Reference to *Talaq Al Tafwid* Provisions in Pakistan in (2005–2006)' 12 *Yearbook of Islamic and Middle Eastern Law* 235, 245.
61. Polygyny is a form of polygamy. Polygamy is a sexual relationship (marriage) with two or more spouses. When a husband has more than one wife it is technically polygyny, as 'poly' in Greek means many and 'gyny' is wives. When a wife has more than one husband, it is polyandry. However, the terms are often used interchangeably, so legislation may refer to a polygamous marriage when technically it is polygynous.
62. Abdullah Yusuf Ali, *The Qur'an: Text, Translation and Commentary* (Tahrike Tarsile Qur'an, New York, 2005), 179.
63. Ibid., 221.
64. *Family Protection Law* 1975, Iran, Article 14; *Islamic Family Law Order* 1999, Brunei Darussalam, section 23.
65. *Muslim Family Law Ordinance* 1961, Bangladesh, section 6.
66. Zainah Anwar, 'Advocacy for Reform in Islamic Family Law', in Asifa Quraishi and Frank E. Vogel (eds), *The Islamic Marriage Contract* (Harvard University Press, Cambridge, MA, 2008), 275.
67. Ibid., 277, 281.
68. Ibid.
69. *Turkish Civil Code* (1926).
70. 1997 [17] BLD 4.
71. In 2011, Mustafa Abdul-Jalil of the Interim government announced that the ban on polygamy would be repealed in order that the regime fully complied with Islamic law.
72. Prakash Shah, Attitudes to Polygamy in English Law, http://www.casas.org.uk/papers/pdfpapers/polygamy.pdf. Marrying a second wife, known as a *kuma*, continues amongst Turkey's urban rich and in some rural parts.
73. L. Clarke and P. Cross, *Muslim and Canadian Family Laws: A Comparative Primer* (Canadian Council of Muslim Women, Ontario, 2006), 43.
74. *Matrimonial Causes Act* 1973 UK section 11(d).
75. L. Clarke and P. Cross, *Muslim and Canadian Family Laws: A Comparative Primer* (Canadian Council of Muslim Women, Ontario, 2006), 43.
76. Susan A. Spectorsky, *Women in Classical Islam: A Survey of the Sources* (Brill, Leiden, 2010), 93.
77. Ibid., 94.
78. Ziba Mir-Hosseini, 'A Woman's Right to Terminate the Marriage Contract Law', in Asifa Quraishi and Frank E. Vogel (eds), *The Islamic Marriage Contract* (Harvard University Press, Cambridge, MA, 2008), 218.
79. Oussama Arabi, *Studies in Modern Islamic Law and Jurisprudence* (Kluwer Law International, The Hague, 2001), 148.
80. Ibid., 147.
81. Abdullah Yusuf Ali, *The Qur'an: Text, Translation and Commentary* (Tahrike Tarsile Qur'an, New York, 2005), 90.
82. Ziba Mir-Hosseini, 'The Delegated Right to Divorce: Law and Practice in Morocco and Iran' in Lucy Carroll and Harsh Kapoor (eds), *Talaq-i-Tafwid: The Muslim*

Woman's Contractual Access to Divorce (1996), 37–40, 45, available at http://www.wluml.org/sites/wluml.org/files/import/english/pubs/pdf/misc/talaq-i-tawfid-eng.pdf

83. Laleh Bakhttiar, *Encyclopedia of Islamic Law: A Compendium of the Views of the Major Schools* (ABC International Group, USA, 1996), 383–484.
84. Abdullah Yusuf Ali, *The Qur'an: Text, Translation and Commentary* (Tahrike Tarsile Qur'an, New York, 2005), 1565.
85. Quran, Súra Talaq, 65:4: 'for those who carry (life within their wombs), their period is until they deliver their burdens'; Abdullah Yusuf Ali, *The Qur'an: Text, Translation and Commentary* (Tahrike Tarsile Qur'an, New York, 2005), 1564.
86. Abdullah Yusuf Ali, *The Qur'an: Text, Translation and Commentary* (Tahrike Tarsile Qur'an, New York, 2005), 94–5.
87. *Islamic Law Family Order* 1999, Brunei Darussalam, section 57.
88. Abdullah Yusuf Ali, *The Qur'an: Text, Translation and Commentary* (Tahrike Tarsile Qur'an, New York, 2005), 96.
89. *Islamic Family Law Order* 1999, Brunei Darussalam, sections 2 and 61 (2).
90. Abdullah Yusuf Ali, *The Qur'an: Text, Translation and Commentary* (Tahrike Tarsile Qur'an, New York, 2005), 190–91.
91. *Islamic Family Law Order* 1999, Brunei Darussalam, section 130 creates the offence of wilful disobedience of a wife.
92. Ashghar Ali Engineer, *The Quran, Women and Modern Society* (New Dawn Press Group, New Delhi, 1999), 48.
93. Ibid., 49.
94. Ibid.
95. Ibid., 50–52.
96. Lynn Welchmann (ed.), *Women's Rights and Islamic Family Law: Perspectives on Reform* (Zed Books, New York, 2004), 9.
97. Essam Fawzy, 'Personal Status Laws in Egypt: an Historical Overview' in Lynn Welchmann (ed.), *Women's Rights and Islamic Family Law: Perspectives on Reform* (Zed Books, New York, 2004), 30, 42.
98. Turkish *Civil Code* (1926) Article 110. Otherwise, the couple is in breach of the Turkish *Penal Code* (2004) Article 230. Furthermore, if the religious official conducts the religious ceremony without documentary proof that the civil ceremony has already been completed in accordance with the law, he too is committing an offence that is punishable under the terms of the *Criminal Code.*
99. Abdullahi A. An-Na'im (ed.), *Islamic Family Law in a Changing World* (Zed Books, London, 2002), 32.
100. Andrea Buchler, *Islamic Law in Europe? Legal Pluralism and its Limits in European Family Laws* (Ashgate, Farnham, 2011), 77.
101. *Marriage Act 1961* (Cth) section 5 (a) a minister of religion registered under Subdivision A of Division 1 of Part IV; or (b) a person authorized to solemnize marriages by virtue of Subdivision B of Division 1 of Part IV; or (c) a marriage celebrant.
102. *Marriage Act 1961* (Cth) section 1: 'Subject to section 12, a person is of marriageable age if the person has attained the age of 18 years'. Section 12 allows a person who has attained the age of 16 years but has not attained the age of 18 years to apply to a judge or magistrate for an order authorizing him or her to marry a particular person of marriageable age. The judge will require the circumstances of the case to be so exceptional and unusual as to justify the making of the order. An underage marriage is unlawful and also an offence under section 95 of the *Marriage Act.* It is a defence to a prosecution under section 95 for the defendant to prove that he or she believed on reasonable grounds that the person with whom he or she went

through the form or ceremony of marriage was of marriageable age, or had previously been married, or had the consent of the court to do so in accordance with the Act.

103. Bigamy, see *Marriage Act 1961* (Cth) section 94.
104. Attorney-General's Department, *Discussion Paper: Forced and Servile Marriages* (2011), available at http://www.ag.gov.au/www/agd/rwpattach.nsf/VAP/(9A5D88DBA63D32A661E6369859739356)~Discussion+Paper+for+Public+Release+-+forced+and+servile+marriage.pdf/$file/Discussion+Paper+for+Public+Release+-+forced+and+servile+marriage.pdf
105. Ibid., 77.
106. Pakistan, India, Bangladesh, Turkey, Iran, Sudan, Somalia and other parts of northern Africa. See Sundari Anitha and Aisha Gill, 'Coercion, Consent and the Forced Marriage Debate in the UK' (2009) 17 *Feminist Legal Studies* 165.
107. *NS v MI* [2007] 1 FLR 444.
108. German Federal Ministry of the Family, 'Forced Marriages in Germany: Number and Analysis of Cases' 2011, available at http://www.bmfsfj.de/BMFSFJ/Service/Publikationen/publikationen,did=175410.html
109. Ibid.
110. Sundari Anitha and Aisha Gill, 'Coercion, Consent and the Forced Marriage Debate in the UK' (2009) 17 *Feminist Legal Studies* 165, 167.
111. Kecia Ali, 'Marriage in Classical Islamic Jurisprudence', in Asifa Quraishi and Frank E. Vogel (eds), *The Islamic Marriage Contract* (Harvard University Press, Cambridge, MA, 2008), 17.
112. Raffia Arshad, *Islamic Family Law* (Sweet & Maxwell, London, 2010), 67.
113. And noting that loud crying and verbalized objections to a marriage were always taken as non-consent: Kecia Ali, 'Marriage in Classical Islamic Jurisprudence', in Asifa Quraishi and Frank E. Vogel (eds), *The Islamic Marriage Contract* (Harvard University Press, Cambridge, MA, 2008), 19.
114. Sundari Anitha and Aisha Gill, 'Coercion, Consent and the Forced Marriage Debate in the UK' (2009) 17 *Feminist Legal Studies* 165.
115. *Mahmud v Mahmud* [1994] SLT 599.
116. Attorney-General's Department, *Discussion Paper: Forced and Servile Marriages* (2011), available at http://www.ag.gov.au/www/agd/rwpattach.nsf/VAP/(9A5D88DBA63D32A661E6369859739356)~Discussion+Paper+for+Public+Release+-+forced+and+servile+marriage.pdf/$file/Discussion+Paper+for+Public+Release+-+forced+and+servile+marriage.pdf/
117. *Norwegian Penal Code* section 222(2).
118. Directorate General of Human Rights, *Forced Marriages in Council of Europe Member States – A Comparative Study of Legislation and Political Initiatives* (2005), 107.
119. Details of the Forced Marriage Unit available at http://www.fco.gov.uk/en/travel-and-living-abroad/when-things-go-wrong/forced-marriage/
120. *The Forced Marriage (Protection and Jurisdiction) Scotland Act* 2011.
121. 'Forced Marriage Parents Face Jail under New Laws', BBC News, 8 June, 2012, available at http://www.bbc.co.uk/news/uk-politics-18356117
122. Ibid.
123. Ian McPhedran, 'Law Hits Forced Marriage', *The Courier Mail*, 24 November, 2011.
124. Quran, Súra Baqarah, 2:229, in Abdullah Yusuf Ali, *The Qur'an: Text, Translation and Commentary* (Tahrike Tarsile Qur'an, New York, 2005), 90.
125. Quran, Súra Nisáa 4:128 and 4:35, in Abdullah Yusuf Ali, *The Qur'an: Text, Translation and Commentary* (Tahrike Tarsile Qur'an, New York, 2005).

126. Ziba Mir-Hosseini, 'A Woman's Right to Terminate the Marriage Contract: The Case of Iran' in Asifa Quraishi and Frank E. Vogel (eds), *The Islamic Marriage Contract* (Harvard University Press, Cambridge, MA, 2008), 215.
127. This is based on the Quran, Súra Baqarah 2:228 'Divorced women shall wait concerning themselves for three monthly periods. Nor is it lawful for them to hide what God hath created in their wombs, if they have faith in God and the Last Day. And their husbands have the better right to take them back in that period, if they wish for reconciliation. And women shall have rights similar to the rights against them, according to what is equitable; but men have a degree (of advantage) over them. And God is Exalted in Power Wise'. Abdullah Yusuf Ali, *The Qur'an: Text, Translation and Commentary* (Tahrike Tarsile Qur'an, New York, 2005), 89–90.
128. Sexual intercourse is generally accepted as sufficient.
129. L. Clarke and R. Cross, *Muslim and Canadian Family Laws: A Comparative Primer* (Canadian Council of Muslim Women, Ontario, 2006), 49. However, it is not necessary, see Laleh Bakhtiar, *Encyclopedia of Islamic Law: A Compendium of the Views of the Major Schools* (ABC International Group, USA, 1996), 533.
130. Abdullah Yusuf Ali, *The Qur'an: Text, Translation and Commentary* (Tahrike Tarsile Qur'an, New York, 2005), 90.
131. Mona Zulficar, 'The Islamic Marriage Contract in Egypt', in Asifa Quraishi and Frank E. Vogel (eds), *The Islamic Marriage Contract* (Harvard University Press, Cambridge, MA 2008), 232.
132. Abdullah Yusuf Ali, *The Qur'an: Text, Translation and Commentary* (Tahrike Tarsile Qur'an, New York, 2005), 90–1 (italics added).
133. Susan Spectorsky, *Women in Classical Islamic Law: A Survey of the Sources* (Brill, Leiden, 2010), 125.
134. *Personal Status Law* (2000), Egypt; *The Dissolution of Muslim Marriages Act* (1939), Bangladesh; The *Dissolution of Muslim Marriages Act* of Pakistan (1939), cited in Abdullahi A. An-Na'im (ed.), *Islamic Family Law in a Changing World* (Zed Books, London, 2002), 159, 166 and 235.
135. Abdullahi A. An-Na'im (ed.), *Islamic Family Law in a Changing World* (Zed Books, London, 2002), 166.
136. Ibid., 278. While the *Administration of Muslim Law Act* 1968 does not specify this, the Sharia Court has ruled in accordance with traditionalist juristic opinion to require husband's consent as a pre-condition for *khula* divorce. See Noor Aisha Bte Abdul Rahman, 'Traditionalism and its Impact on the Administration of Justice: The Case of the Syariah Court of Singapore' (2006) 5(3) *Inter-Asia Cultural Studies* 415, 425.
137. Abdullahi A. An-Na'im (ed.), *Islamic Family Law in a Changing World* (Zed Books, London, 2002), 177.
138. Nik Noriani Nik Badli Shah, 'The Islamic Marriage Contract in Malaysia', in Asifa Quraishi and Frank E. Vogel (eds), *The Islamic Marriage Contract* (Harvard University Press, Cambridge, MA, 2008), 191. Also *Islamic Family Law (Federal Territories) Act* 1984, section 49.
139. Kecia Ali, 'Marriage in Classical Islamic Jurisprudence', in Asifa Quraishi and Frank E. Vogel (eds), *The Islamic Marriage Contract* (Harvard University Press, Cambridge, MA, 2008), 24. The Hanafi school traditionally only allowed *faskh* in cases where impotence of the husband prevented consummation of the marriage, whereas the Maliki school had a wider range, including abandonment, harm and failure to maintain his wife or children.
140. *Islamic Family Law Order* (1999) Brunei Darussalam section 46 (1).
141. Zainah Anwar, 'Advocacy for Reform in Islamic Family Law', in Asifa Quraishi and Frank E. Vogel (eds), *The Islamic Marriage Contract* (Harvard University Press, Cambridge, MA, 2008), 276.

142. Nik Noriani Nik Badli Shah, 'The Islamic Marriage Contract in Malaysia', in Asifa Quraishi and Frank E. Vogel (eds), *The Islamic Marriage Contract* (Harvard University Press, Cambridge, MA, 2008), 192.
143. Page 181.
144. Nik Noriani Nik Badli Shah, 'The Islamic Marriage Contract in Malaysia', in Asifa Quraishi and Frank E. Vogel (eds), *The Islamic Marriage Contract* (Harvard University Press, Cambridge, MA, 2008), 193.
145. The case of *Aklima Khatun v Mahibur Rahman* [1963] Decca High Court 602 upheld a completely unconditional delegation to a wife to exercise *talaq* on behalf of her husband.
146. In Morocco it is irrevocable, but in Bangladesh and Pakistan, like *talaq* by the husband, it must come to court or to the arbitration council. In Brunei and Malaysia (where *talaq-i tafwid* is *ta'aliq*) the court has the power to confirm that such a *talaq* has taken place. See Lucy Carroll and Harsh Kapoor (eds), *Talaq-i-Tafwid: The Muslim Woman's Contractual Access to Divorce* (1996), 37–40, 45, available at http://www.wluml.org/sites/wluml.org/files/import/english/pubs/pdf/misc/talaq-i-tawfid-eng.pdf
147. Ibid., 44.
148. Ibid.
149. Ibid.
150. Ziba Mir-Hosseini, 'The Delegated Right to Divorce: Law and Practice in Morocco and Iran', in Lucy Carroll and Harsh Kapoor (eds), *Talaq-i-Tafwid: The Muslim Woman's Contractual Access to Divorce* (1996), 127, available at http://www.wluml.org/sites/wluml.org/files/import/english/pubs/pdf/misc/talaq-i-tawfid-eng.pdf
151. Ibid., 125.
152. Amira el-Azhary Sonbol, 'A History of Marriage Contracts in Egypt', in Asifa Quraishi and Frank Vogel (eds), *The Islamic Marriage Contract* (Harvard University Press, Cambridge, MA, 2008), 115.
153. For a summary of the jurisprudence and variation between schools see Laleh Bakhtiar, *Encyclopedia of Islamic Law: A Compendium of the Views of the Major Schools* (ABC International Group, USA, 1996), 544–45; and Susan Spectorsky, *Women in Classical Islamic Law: A Survey of the Sources* (Brill, Leiden, 2010), 36–7.
154. See Susan Spectorsky, *Women in Classical Islamic Law: A Survey of the Sources* (Brill, Leiden, 2010), 36–7 and Laleh Bakhtiar, *Encyclopedia of Islamic Law: A Compendium of the Views of the Major Schools* (ABC International Group, USA, 1996), 542–4.
155. Family Law Council of Australia, *Report on Cultural Community Divorce and the Family Law Act 1975* (2001), 4 (Executive Summary, 17); Ann Black, 'In the Shadow of our Legal System: Shari'a in Australia', in Rex Ahdar and Nicholas Aroney (eds), *Shari'a in the West* (Oxford University Press, Oxford, 2010), 240–54.
156. Law Commission UK (Law Com. No. 48) *Family Law: Report of Jurisdiction in Matrimonial Causes* (1972); Ishan Yilmaz, 'Muslim Alternative Dispute Resolution and Neo-Ijtihad' (2003) 2(1) *Alternatives* 1; Muslim Arbitration Tribunal, *Family Dispute Cases*, available at http://www.matribunal.com/cases_faimly.html/
157. Ishan Yilmaz, 'Non-recognition of Post-modern Turkish Socio-political Reality and the Predicament of Women' (2003) 30(1) *British Journal of Middle Eastern Studies* 25–41.
158. Pascale Fournier, 'Transit and Translation: Islamic Transplants in North America and Europe' (2009) 4(1) *Journal of Comparative Law* 1–38.
159. Raffif Arshad, *Islamic Family Law* (Sweet & Maxwell, London, 2010), 149.
160. Quran 2:220; and 4:2, 4:3; 4:6; 4:8; 4:10; 4:36; 4:127; 6:153; and 90:15.

161. Raffif Arshad, *Islamic Family Law* (Sweet & Maxwell, London, 2010), 171.
162. 'We have enjoined on man kindness to his parents: in pain did his mother bear him, and in pain did she give him birth. The carrying of the (child) to his weaning is (a period of) thirty months. At length, when he reaches the age of full strength and attains forty years, He says, "O my Lord Grant me that I may be grateful for thy favour which Thou has bestowed upon me, and upon both my parents, and that I may work righteousness such as Thou mayest approve and be gracious to me in my issue. Truly have I turned to Thee and truly do I bow (to Thee) in Islam"'. Abdullah Yusuf Ali, *The Qur'an: Text, Translation and Commentary* (Tahrike Tarsile Qur'an, New York, 2005), 1370.
163. Quran 33:4, 33:5.
164. *Islamic Adoption of Children Order* 2001 Brunei Darussalam.
165. *Codigo Civil* Spain, Article 173 and *Adoption and Children Act* 2002 UK. France forbids adoption if the child or their adoptive parents are nationals of a Muslim country that recognizes the Quranic prohibition.
166. Reform to this section of the *Iranian Civil Code* was supported by the Council of Expediency after prolonged disputes between the progressive Parliament under the Presidency of Muhammad Khatami and the conservative Council of Guardians. The law prior to this reform was that 'a mother has custody preference over others for two years from the birth of her child and after the lapse of this period custody will devolve to the father except in the case of a daughter who will remain under the custody of the mother till 7 years'.
167. *Mumaiyiz* is the term used in Shafi'i school, see *Islamic Family Law Order*, 1999, Brunei Darussalam, Part V11.
168. *Islamic Family Law Order*, 1999, Brunei Darussalam, section 90.
169. *Children's Law Reform Act* (Canada) section 24.
170. Abdullahi A. An-Na'im (ed.), *Islamic Family Law in a Changing World* (Zed Books, London, 2002), 20.
171. In Saudi Arabia and several Arab states in the Persian Gulf, women's access to divorce is now regulated by statutes. Statutes give governments rather than jurists greater control.
172. Lucy Carroll and Harsh Kapoor (eds), *Talaq-i-Tafswid: The Muslim Woman's Contractual Access to Divorce* (1996), 16, available at http://www.wluml.org/sites/wluml.org/files/import/english/pubs/pdf/misc/talaq-i-tawfid-eng.pdf
173. Mona Zulficar, 'The Islamic Marriage Contract in Egypt', in Asifa Quraishi and Frank E. Vogel (eds), *The Islamic Marriage Contract* (Harvard University Press, Cambridge, MA, 2008), 252, noting that it saves the wife lengthy, costly and strenuous procedures before the court and would save her the loss of her financial rights to deferred *mahr* and financial maintenance as in the case of *khul'*.
174. Christina H. Jones-Pauly and Abir Dajani Tuqan, *Women under Islam: Gender, Justice and the Politics of Islamic Law* (I.B. Tauris, London, 2011), 2.
175. Ekaterina Yahyaoui Krivenko, *Women, Islam and International Law* (Martinus Nijhoff/Brill, Leiden, 2009), 212.
176. Noor Aisha Bte Abdul Rahman, 'Traditionalism and the Administration of Justice: The Case of the Syariah Court of Singapore' (2006) 5(3) *Inter-Asia Cultural Studies* 415, 429.

6. Mediation, arbitration and Islamic alternative dispute resolution

> Courts (and other official agencies) comprise only one hemisphere of the world of regulating and disputing.[1]

1. INTRODUCTION

In every society, as Galanter observes, most disputes are not settled in courts or formal state forums,[2] but are resolved in variety of extra-judicial ways, including by negotiation,[3] mediation[4] and arbitration.[5] This is certainly the case in Muslim societies, where there has been a long tradition of adjudication by a judge (*qadi*) co-existing and intersecting with a range of complementary dispute resolution processes. The rich and lengthy history of complementary dispute resolution in the Islamic world has led some writers to postulate that the Islamic dispute resolution processes influenced the birth of alternative dispute resolution (ADR) in the West,[6] or that the Islamic model is one from which the West should learn.[7] Similar to the focus on courts and judges as the primary dispute resolution forum in Western cultures, there has also been far greater focus and commentary in Muslim cultures on the Islamic judicial institution of the court (*qada*), and the role of the judge (*qadi*). Modern perspectives on the traditions of amicable settlement (*sulh*), either through mediation or conciliation, and arbitration (*tahkim*) are however evident and their contribution to Islamic justice is increasingly acknowledged. Othman explains that, while there is an assumption, corresponding with popular perceptions, that adjudication is the superior mechanism for dispute resolution in Islamic law, neither the Quran nor hadith stress the virtue or necessity for *qada*.[8] Rather they 'unambiguously uphold the values of conciliation, magnanimity and forbearance over exacting one's legal rights'.[9] In light of the clear foundation for these guiding principles to govern Islamic dispute resolution, this chapter will outline the foundations for alternative dispute resolution in Islam and assess the theory and practice of *sulh* and *tahkim* in contemporary times.

Although not considered in this chapter, mention is warranted of additional 'alternatives' within the Islamic justice system. These include forms of third-party intercession or agency known as intercession (*wasita*) or representation (*wakalah*), which use the intervention of an intermediary or agent to negotiate and settle matters on behalf of their principal, but the intermediary or agent remains bound by the terms of the delegation. This delegation can extend to dispute settlement on a matter involving the principal and another party. *Wakalah*, which is similar to modern forms of legal representation, is accepted by *ijma* and has its basis in the Quran, at Súra al-kahf 19.[10] Another avenue in Islam to settle a dispute when it pertains to a specific legal issue or its factual application is a request for a legal opinion (*fatwa*), which by tradition is given by a great legal scholar, a mufti in the Sunni schools, or an Ayatollah in the Shia tradition, or a panel of scholars (*ulama*).[11] This can be likened to the Western ADR strategy of referral for expert determination. This topic is important and is covered in Chapter 4. In addition, international arbitration is used by many Muslim states for state-to-state disputes, and in regard to transnational commercial matters, state agencies, corporations, banks, airlines, investment agencies and individuals have used the mechanisms of international arbitration[12] to settle transnational disputes. While the law chosen to apply may be Islamic law or the law of a Muslim nation, analysis of international arbitration is too extensive for inclusion in this chapter.

The chapter will, however, consider a 'hybrid' form of Islamic dispute resolution that is a product of contemporary times and a response to modern challenges. This hybrid model can be seen in Muslim nations where aspects of Western mediation have been incorporated into the mediation within the Sharia courts. Malaysia, for example, has incorporated aspects of the Western mediation model into the Sharia courts.[13] This hybrid model is also an important development, particularly in Western countries, where Muslims seek to draw on Islamic law to resolve disputes and legal issues within their communities, but do so by adopting Western mechanisms, notably civil arbitration and Western mediation. A pertinent example is the UK's Muslim Arbitration Tribunals, which function under the rules and terms of the *Arbitration Act* 1996 (c23) (Eng), and also the network of Sharia Councils, which employ mediation that has features of both Islamic and Western approaches as well as mediation and arbitration to give non-binding legal decisions. These hybrids are a modern response by Muslims adapting to life in secular societies without the institution of Sharia courts.

2. FOUNDATIONS IN ISLAM FOR DISPUTE RESOLUTION

The origin of contemporary Islamic dispute resolution lies in the customary practices of pre-Islamic Arabia. Conciliation and peace-making were vital for survival in a tribal society. Tribal chiefs, soothsayers, elders and other persons of influence were called on to settle disputes within their own tribe and also between members of different tribes. The process of arbitration (*tahkim*) became well established in early Arabian society, designed to prevent disputes from escalating into vengeance and tribal warfare.[14] When disputing parties could not settle a matter amicably, they had the option to voluntarily present their arguments and grievances to a third person or persons to decide the matter for them. This person, the arbitrator (*hakam*), had to have the trust of both sides or each side selected their own *hakam* or a panel on the basis on personal qualities, community standing, competence and supernatural or soothsaying powers. The Prophet Mohammad approved of *tahkim* but rejected all its pagan elements and in this way laid the foundation for Islamic arbitration. He was an arbitrator, conciliator and mediator for a range of disputes that arose amongst his followers,[15] and by applying God's law to it, the Prophet revolutionized *tahkim*. He also recommended that others who possessed the right religious character and knowledge become arbitrators,[16] and it is reported that the Prophet submitted a minor disagreement between himself and his wife, A'isha, to Abu Bakr for arbitration.[17] However, the first aim of dispute resolution was an amicable settlement (*sulh*) rather than imposing an award or decision on an unwilling party. Sayen writes that *sulh* gets 'far more elaborate treatment than *tahkim* both in the hadith literature and *fiqh* treatises'.[18] After the death of the Prophet, his companions and followers recognized the validity of the processes of *tahkim* and *sulh* and exhorted the role of those who arbitrate and conciliate,[19] in the advice that 'composing of differences between men is better than all fasts and prayers'.[20] Islamic arbitration[21] and mediation evolved in the centuries that followed and, like other aspects of law considered in this book, although both were derived and functioned in accordance with the Sharia, doctrinal variations between the major schools of law developed.

A. Mediation (*sulh*)

> there is no blame on them if they arrange an amicable settlement between themselves; and such settlement is best. (Súra Nisáa 4:128)[22]

The maxim '*sulh* is best' re-iterates and confirms the words of the Quran.[23] Although used in the specific context of a husband's ill-treatment of his wife by cruelty or desertion, the passage 4:128 has been used more widely in support of compromise settlements. Indeed this legal maxim is based on a long-standing Islamic tradition that Hallaq attributes to several factors, including the sociological foundation of early societies in which 'clan-centered and localized conflict resolution of the informal type historically preceded any extra-filial, formal and exogenous modes of adjudication'.[24] He notes that Islamic rulers depended and encouraged this, while families valued their disputes and private matters being resolved away from public scrutiny.[25]

The objective of reaching an amicable agreement and avoiding a court-imposed decision has been pursued in a wide range of commercial, industrial, tortious and even criminal contexts. Most commonly translated in English as 'compromise', 'conciliation', 'mediation' or 'amicable settlement', *sulh* is not only a method but also an outcome in the form of a contract consensually entered into by both disputants that will be enforced, if necessary, on that basis. The dual character of *sulh* is seen in the Ottoman Code, the *Majelle*, which defines *sulh* as 'a contract concluded by offer and acceptance, and consists of settling a dispute by mutual consent'.[26]

Sulh not only is regarded as an accepted method of dispute resolution within the Islamic justice system, but for some is seen as the 'ethically and religiously superior' means for settling disputes.[27] Omar, the second caliph of Islam, recommended *sulh* over adjudication, stating 'Dispel the disputants until they settle amicably with one another; for adjudication truly leads to rancour'.[28] Yet to be successful *sulh* does require willingness to compromise on both sides and for this reason can sometimes be preliminary to an imposed outcome by way of an arbitral award or a judgment of a court or other adjudicative body, such as Saudi Arabia's Board of Grievances.

While the Quran recommends *sulh*,[29] it is the practices of the Prophet and the guidance given by leaders of the early Muslim community that define its scope. *Sulh* is not limited to disputes between individuals, as the Prophet also mediated disputes between clan members. Today, organizations and institutions may prefer *sulh*, because as with Western mediation, it is not played out in a public forum and its inherent flexibility allows for solutions that may be quite different from an anticipated adjudicated outcome. Unlike a *hakam* or *qadi*, the mediator or other third party who assumes the role of facilitator in the search for compromise is not required to have specific qualifications, nor are they required to follow any particular format. It is also possible for an amicable settlement to be reached without the third party's intervention or for several interveners to be involved.

While flexibility is a strength of *sulh*, there are however boundaries and limits. Caliph Omar wrote that for Muslims 'compromise (*sulh*) is permissible between people, except a compromise which would make licit (*halal*) that which is illicit (*haram*) or make illicit that which is licit'.[30] So, any settlement will only be valid to the extent that its outcome is not contrary to Islam. A compromise that allowed for a payment of interest (*riba*), or an exchange involving the sale of alcohol or other illicit substances, or one ignoring the Quranic rules on inheritance, would not be permissible. A second boundary is derived from another part of the Quran. Súra Hujurát 49:10 states: 'The Believers are but a single Brotherhood: so make peace and reconciliation between your two (contending) brothers; and fear God, that ye may receive Mercy'.[31] The preceding verse demands that peace must be 'with justice, and be fair: for God loves those who are fair (and just)'.[32] This means that, for a *sulh* settlement to be valid, it must also be fair and just.

As *sulh* is seen as having a de-escalating and preventative role, some disputes particularly warrant its use. Rosen gives an example from his work in Morocco: where heirs cannot agree on the division of an estate,[33] an early *sulh* intervention can ensure that others are not adversely affected and implicated. Similarly when the parties are closely related to each other, even if it is a commercial matter, *sulh* should be kept in mind as 'preservation of family harmony should receive consideration'.[34] If conflict and hostility can be quelled and good family relationships restored, then *sulh* has served its religious and practical role. In this way it links into arbitration for family disputes, as an integrated process. Other priority situations for using *sulh* are when both parties are virtuous, or where the situation is already hostile and there is fear of further irrevocable deterioration.[35]

As noted above, *sulh* can stand alone or can be woven into court and arbitral processes, unlike Western mediation, which operates in tandem with, but independently of, any adjudicative process. Even when mediation may be mandatory under legislation or is ordered by the court, the Western judge will not slip from mediator into judge or vice versa when conducting the trial. Although Islamic jurists are not unanimous on this point, with classical jurists recommending that judges should only perform adjudications, and leave *sulh* to others,[36] in practice in many Islamic courts, judges perform dual roles as mediators and adjudicators in the same case. Vogel in his study of the courts in Saudi Arabia found that Saudi *qadis* possess great skill as mediators and conciliators.[37] He reports that, in the four months spent observing one *qadi* in the Great

Sharia Court in Riyadh in 1983, only two of the civil disputes before the court ended in a *qadi* judgment. The majority were settled by amicable agreement, often within 30 minutes, even when large sums of money were involved.[38] He writes that the *qadi* 'routinely encourage[d] the parties to settle their differences by religious exhortations invoking immunity from blame, peace of mind, charity and brotherhood, and it worked'.[39] Similarly, Othman writes that the Ottoman *qadi* court records reveal that a considerable portion of court registries recorded dispute settlement by *sulh*. This should not be surprising given that the *Ottoman Code*, the *Majelle* of 1885,[40] allocated a full chapter to *sulh*.

The traditional Islamic model of adjudication is suited to this integrative and inter-connected model for dispute resolution. Parties typically represent themselves in court, with a lawyer or *wakil* (agent) rarely appointed;[41] the judge is in full dialogue with the parties, rather than listening to question and answers, a mode that gives control to the barristers; the procedure is less formal than in Western courts; rules of evidence are less rigid; and as the approach is non-adversarial, levels of hostility between parties are reduced. The result is that, through dialogue and direct conversation with the parties, solutions and compromise become self-evident and in this way an amicable settlement can be reached. Either the settlement may be noted in the record of the court, or if parties wish the reconciliation to remain private, the suit is withdrawn and the agreement is a private one between them.[42]

Walid Iqbal gives two juristic reasons for reconciliation through *sulh*. The first is that *sulh* confers 'religious blamelessness' on the *qadi* and the parties, and the second is that formal court adjudication may breed 'hatred' while reconciliation and agreement can bring parties together.[43] However, it is not always so straightforward. Jurists have reflected on inherent difficulties when a judge considers *sulh* knowing where in law the judgment should lie. This could mean that one party may be denied their full legal rights if there is a compromise settlement. Othman concludes that, if it is clear what a judgment would determine, the judge is prohibited from considering *sulh*.[44] However, despite the technical legal strength of one side, the desire to achieve fairness to both can prevail. Vogel found this outcome in Saudi Arabia where a resolution that was advantageous to both parties would be encouraged.[45] *Sulh* also has practical advantages as it lessens pressures on the justice system as amicable settlement usually takes less time and resources than a contested adjudication. However, it is noted by Vogel and others that the broad discretion given to *qadis* to mediate can be used to cover up 'ineptitude, laziness or dilatoriness especially since terminations by *sulh* are not appealable'.[46]

The endorsement of *sulh* in Islamic jurisprudence has been sustained over many centuries. It remains a flexible process that continues to be used throughout the Muslim world. Some countries, like Saudi Arabia, maintain its traditional role as an integrated component with judicial adjudication and arbitration, while others, like Malaysia, have revised, codified and allocated the task of determining *sulh* outcomes to trained personnel with the Sharia Court system. Malaysia's support for the practice of *sulh* can be seen from the fact that some Malaysian state parties to civil and family disputes are required to have attempted an amicable settlement with the court's *sulh* officials prior to any adjudication.[47] In Iran *sulh* as prescribed in *fiqh* is codified in Chapter 17 of the *Iranian Civil Code*, where it is considered as a form of agreement (*aqd*) that may be used to settle existing disputes or prevent possible disputes in the future.[48]

B. Arbitration (*Tahkim*)

> If ye fear a breach between [a married couple], appoint (two) arbiters, one from his family, and the other from hers; if they wish for peace, God will cause their reconciliation: for God hath full knowledge and is acquainted with all things. (Súra Nisáa 4:35.)[49]

This passage in the Quran gives clear endorsement for arbitration, particularly in cases of marriage discord (*shiqaq*). As noted earlier, arbitration was a well-known practice in pre-Islamic Arabia. Even before the revelations, the Prophet was respected as an arbitrator, with his resolution of the dispute over the replacement of the black stone of the Kabah an early example. The verses of the Quran in support of *tahkim* together with the hadith of the Prophet show that the coming of Islam sanctioned the *tahkim*'s continuance but reformulated it to embody Islamic law as the choice of law[50] and to lay down requirements for persons who could arbitrate for Muslims. There was consensus (*ijma*) of the jurists for *tahkim* and it was widely employed to settle disputes in the time of the caliphs. The best-known example is the arbitration in the dispute between the fourth Caliph Ali and his political rival Mu'awiyyah, the governor of Syria concerning the future of the caliphate.[51] Arbitration was quite well established for family or commercial matters, reasoning (*qiyas*) was used to extend *tahkim* to a dispute over leadership and political authority.[52] However, the disastrous consequences of this arbitration, which contributed to the Sunni–Shia split, meant that *tahkim*'s importance declined, especially as Mu'awiyyah as caliph of the new Ummayad Dynasty strengthened the mandatory jurisdiction of the *qadi*.

Tahkim did not disappear but continued and over time strengthened as a voluntary dispute resolution mechanism for parties in a wide range of matters. Scholars and jurists in each of the schools of law refined their procedure and practice in the centuries that followed. Differences between the schools on several of these aspects of procedure and practice remain.

i. Features of *Tahkim*

Tahkim is the process by which parties voluntarily submit their dispute to a third person or persons, a Muslim arbitrator (*hakam*), in order to resolve the matters in dispute by reference to the law of Islam.[53] There were often aspects of conciliation (*sulh*) incorporated into *tahkim*. Attempts were first made to conciliate the parties, to persuade rather than to coerce, with the *hakam* endeavouring to create a cooperative atmosphere conducive to amicable settlement. If *sulh* could not be attained then the *hakam* guided by the Sharia reached a decision for the parties. The voluntary nature of *tahkim* is its defining feature that distinguishes it from *qada*, or court judgment. While adjudication can proceed without the consent of the parties, both parties must consent to arbitration,[54] otherwise any arbitral award given will be invalid.

Although there are differences in the process of appointment of the *hakam*,[55] no school allows a third party, even a *qadi* or ruler, to appoint an arbitrator who is unacceptable to the parties. There is a difference of opinion on who can serve as an Islamic arbitrator. The main points of contention are: whether a *hakam* should have the same qualifications as a judge; whether women can be arbitrators; whether family disputes require two *hakam* to reflect Quranic verse 4:35; and whether legal expertise is an essential pre-requisite for appointment as an arbitrator. Shia, and the Sunni Shafi'i school, hold that the qualifications for an Islamic arbitrator are essentially the same as for a *qadi*, except in marital disputes where there can be some relaxation of these standards. By contrast, the Hanafis do not require an arbitrator to have the same level of legal competence as a judge, but must have similar physical, ethical and religious standing to a *qadi* to make them beyond reproach in religious and worldly matters. It seems in all schools that a person who is qualified to be a *qadi* will meet the standard required to be a *hakam*; thus, arbitrators need to be an adult, credible (*adil*), just and trustworthy, without mental or physical defects, and a Muslim, although on the latter point there is some debate. Shah writes that a non-Muslim can have no jurisdiction over a Muslim,[56] but El-Ahdab asserts that, when the arbitration is taking place in a non-Muslim country between a Muslim and a non-Muslim party over a purely commercial matter, rather than family or personal one,[57] it may be permissible for the arbitrator to be non-Muslim. There is also some leeway on the degree to which an arbitrator needs to be 'learned in the Sharia'.[58] The Hanafi position is that an arbitrator can avail himself of professional advice,[59] so willingness to consult may replace actual *fiqh* knowledge. For family law matters knowledge of Islamic family law can suffice. Whether a woman can be an arbitrator parallels the debate in regard to whether judges can be arbitrators. The Hanafi school permits female-led *tahkim*,[60] but the other schools by tradition have rejected it mainly on the basis of hadith.[61] Modern perspectives on this question are coming to the fore. Zahraa and Hak argue there is no explicit prohibition supporting this in the Quran and, as the emphasis is on making peace between disputing parties, 'women might be in a better position to deliver this … as conciliators, mediators, social welfare officers and counsellors are women'.[62] In Iran, for example, Shia law allows an arbitrator to be male or female, provided he or she is at least 40 years old, Muslim, married, trustworthy and knowledgeable of the basics of Sharia.[63]

For most matters, the number of *hakam* to be appointed for an arbitration rests with the parties. As verse 35 of Súra Nisáa indicates, two *hakam* should be appointed for marital disputes (*shiqaq*), one from the husband's family and one from his wife's, but questions arise to whether two arbitrators are essential, whether they must be relatives or whether one professional arbitrator is equally valid. Zahraa and Hak point out that, as the purpose of arbitration is to find a solution to the dispute, if this goal is better served by a non-relative then that course should be taken. However, they note that relatives of the parties are likely to be more interested in seeing a reconciliation and have greater knowledge of the issues, and that parties may feel freer to discuss 'inner-most' secrets with family members than with outsiders.[64] Shah also explores these issues and reviews the juristic opinions on both sides of the debate. He concludes that it is recommended but not mandatory that an arbitrator be related to the disputants.[65] He also notes that it is logical in modern times to allow interventions that provide 'efficacious and effective implementation, especially in our age of specialisation and technical expertise'.[66] Shah also separates the theory from the actual practice. In Malaysia, he writes, 'reconciliation is in theory the job of arbitrators' as state legislation (in Selangor State) specifies that the court *may* appoint two arbitrators to act for the husband and wife respectively, but in practice, even when close relatives may be appointed, it is the state officials, the *sulh* counsellor and *qadi* who are the nuclei of any mediating forum. He also illustrates further departures from theory when judges while hearing a case in court resort to private mediation 'in [the judge's] office' in which reconciliation or a particular settlement is urged by the judge, making the demarcation between arbitration, mediation and reconciliation unclear.[67] Similarly to the number of arbitrators, if the objective of reconciliation is served by one arbitrator and the parties are agreeable to this, then the 'end goal' of the law has been served.[68]

There are also juristic differences on the scope and subject matter that can be arbitrated. For example, the Hanafi school allows arbitration for all matters, apart from *hadd* and *qisas* offences[69] (as these regard the rights of God), while the Maliki school permits arbitration for all commercial and financial matters, also allowing for *qisas*, excluding homicide, but excluding *hadd* offences, *li'an*,[70] guardianship, property of orphans and divorce, on the ground that each of these is within the exclusive jurisdiction of the judge.[71] In reviewing the differences between each of the schools, Hassan concludes that employment and industrial relations can be subject to arbitration as these areas pertain to the 'rights of man' category, in particular to proprietary rights with commercial and financial implications.[72] There is also debate on whether an agreement to arbitrate in a possible future dispute is valid in Islamic law, or void for uncertainty.[73]

The arbitral award will be valid if it is a matter that can be lawfully arbitrated, was given by a qualified arbitrator or arbitrators in conformity with the applicable tenets of Islamic law, and the arbitration was with the consent of the parties. There is some juristic divergence on whether the giving of the award must be done with the consent of the parties. The Hanbali school holds that parties can withdraw their consent for *tahkim* up until the time of the award, and if given when one party has withdrawn their consent the award is invalid and not binding.[74] In contrast, the Malaki school holds that consent of the parties at the outset is sufficient and it is not possible to withdraw consent once the arbitral process has commenced, so the award remains binding even when parties have withdrawn consent. Imam Shafi'i considered that an arbitral award would only be enforceable if both parties agreed to it,[75] which in many ways renders it closer to a form of conciliation or mediation. There does seem to be agreement between schools and jurists that an arbitration award should be in writing and witnessed. If the conditions for a valid arbitration are satisfied, then the award should be enforced, if necessary by a court, as enforcement falls outside the arbitrator's powers. Again there are differences of opinion on whether an award is judicially reviewable and whether either party can challenge the award, once given, in a court. Some scholars hold that a *hakam*'s decision is legally equal to that of a *qadi*, making it non-reviewable. This appears to be the majority view, namely, that if all conditions for validity are met, an award is not reviewable by a judge. Therefore, a *qadi* should enforce the award even if they would have concluded differently.[76] The one proviso is that, even though the merits and reasoning of the arbitrator cannot be reviewed, an award that contains a 'flagrant error or injustice' or is contrary to public order can be overturned by a *qadi*.[77]

Since the birth of Islam, when the prior customary process was reformed to align with the Quran and the practices of the Prophet, *tahkim* has been an important component of the Islamic justice system. As with many other practices in Islamic law, the jurists in the centuries that followed the death of the Prophet employed independent scholarly endeavours (*ijtihad*) to extend and refine *tahkim*.[78] Scholars and jurists have diverged on some key points of implementation and interpretation, but the overall consensus is that *tahkim*, alongside *sulh*, are not only *halal* but are to be encouraged as worthy complementary processes to adjudication. Today, Islamic arbitration remains a recognized process for dispute resolution in all Muslim countries[79] and has been brought into secular countries by Muslim migration as well.

3. IN THE WEST: EMERGING HYBRID FORMS OF ISLAMIC DISPUTE RESOLUTION

Many Muslims living in the West retain a strong preference to have disputes settled by persons with Islamic credentials and in accordance with Islamic principles. This does not indicate a rejection of national laws but instead a desire to conform with Islamic law when it is possible to do so. As formal Sharia courts do not exist in most Western countries, alternative dispute resolution mechanisms provide valuable avenues for resolving legal issues in accordance with Islamic law. As shown in this chapter, Islamic law provides and endorses dispute resolution processes other than adjudication, so it is logical that Muslims in the West utilize such options. Muslim community leaders and imams at local mosques and Muslim community centres provide advice, counselling, *sulh*-informed mediation and *tahkim* processes along the lines already outlined. In addition, family members will bring disputing couples together to arbitrate towards reconciliation in traditional ways. However, Muslims have also looked to mediation and arbitration models used in the common law and civil law systems and adapted these mechanisms to apply tenets of Islamic law. Just as Sharia informs Islamic dispute resolution processes, the processes in the common law and civil law countries are informed by European values and legal principles. Western mediation, which has been variously labelled modern mediation,[80] or independent mediation,[81] was consciously formulated and promoted to be an alternative process either in competition with, or complimentary to, litigation. The common law setting informed the development of mediation: some features of mediation were designed to ameliorate perceived problems identified with litigation, while other features of the common law were considered so important that they were incorporated into Western mediation process and theory. Significant amongst the latter was the principle of independence of the judiciary making the hallmark of Western mediation (also arbitration) the intervention of a neutral, independent, impartial and accredited professional,[82] thus the mediator cannot pursue agendas such as reconciliation or use of persuasion. In response to these characteristics of Western mediation, and in order to prioritize an Islamic imperative, a new concept of 'faith-based' mediation and arbitration has developed in many Western countries in which there is a fusion of components of Western-style ADR overlaid with principles and approaches that come with religious law,[83] for the purposes of this chapter, Islam. Fusions are taking place in Canada,[84] North America[85] and Australia, but it is the UK with its significant Muslim population of 1.5–2 million, which has become a social laboratory for hybrid forms of Islamic ADR.

A. Islamic ADR in the UK

Without a formal Sharia Court in existence in the UK, proactive Muslims in the 1980s set up Sharia Councils across the UK. These Councils were closely associated with mosques,[86] which meant that to some extent the Councils reflected the background, position and credentials of the imam and religious scholars (usually from Pakistan or Bangladesh) involved with the mosque and its ties to any home institution.[87] Amongst the Council's stated roles is to give 'judgments' in divorce, custody and other family matters. Currently, 85 Sharia Councils, colloquially known as Sharia courts, are situated across the UK to assist Muslims with financial, social, family and matrimonial, notably divorce, matters and also to provide Islamic legal opinions (fatwas). In the UK, UK law accepts private arrangements for dispute resolution, but any Sharia Council decision is not legally binding, nor will it be recognized by UK courts, although it may be by some Muslim countries, such as Pakistan. Any matter determined by a Sharia Council can always be brought to the civil courts for a legal determination under UK law, and many custody and financial matters do in fact come to the civil courts. Forms and applications relevant to marriage and divorce can be downloaded from Council website.[88] Fees are charged for the services. Guidance and decisions on legal issues are given by an Islamic scholar or scholars, with reassurances that these Sharia councillors represent a cross-section of *fiqh*, ethnicity and training, whether as imams, juristic scholars or lawyers. It is reported that 95 per cent of matters dealt with are in relation to matrimonial issues,[89] mainly divorce applications by wives.

Mediations often begin at a mosque or an Islamic community centre, and then progress to the Council, but a party can go directly to the Council. In keeping with Islamic principles, the first goal is to bring about reconciliation. If the couple do not reconcile, the scholar mediator draws on his understanding of applicable Islamic law to decree a divorce in one of the forms described in Chapter 5, and then decides on its terms and consequences, for example, on dower (*mahr*), arrangements for children, property distribution and spousal and child support. Yilmaz describes the Councils as a quasi-Islamic court.[90] Rather than following one particular school of law, they employ, he suggests, 'neo-*ijtihad*' to reconstruct Muslim family laws into an English Sharia (*Angrezi shariat*) to deliver new Islamic solutions in tune with modern times.[91] This, he believes, better accords with the needs of the Muslim community in Britain.[92] The notion of *Angrezi Shariat* was first described by Menski as a combination of Islamic and English law to form a distinctive hybrid.[93] An example is the reconstructed stance on divorce. The Council reached consensus that a pre-requisite for Islamic divorce in the UK is a proven 12 month period of separation.[94] This is interesting as it shows some convergence with civil law as one way to demonstrate 'irretrievable breakdown of marriage' under the civil divorce law is a period of separation, albeit for two years.[95] In Australia, it is evidenced by 12 months' separation. Through such adjustments by Islamic entities in Britain, Sano believes that a new form of 'Muslim family justice' has emerged.[96]

Since 2007, the UK also has Muslim Arbitration Tribunals (MAT),[97] which are registered and operate under the *Arbitration Act* 1996 (c23) (Eng). The Act allows for 'fair resolution of disputes by an impartial tribunal' when parties have agreed to it, and subject only to such safeguards as are necessary in the public interest.[98] The MAT Procedural rules require a tribunal to be constituted by at least one scholar of 'Islamic Sacred law' and one English registered barrister or solicitor. The website states that these tribunals 'offer the Muslim community a real and true opportunity to settle disputes in accordance with Islamic sacred law with the knowledge that the outcome as determined by MAT will be binding and enforceable'.[99] However, while the *Arbitration Act* does allow for legal recognition of arbitration agreements, and enables parties to agree on the law to be applied in the arbitration, and for arbitral awards to be enforced by UK Courts, not every matter can be arbitrated nor will all MAT awards be enforced by the UK courts. Certain matters are excluded, including a party's liability for a criminal penalty, the grant of divorce and the custody of children.[100]

A large proportion of cases that come to the MAT are wives seeking to divorce their husband. MAT can only grant a religious divorce, such as *kuhl'* or *faskh*,[101] which has no legal effect on a wife's status under UK law. This is because divorce 'is not a matter of private law which is capable of being decided by an arbitral tribunal'.[102] A grant of religious divorce by MAT will not be legally recognized as a civil divorce, just as obtaining a civil divorce will not of itself be recognized as an Islamic divorce by the Muslim community.[103] This creates the limping marriage phenomenon, discussed in Chapter 5, which the UK has tried to address by allowing a court to require dissolution of a religious marriage before granting a civil divorce.[104] An important exclusion is arbitral awards regarding the custody and care of children. Any MAT arbitration award concerning children will be subject to the civil courts' overriding power to intervene and make orders in the 'best interests of the child'.[105] The jurisdiction of the the UK courts over the rights of children and the obligations of parents towards their children cannot be displaced by a religious or other authority, including the MAT. Lastly, if a MAT award comes to the UK courts seeking enforcement,[106] it is open for the award to be challenged not only on grounds that it is a non-arbitral matter, but also if one party argues that there was no valid agreement to arbitrate because of duress, incapacity or undue influence, or that the arbitrator was biased or the procedure followed was unfair.[107]

While the majority of cases heard in the MAT fall into the category of family law, it does arbitrate other types of cases, including contract, commerce and employment. It also resolves matters involving Muslim organizations and institutions. Unlike the civil courts, which will only apply national 'foreign law', such as the law of Saudi Arabia, and not general law such as Sharia law, the *Arbitration Act*, section 46, allows this broad 'Sharia law' to be chosen.

Although there are different and contested views as to whether the majority of British Muslims favour institutions that apply Islamic law,[108] it appears that the Sharia Councils and the Muslim Arbitration Tribunals are well used and have a steadily increasing demand for their services. The Sharia Law Council reports that around 1000 cases of disputes involving Muslims are investigated, deliberated and then adjudicated successfully per year. The reasons for the take-up rates of Islamic ADR are varied and complex. As seen throughout this chapter, dispute resolution alternatives to adjudication have always had an important place in the Islamic justice system, and this has not changed because of immigration to the West. Yilmaz also sees the popularity of Islamic ADR in Britain as evidence of distrust of official (UK) law and a lack of respect for its law-makers.[109] Through 'chain migration', he argues that it has been possible for Muslims to 'reconstruct their traditional milieus in Britain', which enable the setting up of their own internal regulatory frameworks.[110] In addition, cultural factors including notions of honour and shame may mitigate against family disputes being discussed in the public sphere, giving private religious forums considerable legitimacy within Muslims communities. Reiss feels that, in reaction to the hegemonic British identity that creates 'resentment towards assimilation and pride in one's culture', which takes a form of 'unbelonging', a culture of 'resistance' has been fuelled.[111] Bowen suggests that a practical reason for the strong uptake of Muslim ADR in divorce cases is linked to the fact that one-half of British South Asian Muslims have transnational marriages; for example, they were married in Pakistan[112] but now live in the UK. For these couples, uncertainty about the equivalence of laws across the two countries' legal systems and a general ignorance of either system lead many Muslims to avoid the civil law system in favour of the quicker, seemingly more familiar, Islamic one.[113] On the other hand, divisions amongst Britain's Muslims have meant that calls by some for the implementation of formal Sharia courts have been met by counter argument by others content with the existing legal pluralism whereby British Muslims have the choice to turn to private institutions like Sharia Councils and the MAT or to the secular civil courts, or to both, or to neither.[114]

4. CONCLUSION

The sources of Islamic law give a clear message that adjudication is but one avenue for resolving disputes and alternatives to judicial fiat should be prioritized and supported. This has been so since the dawn of Islam when the Prophet endorsed both amicable settlement (*sulh*) and arbitration (*tahkim*). In contemporary times, these processes of dispute resolution continue to have relevance for Muslims not only in Muslim nations but also in the West, enabling principles of Islamic law to be applied by Islamic scholars to matters of importance in their lives.

NOTES

1. Mark Galanter, 'Justice in Many Rooms: Courts, Private Ordering and Indigenous Law' (1981) 19 *Journal of Legal Pluralism and Unofficial Law* 1, 34.
2. Galanter contends that there is a paradigm of legal centralism common among legal professionals, that is, an assumption that disputes require access to a forum external to the social setting of the dispute, where remedies are provided as prescribed by a body of specialized learning, and dispensed by experts operating under the auspices of the state; ibid.
3. Negotiation is dialogue between two or more people or parties, intended to reach an understanding or resolve point of difference in order through compromise to reach an agreement. There need be no third party involvement.
4. Mediation is a process in which a third person or persons seek to assist the parties to resolve a dispute without imposing a binding decision. The parties in dispute are assisted by the mediator, who facilitates a process of discussion to enable them to reach an outcome to which each can assent.
5. Arbitration is a process in which a dispute is referred to the adjudication of a third party chosen by the disputing parties and whose decision will be binding on them.
6. Kamal Halili Hassan, 'Employment Dispute Resolution Mechanism from the Islamic Perspective' (2006) 20(2) *Arab Law Quarterly* 181, 182.
7. Ann Black and Jamila Hussain, 'Responding to the Challenge of Multiculturalism: Islamic Law Courses in law School Curricula in Australia' (2006) 9 *The Flinders Journal of Law Reform* 205, 214.
8. Aida Othman, '"And Amicable Settlement is Best": *Sulh* and Dispute Resolution in Islamic Law' (2007) 21 *Arab Law Quarterly* 64.
9. Ibid., 68.
10. See Abdurraham Al-Juziry, *Kita al-Fiqh ala al-Mazahib al-Arba'a* [The Book of Jurisprudence According to Four Schools of Thought], Vol. 3 (Shu'bah-yi matbu'at, Mahakamah-yi Auqaf, Punjab, 1999), 124–34.
11. See Kamal Halili Hassan, 'Employment Dispute Resolution Mechanism from the Islamic perspective, (2006) *20 Arab Law Quarterly*, 181,186.
12. International mechanisms include the permanent Court of Arbitration, the International Centre for Settlement of Investment Disputes, United Nations Commission on International Trade Law arbitration and International Criminal Court arbitration.
13. Sayed Sikander Shah, 'Mediation in Marital Discord in Islamic Law: Legislative Foundation and Contemporary Application' (2009) 23 *Arab Law Quarterly* 329, 330.
14. George Sayen, 'Arbitration, Conciliation, and the Islamic Legal Tradition in Saudi Arabia', (1987) 9(1) *The University of Pennsylvania Journal of International Business Law* 211, 226.
15. For example, the Prophet arbitrated a major dispute between the two large Arab tribes of al-Aus amd al-Khazraj with three Jewish clans.
16. Abdul Hamid El-Ahdab, 'The Moslem Arbitration Law' in *Proceedings of the International Bar Association First Arab Regional Conference*, Vol. 1, (Cairo, February 1987), 342.
17. Sayed Sikander Shah, 'Mediation in Marital Discord in Islamic law: Legislative Foundation and Contemporary Application' (2009) 23 *Arab Law Quarterly* 329, 336.
18. George Sayen, 'Arbitration, Conciliation, and the Islamic Legal Tradition in Saudi Arabia' (1987) 9 (1) *The University of Pennsylvania Journal of International Business Law*, 211, noting that Al Bukhari devoted an entire chapter to *sulh.*

19. Vincent Powell-Smith, *Aspects of Arbitration: Common Law and Shari'a Compared* (Central Law Book, Ampang Jaya, 1995), 4–6.
20. In the Fatamid authority *Da'a'im al'Islam*, cited in Vincent Powell-Smith, *Aspects of Arbitration: Common Law and Shari'a Compared* (Central Law Book, Ampang Jaya, 1995), 6.
21. The early recorded arbitration agreements show many similarities with contemporary ones: the place and time for the arbitration and the procedure and law to be applied are specified; the arbitrators for each party, including provisions for substitution of an arbitrator in certain circumstances such as death, are noted; and the process of enforcement of the award is set out. The arbitrator was required to be strictly neutral between the parties. A famous early arbitration involved a caliph and an ordinary man. When the arbitrator offered the caliph a cushion, in deference to the caliph's importance, the arbitration could not continue as it indicated 'the first act of bias on the part of an arbitrator'. See S.E. Rayner, *The Theory of Contracts in Islamic Law* (Graham & Trotman, London, 1991), 366.
22. Abdullah Yusuf Ali, *The Qur'an: Text, Translation and Commentary* (Tahrike Tarsile Qur'an, New York, 2005), 220.
23. *Al-sulh khayr.* See generally, Mohammad Hashim Kamali, 'Legal Maxims and Other Genres of Literature in Islamic Jurisprudence' (2006) 20(1) *Arab Law Quarterly*, 77–101.
24. Wael B. Hallaq, *Sharia: Theory, Practice, Transformations* (Cambridge University Press, Cambridge, 2009), 162–3.
25. Ibid., 163.
26. The *Majelle*, Article 1531.
27. Aida Othman, '"And Amicable Settlement is Best": *Suhl* and Dispute Resolution in Islamic Law' (2007) 21 *Arab Law Quarterly* 64, 65.
28. Ibid., 69.
29. Súra Nisáa 4:128; 4:35; Súra Anfál 8:1 and Súra Shura 42: 20 in Abdullah Yusuf Ali, *The Qur'an: Text, Translation and Commentary* (Tahrike Tarsile Qur'an, New York, 2005).
30. Omar's instructions in his letter on judging, cited in Frank E. Vogel, *Islamic Law and Legal System* (Brill, Boston, MA, 2000), 153.
31. Abdullah Yusuf Ali, *The Qur'an: Text, Translation and Commentary* (Tahrike Tarsile Qur'an, New York, 2005), 1405.
32. Súra Hujurát 49:9, in Abdullah Yusuf Ali, *The Qur'an: Text, Translation and Commentary* (Tahrike Tarsile Qur'an, New York, 2005), 1405.
33. Lawrence Rosen, *The Justice of Islam: Comparative Perspectives on Islamic Law and Society* (Oxford University Press, New York, 2000), 123.
34. Aida Othman, '"And Amicable Settlement is Best": *Sulh* and Dispute Resolution in Islamic Law' (2007) 21 *Arab Law Quarterly* 64, 77.
35. Ibid.
36. Ibid., 76.
    Ibid., 75.
37. Frank E. Vogel, *Islamic Law and Legal System* (Brill, Boston, MA, 2000) 155.
38. Ibid.
39. Ibid., 156.
40. Discussed in Kamal Halili Hassan, 'Employment Dispute Resolution Mechanism from the Islamic Perspective' (2006) *20 Arab Law Quarterly* 181, 186. See for example, Articles 1532–5 *The Majelle.*
41. A *wakil* is allowed as an agent or proxy appearing in the absence of an actual party rather than as a barrister or counsel of the court.

42. Walid Iqbal, 'Dialogue and the Practice of Law and Spiritual Values: Courts, Lawyering and ADR: Glimpses into the Islamic Tradition' (2001) 28 *Fordham Urban Law Journal* 1035, 1041.
43. Ibid., 1041–2.
44. Aida Othman, '"And Amicable Settlement is Best": *Suhl* and Dispute Resolution in Islamic Law' (2007) 21 *Arab Law Quarterly* 64, 78.
45. Frank E. Vogel, *Islamic Law and Legal System* (Brill, Boston, MA, 2000), 159. Ibid.
46. Ibid., 157.
47. Najibah M. Zin, 'The Training, Supervision and Appointment of Islamic Judges in Malaysia' (2012) 21(1) *Pacific Rim Law and Policy Journal* 115, 125.
48. Section 752 *Civil Code of Iran* 1928.
49. Abdullah Yusuf Ali, *The Qur'an: Text, Translation and Commentary* (Tahrike Tarsile Qur'an, New York, 2005), 191.
50. The Quranic injunction at Súra Máida 5:49 is for Muslims to 'judge thou between them by what God has revealed and follow not their vain desires'. Abdullah Yusuf Ali, *The Qur'an: Text, Translation and Commentary* (Tahrike Tarsile Qur'an, New York, 2005), 259.
51. George Sayen, 'Arbitration, Conciliation, and the Islamic Legal Tradition in Saudi Arabia' (1987) 9(1) *The University of Pennsylvania Journal of International Business Law* 211, 229.
52. Mahdi Zahraa and Nora A. Hak, 'Tahkim (Arbitration) in Islamic Law Within the Context of Family Disputes' (2006) 20 *Arab Law Quarterly* 2, 7.
53. Abd al-Majid Mohammad al-Susu, 'Athar al-Takhim Fi al-Fiqh al-Islamiyah' [The Effect of Arbitration in Islamic Jurisprudence] (2005) 22 *Majjallah al-Sharia wa al Qanoun* [*Journal of Sharia and Law*], 101, 102.
54. The issue of consent is covered in Chapter 5 and the same requirements apply here as they do for consent to marriage.
55. In the Shafi'i, Hanafi and Hanbali schools, the appointment of the *hakam* could be revoked by either of the disputing parties or by the *hakam* himself, up until the announcement of the decision. In the Maliki texts it was irrevocable. Where the appointment of a *hakam* was ratified by a *qadi*, it could not be revoked. See George Sayen, 'Arbitration, Conciliation, and the Islamic Legal Tradition in Saudi Arabia' (1987) 9(1) *The University of Pennsylvania Journal of International Business Law* 211, 230.
56. Sayed Sikander Shah, 'Mediation in Marital Discord in Islamic Law: Legislative Foundation and Contemporary Application' (2009) 23 *Arab Law Quarterly* 329, 338.
57. Abdul Hamid El-Ahdab, 'The Moslem Arbitration Law' in *Proceedings of the International Bar Association First Arab Regional Conference*, Vol. 1, (Cairo, February 1987), 377.
58. The Hanafis do not hold this as an essential requirement, as an arbitrator can avail himself of professional advice. See also Jamila Hussain, *Islam: Its Law and Society* (Federation Press, Leichhardt, 2011), 214.
59. Ibid.
60. Also in the Maliki and Hanbali schools. However, the Hanafi school permits a woman to sit as a *qadi* in financial and commercial matters and hence she is also able to arbitrate in these matters. Indonesia allows female *qadis*, and so women could also be arbitrators.
61. The Prophet warned that 'a community will not prosper if its affairs are administered by a woman'. Al Bukhari, Vol. 9, Book 88, 219. This is also discussed by Shah, see Sayed Sikander Shah, 'Mediation in Marital Discord in Islamic law:

Legislative Foundation and Contemporary Application' (2009) 23 *Arab Law Quarterly* 329, 339, fn 42.
62. Mahdi Zahraa and Nora A. Hak, '*Tahkim* (Arbitration) in Islamic Law Within the Context of Family Disputes' (2006) 20 *Arab Law Quarterly* 2, 21.
63. Regulations concerning Article 1 of the Law relating to Reform of Divorce Law (Iran) 1992, section 4.
64. Mahdi Zahraa and Nora A. Hak, '*Tahkim* (Arbitration) in Islamic Law Within the Context of Family Disputes' (2006) 20 *Arab Law Quarterly* 2, 22.
65. Sayed Sikander Shah, 'Mediation in Marital Discord in Islamic law: Legislative Foundation and Contemporary Application' (2009) 23 *Arab Law Quarterly* 329, 336–337.
66. Ibid., 337.
67. Ibid., 342–5.
68. Ibid., 336–40.
69. The nature of *hadd* and *qisas* offences is discussed in Chapter 9.
70. Divorce by way of *li'an* is laid down in the Quran 24:6–9, see Chapter 6.
71. Kamal Halili Hassan, 'Employment Dispute Resolution Mechanism from the Islamic Perspective' (2006) 20(2) *Arab Law Quarterly* 181, 194.
72. Ibid.
73. The uncertainty (*gharar*) is based on the possibility of a dispute arising at some future time over an aspect of the contract that was unknown at the time of agreement.
74. Mahdi Zahraa and Nora A. Hak, '*Tahkim* (Arbitration) in Islamic Law Within the Context of Family Disputes' (2006) 20 *Arab Law Quarterly* 2, 30.
75. Abdul Hamid El-Ahdab, 'The Moslem Arbitration Law' in *Proceedings of the International Bar Association First Arab Regional Conference*, Vol. 1 (Cairo, February 1987), 341.
76. Mahdi Zahraa and Nora A. Hak, '*Tahkim* (Arbitration) in Islamic Law Within the Context of Family Disputes' (2006) 20 *Arab Law Quarterly* 2, 30.
77. Kamal Halili Hassan, 'Employment Dispute Resolution Mechanism from the Islamic Perspective' (2006) 20(2) *Arab Law Quarterly* 181, 203.
78. See Chapter 1 for a discussion of *ijtihad.*
79. Saudi Arabia, Egypt, Jordan, Sultanate of Oman, Qatar, Bahrain, Yemen Arab Republic and United Arab Emirates.
80. Also referred to as the North American model of mediation because of its revival in that jurisdiction. Mediation does have a long history in Europe, but it fell into disuse until the modern ADR movement of the 1970s.
81. Christopher W. Moore, *The Mediation Process: Practical Strategies for Resolving Conflict* (Jossey-Bass, San Francisco, CA, 1996), 41–53.
82. Mediators are guided by codes of conduct and statutes, with considerable focus on process, skills and techniques. Accreditation does not come from qualities of character but from objective, mandatory professional qualifications.
83. Judaism is the other main religion that has adopted this 'faith-centred' approach.
84. While religious arbitration was abolished in Ontario in 2005, other forms of mediation with Islamic parameters have been adopted.
85. The United States accepts faith-based arbitrations, for an elaboration see Caryn Litt Wolfe, 'Faith-based Arbitration: Friend or Foe? An Evaluation of Religious Arbitration Systems with their Interaction with Secular Courts' (2006–2007) 75 *Fordham Law Review* 247, 249.
86. Samia Bano, 'Islamic Family Arbitration, Justice and Human Rights in Britain' (2007) 1 *Law, Justice and Global Development Journal* 2, 12–14.
87. Samia Bano, 'Muslim Family Justice and Human Rights: The Experience of British Muslim Women' (2007) 1(4) *Journal of Comparative Law* 1, 9.

88. The Muslim Law Sharia Council, London: http://www.shariahcouncil.org/
89. Raffia Arshad, *Islamic Family Law* (Sweet & Maxwell, London, 2010), 37.
90. Ihsan Yilmaz, 'Muslim Alternative Dispute Resolution and Neo-Ijtihad in England' (2003) 91(2) *Alternatives* 117, 118.
91. Ibid.
92. Ibid., 132.
93. David Pearl and Warner Menski, *Muslim Family Law* (Sweet & Maxwell, London, 1998).
94. John R. Bowen, 'How Could English Courts Recognise Shariah?' (2010) 7(3) *University of St Thomas Law Journal* 411, 421.
95. *Matrimonial Causes Act* 1973, section 18 (UK) gives five grounds for establishing irretrievable breakdown: (1) adultery; (2) unreasonable behaviour; (3) desertion for a continuous period of two years; (4) a two-year separation immediately prior to the divorce request with the other spouse's consent; (5) a five-year separation immediately prior to the divorce request.
96. Samia Bano, 'Muslim Family Justice and Human Rights: The Experience of British Muslim Women' (2007) 2 *Journal of Comparative Law* 1, 9.
97. In London, Birmingham, Bradford, Manchester, Nuneaton, and planned for Glasgow and Edinburgh.
98. Section 1, *Arbitration Act*,1996, c. 23, 58 (UK).
99. Muslim Arbitration Tribunal: http://www.matribunal.com/>/
100. Robert Blackett, 'The Status of Religious "Courts" in English Law' (2011) *Dispute Resolution and International Arbitration Newsletter* 11, 13.
101. See Chapter 5.
102. Ibid.
103. However, Sameer Ahmed notes that some British Muslims believe a British civil divorce fulfills the general objective of the Sharia, making a Sharia Council divorce redundant; see Sameer Ahmed, 'Pluralism in British Islamic Reasoning: The Problem with Recognising Islamic Law in the United Kingdom' (2008) 33 *Yale Journal of International Law* 491, 495.
104. *Divorce (Religious Marriages) Act*, 2002 (UK).
105. *Children's Act*, 1989, c. 41 (UK).
106. Only the civil court has the power to make orders on the distribution of marital assets though property awards from MAT.
107. Robert Blackett, 'The Status of Religious "Courts" in English Law' (2011) *Dispute Resolution and International Arbitration Newsletter* 11, 13.
108. Maria Reiss, 'The Materialisation of Legal Pluralism in Britain: Why Shari'a Council Decisions Should be Non-binding' (2009) 26 *Arizona Journal of International and Comparative Law* 739, 741.
109. Ihsan Yilmaz, 'Muslim Alternative Dispute Resolution and Neo-Ijtihad in England' (2003) 2(91) *Alternatives* 117, 118.
110. Ibid., 121.
111. Maria Reiss, 'The Materialisation of Legal Pluralism in Britain: Why Shari'a Council Decisions should be non-binding' (2009) 26 *Arizona Journal of International and Comparative Law* 739, 760.
112. John Bowen, 'Private Arrangements' (March/April 2009) *Boston Review*; for the percentage from Pakistan, see Samia Bano, 'Muslim Family Justice and Human Rights: The Experience of British Muslim Women' (2007) 1(4) *Journal of Comparative Law* 1, 9.
113. John R. Bowen, 'How Could English Courts Recognise Shariah?' (2010) 7(3) *University of St Thomas Law Journal* 411, 413.

114. Sameer Ahmed, 'Pluralism in British Islamic Reasoning: The Problem with Recognizing Islamic Law in the United Kingdom' (2008) 33 *Yale Journal of International Law* 491, 492.

7. Islamic law and economics

1. INTRODUCTION

Western influence has dominated the areas of trade and finance in the Muslim world. Traditional Islamic contracts and financial instruments have been replaced by Western financial instruments and institutions through either colonialism or capitalism. The wholesale adoption of the French Civil Code (or the Napoleonic Code) by most Middle Eastern countries demonstrates the magnitude of the European commercial influence. However, most of the world's Muslim countries are poor. In the year 1000, the economy of the Middle East was at least as advanced as that of Europe, but by 1800, the region had fallen dramatically behind, in living standards, technology and economic institutions. By the nineteenth century, modern economic institutions began to be transplanted to the Middle East, but even in the twenty-first century, the Middle East's economies have not caught up with those of the West. In other words, the transplanting of the Western commercial system into the Middle East did not automatically produce wealth. In short, over the past two centuries the Middle East has failed to modernize economically even as the West surged ahead. The reasons for this are complex and divergent.[1]

In *The Long Divergence: How Islamic Law Held Back the Middle East*, Timur Kuran, a Turkish-American economist at Duke University, argues that Islam, liberated from stagnant interpretation and practice, is very adaptable to modern institutions.[2] However, the Middle East fell behind the West because it failed to produce commercial institutions (for example, joint-stock companies) that could be distanced from individuals or partnerships and could endure for long periods of time and mobilize large quantities of resources.

The notion that religion plays a central role in economic development is not new at all, and can be traced to Max Weber's 1905 treatise, *The Protestant Ethic and the Spirit of Capitalism*. Following Weber's reasoning, if it is true that capitalism is based on a 'Protestant ethic',[3] could Islamic law produce a new modern Islamic economic system based on the reinterpretation of the Quran and hadith? It does not seem too great a stretch: after all, the Prophet Mohammad was a merchant and the Quran praises commerce. Furthermore, great commercial centres, such as Baghdad, Istanbul and Isfahan, were the centres of European and Asian trade for centuries during the flourishing periods of Islamic civilization (eleventh to seventeenth centuries). In order to respond to the current economic conditions of the Muslim world, two different approaches have emerged amongst Muslim scholars.[4] First, some writers focus on highlighting a socio-political economic approach as part of overall reform of Muslim societies. The economic system of Islam is not conceptualized simply on the basis of arithmetical calculations and productive capacities. Rather, it is drawn and conceived in the light of a comprehensive system of morals and principles. The works of Abul A'la alMawdudi[5] and Sayyid Qutb[6] reflect this approach, which presents Islamic economic and financial concepts as a response to demands for social justice and economic opportunity, while at the same time complying with Islamic legal and moral principles. These scholars tend to see problems facing Muslim societies as being due to 'foreign' economic concepts imposed by colonialism and capitalism. Such scholars take the view that Muslims need to go back to the basic teachings of Islamic commerce and trade.

The second approach adopts a more pragmatic method aimed at elucidating the optimal structure of Islamic financial institutions that could efficiently function as lawful or permissible (*halal*) platforms for offering conventional banking and financial services. This approach is more legalistic than the socio-political economic enquiries of the first approach. Scholars who favour this approach are of the view that the failure of the first approach is due to the political agendas being pursued by those who advocate it, which is generally to establish an Islamic state. Pragmatic scholars, like Muhammad Baqir al-Shadr, also criticize the first approach for failing to recognize that there is a lack of financial institutions in the Quran and hadith that can drive reforms based on socio-political and economic justice.[7] For instance, without creating a separate concept of Islamic banking, the socio-political economic approach will fail to implement their ideas on a practical level.

It is worth noting that, since 2007, governments worldwide have been struggling to manage the global financial crisis, which is considered by many economists to be the worst financial crisis since the Great Depression of the 1930s. As a result, what we have seen is the collapse of large financial institutions, the bailout of banks by national governments and downturns in stock markets around the world. In many areas, the housing market has also suffered, resulting in evictions, foreclosures and prolonged unemployment. The crisis has played a significant role in the failure of key businesses, declines in consumer wealth estimated in trillions of US dollars, and a downturn in economic activity leading to the 2008–2012 global recession and contributing to the European sovereign debt crisis. The bursting of the US housing bubble, which peaked in 2007, caused the values of securities tied to US real estate pricing to plummet, damaging financial institutions globally.[8]

However, at least so far, one sector has been unscathed: the US$1 trillion-and-growing business of Sharia-compliant banking.[9] Justice, partnership and opposition to excessive risk are the main principles guiding Islamic banks, as will be discussed later. The biggest difference compared with the Western economic system is that interest is banned. In short, Islamic finance prohibits some of the excess that has brought the West's financial system to its knees: speculation, borrowing based on interest and investments deemed unethical by Islamic scholars, such as casinos. Islamic finance's more prudent rules on debt look attractive in light of the West's financial woes. More fundamentally, proponents say that Islamic finance provides a better way to link the financial system to the 'real' economy: as Islamic banks retain ownership of assets until the loan is repaid, they have a greater incentive to make sure borrowers do not bite off more than they can chew. Islamic banks therefore share in the upside risks of the entrepreneur but also bear the risk of financial failures, the argument goes. These characteristics of Islamic finance have led some to ask whether Islamic financial institutions could rescue the world economy from the global financial crisis, or prevent future crises from eventuating.

Although some of the modern Islamic economic concepts have developed as a reaction to colonialism and capitalism, as this chapter will demonstrate, these ideas could be adopted in both Muslim and non-Muslim countries without necessarily accepting at the same time the political ideas of al-Mawdudi or Sayyid Qutb, both of whom are controversial historical figures who have been labelled by some as fundamentalists or even extremists. Islamic financial institutions and/or Sharia-compliant products should be seen as an alternative option for a more ethical economic regime. Even the Vatican has put forward the idea that 'the principles of Islamic finance may represent a possible cure for ailing markets'.[10] The Osservatore, the Vatican Official newspaper's editor, Giovanni Maria Vian, stated that 'the great religions have always had a common attention to the human dimension of the economy'.[11] The appeal and currency of Islamic finance can be seen from the fact that high-profile Western banks such as HSBC, Citigroup and Deutsche Bank have been at the forefront of developing Islamic financial instruments.[12] Moreover, the International Monetary Fund has built up cordial relationships with the Islamic financial world.[13]

In this chapter, the basic concept of trade and commerce in the Quran and hadith will be introduced. Second, the issue of whether or not interest is considered as *riba* amongst Muslim legal scholars will be discussed. Finally, the establishment of Islamic financial institutions and the operation of Sharia-compliant products in Muslim and nonMuslim countries will be examined.

2. PRINCIPLES OF ISLAMIC ECONOMY

Islamic economics is first and foremost the application of ethical and legal principles derived from what is seen as divine law: Sharia. In trade and commerce, everything that is not prohibited is permissible, in other words, nothing is *haram* except what is prohibited by Allah. Muslims are therefore free to indulge in all forms of business, as long as they do not transgress into areas that are specifically forbidden. Commercial activities are basically permitted under Islam, subject to some restrictions such as risk or uncertainty (*gharar*) and gambling or speculation (*maysir*). The Sharia ban on *gharar* implies that 'commercial partners should know exactly the countervalue that is offered in a transaction'.[14] Of course, risk can never be totally avoided, certainly not by entrepreneurs, and no productive or commercial activity would be possible without a certain degree of risk and uncertainty. Only conditions of excessive risk have to be avoided. Ibn Hazm clarifies this: '*Gharar* in sale occurs when the purchaser does not know what he has bought and the seller does not know what he has sold'.[15] A *gharar* situation could be one where there is uncertainty about the price or the goods or services for one or both parties. Selling goods without specifying the price, such as selling at the 'going price', is *haram*, as is selling goods without allowing the buyer to properly examine the goods. To avoid *gharar*, all parties need to specify the characteristics and the amounts of the countervalues, and to define the quantity, quality and date of future delivery (if any). The ban on *gharar* provides transparency and fairness in transactions.

The need for transparency and fairness can be seen from the rulings of the Prophet, as he forbade the purchase of the unborn animal in the mother's womb, the sale of the milk in the udder without measurement, the purchase of spoils of war prior to distribution, the purchase of charities prior to their receipt and the purchase of the catch of a diver.[16] All Islamic financial and business transactions must be based on transparency, accuracy and disclosure of all necessary information so that no one party has an advantage over the other party. For instance, Sharia does not permit interdependent contracts such as combining two sales in one contract, or linking two sales jointly.[17] *Gharar* will also be established if the sale price is dependent on a specific event, or the parties are not sure if the sale may or may not take place.

In contemporary financial transactions, the two areas where *gharar* most profoundly affects common practice are insurance and financial derivatives. Some Islamic jurists often argue against financial insurance contracts, where a premium is paid regularly to the insurance company, and the insured receives compensation for any insured losses in the event of a loss. In this case, the jurists argue that the insured may collect a large sum of money after paying only one monthly premium. On the other hand, the insured may also make many monthly payments without ever collecting any money from the insurance company. Since 'insurance' itself cannot be considered an object of sale, this contract is rendered invalid because it is considered to be *gharar*.[18]

The ban on *gharar* might also mean that one could not sell agricultural products before they were harvested. After all, it is not certain what the harvest will be and the buyer is unable to examine the goods at the time of purchase.[19] As a general rule, futures, forwards and other derivatives are seen as *gharar*, as there is no certainty that the object of the sale will exist at the time the trade is to be executed.

Maysir is prohibited in Islam (Quran, Súra Máida 5:90) and this is another restriction in Islamic economics. *Maysir* (gambling) and *gharar* are inter-related. Where there are elements of *gharar*, the elements of *maysir* are also usually present. *Maysir* exists in an insurance contract when the policy-holder contributes a small amount of premium in the hope of gaining a larger sum; the policy-holder loses the money paid for the premium when the event that has been insured for does not occur, or if the company registers a deficit as the claims are higher than the amount contributed by the policy-holders.[20]

The third restriction in Islamic finance is the prevention of surplus value without a corresponding gain (*riba*). If there is one distinguishing characteristic of the Islamic economy, it is the prohibition of *riba*. The prohibition of *riba* is based on a number of verses from the Quran, in particular Súra Baqarah 2:275, 276 and 278, and Súra Áli'Imrán 3:130. The literal meaning of *riba* is 'increase' or 'addition' or 'surplus'. In the Sharia, *riba* stands for an addition to the principal and, by implication, a payment for the use of a sum of money that was fixed beforehand. It is a form of excess, of unjustified appropriation of income. One form of *riba* concerned a pre-Islamic Arabic custom that prevailed in transactions of gold and silver. If a debt was not paid on maturity (after one year), the principal was doubled. Thus, the principal due from the debtor was described in the Quran as *riba* 'doubled and multiplied'.[21]

There are a number of reasons for the prohibition of *riba*: first, one might potentially exploit poor debtors who need to borrow money or commodities; second, trading money may lead to fluctuations in currency values and monetary uncertainty; and third, trading foodstuffs for larger amounts of future foodstuffs would lead to shortages in spot markets for those foodstuffs, presumably because many traders would withhold the goods in the hope of getting more in the future.[22] The ban on *riba* was aimed, in the view of some commentators, to prevent the debtor being enslaved.[23]

There are two types or classes of *riba*. The first is *riba al-nasi'ah*, which is defined as an increase over the original value of capital given, usually by putting a condition in the loan agreement indicating that the lender will be entitled to an increase over the original value if the borrower asks for an extension of the term of the credit. The second is *riba al-fadl*, which is defined as selling [real] money for [real] money, commodity for commodity, such as food for food, with an increase over the original value. This is based on the hadith:

> Ubida b. al-Simit reported Allah's Messenger (may peace be upon him) as saying: Gold is to be paid for by gold, silver by silver, wheat by wheat, barley by barley, dates by dates, and salt by salt, like for like and equal for equal, payment being made hand to hand. If these classes differ, then sell as you wish if payment is made hand to hand.[24]

It is worth considering that some jurists agreed that those six commodities mentioned in the hadith were given only as examples. Hanafi jurists extended the prohibition to all fungible goods measured by weight or volume, whereas Shafi'i and Maliki jurists restricted it to monetary commodities (gold and silver) and storable foodstuffs.[25]

As for the moral justification for the prohibition of *riba*, it is seen as unfair, exploitative and unproductive. It tends to favour the rich, who are guaranteed a return, at the expense of the vulnerable, who assume all the risk. When a person having money is allowed to earn more money on the basis of interest, either in spot or in deferred transactions, it becomes easy for them to earn without bothering to take pains to pursue 'real' economic activities. Therefore, Islam prohibits *riba* in its old forms in order to protect society, particularly the vulnerable and poor people, who may be exploited. Similarly, the common law, in developing the principle of unconscionability, views the lending of money, by mortgage or otherwise, with considerable suspicion and courts are alerted 'to discover want of conscience in terms imposed by lenders'.[26]

The Islamic economic system prohibits *riba*, excessive uncertainty (*gharar*), gambling and all other games of chance and emphasizes a social welfare system based on mutual help, character building, behavioural changes, the system of charitable giving (*zakat*)[27] and care and dignity for the poor. Muslim scholars take the view that the injection of a moral dimension into the financial system along with greater equity and market discipline makes the financial system more equitable, healthier and stable.

3. *RIBA*, FATWAS AND INTEREST

All Muslim scholars agree that *riba* is prohibited in Islam. However, they provide different answers to the question: is *riba* the same as 'interest'? Different scholars have varying approaches to the meaning of *riba* or what constitutes *riba*, which is an activity, as set out above, that must be avoided to enable economic activities to conform with the tenets of the Sharia.[28]

One group of Muslim scholars takes the view that the Quranic principle is that the creditor has the right to the principal amount only for both loans and debts. In the case of loans, exactly the amount agreed as the loan must be repaid, and in the case of debts, only the liability or the amount of debt generated from the credit transaction can be recovered. Any amount, big or small, over and above the principal of a loan or debt would be *riba*. As conventional banks' financing falls into the category of loans for which a premium is charged, bank financing falls under the scope and meaning of *riba* as prohibited by the Quran. Scholars supporting this view include Mufti Taqi Usmani of Pakistan, who has declared that bank interest is not permitted in Islam.[29] Also, the Indonesian Council of Ulama (Majelis Ulama Indonesia) issued a fatwa in 2003 that bank interest is considered *riba*, and therefore is prohibited in Islam.[30] The Islamic Fiqh Institute of Qatar have also concluded that bank interest is considered to be *riba*.[31]

Setting aside Islamic moral arguments here, one need only look at the effect of the recent United States subprime mortgage crisis that led to the global financial crisis to understand that bank interest, as some economists would argue,[32] can be exploitative and unfair. Traditionally, banks financed their mortgage lending through the deposits they received from their customers. This limited the amount of mortgage lending they could do. In recent years, banks moved to a new model where they sell on the mortgages to the bond markets. This has made it much easier to fund additional borrowing, but it has also led to abuses as banks no longer have the incentive to check carefully the mortgages they issue.

Banks and other lenders are now cutting back on how much credit they make available. They are rejecting more people who apply for credit cards, insisting on bigger deposits for house purchase and looking more closely at applications for personal loans.[33] The mortgage market has been particularly badly affected, with individuals finding it very difficult to get non-traditional mortgages, both sub-prime and 'jumbo' (over the limit guaranteed by government-sponsored agencies). The banks have been forced to do this by the drying up of the wholesale bond markets and by the effect of the crisis on their own balance sheets. In late 2011 there were about a million homes in foreclosure in the United States, several million more foreclosures in the pipeline and 872,000 previously foreclosed homes in the hands of banks. The International Monetary Fund estimated that large US and European banks lost more than US$1 trillion on toxic assets and from bad loans from January 2007 to September 2009. These losses were expected to top US$2.8 trillion from 2007 to 2010. Losses of US banks were forecast to reach US$1 trillion and those of European banks to reach US$1.6 trillion.[34] As a result, the interest rate in United States in 2012 was nearly zero (0.25 per cent).[35]

In contrast, other Muslim scholars such as the late Grand Sheikh of al-Azhar University in Cairo, Sayyid Tantawi, are against the view that interest should be considered *riba*. In 1989, Tantawi issued a fatwa in which it was stated that the reason for the prohibition of *riba* was the harm caused to the debtor, and this rationale did not apply to deposits with banks. Therefore, he argued, bank interest was not forbidden as *riba*.[36] In 2002, the Islamic Research Institute (*Majma' al-Buhuts al-Islamiyah*) in Cairo reiterated the fatwa that all banking transactions are permitted in Islam.[37] The Egyptian Mufti Nasr Farid Wasil supported this view when he said: 'I will give you a final and decisive ruling … So long as banks invest the money in permissible venues (*halal*), then the transaction is permissible … there is no such thing as an Islamic or non-Islamic bank. So let us stop this controversy about bank interest'.[38]

It is worth noting that, when the Quran was revealed, the economic system was based on gold. If one borrowed 1000 dinar during the Prophet's time for one year, after one year the value of 1000 dinar would be the same as 1000 gold pieces: there was no inflation, fluctuation or different monetary policy from year to year. Therefore, there was no justification for a lender to ask for additional money (say 1200 dinar) after one year. However, the current economic system is based on paper money and electronic transactions. After President Nixon abolished the gold standard in the 1970s (by cancelling the direct convertibility of the

US dollar to gold) and currencies started to float, the world changed.[39] In 2012 if one borrows money from the bank to buy a car (for example, US$50,000), the real value of the borrowed money will decrease over the following five years. This is one of the reasons that the bank needs to charge interest. Without charging interest, the bank or the lender will have to absorb the decreased value of the money. This new situation needs to be addressed by Muslim scholars and jurists.

The Sharia Appellate Bench of Pakistan's Supreme Court says in this regard: 'Today's paper money has practically become almost like natural money equal in terms of its facility of exchange and credibility to the old silver and gold coins. It will, therefore, be subject to the injunctions laid down in the Qur'an and the hadith, which regulated the exchange or transactions of gold and silver'.[40] The Islamic Fiqh Academy (*Majma' al-Fiqh al-Islamiy*) of the Organisation of Islamic Conference (OIC) in its third session (11–16 October, 1986) also resolved that paper money should be considered 'real' money, possessing all the characteristics of value, and subject to Sharia rules governing gold and silver, including *riba*, *zakat* and the rules governing all other transactions.[41]

While scholars of the second view accept the charging of interest in all transactions, those of the first view must face the hard question: can we live without interest in our modern economy? This question leads scholars of the first view to propose the establishment of Islamic financial institutions that do not charge interest as an option for the current modern economic system.

4. ISLAMIC FINANCIAL INSTITUTIONS AND THEIR PRODUCTS

The phrases 'Islamic finance' or 'Islamic banking' simply refer to a state of affairs wherein the financial institutions and the clients have to fulfil the relevant principles of Islamic jurisprudence. By the 1960s, the first Islamic finance-based institutions were appearing; for example, in Egypt, Ahmad En-Najjar established the Mit Ghamr Savings Association.[42] Importantly, Mit Ghamr was modelled on Western banking institutions (specifically, German regional savings banks) and was not a bottom-up creation for Islamic finance. Despite its Islamic orientation, the Mit Ghamr Bank could not operate openly under an Islamic banner owing to the government's hostility towards Islamic movements. The bank was a successful business and particularly appealed to devout Egyptian farmers, but it was closed in 1968 by the Egyptian government, which was unsympathetic to private enterprise.

In addition to the Mit Ghamr Bank, a number of Islamic financial institutions oriented towards the socio-economic approach to Islamic economics discussed above were established during the 1960s and 1970s, particularly in non-Arab Muslim countries such as Pakistan and Malaysia. One example of such an institution is the Muslim Pilgrims Savings Corporation, which was established in 1963 as a savings fund for Muslims planning to perform the religious duty of pilgrimage (*hajj*). Within two decades the Malaysian pilgrim fund, which became known as Tabung Haji, was able to achieve wide recognition as a successful Islamic investment company in Malaysia. The success of Tabung Haji encouraged the Malaysian government to establish the first full-fledged Islamic commercial bank in the country, the Bank Islam Malaysia Berhad.[43]

The 1970s saw the emergence of a number of Gulf-based Islamic banks, notably Dubai Islamic Bank and the Islamic Development Bank. The Islamic Development Bank was primarily engaged in intergovernmental activities to provide funds for development projects running in member countries. Its business model involved fees for financial services and profit-sharing financial assistance for projects. Not only were Islamic banks established, but Islamic insurance (*takaful*) companies were also established. The first *takaful* company was established in 1979, the Islamic Insurance Company of Sudan. In 1985, the High Council of OIC declared *takaful* to be Sharia compliant.[44]

In 1991 the Accounting and Auditing Organization for Islamic Financial Institutions was established to advise on Islamic finance standards all over the world. Later, the development of uniform standards was supported by other organizations such as Islamic Financial Services Board in Malaysia in 2002. The Islamic economic institutional infrastructure started to become much more sophisticated and Western banks and institutions started to involve themselves through offering non-interest-bearing bonds and indices designed for the Sharia market. The new, wider spectrum of Islamic finance covers not only banking activities but also capital markets, capital formation and other financial instruments and intermediaries. During the last 30 years Islamic banking has emerged as another viable way of financial intermediation. It has gained credibility and respect in international financial circles. The presence of Islamic financial institutions has spread to all corners of the globe. Islamic finance is one of the fastest growing industries, posting double-digit annual growth rates for more than 30 years.[45]

The practice of Islamic banking is now not limited to Arab and Muslim countries but has spread from East to West, all the way from Indonesia and Malaysia towards Europe and the Americas. Many conventional banks, including some major multinational Western banks, have also started using Islamic banking techniques or accommodate Sharia-compliant products.[46] In Australia in 2010, for instance, the then Trade Minister, the Honourable Simon Crean MP, launched the Australian Government's first-ever comprehensive publication on Islamic finance. The booklet *Islamic Finance* provides a detailed explanation of the opportunities that the booming Sharia-compliant investment and banking market offers Australia's financial services sector.[47]

It has been reported that in the last 30 years there have been approximately 280 Islamic banks in 48 countries, whose total deposits have reached around US$400 billion, in addition to 300 conventional banks that have opened branches or windows or provided Islamic financial products. Major international institutions such as Citibank, Deutsche Bank and HSBC have had a presence in the Middle East and Southeast Asia for a number of years. As a result, they have developed considerable knowledge and experience of local markets, including Islamic markets. To accommodate the new and growing demand for Islamic products, they have established business lines known as 'Islamic windows', some of which are based in the UK and others in the Middle East and Southeast Asia. These windows have contributed significantly to the development of Islamic finance because of the institutions' global experience in product development and their access to far greater resources than those available to local institutions in the Middle East and Southeast Asia. However, it is worth noting that, if the assets of all Islamic banks were pooled, they would still be less than those of any single one of the top 50 banks worldwide, and the assets of the largest Islamic bank are equal to only 1 per cent of the assets of the largest bank in the world.[48]

What are the main differences between conventional banks and Islamic banks? Conventional banks deal in money: they get money from the public as loans and pay them interest; they give advances to people or firms in the form of money and charge them interest. In domestic or foreign trade financing activities or even in the case of finance leases, goods are also involved, but conventional banks have no concern with the goods or assets themselves; their main concern is with financing the purchase of goods and for that purpose they also deal in documents to facilitate the trading of goods. As such, banks deal in documents, not in goods. They assume no responsibility or risk in respect of the subject of the contracts and their counter payments or price.

In contrast, Islamic banks deal in goods and documents and not in money. They use money only as a medium of exchange for purchasing the goods for the purpose of leasing or selling onward, thereby earning income or profit. In this process they also use documents for executing sale and lease contracts, while upholding the principles of Sharia and facilitating the bank's operations. Islamic banks intermediate between savers/investors and fund-users by holding certain goods and assets or papers representing ownership of real assets. Therefore, financial transactions, in order to be permissible in Islam, should be associated with goods, services or benefits. While at a micro-level this feature of Islamic finance leads to the generation of real economic activity and stable growth, at a macro-level it can be helpful in creating better discipline in the conduct of fiscal and monetary policies.[49]

Islamic financial institutions have designed a number of products that aim to comply with Sharia, including trustee finance contracts or trust financing (*mudaraba*); profit-margin sales (*murabaha*); leasing (*ijara*); Islamic bonds (*sukuk*); and Islamic insurance (*takaful*). These products will be reviewed in the next section of this chapter.

Trustee finance contracts or trust financing (*mudaraba*) is a form of profit-sharing contract. *Mudaraba* is therefore reserved for business finance, and is not suitable for consumer finance. The bank, or any other money provider, acts as financier or capital owner (*rabb al-mal*) and provides the entire capital needed for financing a project. The other party, the agent (*mudarib*), manages the venture and brings in their labour and expertise. The capital provider is similar to a sleeping partner. Parties agree beforehand on the proportion in which they share any profits. Losses are borne exclusively by the capital provider. The *mudarib* cannot share in any loss, because the Sharia stipulates that one cannot lose what one does not contribute. Even poor management is no reason to hold the *mudarib* responsible, unless there is evidence of wilful or culpable negligence. For investment funds, *mudaraba* are considered to be high-risk ventures.[50]

A low-risk category of Islamic financial products is profit-margin sales (*murabaha*), which comprise the most widely used Islamic financial contract. *Murabaha* is an agreed profit-margin sale with spot or deferred payment of the sale price. The term '*murabaha*' means the sale of goods by one party to another under an arrangement whereby the seller is obliged to disclose to the buyer the cost of the goods sold on either a spot basis or a deferred payment basis, and a profit margin is included in the sale price. It is suitable for corporate, consumer, agriculture, micro-finance and other sectors where the client needs finance to purchase goods. For instance, in an Islamic mortgage transaction using *murabaha*, instead of loaning the buyer money to purchase the item, a bank might buy the item itself from the seller, and re-sell it to the buyer at a profit, while allowing the buyer to pay the bank in instalments. However, the bank's profit cannot be made explicit and therefore there are no additional penalties for late payment. In order to protect itself against default, the bank asks for strict collateral. The goods or land are registered to the name of the buyer from the start of the transaction.[51]

One might argue that the increase in price in a credit sale, being in consideration of the time given to the purchaser, should be treated analogously to the interest charged on a loan, because in both cases an additional amount is charged for the deferment of payment. On this basis one could argue that *murabaha* transactions, as practised in the Islamic banks, are not different in essence from the interest-based loans advanced by conventional banks. *Murabaha* could be considered as a kind of permanent fixed-term interest. It would undermine the foundations of Islamic finance if *murabaha* was used as a trick to do what conventional finance is doing, which is lending on the basis of interest. Only the practitioner can ensure that *murabaha* does not degenerate to that level.

The Australian Government in the Board of Taxation's 2012 Review of the Taxation Treatment of Islamic Finance Products is addressing a major issue with Islamic banking: that Islamic banking and financial contracts are treated as buying and selling properties and hence are taxed twice. In some countries, such as the UK and Singapore, double stamp duty on some Islamic home finance schemes has been abolished so as to provide tax neutrality.[52] This change, if enacted in Australia, would make *murabaha* transactions easier to take up.[53]

Another Islamic financial product is leasing (*ijara*), which is equivalent to conventional leasing but with some key differences, such as the requirement of the lessor to assume the risk relating to ownership of the leased asset at all times, and that any sale to the lessee at the end of the lease period must not be a condition of the leasing contract. An Islamic bank's income is derived from the profit charged on the cost of a leased asset, and this profit is included with the cost in the lease repayments. In an alternative approach, the lessee can agree at the outset to buy the asset at the end of the lease period, in which case the lease takes on the nature of a hire purchase known as *ijara wa iqtina* (literally, lease and ownership).[54] Some jurists do not permit this latter arrangement on the basis that it represents more or less a guaranteed financial return at the outset to the lessor, in much the same way as a modern interest-based finance lease. Although *ijara* is not strictly a financing mode, Islamic banking institutions use it extensively as such to acquire fixed assets for their clients because it does not involve interest payments, is easily understood and can be used in order to obtain tax concessions in certain countries.[55]

Sukuk are tradable, asset-backed, medium-term notes. The name *sukuk* is sometimes translated as certificates, or as Islamic bonds. It is the plural of the word *sakk*, from which the term 'cheque' was derived. *Sukuk* are backed by real assets and often, but not always, represent ownership of real assets.[56] The first Islamic global bond issue was floated in 2002 by the Malaysian government. *Sukuk* are mainly aimed at institutional investors, although there have been issues with a minimum value of each *sukuk* below the equivalent of €2000.[57] The Fiqh Academy of the Organization of the Islamic Conference legitimized the use of *sukuk* in February 1988, but it took some years before the market developed. *Sukuk* are not only issued by or on behalf of governments and quasi-sovereign agencies, but also on behalf of corporations. The first *sukuk* was listed on the London Stock Exchange in July 2006.[58]

Sukuk are widely regarded as controversial owing to their perceived purpose of evading the restrictions on *riba*.[59] Conservative scholars do not believe that this is effective, citing the fact that a *sakk* effectively requires payment for the time-value of money. This can be regarded as the fundamental test of interest. *Sukuk* offer investors a fixed return on their investments, which is also similar in appearance to interest in that the investor's return is not necessarily dependent on the risks of that particular venture. However, banks that issue *sukuk* are investing in assets, not currency. The return on such assets takes the form of rent, and is evenly spread over the rental period. The productivity of the asset forms the basis of the fixed income stream and the return on investment. Given that there is an asset underlying the value of the certificate, there may be, depending on the value of the asset, more security for the investors involved, accounting for the additional appeal of *sukuk* as a method of financing for investors.[60]

Certain common structuring elements for *sukuk* were criticized by Mufti Taqi Usmani, President of the Sharia Council of the Accounting and Auditing Organisation for Islamic Financial Institutions.[61] Usmani argues that *sukuk* have taken on the same characteristics as conventional interest-bearing bonds, as they do not return to investors more than a fixed percentage of the principal, based on interest rates, while guaranteeing the return of the investors' principal at maturity. Moreover, Usmani estimated that 85 per cent of all *sukuk* in issuance were not Sharia-compliant owing to the existence of guaranteed returns and/or repurchase obligations from the issuer.

Another Islamic financial product is Islamic insurance (*takaful*). The term '*takaful*' derives from the verb *kafala*, meaning to help or to take care of one's needs. The Fiqh Councils of the World Muslim League and the Fiqh Academy of the Islamic Conference resolved in 1978 and 1985, respectively, that conventional insurance in its existing form is *haram*, but that *takaful*, that is, cooperative or mutual insurance, is permissible (*mubah*).[62] The conventional model of insurance is considered technically wrong from the Sharia perspective because of concerns about insurance's interaction with the principles of uncertainty (*gharar*), gambling (*maysir*) and interest (*riba*). The insurance scenario, where an insured person or entity contributes a small amount as a premium in the hope of gaining a large sum, contains elements of *gharar* and *maysir*; the participant loses the money paid for the premium when the insured event does not occur, which is *gharar*; and finally, the insurance company will be in deficit if the claims are higher than the amount contributed by the participants, which is *gharar*.[63]

As a solution, *takaful* operates in the following way: since *gharar* is not allowed in compensatory contracts, risk mitigation may be accepted on a voluntary basis.[64] The voluntary basis of risk mitigation means that an amount of money or valuables is jointly pooled by a group of people in order to be prepared to meet any unexpected events for any member of the group. *Takaful* is based on the principle of mutual assistance (*ta'awun*) and voluntarism (*tabarru*) from the participants (policy-holders) to create a fund that will provide financial help at the occurrence of certain losses. Such principles are based on the Quran, Súra Máida 5:2: 'Help ye one another in righteousness and piety, but help ye not one another in sin and rancour'.[65] Despite the justifications for the compliance of *takaful* with Sharia, one might wonder whether *takaful* insurance does not involve *gharar*, in the same way as does conventional insurance. After all, under *takaful* insurance the insured party may receive a large sum after having paid a low sum in the form of premiums, or receive nothing, although having paid a large premium. Indeed, one commentator has branded it an unequal exchange (*riba al-fadl*).[66]

5. CONCLUSION

As this chapter has demonstrated, Islamic financial institutions are striving to produce Sharia-compliant products that are free from *gharar*, *maysir and riba*. However, Islamic financial institutions tend to be pragmatic in the sense that many of their products (if not all) are merely Islamic reinventions of conventional Western financial products. Instead of creating new, fresh and different products based on Sharia, these institutions tend to 'Islamicize' Western conventional products. Some Muslim jurists are unhappy with the pragmatic approach of the Islamic financial institutions, as they perceive that fundamental problems with the

Western financial products have not been resolved in the Islamic versions. That is the most challenging issue facing Islamic financial institutions.

NOTES

1. See Murat Çizakça, *Islamic Capitalism and Finance: Origins, Evolution and the Future* (Edward Elgar Publishing, Cheltenham, UK and Northampton, MA 2011); M. Henry Clement and Rodney Wilson (eds), *The Politics of Islamic Finance* (Edinburgh University Press, Edinburgh, 2005); M. Umer Chapra, *The Future of Economics: An Islamic Perspective* (The Islamic Foundation, Leicester, 2000).
2. Timur Kuran, *The Long Divergence: How Islamic Law Held Back the Middle East* (Princeton University Press, Princeton, NJ, 2010).
3. Max Weber, *The Protestant Ethic and the Spirit of Capitalism* (Allen and Unwin, London, 1930).
4. Walid S. Hegazy, 'Contemporary Islamic Finance: From Socioeconomic Idealism to Pure Legalism' (2007) 7 *Chicago Journal of International Law* 589.
5. Abul A'la al-Mawdudi, *The Economic Problem of Man and its Islamic Solution* (Islamic Publications, Lahore, 1955).
6. Sayyid Qutb, *Social Justice in Islam* (translated and published in English by American Council of Learned Societies, Washington, DC, 1953).
7. Muhammad Baqir al-Shadr, *Iqtishaduna* (1961), available at http://www.wofis.com/DownloadFilePage.aspx?fileName=asset/Books/IQTISADUNA1-1.pdf
8. See Yuliya Demyanyk and Otto Van Hemert, 'Understanding the Subprime Mortgage Crisis' (2011) 24(6) *Review of Financial Studies* 1773–81.
9. Maher Hasan and Jemma Dridi, 'The Effects of the Global Crisis on Islamic and Conventional Banks: A Comparative Study' (2010) IMF Working Paper, WP/10/201.
10. See Lorenzo Totaro, 'Vatican Says Islamic Finance May Help Western Banks in Crisis', *Bloomberg*, 4 March 2009, available at http://www.bloomberg.com/apps/news?pid=newsarchive&sid=aOsOLE8uiNOg&refer=italy
11. Ibid.
12. Hans Visser, *Islamic Finance: Principles and Practice* (Edward Elgar Publishing, Cheltenham, UK and Northampton, MA, 2009), 7.
13. See Juan Solé, 'Introducing Islamic Banks into Conventional Banking Systems' (July 2007) IMF Working Paper, WP/07/175.
14. Hans Visser, *Islamic Finance: Principles and Practice* (Edward Elgar Publishing, Cheltenham, UK and Northampton, MA, 2009), 45.
15. Ibn Hazm, *Al-Muhalla*, Vol. 8 (Dar al-'Uruba, Cairo, 1960), 343.
16. These requirements were narrated by Ahmad and Ibn Majah.
17. See Mohammed Obaidullah, 'Islamic Financial Services' (Islamic Economics Research Center at King Abdul Aziz University, Jeddah, 2005), available at http://islamiccenter.kau.edu.sa/english/publications/Obaidullah/ifs/ifs.html
18. Wahbah al-Zuhayli, *al-Fiqh al-Islamiy wa Adillatuh*, Vol. 5 (Dar al-fikr, Beirut, 1997), 3415–20.
19. However there are some exceptions discussed amongst different schools of thought (*madhhab*). With the exception of prepaid forward sales (*salam*) and commissions to manufacture (*istisna*), objects of sale must exist at the time of the contract. *Bay' salam* is a contract that demands a payment of a good or service that will be delivered eventually. The money owed should be submitted to the supplier. The supplier will receive the full price for his commodity. It is necessary that the details

of the transfer of the commodity are specified to prevent disagreement with a partner later. These commodities have to exclude gold, silver and currencies based on these specific metals. *Istisna* is translated as 'commission to manufacture'. The price due is paid in instalments as investment progresses. The prepaid instalments will be lower in price in relation to the purchasing of the final product. See Mahmoud A. El-Gamal, *Islamic Finance: Law, Economics, and Practice* (Cambridge University Press, Cambridge, 2006), 81–91.

20. Mohd Daud Bakar, 'Shari'ah Principles Governing Takaful Models' in Simon Archer, Rifaat Ahmed Addel Karim and Volker Nienhaus (eds), *Takaful Islamic Insurance: Concepts and Regulatory Issues* (Wiley, Singapore, 2009).
21. The condemnation of interest has not been confined to Islam. Based on passages from the Bible, the Christian Church at various times took a strong stand against demanding and paying interest. See Hans Visser, *Islamic Finance: Principles and Practice* (Edward Elgar Publishing, Cheltenham, UK and Northampton, MA, 2009), 39–45.
22. The Quran, Súra Ál i 'Imrán 3:130, in Abdullah Yusuf Ali, *The Qur'an: Text, Translation and Commentary* (Tahrike Tarsile Qur'an, New York, 2005), 156. See also Wahbah al-Zuhayli, *al-Fiqh al-Islamiy wa Adillatuh*, Vol. 5 (Dar al-fikr, Beirut, 1997), 3713.
23. See Timur Kuran, 'Islamic Economics and the Islamic Subeconomy' (1995) 9(4) *Journal of Economic Perspectives* 155–73, reprinted as Chapter 2 in Timur Kuran, *Islam and Mammon: The Economic Predicaments of Islamism*, 3rd edn (Princeton University Press, NJ, 2006), 38–54.
24. Hadith narrated by Muslim.
25. Ibn Rushd, *Bidayah al-Mujtahid* (Dar al-Fikr, Beirut, 1980) 2/135.
26. *Kreglinger v. New Patagonia Meat and Cold Storage* [1914] AC 25, 36.
27. *Zakat* is the religious obligation of every Muslim who has wealth in excess of his consumption needs at the nonprogressive rate – generally 2.5% of net wealth or 5 or 10% in the case of agricultural produce above a minimum limit. *Zakat* money must be distributed among the have-nots and the needy as per the tenet of the Quran given in Súra Tauba 9:60 – 'Alms are for the poor and the needy, and those employed to administer the (funds); for those whose hearts have been (recently) reconciled (to Truth); for those in bondage and in debt; in the cause of God; and for the wayfarer: (thus is it) ordained by God, and God is full of knowledge and wisdom'; Abdullah Yusuf Ali, *The Qur'an: Text, Translation and Commentary* (Tahrike Tarsile Qur'an, New York, 2005), 458.
28. More information can be found in Abdelkader S. Thomas (ed.) *Interest in Islamic Economics: Understanding Riba* (Routledge, London, 2006).
29. The full text of his statement can be read at: http://www.albalagh.net/Islamic_economics/riba_judgement.shtml
30. MUI's fatwa No. 1 of 2004 on Banking Interest can be read at its website, at: http://www.mui.or.id/
31. Excerpt of its fatwa can be read in Mahmoud A. El-Gamal, '"Interest" and the Paradox of Contemporary Islamic Law and Finance', available at http://www.ruf.rice.edu/~elgamal/files/interest.pdf
32. See for example Renáta Janka Tóth, 'Islamic Economics and the Effect of the Global Financial Crisis', available at http://www.atlantic-community.org/app/webroot/files/articlepdf/IslamicEconomics.pdf
33. See 'The Downturn in Facts and Figures', *BBC News*, 21 November 2007, available at http://news.bbc.co.uk/2/hi/business/7073131.stm
34. See 'Bloomberg–U.S. European Bank Writedowns & Losses', *Reuters*, 5 November 2009.

35. The information above has been taken from: http://www.tradingeconomics.com/united-states/interest-rate
36. See Frank Vogel and Samuel Hayes, *Islamic Law and Finance: Religion, Risk and Return* (Kluwer Law International, The Hague, 1998), 46.
37. Text of the fatwa can be read in Mahmoud A. El-Gamal, *Islamic Finance: Law, Economics, and Practice* (Cambridge University Press, Cambridge, 2006), 139–41.
38. Ibrahim Warde, *Islamic Finance in the Global Economy* (Edinburgh University Press, Edinburgh, 2000), 57.
39. Detlev S. Schlichter, 'Forty Years of Paper Money', *The Wall Street Journal*, 15 August 2011, available at: http://online.wsj.com/article/SB10001424053111903918104576500811399421094.html
40. Shariat Appellate Bench, 'Judgement on Riba', *Shariat Law Reports* (2000), as quoted in Muhammad Ayub, *Understanding Islamic Finance* (Wiley, Chichester, 2007), 91.
41. Ibid.
42. Hans Visser, *Islamic Finance: Principles and Practice* (Edward Elgar Publishing, Cheltenham, UK and Northampton, MA, 2009) 94.
43. Walid S. Hegazy, 'Contemporary Islamic Finance: From Socioeconomic Idealism to Pure Legalism' (2007) 7 *Chicago Journal of International Law* 589. See also Ibrahim Warde, *Islamic Finance in the Global Economy* (Edinburgh University Press, Edinburgh, 2000).
44. Muslehuddin, *Insurance and Islamic Law* (Islamic Publications, Lahore, 1995).
45. V. Sundararajan and Luca Errico, 'Islamic Financial Institutions and Products in the Global Financial System: Key Issues in Risk Management and Challenges Ahead' (2002), IMF Working Paper, WP/02/192; Saiful Azhar Rosly, *Critical Issues on Islamic Banking and Financial Markets* (Dinamas, Kuala Lumpur, 2005).
46. Zamir Iqbal and Abbas Mirakhor, *An Introduction to Islamic Finance* (Wiley, Singapore, 2011).
47. See 'Islamic Finance' at: http://www.austrade.gov.au/ArticleDocuments/2792/Islamic-Finance-Publication.pdf.aspx
48. See Munawar Iqbal and Philip Molyneux, *Thirty Years of Islamic Banking: History, Performance and Prospects* (Palgrave Macmillan, New York, 2004), 130–32.
49. See Institute of Islamic Banking and Insurance, *A Compendium of Legal Opinions on the Operations of Islamic Banks* (IIBI, London, 2000).
50. Yahia Abdul-Rahman, *The Art of Islamic Banking and Finance* (Wiley, Hoboken, NJ, 2010), 59.
51. See Daud Vicary Abdullah and Keon Chee, *Islamic Finance: Why It Makes Sense* (Marshall Cavendish, Singapore, 2010), 137–40.
52. Mohammed Amin, *UK Taxation of Islamic Finance: Where Are We Now?* (IIBI, London, 2006).
53. See Kerrie Sadiq and Ann Black, 'Embracing Sharia-compliant Products Through Regulatory Amendment to Achieve Parity of Treatment' (2012) 34(1) *Sydney Law Review* 189–211.
54. See M. Tahir Mansoori, *Islamic Law of Contracts and Business Transactions* (Adam, New Delhi, 2005).
55. Abdullah Alwi Haji, *Sales and Contracts in Early Islamic Commercial Law* (Islamic Research Institute, Islamabad, 1993); see also Mabid Ali Jarhi and Iqbal Munawar, *Islamic Banking: Answers to some Frequently Asked Questions* (Islamic Research and Training Institute, Saudi Arabia, 2001).
56. Hans Visser, *Islamic Finance: Principles and Practice* (Edward Elgar Publishing, Cheltenham, UK and Northampton, MA, 2009), 63–6.
57. Ibid.

58. Nathif Jama Adam, 'Sukuk: A Panacea for Convergence and Capital Market Development in the OIC Countries' (2005), compiled papers presented at the *6th International Conference on Islamic Economics and Banking in the 21st Century*, Jakarta, 21–24 November.
59. Mohamed Ariff, Munawar Iqbal and Shamsher Mohamad (eds), *The Islamic Debt Market For Sukuk Securities: The Theory and Practice of Profit Sharing Investment* (Edward Elgar Publishing, Cheltenham, UK and Northampton, MA, 2012).
60. See also Ravindran Ramasamy, Shanmugam Munisamy and Mohd Hanif Mohd Helmi, 'Relative Risk of Islamic Sukuk Over Government and Conventional Bonds' (2011) 11(6) *Global Journal of Management and Business Research* 5–11.
61. Sheikh Muhammad Taqi Usmani, 'Sukuk and their Contemporary Applications' (November 2007), available at http://www.pdftop.com/view/aHR0cDovL3d3dy5mYWlsYWthLmNvbS9kb3dubG9hZHMvVXNtYW5pX1N1a3VrQXBwbGljYXRpb25zLnBkZg
62. Hans Visser, *Islamic Finance: Principles and Practice* (Edward Elgar Publishing, Cheltenham, UK and Northampton, MA, 2009), 104.
63. See Saiful Azhar Rosly, *Critical Issues on Islamic Banking and Financial Markets* (Dinamas, Kuala Lumpur, 2005).
64. Abdul Rahim Abdul Wahab, Mervyn K. Lewis and M. Kabir Hassan 'Islamic Takaful: Business Models, Shariah Concerns, and Proposed Solutions' (2007) 49 *Thunderbird International Business Review* 371–96.
65. Abdullah Yusuf Ali, *The Qur'an: Text, Translation and Commentary* (Tahrike Tarsile Qur'an, New York, 2005), 239.
66. Hans Visser, *Islamic Finance: Principles and Practice* (Edward Elgar Publishing, Cheltenham, UK and Northampton, MA, 2009), 105.

8. Property rights, inheritance law and trusts (*waqf*)

1. INTRODUCTION

Property rights and interests, particularly land interests, and legal principles and laws regulating the use and ownership of land are important features of every legal system. According to one commentator:

> From the earliest settlement until the industrial revolution the economic basis of society was agrarian. Land was wealth, livelihood, family provision, and the principal subject-matter of the law. To begin with, moreover, land was also government and the structure of society.[1]

In modern legal systems, such as the common law and civil law systems, property law has always been a major area of law, and many legal and philosophical principles have been developed based on the notions of property and ownership. Owing, however, to the development of intellectual property rights in recent decades, traditional real property interests may not now be as important as they were in the past. Furthermore, property institutions, including trusts, are important features of common law legal systems. According to Blackstone:

> There is nothing which so generally strikes the imagination, and engages the affections of mankind as the right of property; or that sole and despotic dominion which one man claims and exercises over the external things of the world, in total exclusion of the right of any other individual in the universe.[2]

In both natural law and positivist legal theories the concept of property is considered significant. According to natural law theory, property is approached as a 'state of nature' and is considered a natural right. Alternatively, legal positivists, such as Jeremy Bentham, believe that 'property and law are born together and die together'.[3] This means that property and its limits are created by law. Therefore, property is not a natural right but instead a legal construct. There are also varying views of the definition of property in the Western legal tradition. The concept of the 'property' in Western legal systems is elusive and fragile.[4] The High

Court of Australia has held that property is not a thing but 'is a description of a legal relationship with a thing'.[5]

In addition to the importance of property law in legal systems, property rights are linked to economic development,[6] and even to the establishment of the rule of law and democracy.[7]

In Islam, the theory of property law has also developed a number of fundamental principles relating to land. According to Joseph Schacht:

> The theory of Islamic law has … developed only a few rudiments of a special law of real estate; conditions of land tenure in practice were often different from theory, varying according to place and time, and here the institution of wakf has become of great practical importance.[8]

Apart from property law and trusts, the inheritance law of Islam has its own features. While there are some similarities with the inheritance laws of modern Western legal systems, two important principles of Islamic inheritance law make the Islamic inheritance system different from other modern legal systems. These are that testators are limited to disposing of no more than one-third of his or her property in a will, and that the remainder of the estate is to be distributed to certain heirs in fixed shares in accordance with the Quran. Although individuals may dispose of their property as they wish during their lifetime, their estates will be divided according to the inheritance law of Islam after their death. Historically, this has led to the diffusion of capital in Muslim societies.

The legal nature of the Islamic trust (*waqf*) institution in Islamic law has distinct differences from the institution of 'trust' and real property law in common law countries. In particular, the principle of perpetuity and their charitable nature are important features of trusts in the Islamic legal system. The institution of *waqf*, which was established as an innovative institution from the early stages of development of Islamic law, has frozen in time and arguably has not significantly contributed to effective wealth management in Islamic societies in the past. It has also been argued that *waqf*, which locks wealth and resources into unproductive institutions, has contributed to the weakening of civil society in the Muslim world.[9] There is a reasonable amount of literature available on this topic in both English and Middle Eastern languages (Arabic, Persian and Turkish).

This chapter briefly reviews the historical background of the theories of property and inheritance in Islamic law, and considers basic principles of *waqf* under Islamic law. The chapter investigates property, inheritance and *waqf* as economic instruments developed in the history of the Middle

East, and examines the relationship between these institutions and the rule of law in Middle Eastern and Muslim countries' legal systems.

2. PROPERTY LAW IN ISLAM

Under Islamic law a distinct area or systematic field of land or property law does not exist. In jurisprudence texts as scholarly works on Islamic law there are very simple and concise references to property or land law. Ironically, while interests in land and property rights were well protected under Islamic law, before the recognition of individuals' property rights under common law, classical Muslim jurists have contributed minimally to the discussion on property law. Classical Islamic law, and jurisprudence texts, contain chapters and sections (known in Arabic as *kitab*) on proprietary interests, such as leases, partnerships, treasure troves, gifts, wills and taxes (*zakat*), but there is no specific chapter on land ownership.[10] In some classical texts, the issues relating to land law are discussed under the concept of reclaiming or reviving dead land (*ahya al-mawat*).[11] Also, Hanafi jurists cover the area of real property law under the area of *siyar*. The term *siyar* in Arabic literally means 'the conduct and method' and is taken as the conduct of government in its relations with non-Muslims, which is part of Islamic international relations. From the early stages of the expansion of Islam, most land was acquired through conquest by means of military expansion (*jihad*) or taxation imposed on lands of non-Muslims who opted to keep their religion and not convert to Islam. Therefore, land law became a part of *siyar*. Hanafi jurists classified both the lands taken by Muslims as spoils of war and the lands of those who chose to convert to Islam together as one category. The second category included the land of the owners who did not convert to Islam and paid a special tax (*kharaj*).[12]

While a distinct area of law in the area of property and land law has not developed in Islamic jurisprudence texts, legal principles in relation to personal property and land law are present in the sources of Islamic law, particularly the Quran and the Sunna. These legal principles have also developed sporadically in other areas of law, such as taxation law, commercial transactions law, inheritance law and the Islamic law of partnership (*shirka*).

A. Basic Concepts

In Islam there are a number of key terms used in the Quran, and in other Islamic law original texts, that well describe the concept of property and property rights. These include property (*mal*, which generally refers to a thing; the plural of *mal* is *amwal*); relationship with a thing (*milk*, a concept close to ownership); ownership (*malikiat*); and vacant land (*mewat*).

In this section the classifications of property (*mal*), ownership (*milk* or *malikiat*), other propriety rights, mortgage (*rahn*), real property (land law) and water law will be discussed.

i. Property (*mal*)

Unlike common law, Islamic law does not strictly make a distinction between tangible and intangible things. However, interests are divided into things (*aeini*) and claims or debt (*deini*). Equivalent concepts in common law legal systems for *aeini* interests and *deini* interests are proprietary interests and personal interests, respectively. It also seems that *aeini* rights are similar to rights *in rem* and *deini* rights are similar to rights *in personam*. According to Professor Nasser Katouzian, tangible things are called *mutlaq* interests and can be enforced against the world, but intangible things are *nisbi* and can only be enforced against a person.[13] However, Katouzian does not clearly explain whether this is the position of Islamic law or the interpretation of the *Iranian Civil Code* of 1928. The *Iranian Civil Code* is predominantly based on Islamic law but has also adopted principles of modern European civil codes. Islamic traditional law does consider debt to be a personal right, but it can be enforced against an individual's real property, in particular against the land that may be inherited by the individual's heirs.

ii. Ownership (*milk* or *malikiat*)

Milk concerns a relationship between a person and a thing. The relationship creates absolute, exclusive and permanent control over property. However, the absolute control is subject to certain restrictions. According to Muslim jurists, the absolute owner of any property (*mal*), particularly land, is God. However, individuals have absolute and exclusive rights to enjoy property.[14] There are two maxims applicable to ownership of property in Islam: the maxim of control (*taslit*) and that of no harm (*la-zavar*). According to the principle of *taslit*, individuals have exclusive control over and possession of their property. However, this maxim is limited by *la-zavar*, which states that the enjoyment of property shall not result in the harming of others. Private ownership can be acquired through a number of legitimate means under Islamic law. These are through physical work and production, farming, trade and commerce, inheritance and by gift.

Under Islamic law, in certain circumstances, people may acquire ownership of land by working on the land.[15] Traditionally, individuals were able to claim vacant land by the means of *tahjir*, which means making a fence around the land and is similar to the Western concept of squatting. Also, people could acquire the land through developing and utilizing vacant land.[16]

Ownership of property rights can also be obtained through contract and other commercial transactions. As seen in Chapter 7, Islam generally encourages trade and forbids usury.[17] Similar to the Western tradition, land in Islam is not spiritual and is a commercial commodity.

Land and other properties are transferred through inheritance and bequest in Islam. Gifts of land and other properties are subject to specific regulation in Islamic law, known as *hibah*.

iii. Private and public land

While individual ownership of property and land is well recognized in Islam, public ownership of property and land is also recognized. Traditionally, and in the Quran, public ownership of land is known as *anfal*. This includes property and lands obtained through conquest of non-Muslim land and property, unoccupied land within the territory of a Muslim state, and mining and water resources found on public land. In modern times, Muslim states, such as Iran, Saudi Arabia and Malaysia, have claimed state ownership of forests, rivers, land not owned by individuals and mineral resources, notably natural gas and petroleum. According to the constitution of Iran, *anfal* and public properties such as dead land, abandoned land, minerals, the sea, lakes, rivers, mountains, jungles, pastoral land and unclaimed estates must be controlled by the Islamic state.[18]

B. The Doctrine of Tenure

The doctrine of tenure underpins the modern land laws of England, Australia and other common law countries. This doctrine is linked to the historical social and economic system of feudalism. Although there is disagreement among historians about the origin of feudalism in England, according to the predominant view, the feudal system of land ownership dated from the Norman Conquest of England in 1066.[19]

The Islamic system of land ownership is similar to the doctrine of tenure in two ways. First, under Islam the real owner of land is Allah and individuals own the land on God's behalf. According to the Quran, the sole owner of the land and whatever is under the land, and is over the land, is Allah.[20] However, Allah has made humans as stewards (*kholafa*) and trustees to inherit the earth.[21] In practice this means that individuals can own private property in the same way as in a capitalist system. The absolute ownership of land by God does not give the Islamic state the equivalent right to ownership that the Crown has under common law doctrine of tenure. Second, apart from the land that an individual may own (such as residential and farming lands), a significant part of land, whether gained by conquest or vacant and dead land, is the property of the Imam or the Islamic state. This was particularly articulated in the work of the eighth-century Muslim jurist Abu Yusof in his book *Kharaj* (Tribute). However, this type of land, when granted to individuals, provides unconditional ownership to land owners, subject to the absolute ownership of God.

C. The Theory and Principles of Islamic Property Law

Generally, ownership and the concepts and values of land in Islamic property law are similar to Western concepts of property and land ownership. Unlike the communal and spiritual concepts of property in certain indigenous, animistic or chthonic societies, such as some of the concepts of Australian Indigenous peoples, Islamic law accepts individual ownership of land and confirms the commercial value of land, similar to the common law and civil law systems. The notion of absolute ownership of land by God, and the role of the Islamic state in distrusting land conquered from nonMuslims, resembles the doctrine of tenure in common law. Although property law is not a well-developed area of Islamic law, its fundamental principles do not create any potential obstacles to the establishment of modern and progressive systems of land and property ownership. This means that individuals can own property without limitations. The private ownership of property, particularly land, is well developed in Islamic law. The public ownership of certain properties, such as vacant lands, forests and minerals, is also accepted.

It seems that individuals who own property, whether personal property or land, must protect the property, as long as they do not damage the property of others. The principle of control (*taslit*) sets out that owners of real and personal property can have the absolute rights to control and use the property. However, according to the principle of no harm (*la-tharar*), individuals should not cause damage or harm to others when using their property. The *la-tharar* principle imposes a limit on how a person may control or use property. These two basic principles of Islamic law relating to ownership of private property are to some extent similar to certain common law principles of torts law, such as trespass and damages. As with common law and civil law systems, Islamic law recognizes public and statutory duties that may limit the use of property. For example, wasting properties (*israf*) is considered a sin under Islam, but unlike other legal systems, Islamic law does not provide general legal sanctions for *israf*, which it applies only to private property. However, if wasting of the property is adverse to the public's interests, then such wasting may be subject to legal sanctions. For example, wasting water may be sanctioned by law, which could be a limitation on an individual's property rights. In the course of interpreting certain Quranic verses relating to property, one commentator stated that the public's interests must be observed when controlling and using private property.[22]

3. INHERITANCE LAW

The law of inheritance in Islam is one of the most important areas of Islamic law, both in theory and in practice. Historically, the inheritance law of Islam revolutionized the inheritance system of Arabia, despite many elements of pre-Islamic Arabian customs being retained. The Islamic inheritance system is therefore based on some Arabian traditional customs, as well as the Quranic reforms and sayings and practices of the Prophet of Islam. Unlike some other areas of Islamic law that are not practised in many modern Muslim countries' legal systems, the Islamic law of inheritance is part of almost all Muslim countries. As a result, the system is well developed and comprehensive. The broad and inclusive nature of Islamic inheritance law led Sir William Jones to state: 'I am strongly disposed to believe, that no possible question could occur on the *Mohammedan* law of succession, which may not be rapidly and correctly answered'.[23]

A. Pre-Islamic Arabian Custom of Inheritance

Under the Arab customary law of the pre-Islam era, inheritance was based on blood relationship only, and hence there were no inheritance rights for people related through marriage. Females were generally excluded from inheritance, and in some instances they would actually be considered part of the estate to be inherited.[24] The entire estate of the deceased was inherited by the nearest adult male, which included adopted sons. Also, mutual inheritance between two men was possible through a contract of alliance.

As it can be seen in the following section, Islam did not entirely abolish the Arab customary law of inheritance, but made significant reforms, including prohibiting women from becoming part of the estate, providing inheritance rights for daughters and spouses, including wives and abrogating inheritance through adoption.[25] Notably, the Quran itself laid down a number of principles of inheritance.

B. The Quranic Principles of Inheritance

Although the inheritance law of Islam is relatively well developed in Islamic jurisprudence, some of its basic principles are laid down in the Quran. First, the Quran provided inheritance for women. According to Súra Nisáa 4:7 '[f]rom what is left by parents and those nearest related there is a share for men and a share for women, whether the property be small or large, – a determinate share'.[26] Further, the Quran lays down certain principles of inheritance law as follows:

> God (thus) directs you as regards your children's (inheritance): to the male, a portion equal to that of two females; if only daughters, two or more, their share is two thirds of the inheritance; if only one, her share is a half. For parents, a sixth of share of the inheritance to each, if the deceased left children; if no children, and the parents are the (only) heirs, the mother has a third; if the deceased left brothers (or sisters), the mother has a sixth. (The distribution in all cases is) after the payment of legacies or debts. Ye know not whether your parents or your children are nearest to you in benefit. These are settled portions ordained by God; and God is All-Knowing, All-Wise.[27]
>
> In what your wives leave, your share is a half, if they leave no child; but if they leave a child, ye get a fourth; after payment of legacies and debts. In what you leave, their share is a fourth, if ye leave no child; but if ye leave a child, they get an eighth; after payment of legacies and debts. If the man or woman whose inheritance is in question, has left neither ascendants nor descendants, but has left a brother or a sister, each one of the two gets a sixth; but if more than two, they [share] in a third; after payment of legacies and debts; so that no loss is caused (to anyone). Thus it is ordained by God; and God is All-Knowing, Most Forbearing.[28]

The Quranic principles of inheritance have been interpreted differently by the Sunni and Shia schools of law. While the two schools are very similar in most other areas of Islamic jurisprudence and law, there are some notable differences between the Shia and Sunni laws of inheritance. The differences are well articulated by Muslim jurists as follows:

> I. The Hanafis allow the frame-work or principles of the pre-Islamic customs to stand: they develop or alter those rules in the specific manner mentioned in the Quran, and by the Prophet.

> II. The Shias deduce certain principles, which they hold to under-lie the amendments expressed in the Quran, and fuse the principles so deduced with the principles underlying the pre-existing customary law, and thus raise up a completely altered set of principles and rules derived from them.[29]

The major difference between the two schools is that the Sunni schools of law make a distinction between agnates (relatives related through a male) and cognates (relatives related through a female), whereas Shia schools do not make such a distinction.[30]

C. Basic Principles

The basic principles of Islamic law of inheritance are the classification of heirs and the specific rules for distribution and exclusion. Since there are significant differences between Sunni and Shia schools of law, the principles of inheritance law of each school will be discussed separately here.

i. The Sunni law of inheritance

Inheritance law in most Sunni jurisprudence texts is discussed under a section called 'bequests and shares' (*wasaya wa fraeidh*). A Muslim may only make a bequest of one-third of their property. The remainder must be distributed after the death of the person according to the inheritance law of Islam. This principle is also a rule of the Shia law of inheritance. The principle is based on the Sunna.[31]

The classes of heirs under the Sunni law of inheritance are sharers (*fraeidh*), residuals (*asabah*) and distant kindred. The sharers are entitled to a fixed share of the estate and mainly include those individuals who were excluded from inheritance by pre-Islamic Arab custom. They include daughters, wives, full sisters, sons' daughters, husbands, fathers, mothers, true grandparents (an ancestor in the male line) and half brothers. Notably, sons are omitted from the list of sharers, probably because they were made heirs under pre-Islamic Arab tradition. They are, however, part of the second class of heirs, which are residuals. While the first class only get their specific share of the estate, the second class, residuals, may get the whole estate if there are no living beneficiaries of the first class. The residuals, who inherit the remainder of the estate after the shares in the first class have been distributed, are separated into three categories. They are the 'residuals in their own right' (*asabah bi al-Nafs*), which includes all agnate male relatives of the deceased person: the son and his sons; the father, his father and any other sons of his; full brothers; and descendants of his father's father, such as parental uncles, great uncles and their sons. The second category is 'residuals through another' (*asabah bi al-Gahyr*), which includes a daughter with a son, the son's daughter, a full sister if there is also a full brother, and a half-sister from the father's side if there is also a half-brother. The third category is 'residuals with another' (*asabah ma'a al-Gahyr*), and this category includes only two classes of people: full and half-sisters (from the father's side only) who do not have a male agnate, but become residuals with the daughters of the son or the sons of daughters. Distant kindred, the third class of heirs, are only entitled to inherit if there are no surviving members of the first two classes. They include females and males that are related to the deceased person through a female link known as 'relatives by ritual of the womb' (*ulul-Alarham*). This class itself is divided into four categories of people in order of the priority: (1) descendant of the deceased through a female link (daughter's children and children of son's daughters); (2) ascendants of the deceased through a female link (mothers, fathers); (3) descendants of the deceased's parents who are neither sharers or residuals; and (4) descendants of the deceased's immediate grandparents.

ii. The Shia law of inheritance

Shia inheritance law is much simpler than that Sunni inheritance law. Generally, under Shia law, heirs inherit for two reasons, which are 'blood relationship' (*nasab*) and marriage relationship (*sabab*). People who inherit because of *nasab* are classified into three categories: (1) parents, children and grandchildren; (2) grandparents and siblings and their children; and (3) uncles and aunts and their children. People in the second and third categories will only inherit if there are no living members of a higher category. Wives and husbands that inherit through *sabab* will receive their share along with any blood relatives. However, the amount of their share could be different depending on who the surviving blood relatives are. In any case, a husband will always inherit a half or quarter share, and a wife a quarter or eighth share.

D. Inheritance Law of Modern Muslim Countries

The Sunni law of inheritance applies in most Muslim countries, including Egypt, Jordan, Iraq, Saudi Arabia, Indonesia and Malaysia. The Shia law of inheritance is applied in Iran, and for Shia Muslims in countries such as Lebanon, India and Pakistan.

In Egypt, the Islamic inheritance law is based on the Hanafi school of law, which is the dominant system of Sunni inheritance law.[32] Egypt has passed a number of pieces of legislation that provide rules relating to succession, including those relating to inheritance law, the law of wills and the law of obligatory bequests.[33]

4. ISLAMIC TRUSTS (*WAQF*)

A. Historical Background of *Waqf* in Islam, Compared with Trust in the Common Law System

i. Development of the trust in the common law system

The trust, which comprises the major part of the equity system, is an important area of common law legal systems. According to Frederic Maitland, 'the greatest and the most distinctive achievement performed by Englishmen in the field of jurisprudence … [is] the development from century to century of the trust idea'.[34] The origin of trust in the common law system goes back to medieval England.[35]

After the Normans conquered England in 1066, most of the land in England became the property of the king. In order to effectively administer the land, the king granted land to noblemen in exchange for the rendering of military services. These noblemen, in turn, granted smaller parcels of land to other noblemen. These grants of land formed the basis of the feudal system of land ownership in England.[36] By 1086 and the compiling of the Domesday Book, the feudal system was well established in England, and the land surveyed in the Domesday Book was held by the king (one-fifth), the Church (one-quarter), and by the king's followers (one-half).[37] The king's followers, numbering about 1500, known as 'tenants in chief', provided services to the king.[38] However, the king remained the paramount landlord. The granting of land on behalf of the king was the basis of all landholding in England. This doctrine of absolute land-holding by the king, and granting to tenants in chief in return for military and other services, is known as the doctrine of tenure,[39] which became the basis of land law in English common law.[40]

Over time, an intricate set of hierarchical relationships grew up through the tenurial system, with the king at the top and various groups of landholders possessing rights to parcels of land. By the thirteenth century the complexity of the system resulted in the feudal system becoming both unwieldy and open to numerous claims to the same parcel of land.[41]

By the end of the thirteenth century, the common law system, originating from the Norman Conquest of England in 1066, became bound by a rigid formalism in which remedies could only be obtained through existing forms of writs, and further, there were only a limited numbers of writs in land law.[42] In addition, the alienation of land by ordinary tenants was limited by the claims of the feudal overlord and the tenant's own heirs (whether *inter vivos* or by will).[43]

Landowners turned to a new innovative legal institution in order to avoid those obstacles in managing their land interests. The institution known as the 'use' is the basis of trust law and the equity system in common law systems. A trust exists in the case when the owner of a legal interest, for example, a landowner, transfers the legal title to another person, to be used for the benefit of other person or persons, or for some other purpose.[44] In other words, through a trust, equitable obligations will be created to deal with property in a particular way.[45] Indeed, by the creation of a trust, the legal title (in law), the equitable title (in equity) and the beneficial title are separated into three elements, which are the trustee (title holder), trust property and the beneficiary or object of the trust. Initially, the courts of common law in England did not recognize the 'use' (*feoffees to uses*),[46] but the practice was widespread and impacted on royal revenues to the extent that Henry VIII, in 1530, enacted legislation to abolish uses.[47] However, land owners and lawyers developed the device of a 'use upon a use', which was accepted by 1635,[48] by which people created an extra 'use' to bypass the Statute of Uses. Following the passing of the Statute of Uses, and under pressure from the landholders, in 1540, the *Statute of Wills* (32 Hen VIII c 1) was passed, in which a statutory right was created to enable landholders to make conditional testamentary gifts of land.[49] In addition, in 1645, the feudal tenure was abolished and the modern trust emerged.[50] In common law countries, the law of trusts has been consistently amended and has acted to counter state intervention in wealth transmission and management by eliminating or reducing taxes, and limiting the government's regulation of individuals' wealth and property.[51] According to Austin W. Scott:

> It was chiefly by means of uses and trusts that the feudal system was undermined in England, that the law of conveyancing was revolutionized, that the economic position of married women was ameliorated, that family settlements have been effected, whereby daughters and younger sons of landed proprietors have been enabled modestly to participate in the family wealth, that unincorporated associations have found a measure of protection, that business enterprises of many kinds have been enabled to accomplish their purposes, that great sums of money have been devoted to charitable enterprises; and by employing the analogy of a trust, by the invention of the so-called constructive trust, the courts have been enabled to give relief against

> all sorts of fraudulent schemes whereby scoundrels have sought to enrich themselves at the expense of other persons.[52]

Therefore, in contemporary common law systems, the trust acts as an important economic institution for the management of property, particularly for future purposes, as well as a legal mechanism in equity to provide a cushion against instances of rigidness in common law principles. Indeed, the success and effectiveness of common law systems in the contemporary world can, to a great extent, be attributed to the development of a flexible equitable system within the English common law system. Furthermore, most of the principles of equity have been developed through trust law. Therefore, the trust is both an important economic institution that enhances flexible economic activities and a legal mechanism that provides for more effective justice.

ii. Historical background of *waqf* in Islam

Under Islamic law, *waqf* (plural *awqaf*) is an Islamic law institution that originated in the sayings of the Prophet Mohammad (the Sunna), which has had an important impact on the social and economic life of Muslim societies for centuries. According to Islamic jurisprudence texts, *waqf* did not exist in pre-Islamic Arabia (*jahiliya*, before 610 CE) and was inferred by the Prophet Mohammad.[53] In early sayings of the Prophet (hadiths), what is now known as *waqf* is referred to as ‘continuous charity’ (*sadaqato jariyeh*).[54] During the time of the Prophet, properties such as mosques, water bores, land and horses were made *waqf* for charitable purposes.[55] According to Islamic jurisprudence texts, and leading hadith scholars,[56] real property was the first incident of *waqf* in Islam, made by the second caliph on the order of the Prophet.[57]

B. Basic Principles of *Waqf* in Islam

The *waqf* institution has a great potential to contribute to the reconstruction of the social, economic and legal affairs of Muslim societies in the future. *Waqf* is an Arabic word and literally means ‘detention’ (*habs*) and in Islamic Sharia law means ‘keeping the property (surrendering the title) for separate use for a particular purpose’.[58] *Waqf* under Islamic law is classified in two categories, which are *waqf* for children and the family (*waqf al-ahli*), and charitable *waqf* (*waqf al-khayri*).[59]

According to the Shafei school of jurisprudence, when a property is made *waqf*, the ownership of the property is transferred to God, and hence there is no legal title for the endower or the beneficiary (*mawqouf alayh*).[60] However, according to the Maliki and Hanbali schools of jurisprudence, by endowing a property as *waqf*, the endower transfers the ownership to the beneficiary.[61] According to the Hanafi school, the *waqf* property may be sold.[62]

The land subject to *waqf* is not alienable, not to be gifted, not to be inherited, and its benefits should be used for poor people, relatives of the endower, slaves, itinerant travellers and guests.[63] The trustee (*mutawali*) may eat (be paid) from the benefit and may use the benefit to feed the needy (but not the wealthy).[64]

Both real property and chattels, including animals, can be the subject of *waqf*, except in the Hanafi school, in which animals cannot be included.[65] *Waqf* for non-Muslims who are people of the Book (Christians and Jews) is allowed.[66] Saphia, one of the Prophet's wives, made certain properties *waqf* for her brother, who was Jewish.[67] According to some scholars, and according to the Hanafi school, a person may make *waqf* for himself or herself, and for their children and grandchildren.[68]

According to some, a person may not make their property *waqf* if it is intended to harm their heirs.[69] However, this proposition may make most *waqf* incidents impossible according to Sharia, given that most *waqf*s may potentially harm the interests of the endower's heirs.

C. Development of *Waqf* Institution as an Economic Instrument in the Middle East

Waqf law was not developed until the second century of Islam, when Islamic schools of law took shape. Given that there is no provision in the Quran on the nature of *waqf*, and it was not commonly practised during the time of the Prophet Mohammad and the Righteous Caliphs, there was much uncertainty about the law of *waqf*, and different legal principles developed according to the various schools of law.

Generally, *waqf* originated as a charitable institution in Islam. Later, during the Umayyad and Abbasid dynasties, when new territories, particularly from the Roman Empire, were conquered by Muslims, they encountered the considerable pre-existing endowments for churches, orphanages, monasteries and poorhouses in the conquered lands.[70] Inspired by charitable impulses and by the endowments they had observed, Muslims extended the *waqf* institution to a wide variety of property.[71]

During the Ottoman Empire (1299–1923) and the Safavid Persian Empire (1501–1726), the institution of *waqf* became an important part of the economic system of those two Islamic empires. In 1826, through certain law reform initiatives in the Ottoman Empire, the *waqf* properties and administration were placed under the control of an Imperial ministry, and the income from major *waqf* properties was seized by the state.[72] As a result, the Empire brought under its control major private investments and properties, including the public water supply (largely constituted as *waqf*). It is estimated that more than half of the real property in the Ottoman Empire, which included most of the current Middle Eastern countries, was under *waqf* endowment.[73] Similarly, another major Muslim empire, Iran, under the Qajar dynasty (1779–1924), created a Ministry for *waqf* in 1854, which is still a current government department, but under the authority of the Supreme Leader.

The growth of *waqf* in the Muslim world can be attributed to a number of factors. First, the strong religious and charitable impulses of many in the Muslim world have led people to make at least part of their property *waqf*. As was mentioned above, *waqf* originally was named by the Prophet as 'continuous charity' (*sadaqato al-jariyeh*). There is also extensive literature, including Quranic verses and the hadith, recommending Muslims to spend money and property in the way of Allah (*fi sabil Allah*). Indeed, the *waqf* system acted in a similar way to the social security system in a modern state like Australia, and Muslims contributed to the charitable system by making their properties *waqf*. Second, *waqf* was a means of safeguarding property against the risk of expropriation by the state or other powerful individuals and nobles, who were able to confiscate weaker parties' property, as all groups would respect *waqf* property. The endower of *waqf* property was still able to control and maintain the property by making themselves and their heirs the trustee (*mutawali*). The only power that an endower of *waqf* property would forfeit would be the right of alienation of the property. Third, *waqf* has been used as a method to evade taxation. Finally, major landholders have occasionally made part of their properties *waqf* to avoid the claims of other potential interest holders to the property.[74]

D. *Waqf* and the Rule of Law

Today there is intense debate among Muslim and non-Muslim legal scholars and economists about the role and performance of *waqf* in Muslim societies. Although *waqf* as a social institution has significantly contributed to the social welfare of Muslim communities for centuries,[75] some argue that the institution has locked considerable properties and investments into an unprofitable system.[76]

Establishing societies based on a 'rule of law' system, where the 'law' is supreme and protects people against the arbitrary power of the state and individuals,[77] is a tradition of Western legal systems, but is also cherished in other parts of the world, including in Muslim countries. In most Muslim countries an effective 'rule of law'[78] system to protect both individuals and the community against the powerful state is, as yet, unavailable.

Many reasons, historical, cultural, religious, political and economic, are cited for the lack of a 'rule of law' system in the Muslim world. Colonialism, a lack of water resources and the discovery of huge oil reserves in the early nineteenth century are also factors contributing to the failure of civil society and the rule of law.

Waqf is an economic institution, so by linking its operation to civil society, the role of the economy and the establishment of a 'rule of law' system are emphasized. There is no doubt that the economy and its institutions play an important role in the social, political and legal affairs of every society. Historically, feudalism in Europe, land and water ownership, the establishment of corporations, the revival of commerce and banking and agricultural productivity made states weaker and corporations stronger. The equivalent to corporations and social association in the Muslim world, particularly in the Middle East, was tribalism. While tribe structure played an important role in the power structure of Islamic empires such as the Ottoman, Mughul and Safavid empires, the system was more family and socially based than economically oriented. However, in the West the feudal system was replaced by a capitalist system by the sixteenth century, in which big corporations and individual workers and farmers were able to influence weak Western states.

i. *Waqf* as a factor in the lack of the rule of law in the Muslim world

According to some scholars, the institution of *waqf* played an important role in the economic underdevelopment of the Middle East and is therefore an important factor for the lack of rule of law in the Middle East and Islamic world. In the view of these scholars, economy and economic institutions are the main reason behind the establishment of cultural and legal systems in Muslim societies. In addition to the *waqf* institution, Islamic contract law and Islamic inheritance law are cited as important factors in the underdevelopment of Islamic economic systems and the lack of an effective rule of law-based legal system.[79]

Historically, as discussed, *awqaf* played important roles in the social and economic order of Islamic states, particularly in the Ottoman Empire (1299–1923), Mughal Empire (1526–1825) and Safavid Persian Empire (1501–1726). Generally, *awqaf* properties were charitable institutions in the agricultural economies, holding thousands of farms, villages and urban lands.[80] The *waqf* institutions are described as 'redistributive institutions and poor relief agents'.[81] They were not designed as special ventures for profit maximization, or for establishing large corporation-style institutions.[82]

According to Timur Kuran, *waqf*, as an unincorporated trust established under Islamic law, had an important contributory role to the shortcomings of economic development in the Middle East.[83] *Waqf* had to be fixed in perpetuity in order to establish a balanced arrangement between the Islamic state and the founder of the *waqf*, which made the *waqf* properties unproductive and inflexible.[84] As a result, modern institutions such as modern schools, corporations and universities, were developed outside of *waqf*.[85] While in the nineteenth century, corporations with freedom of association and organizational autonomy were developed in the West, *waqf* institutions in the Muslim world, although providing a kind of associational freedom, restricted self-governance and the evolution of big corporations with significant economic power to balance the power of the state.[86]

In addition, *waqf* in Islamic societies did not remain as private institutions, struggling for autonomy and recognition by the state. Rather, Islamic states, by establishing *awqaf* state-controlled institutions, co-opted *waqf* for their own purposes. For example, in Iran, the *awqaf* organization (*sazman awqaf*), which is a department of the Ministry of Culture and Islamic Guidance, manages most *waqf* properties that do not have a specific trustee (*mutawali*).[87] Similarly, in many other Muslim countries, government departments have taken over the administration of *awqaf* properties.[88]

ii. *Waqf* as a social institution and a welfare mechanism

Both in historical terms and in contemporary Muslim societies, *waqf* has acted as a social institution. It has been a mechanism for the elimination of poverty, supporting families, low socio-economic groups and professions. Historically, Islamic states and caliphates did not have special departments to support low socio-economic groups or to provide for public works, such as roads, bridges, mosques, inns and hospitals.[89] One important function of the Islamic *waqf* was to support social units and to provide for public institutions, such as schools and mosques. For example, the health, education and welfare systems of the Ottoman Empire were financed to a great extent by *waqf*.[90]

It is also argued that *waqf* and the administration of *waqf* properties has an important role in the alleviation of poverty in Muslim societies.[91] *Waqf* in Muslim states provides educational institutions, including universities, colleges and schools; orphanages; mosques, which provide religious and cultural activity centres; charitable clinics; and shopping complexes and commercial centres where the income is used for social and charitable purposes.[92]

In the contemporary world, it is argued that the existing *waqf* institutions could be better managed and used in establishing an effective welfare system, assisting in resource mobilization and redistribution, and strengthening civil society.[93]

5. CONCLUSIONS

The principles of property law in Islam are similar to the principles of other modern legal systems, such as the civil law and common law systems. Unlike the common law legal system in which property law is very well developed and underlies many aspects of society, such as wealth management, family provision and human rights, Islamic property law is in its early stages of development, despite having the potential to develop similar principles.

The inheritance law of Islam is relatively comprehensive. Unlike other aspects of Islamic property law, such as property ownership, mortgages and easements, which are not of such significant practical importance, the law of inheritance in Islam is well developed and applicable in the legal system of most modern Muslim countries. The scheme of mandatory fixed shares is the main feature of Islamic inheritance law. Although individuals can distribute and alienate their property without any limitation during their lifetime, they only can distribute one-third of their estate through bequest. In practice, this principle makes it difficult for individuals to manage and distribute their estate in a way different to the way set out in Islamic inheritance law. The institution of inheritance in Islam therefore has its own distributive justice.

The institutions of trust in common law systems and *waqf* in Islamic law systems, which have certain similarities and differences, are important legal and economic mechanisms. In common law systems, trust, as the major part of the equity system, has been a very effective economic and legal instrument in facilitating economic activity, as well as making rigid legal systems more flexible and just. Under Islamic law, *waqf* has acted as more of a social welfare mechanism and arguably has not contributed to the development of large economic institutions and corporations. The lack of major economic associations may be cited as one reason for the lack of 'rule of law' systems in many Middle Eastern countries. While *waqf* is cited as a reason for the failure of Islamic economic systems to develop major corporations, it may still be managed in such a way as to enhance support for social institutions and civil society organizations.

NOTES

1. S.F.C. Milsom, *Historical Foundations of the Common Law* (Butterworths, London, 1969), 88.
2. William Blackstone, *Commentaries on the Law of England*, Vol. 2 (Clarendon Press, Oxford, first published 1766), 2.
3. Jeremy Bentham, *Theory of Legislation* (Routledge & Kegal Paul, London, 1931, first published 1802), 113.
4. Kevin Gray and Susan Gray, *The Idea of Property in Land* (Oxford University Press, Oxford, 1998), 15.
5. *Yanner v Eaton* (1999) 201 CLR 351 at [17].
6. See Timothy Besley, 'Property Rights and Investment Intensives: Theory and Evidence from Ghana' (1995) 103 *Journal of Political Economy* 903.
7. Kazem Alamdari, *Chera Iran Aghab mand wa Gharb Pish Raft* [Why Iran Lagged Behind and the West Moved Forward], 6th edn (2001). The author argues that the main reason for the lack of development in Iran is that the feudalism system of land ownership did not occur in Iran: at 176.
8. Joseph Schacht, *An Introduction to Islamic Law* (Oxford, Clarendon Press, 1965), 142.
9. Timur Kuran, 'The Provision of Public Goods under Islamic Law: Origins, Impact, and Limitations of the Waqf System' (2001) 35(4) *Law & Society Review* 841, 844.
10. See for example, Ibn Rushd al-Qurtbi and Muhammad ibn Ahmaed (known in English as Averroes), *Bidayato al-Mujtahid wa Nihayato al-Muqtasid* [The Distinguished Jurist's Primer, written in the twelfth century] (Garnet, Reading, 1988).
11. An example is Muhaqiq Helli, Abolqasim Najm al-din Jafar ibn Muhammad ibn al-Hassan, *Sharaye al-Islam* [Laws of Islam], written in the thirteenth century (Dar al-Awa, Beirut, 1983).
12. See generally Abu Yusuf, *Kitab al-kharj* [Taxation in Islam] (Luzac, London, 1969).
13. Nasse Katouzian, *Hoqouq Madaini, Amwal wa Malikiat* [Civil Law: Property and Ownership], 11th edn (Nahher Mizan, Tehran, 2006), 18.
14. Abi al-Faraj and Abdu al-Rahman bin Rajab, *al-Qavaid Fi al-Fiqh al-Islam* [Basis of Islamic Jurisprudence] (Dar al-Kotob al-Elmiah, Beirut, n.d.), 188.
15. The Quran, Súra Tauba 9:105; Abdullah Yusuf Ali, *The Qur'an: Text, Translation and Commentary* (Tahrike Tarsile Qur'an, New York, 2005), 472.
16. Abdel Hameed M. Bashir, 'Property Rights, Institutions and Economic Development: An Islamic Perspective' (2002) 18 *Humanomics* 75, 78.
17. The Quran, Súra Baqarah 2:275; Abdullah Yusuf Ali, *The Qur'an: Text, Translation and Commentary* (Tahrike Tarsile Qur'an, New York, 2005), 111–12.
18. The Constitution of the Islamic Republic of Iran 1980, amendments 1990, Article 45.
19. See C. Warren Hollister, *The Impact of the Norman Conquest* (Krieger, Melbourne, 1982) and Allen Brown, *Origins of English Feudalism* (Allen & Unwin, London, 1973).
20. The Quran, Súra Tá Há 20:6; Abdullah Yusuf Ali, *The Qur'an: Text, Translation and Commentary* (Tahrike Tarsile Qur'an, New York, 2005), 790.
21. The Quran, Súra An'ám 6:165: Abdullah Yusuf Ali, *The Qur'an: Text, Translation and Commentary* (Tahrike Tarsile Qur'an, New York, 2005), 338.

22. Mohammad Hossein Tabatabei, *Al-Mizan fi tafsir al-Quran* [The Balance Interpretation of the Quran], Vol. 4 (Institute of Al-Alamin, Beirut, 1972), 171.
23. Siraj al-Din Muḥammad ibn Muḥammad Sajawandi, 'Al Sirajiyyah' [The Mohammedan Law of Inheritance] (Joseph Cooper, Calcutta, 1792), vii.
24. According to the Quran, this custom was forbidden: The Quran, Súra Nisáa 4:19; Abdullah Yusuf Ali, *The Qur'an: Text, Translation and Commentary* (Tahrike Tarsile Qur'an, New York, 2005), 184–5.
25. Under Islamic law, the adoption of children was abrogated, although in the modern world the practice is recognized as a form of guardianship (*hadhanah*).
26. Abdullah Yusuf Ali, *The Qur'an: Text, Translation and Commentary* (Tahrike Tarsile Qur'an, New York, 2005), 180.
27. Súra Nisáa 4:11: Abdullah Yusuf Ali, *The Qur'an: Text, Translation and Commentary* (Tahrike Tarsile Qur'an, New York, 2005), 181–2.
28. Súra Nisáa 4:12; Abdullah Yusuf Ali, *The Qur'an: Text, Translation and Commentary* (Tahrike Tarsile Qur'an, New York, 2005), 182.
29. Faiz Badruddin, *Muhammadan Law – The Personal Law of Muslims*, 3rd edn (N.M. Tripathi & Co., Bombay, 1940), 85–6.
30. For a discussion of the historical background of differences between Shia and Sunni laws of inheritance, see Asaf Asaf A.A. Fyzee, *Outlines of Muhammadan Law*, 5th edn, Tahir Mahmood (ed.) (Oxford University Press, New York, 2008, first published 1949), Chapters 13–14; Jamal J. Ahmad Nasir, *The Islamic Law of Personal Status*, 3rd edn (Brill, Leiden, 2009), 199–234.
31. Sheikh Sayyed Sahbeq, *Fiqh al-Sunna* [Sunni Jurisprudence], Vol. 3, 2nd edn (Dar al-Fiker, Beirut, 1998), 299.
32. In modern terms, the law of inheritance was enacted by the Act No. 77-1943.
33. Ian Edge, 'Sunni and Shia Law compared to the laws of Egypt and Iran' (2009) 15 *Trusts and Trustees* 821.
34. Frederic William Maitland, 'The Unincorporate Body' in H.A.L. Fisher (ed.), *The Collected Papers of Frederic William Maitland*, Vol. 3 (Cambridge University Press, Cambridge, 1911), 271, 272.
35. William Fratcher, 'Uses of Uses' (1969) 34 *Missouri Law Review* 39.
36. The origins of feudalism in Europe can be traced to well before 1066, to the collapse of the Roman Empire: Theodore Plunkett, *A Concise History of the Common Law*, 5th edn (Butterworths, London, 2010), 509–15. See also Reginald A. Brown, *Origins of English Feudalism* (Allen & Unwin, London, 1973), 29.
37. Reginald Lennard, *Rural England 1086–1135* (Clarendon Press, Oxford, 1959), 25–6.
38. Peter Butt, *Land Law*, 5th edn (Lawbook Co., Sydney, 2006), 67.
39. Eric John, *Land Tenure in Early England: A Discussion of Some Problems* (Leicester University Press, Leicester, 1960), Chapters 1–3.
40. Peter Butt, *Land Law*, 5th edn (Lawbook Co., Sydney, 2006), 73.
41. Brendon Edgeworth et al., *Sackville and Neave Australian Property Law*, 8th edn (LexisNexis Butterworths, Chatswood, New South Wales, 2008), 196–8.
42. Theodore Plunkett, *A Concise History of the Common Law*, 5th edn (Butterworths, London, 2010), 675; Patrick Parkinson, *Tradition and Change in Australian Law*, 4th edn (Lawbook Co. and Thomson Reuters Professional Australia, Pyrmont, New South Wales, 2010), 74; and Peter Butt, *Land Law*, 5th edn (Lawbook Co., Sydney, 2006), 96.
43. A Simpson, *A History of Land Law* (Clarendon Press, Oxford, 1984), 53–4.
44. Michael Evans, *Equity and Trusts*, 3rd edn (LexisNexis Butterworths, Chatswood, New South Wales, 2012), 389.
45. *Re Williams* [1897] 2 Chapter 12 at 18, as cited by Isaacs J in *Glenn v Federal Commissioner of Land Tax* (1915) 20 CLR 490, 503.

46. Originally, trusts were developed when the landholders (the *feoffors*) conveyed their lands to certain trusted agents (the *feoffees to uses*). The latter were obliged to hold land for the benefit of (*to the use of*) those designated by the landholders (the *feoffors*). In practice, the landholders (*feoffors*) would instruct the *feoffees* to hold the land for the benefit of themselves for life, and to those nominated by them by deed or will after their death. This would give greater power to landholders to manage their real property during their life and after. Further, they could avoid certain legal implications by creating the 'uses'. For a good overview of the development of uses, see R.H. Helmholz, 'The Early Enforcement of Uses' (1979) 79(8) *Columbia Law Review* 1503.
47. The *Statute of Uses 1535* (27 Hen VIII c 10).
48. *Sambach v Daston* (1635) 21 ER 165.
49. Michael Evans, *Equity and Trusts*, 3rd edn (LexisNexis Butterworths, Chatswood, New South Wales, 2012), 7.
50. Ibid.
51. Jeffrey Schoenblum, 'The Role of Legal Doctrine in the Decline of the Islamic *Waqf*: A Comparison with the Trust' (1999) 32 *Vanderbilt Journal of Transnational Law* 1191, 1203.
52. Austin W. Scott, 'The Trust as an Instrument of Law Reform' (1922) 31(5) *Yale Law Journal* 457.
53. Sheikh Sayyed Sahbeq, *Fiqh al-Sunna* [Sunni Jurisprudence], Vol. 3, 2nd edn (Dar al-Fiker, Beirut, 1998), 268.
54. It is narrated from the Prophet Mohammad (by Moslem, Abu Daoud, Al-Termadhi and Al-Nisai) that 'When a person dies, they are survived by three things: *sadaqato jariyeh* [continuous charity], knowledge that benefits society, and their children of good character'. It has been said that *sadaqato jariyeh* means *al-waqf*. See Sheikh Sayyed Sahbeq, Fiqh al-Sunna [Sunni Jurisprudence], Vol. 3, 2nd edn (Dar al-Fiker, Beirut, 1998), 268.
55. Sheikh Sayyed Sahbeq, *Fiqh al-Sunna* [Sunni Jurisprudence], Vol. 3, 2nd edn (Dar al-Fiker, Beirut, 1998), 268–9.
56. Termadhi says that this hadith has been narrated from many scholars and companions of the Prophet, and he knows no one who has raised doubt about this hadith and that this was the first incident of *waqf* in Islam. Sheikh Sayyed Sahbeq, *Fiqh al-Sunna* [Sunni Jurisprudence], Vol. 3, 2nd edn (Dar al-Fiker, Beirut, 1998), 270.
57. It is narrated from Abdullah Ibn Omar that the second caliph (Omar) had a piece of land in Khaybar, on the outskirts of Medina. He came to the Prophet stating that he had never obtained such a valuable property and sought the advice of the Prophet Mohammad on how to deal with it. The Prophet said, 'If you like, make the property inalienable and give the benefits for charity [*Habasat aslaha wa tasaddaqat beha*]'; Sheikh Sayyed Sahbeq, *Fiqh al-Sunna* [Sunni Jurisprudence], Vol. 3, 2nd edn (Dar al-Fiker, Beirut, 1998), 269.
58. *Habs al-asl wa tasbil al-samarehi* [keeping the principle and using the benefit (for the way of Allah)]; Sheikh Sayyed Sahbeq, *Fiqh al-Sunna* [Sunni Jurisprudence], Vol. 3, 2nd edn (Dar al-Fiker, Beirut, 1998), 267.
59. Sheikh Sayyed Sahbeq, *Fiqh al-Sunna* [Sunni Jurisprudence], Vol. 3, 2nd edn (Dar al-Fiker, Beirut, 1998), 267.
60. Ibid., 270.
61. Ibid.
62. Ibid.
63. Ibid., 269.
64. Ibid., 269.
65. Ibid., 271.

66. Mohaqqeq Helli, *Sharayeh al-Islam* [Farsi translation by Abol Qasim Ibn Ahmad Yazdi] (University of Tehran Press, Tehran, 1995), 347; Zaynodeen bin Ali (Shaheed Thani), *Al-Rodha al-Bahiya fi Sharha al-Loma al-Demeshqiya* [Collection of Legal Sections by Asadollah Lotfi] (Majid Press, Tehran, 2009), 38.
67. Sheikh Sayyed Sahbeq, *Fiqh al-Sunna* [Sunni Jurisprudence], Vol. 3, 2nd edn (Dar al-Fiker, Beirut, 1998), 271.
68. Ibid., 271–2.
69. Ibid., 274–5.
70. Asaf Asaf A.A. Fyzee, *Outlines of Muhammadan Law*, 5th edn, Tahir Mahmood (ed.) (Oxford University Press, New York, 2008, first published 1949), 225.
71. Ibid., 276.
72. Wael Hallaq, *An Introduction to Islamic Law* (Cambridge University Press, Cambridge, 2009), 96.
73. Ibid.
74. For an overview of the varying objectives of *waqifs* (endowers of *waqf*) see Robert McChesney, '*Waqf* and Public Policy: The *Waqfs* of Shah Abbas 1011–1023/1602–1614' (1981) 15(2) *Asian and African Studies* 165–90; and Gabriel Baer, 'The Waqf as a Prop for the Social System (Sixteenth-Twentieth Centuries)' (1997) 4(3) *Islamic Law and Society* 264–97.
75. Andrew White, 'The Role of the Islamic Waqf in Strengthening South Asian Civil Society: Pakistan as Case Study' (2006) 7 *International Journal of Civil Society Law* 7–36.
76. Amy Singer, 'A Note on Land and Identity: From Ze'amet to Waqf' in Roger Owen and Martin P. Bunton (eds), *New Perspectives on Property and Land in the Middle East* (Harvard University Press, Cambridge, MA, 2001), 161–73; Jack Goldstone, 'Islam, Development, and the Middle East: A Comment on Timur Kuran's Analysis' (Forum Series on the Role of Institutions in Promoting Economic Growth, Mercatus Center, George Mason University, 24 June 2003), 6–7, accessed on 10 January 2012 at: http://www.usaid.gov/our_work/economic_growth_and_trade/eg/forum_series/f7-comments-on-kuran.pdf; Timur Kuran, 'Why the Middle East is Economically Underdeveloped: Historical Mechanisms of Institutional Stagnation' (2004) 18(3) *The Journal of Economic Perspectives* 71, 81.
77. Albert V. Dicey, *Introduction to the Study of the Law of the Constitution*, 10th edn (Macmillan, London, 1967), 202.
78. While support for the rule of law is worldwide (in both Western and non-Western societies), the definition and the scope of the notion is not clear. There are political and legal theories on the concept and nature of the rule of law. The concept of the 'rule of law' is essentially contested. On the rule of law see Brian Tamanaha, *On the Rule of Law: History, Politics, Theory* (Cambridge University Press, Cambridge, 2004); Ronald Dworkin, *Law's Empire* (Fontana Press, London, 1986); Lon L. Fuller, *The Morality of Law*, 2nd edn (Yale University Press, New Haven, CT, 1969); Joseph Raz, 'The Rule of Law and Its Virtue' in *The Authority of Law* (Oxford University Press, Oxford, 1979).
79. See Timur Kuran, 'Institutional Causes of Economic Underdevelopment in the Middle East: A Historical Perspective' in Janus Kornai, Lazlo Matyas and Gerard Roland (eds), *Institutional Change and Economic Behaviour* (Palgrave Macmillan, Basingstoke, 2008), 64–76; Timur Kuran, 'The Provision of Public Goods under Islamic Law: Origins, Impact and Limitations of the Waqf System' (2001) 35(4) *Law & Society Review* 841; Timur Kuran, 'The Absence of the Corporation in Islamic Law: Origins and Persistence' (2005) 53 *American Journal of Comparative Law* 785.
80. Kayhan Orbay, 'The Economic Efficiency of Imperial Waqfs in the Ottoman Empire', Papers from the *XIV International Economic History Congress*, University

of Helsinki, 22 August 2006, 4, accessed on 11 January 2012 at: http://www.helsinki.fi/iehc2006/sessions81_124.html

81. Ibid., 14.
82. Ibid.
83. Timur Kuran, 'Institutional Causes of Economic Underdevelopment in the Middle East: A Historical Perspective' in Janus Kornai, Lazlo Matyas and Gerard Roland (eds), *Institutional Change and Economic Behaviour* (Palgrave Macmillan, Basingstoke, 2008), 70.
84. Ibid., 72.
85. Ibid.
86. Ibid., 74.
87. See the website of the *sazman awqaf*, accessed on 2 October 2009 at: http://www.iranculture.org/nahad/oghaf.php
88. For the United Arab Emirates: General Authority of Islamic Affairs and Endowments, see: http://www.awqaf.ae/ (accessed 11 January 2012). For Jordan, see Ministry of Awqaf and Islamic Holiness: http://www.awqaf.gov.jo/index.php (accessed 11 January 2012). For Turkish Department of Awqaf and Protection of Cultural Heritage, see: http://www.vgm.gov.tr/ (accessed 9 October 2009). For Syria, see Ministry of Awqaf: http://www.syrianawkkaf.org/ (accessed 11 January 2012). For Saudi Arabia, see Ministry of Islamic Authority, Awqaf, Preaching and Guidance: http://www.al-islam.com/arb/ (accessed 11 January 2012). For Oman, see Ministry of Awqaf and Religious Authorities: http://www.maraoman.net/ (accessed 11 January 2012). For Qatar, see Ministry of Awqaf and Islamic Authorities: http://www.islam.gov.qa/ (accessed 11 January 2012). For Kuwait, see Ministry of Awqaf and Islamic Authorities: http://www.islam.gov.kw/site/ (accessed 11 January 2012).
89. Abul Hasan M. Sadeq, 'Waqf, Perpetual Charity and Poverty Alleviation' (2002) 29(1/2) *International Journal of Social Economics* 135, 140.
90. Siraj Sait and Hilary Lim, *Land, Law & Islam: Property & Human Rights in the Muslim World* (Zed Books, London, 2006), 149.
91. Abul Hasan M. Sadeq, 'Waqf, Perpetual Charity and Poverty Alleviation' (2002) 29(1/2) *International Journal of Social Economics* 135, 140.
92. Ibid., 140–41.
93. Siraj Sait and Hilary Lim, *Land, Law & Islam: Property & Human Rights in the Muslim World* (Zed Books, London, 2006), 171.

9. Islamic criminal law

1. INTRODUCTION

Islamic law has the main objective of producing and realizing and also protecting the good of humankind, whether the good is in the interests of the individual or the public, or both. To guarantee, protect and safeguard these common goods, Islam determines a number of regulations, whether in the form of commands or prohibitions. In certain matters, these regulations are accompanied by the threat of worldly punishment (in addition, of course, to punishment in the hereafter) if they are transgressed. It is this set of regulations that is known as Islamic criminal law (*Fiqh Jinayah*, *at-Tashri' al-Jina'i*).

However, in modern times, most Muslim countries have abandoned the full application of classic Islamic criminal law. It seems that many regard it as a phenomenon of the past. However, from the 1970s the number of countries applying Islamic criminal law slowly increased. One recent application that garnered worldwide media attention occurred in October 2008, when a 13-year-old girl, Aisho Ibrahim Dhuhulow, was buried up to her neck at a Somalian football stadium, then stoned to death in front of more than 1000 people. The stoning occurred after she had allegedly pleaded guilty to adultery in a Sharia court in Kismayo, a city controlled by Islamist insurgents. Since the Sharia legal system was introduced in the predominantly Muslim north of Nigeria in 2000, more than a dozen Nigerian Muslims have been sentenced to death by stoning for sexual offences ranging from adultery to homosexuality.

In this context Professor Tariq Ramadan has called for an immediate international moratorium on corporal punishment, stoning and the death penalty in all Muslim majority countries.[1] However, that call did not stop the practice. In 2008, it was reported that six people convicted by Islamic Sharia courts in a northern Nigerian state were awaiting death by stoning, while 46 others were waiting for amputation. In 2010 the world was shocked with the news of Sakineh Mohammadi Ashtiani's sentence of stoning to death in Iran. She had two sentences, one regarding adultery, for which she was sentenced to stoning, and the other for being an accomplice to murdering her husband, for which she received a 10-year prison term. Mrs Ashtiani's two children began a campaign to overturn their mother's conviction. In June 2010, they wrote a letter to the world asking for help to save their mother, which was first published on 26 June 2010, by Mission Free Iran's International Committee against Stoning. The letter brought widespread attention in 2010 as a result of grassroots campaigning through social networking sites that led to the letter being passed along to mainstream mass media. As of January 2011, her stoning sentence has been suspended, and she remains in prison in Tabriz, Iran.[2]

This chapter seeks to analyse the controversies surrounding modern interpretations of Islamic criminal law by first briefly outlining its basic features. The chapter will then demonstrate how a reinterpretation of Islamic criminal law and the adoption of Western-inspired penal codes explain why most Muslim countries no longer apply Islamic criminal law in its strictest sense. The chapter will also consider Muslim conservatives' response to this situation: their attempts to restore the previous Islamic criminal law as part of their over-arching political agenda.

2. TYPES OF PUNISHMENT

Among the important elements of Islamic criminal law are the categories of prohibition (*jarimah* or *jinayah*) and the threat of punishment (usually termed *'uqubah*). *Jarimah* and *jinayah* are defined by al-Mawardi as 'prohibitions of *shari'a* (Islamic law) that Allah threatens with *hadd* or *ta'zir* punishment'.[3] *'Uqubah* is defined as 'retribution in the form of a threat of punishment whose category is determined by the *shari'ah* in order to prevent the transgression of His regulations',[4] in order that the common good may be realized.[5] The categories of *jarimah* and their *'uqubah* are (mostly) determined in the Quran and hadith.

From the above definition of *jarimah* it can be demonstrated that the punishment may be in the form of *hadd* (plural *hudud*) or *ta'zir*. According to Abu Zahrah,[6] as well as other *ulama*,[7] '*hadd*' refers to all categories of punishment that have been determined by the Quran or the Sunna. Ibn Rushd in his book *Bidayah al-Mujtahid wa Nihayah al-Muqtasid* divided criminal actions into four categories: (1) crimes against physical life, such as injuring people or murdering them; (2) crimes against property, such as robbery or vandalism; (3) crimes against descendants,[8] such as adultery; and (4) crimes against human virtues and chastity, such as a false accusation of unchastity (*qazf*), drinking intoxicants (*shurb*) and apostasy (*riddah* or *irtidad*, understood to mean switching religion from Islam to another, or to no, religion).

Hence, included in the understanding of *hadd* would be *qisas* and *diyah* punishments. On the basis of this description the categories of punishment in Islamic criminal law that will be discussed in this chapter are (1) *qisas* and *diyah*, (2) *hudud* and (3) *ta'zir*.[9]

Apart from the three categories above, one should also understand about *kaffarah*, which is a specific sanction for specific violations (evil-doing) or for unintentional killing, with the intent of cleansing the sin of the violator. The forms of this punishment and the violations to which it applies are determined in the holy texts (Quran and hadith). The forms of sanctions in the *kaffarah* category are of four kinds: (1) freeing a slave; (2) fasting; and (3 and 4) providing for the poor, in the form of food or clothing. Violations that are provided with *kaffarah* are (1) unintentional killing; (2) violating the fast of Ramadan by committing sexual intercourse with one's spouse; (3) breaking an oath; (4) *zihar* sexual intercourse with one's wife;[10] and (5) violation of the state of *ihram*.[11] Generally, however, the *kaffarah* for this last violation is termed *fidyah* or *dam*. Of these five forms of violation, the only one that is usually categorized as a criminal offence is unintentional killing. Muslim scholars (*ulama*), in general, do not view the other violations as *jarimah*. Because of this, it is not usual to speak of there being a *jarimah kaffarah*. On this basis, some scholars take the view that the classification of the categories of punishment (*'uqubah*) in Islamic criminal law generally only includes *qisas-diyah*, *hudud* and *ta'zir* without mentioning *kaffarah*.

From the above explanation it can be concluded that the categories of punishment in Islamic criminal law, generally speaking, are *qisas-diyah*, *hudud* and *ta'zir*. These categories of punishment take a form that varies according to the different types of criminal offence that they apply to. *Qisas* and *diyah*, which concern crimes towards life and body, vary according to the form of the crime. It is the same with *hudud*. The forms of punishment prescribed are the death penalty, amputation (of hands or feet), flogging, stoning and banishment. On the other hand, the *ta'zir* punishments have the most variety of form, because the determination of their form is at the discretion of the judge (or the government).

In the study of Islamic criminal law, generally speaking, the categories of punishment are divided into two groups, Allah's right (*haqqullah*) and man's right (*haqqul adami*). Besides that, there are also punishments that have elements of both *haqqullah* and *haqqul adami* simultaneously. By *haqqullah* it is meant that the punishment cannot be annulled, whether by the aggrieved party or the ruler, because the punishment relates strongly to the interests of the public,[12] whereas what is meant by *haqqul adami* is that the punishment may be annulled by the aggrieved party or the government, because the matter only concerns individual interests.[13]

Haqqullah punishments include all punishments of the *hudud* and *kaffarah* categories in their various forms, other than the *qazf hadd*, according to some *ulama*, as has been mentioned previously. These punishments must be carried out where the necessary conditions are fulfilled. Concerning the *qazf hadd*, the punishment can only be imposed where there is a demand from the aggrieved party (*maqzuf*),[14] and it is annulled if he forgives the crime.[15]

Concerning the position of *ta'zir*, it can be demonstrated that some of these punishments are *haqqullah*, if the sinful act does not cause harm to anyone; and some are both *haqqullah* and *haqqul adami* at once, namely, when the sinful act causes harm to a person, such as a theft that does not fulfil the requirement for *hadd*. Thus, the *ulama* are of the opinion that this punishment can be forgiven and *shafa'ah* (intercession) can be asked for, both by the aggrieved party and by the government (the judge), and the punishment may also be annulled by repentance (*tawbah*).[16]

Following is a brief explanation of each category of punishment.

A. *Qisas* and *Diyah*

Linguistically, *qisas* is *al-musawah wa at-ta'adul*',[17] which means 'equivalence and balance'. Thus, *qisas* is a punishment that is equivalent and proportionate to the crime that has been committed.[18] For example, a murderer is threatened with the death penalty, someone who gouges another's eyes out is threatened with a punishment of eye-gouging himself, and so on. On the other hand, *diyah* is a given amount of wealth that must be given by the one who commits a crime against life or body to the victim (or his family) as a punishment. Generally speaking *qisas* and *diyah* are types of punishment that are provided for criminal acts that are crimes against life or body in their various forms, or in other words, acts that take life (murder) or harm the body. However, in addition to *qisas* and *diyah*, these crimes are also provided with *kaffarah*.

Qisas is the penalty for intentional killings and intentional bodily injury. This is affirmed in a number of Quranic verses and hadith. Allah reveals in the Quran: 'O ye who believe! The law of equality is prescribed to you in cases of murder: the free for the free, the slave for the slave, and the woman for the woman';[19] 'We ordained therein for them: "Life for life, eye for eye, nose for nose, ear for ear, tooth for tooth, and wounds equal for equal".'[20]

Diyah is provided for semi-intentional killings (*shibh al-'amd*) and unintentional killings (*alkhata'*) and unintentional injury. It is also threatened for intentional killings where the family of the victim does not demand *qisas*. Some critics have labelled 'blood money' barbaric, and have criticized the practice of *diyah* as undemocratic and inhumane. *Qisas* offences are based upon the criminological approach of retribution. The concept of retribution is found in the first statutory 'Code of Hammurabi' and in the Law of Moses in the form of 'an eye for an eye'. Muslims add to that saying 'but it is better to forgive'. The matter of *diyah* is regulated by a number of Quranic verses and hadith, for example, 'But if any remission is made by the brother of the slain, then grant any reasonable demand, and compensate him with handsome gratitude. This is a concession and a mercy from your Lord',[21] and 'Never should a Believer kill a Believer; but (if it so happens) by mistake, (compensation is due): if one (so) kills a Believer it is ordained that he should free a believing slave, and pay compensation to the deceased's family.'[22]

Diyah has its roots in Islamic law and dates to the time of the Prophet Mohammed when there were many local families, tribes and clans.[23] They were nomadic and travelled extensively. The Prophet was able to convince several tribes to take a monetary payment for damage to the clan or tribe. This practice grew and now is an acceptable solution to some *qisas* crimes. The current practice is that the offender pays *diyah* to the victim, if he is alive. If the victim is dead, the money is paid to the victim's family or to the victim's tribe or clan. The assumption is that victims will be compensated for their loss. Criminal compensation schemes are available in common law countries as well, but these are provided by the government – not at the offender-to-victim level. In the application of *diyah*, Islamic law combines tort and criminal law into one. *Qisas* and *diyah* crimes are compensated as restitution under common law and civil law.

B. *Hudud*

Hudud, the plural of *hadd*, is a punishment that is determined with certainty as Allah's right (*haqqullah*). 'Determined with certainty' requires that the punishment has a given limit and amount. The meaning of '*haqqullah*' is that the punishment cannot be annulled, as it is imposed for the sake of the public good, not the individual good. On this basis, *qisas* and *diyah* are not included in *hudud*, because they may be annulled by the aggrieved party (the family of the victim). According to some Muslim jurists, among them al-Mawardi, the *hudud* are divided into two, Allah's right (*haqqullah*) and man's right (*haqqul adami*). The *haqqul adami* comprises the *hadd* of *qazf*, according to some opinions, whereas the other *hudud*, as will be explained, are Allah's right.[24]

This category of punishment (*hudud*) varies in form according to the crime that it applies to, of which there are seven types. Although their form varies, these punishments in the terminology of Islamic Criminal Law are all known as *hadd*. Following is a brief explanation of each of them.

i. The *hadd* for adultery (*zina*)

In Islamic law there are three forms of *hadd* that are threatened for adultery: flogging (*jilid*), banishment (*tagrib*) and stoning (*rajm*). Flogging and banishment can be given for adultery committed by persons who have never married (*gayr muhsan*), whereas stoning is available for adulterers who have been married (*muhsan*).

Concerning the punishment of flogging, the Quran states: ‘The woman and the man guilty of adultery or fornication, – flog each of them with a hundred stripes: let not compassion move you in their case, in a matter prescribed by God, if ye believe in God and the Last Day: and let a party of the Believers witness their punishment’.[25] In addition to incurring a flogging, Muslims who commit adultery risk the possibility of banishment for a year. The basis of this punishment is a hadith of the Prophet that says: ‘[Adultery that occurs between] a male virgin and a female virgin is [threatened with the punishment] of one hundred stripes and banishment for one year’.[26] However, bearing in mind that the authenticity of this hadith is not agreed upon, the *ulama* (Muslim scholars) do not agree whether banishment is a *hadd* that must be imposed for every adulterer or whether it is only a *ta'zir* whose use is at the discretion of the judge (the government).

Rajm is a death sentence, in other words, execution by stoning. It is worth noting that this punishment is not mentioned in the Quran. Some Muslim sects such as Khawarij do not recognize it; however, as it is based in a number of hadith, the majority of Muslim schools and sects do accept it. Supporting this position is the well-known hadith: ‘The blood of a Muslim is not lawful, unless it be for one of three things: *kofr* after belief [apostasy], adultery after marriage (*zina muhsan*), and killing someone without lawful reason’.[27] Other support for *rajm* includes the example of the Prophet, who personally ordered the stoning of Ma'iz, Gamidiyah and also a labourer and his partner in adultery.[28] Thus, the punishment of stoning is based on both verbal Sunna (*sunnah qawliyah*) and Sunna in practice (*sunnah fi'liyah*). It must be noted, however, that this punishment is subject to a very strict evidential requirements and therefore has been applied in very isolated circumstances in the history of Islam. This issue will be discussed later.

ii. The *hadd* for accusation of adultery (*qazf*)

Qazf is a criminal act or crime against a person's honour, in the form of an accusation of adultery. This crime is subject to two types of punishment: the basic punishment (*asliyah*), which is flogging, and an additional one (*tab'iyah*), which is the rejection of the perpetrator's testimony for the rest of his life. The latter seems to be a disqualification rather than a punishment. This is affirmed in the revelation: 'And those who launch a charge against chaste women, and produce not four witnesses (to support their allegations), – flog them with eighty stripes; and reject their evidence ever after: for such men are wicked transgressors'.[29]

Traditionally, the requirements for proving unlawful sexual intercourse are very strict. Full evidence for this crime requires the concurring testimonies of four male eyewitnesses. They must have seen the act in its most intimate details (the penetration). If their testimonies do not satisfy the requirements, the witnesses can be sentenced to 80 lashes, the fixed penalty for unfounded accusation of fornication (*qazf*).[30] It is pertinent to point out that the evidentiary requirement for *zina* was initially intended to protect men and women from frivolous charges. It is believed that the requirement of four witnesses (with all its restrictions and specifications) is considered a merciful measure from God in order not only to avoid incriminating innocent people, but also to preserve the privacy of Muslims, which is one of the most valued principles in Islam. In other words, to fulfil the requirement of four witnesses, *zina* would take place in public space, and any person who committed *zina* in public place would be considered immoral and inhumane and therefore would receive severe punishment.

iii. The *hadd* for drinking intoxicants (*shurb*)

What is meant by *shurb* is the crime of drinking *khamr* (or an intoxicating drink). The punishment for this *jarimah* is not clearly stated in the Quran. In the Quran there is only a prohibition on drinking *khamr* that shows its *haram* status, as is explained in the revelation: 'O ye who believe! Intoxicants and gambling, (dedication of) stones, and (divination by) arrows, are an abomination, – of Satan's handiwork: eschew such (abomination) that ye may prosper'.[31]

Regarding the punishment that applies to this crime, a hadith of the Prophet explains: 'The Prophet once imposed a punishment of flogging for (someone who drank) *khamr* with date palm leaves and sandals. Abu Bakr, the first caliph, also once imposed a punishment of flogging (for someone who drank *khamr*) forty times' (Bukhari, Muslim, Tirmidhi and Abu Daud from Anas ibn Malik).[32] Another hadith affirms: 'Whosoever drinks *khamr*, flog him. If he repeats it, flog him, and if he repeats it again, flog him'.[33] These two hadith only explain that the Prophet imposed the punishment of flogging for the crime of drinking *khamr*, without stating clearly the number of strokes. Because of this, the *ulama* differ in opinion concerning the number of strokes set down as the punishment. Imam Shafi'i was of the opinion that the punishment was 40 strokes, and this punishment, according to him, was not a *hadd* punishment, but fell under the category of *ta'zir*. Meanwhile, other *ulama* have determined that the punishment should be 80 strokes. This number is based on a fatwa of the Companions of the Prophet. During the rule of 'Umar ibn Khattab, 'Umar asked for the opinion of the Companions about the punishment for those who drank *khamr*. 'Ali ibn Abi Talib stated the opinion that the drinker should be flogged 80 times. His argument was that if the drinker drinks *khamr*, he becomes drunk; if he is drunk, he speaks nonsense; and if he is already speaking nonsense, he will say provocative things (*iftira'*). And the punishment for someone who creates a provocation (*fitnah*), meaning someone who accuses another of committing adultery (*qazif*), is 80 strokes. This opinion of 'Ali's was approved by a large proportion of the Prophet's Companions, including the caliph, 'Umar ibn Khattab.

From the above brief explanation, it is clear the *haram* nature of drinking *khamr* is determined by the Quran and the Sunna, while the type of punishment (flogging) is determined by the Sunna, and the number of strokes is based on a fatwa of the Companions.

iv. The *hadd* for theft (*sariqah* or *sirqah*)

The punishment for the crime of theft is amputation. This fact is stated clearly in the Quran: 'As to the thief. Male or female, cut off his or her hands: a punishment by way of example, from God, for their crime: and God is Exalted in Power'.[34]

A number of conditions must be fulfilled before the hand of a thief is cut off. These conditions include: first, the thing should have been taken by stealth; if it was not taken by stealth, then the punishment is not applied, such as when property has been seized by force in front of other people, because in this case the owner of the property could have asked for help to stop the thief. Second, the stolen property should be something of worth, because that which is of no worth has no sanctity, such as musical instruments, wine and pigs. Third, the value of the stolen property should be above a certain limit, which is three Islamic Dirhams or a quarter of an Islamic Dinar, or their equivalent in other currencies. Fourth, the stolen property should have been taken from a place where it had been put away, that is to say, a place where people usually put their property, such as a cupboard, for example. Fifth, the theft itself has to be proven, either by the testimony of two qualified witnesses or by the confession of the thief twice. Also, the person from whom the property was stolen has to ask for it back; if they do not, then (the thief's) hand does not have to be cut off. We will come back to this issue later.

v. The *hadd* for waging war against God (*hirabah*)

Hirabah is a crime against the stability of the state's security, in its various forms. There are four types of punishment for this crime: the death penalty, crucifixion, cutting off the hands and feet, and banishment (*an-nafy*). These four types of punishment are stated in the Quran: 'The punishment of those who wage war against God and His Apostle, and strive with might and main for mischief through the land is: execution, or crucifixion, or the cutting off of hands and feet from opposite sides, or exile from the land'.[35]

A judge can prescribe any of these punishments in accordance with the degree and level of the crime. These punishments can be prescribed for any crime that can threaten the society at large. Examples of these crimes are armed robbery (unlike theft, which has a different punishment), looting and terrorism.

vi. The *hadd* for apostasy (*riddah*)[36]

Apostasy (*riddah* or *irtidad*; another term for apostate is '*murtad*') is turning away and leaving the religion of Islam after having embraced it or been born to Muslim parents. This act is seen as a major crime that is forbidden by religion, since it is seen as bearing false witness to God. Because of this, the person who commits it may be subjected to the death penalty. However, the following Quranic verses do not mention the death penalty: 'And if any of you turn back from their Faith and die in unbelief, their works will bear no fruit in this life and in the Hereafter; they will be Companion of the Fire and will abide therein'.[37] However, the Prophet said: 'Whoever changes his religion, kill him'.[38]

Modern scholars argue against death penalty for apostasy. Mahmoud Ayoub criticizes several key hadith used by legal scholars to address both the existence of the category of crime labelled 'apostasy', and its accompanying punishment of death. He concludes that no Quranic or Prophetic tradition forms a strong, valid basis for assigning apostasy the death penalty.[39] The former Chief Justice of Pakistan, S.A. Rahman, believes that there is no reference to the death penalty in any of the 20 instances of apostasy mentioned in the Quran.[40] The Quranic statement, 'there is no compulsion in religion' is often cited to support the view that death was not an authorized punishment for conversion.

Moreover, the context of the order from the Prophet to kill the apostate should be fully understood. Apostasy in Islam should be seen as equal to treason. At the time of the Prophet, when a Muslim repudiated his faith, he rebelled against the order and endangered the security and the stability of the society to which he belonged. Since apostasy in Islam is not merely a private or ecclesiastical affair (by withdrawal of church membership, for example), as it is in Western society, the state must act. Apostasy is considered treason towards Muslim society (the *ummah*) and undermines the Muslim state, for Islam is the buttress of society and the state itself. Apostasy erodes and shakes the foundations of the order of society and, because it is treason, the state must prosecute it.[41] As the Quran revealed: 'A party of the People of the Book say, "Believe in what has been revealed to the Believers" at the beginning of the day and reject it at the end of it, in order that they may turn back (from Islam)' (Quran 3:72). Therefore, in the modern context, the death penalty could be seen as not an appropriate response to apostasy since apostasy should no longer be seen as treason. Loyalty or disloyalty to God will not constitute treason in modern legal sense.

The apostasy law has been used to target many liberal free-thinking Muslims.[42] In a case in Egypt in 1995, Nasr Hamid Abu Zayd, a lecturer at the American University in Cairo, was labelled an apostate for writing an academic book that Islamic scholars deemed to be offensive to Islam. Abu Zayd had used hermeneutics to interpret the Quran, and the lawyers argued that his findings placed him outside the bounds of Islam. The courts ruled that, as an apostate, he must be divorced from his wife, and upheld the ruling even after he appealed. No longer able to live together as a couple in Egypt, Abu Zayd and his wife left for Holland in 1996.[43]

vii. The *hadd* for rebellion (*bagy*)

Rebellion (*al-bagy*) or conspiracy to bring down a legitimate government is another offence with the death penalty. The legal basis is the Quran and a number of hadith, including the following: 'If two parties among the Believers fall into a quarrel, make ye peace between them: but if one of them transgresses beyond bounds against the other, then fight ye (all) against the one that transgresses until it complies with the command of God'.[44] The Prophet said: 'Whosoever comes to you – while your affairs are with a (legitimate) leader – with the intent of dividing your power and scattering your congregation, kill him'.

Hirabah, mentioned earlier, is dealt with as a crime and the criminal law of the land is applied to those who commit *hirabah* (*muharibin*), while *bagy* is governed by the law of war and the rebels (*bughah*) are dealt with as combatants. In his landmark study of the Islamic law of rebellion, Khaled Abou El Fadl defines rebellion as 'the act of resisting or defying the authority of those in power'.[45] He says that rebellion can occur either in the form of 'passive non-compliance with the orders of those in power' or in the form of 'armed insurrection'.[46] Regarding the target of a rebellion, Abou El Fadl says that that the target could be a social or political institution or the religious authority of the *ulama*.[47]

This chapter so far has discussed the types of *hudud* punishment in their various forms. Now, the third category of punishment, *ta'zir*, will be considered.

C. *Ta'zir*

Ta'zir is a punishment of an educational (*ta'dib*) nature for an act of sin or evil that is not subject to *hadd* or *kaffarah*. In one aspect, *ta'zir* is similar to *hudud* as it is meant to educate, reform and deter, yet in another aspect it is different as it is unspecified and not fixed, unlike *hudud*. By the words 'unspecified punishment', *hudud* and *qisas* are excluded from the concept of *ta'zir* as these punishments are prescribed, specified and fixed by Allah and His Messenger. The determination of the form and substance of *ta'zir* punishment is at the discretion of those who hold power (the government or the court). They have a wide freedom to formulate various types of actions that are categorized as *ta'zir* criminal acts and also determine the type of punishment for them. Adjudicators of *ta'zir* are authorized by Islamic law as long as their decisions are in line with the general spirit and intent of the enactment of Islamic law, namely to realize and protect the common good of humankind. Any sentence or punishment imposed by a judge (*qadi*) and ruler in an Islamic state could be considered *ta'zir*. In other words, every act of evil whose punishment, whether *kaffarah* or *hudud*, is not determined in the Quran or *hadith*, is subject to *ta'zir* punishment.[48]

3. REFORM OF ISLAMIC CRIMINAL LAW IN THE MODERN WORLD

The objective of the enactment of Islamic criminal law or, more particularly as has been discussed in this chapter, criminal law punishment, is no different from the general aim of the enactment of Islamic law. That is, to realize and protect the common good of humankind, for the sake of happiness in this world and the hereafter. From the studies of the *ulama*, there are two main objectives in punishment.[49] The first objective is the 'relative objective' (*al-garad al-qarib*), whose aim is to punish, or produce a feeling of pain in, the perpetrator of the crime. This will generally push the perpetrator to repent, so that they become wary from experience, and do not wish to repeat the *jarimah*, and other people will likewise be afraid of following their path. The second objective is the 'absolute objective' (*al-garad al-ba'id*), which has the aim of protecting the public good. These two objectives are indeed what was intended to be achieved by the punishment of each *jarimah*.

The *ulama* have stated that the functions of punishment are '*zawajir*' (to prevent) and '*jawabir*' (to cleanse the sins). *Zawajir* means that the punishment functions to make the perpetrator of the *jarimah* aware so they do not repeat the crime and so that the punishment will be a lesson to others so that they are afraid of perpetrating the same crime (*jarimah*). The function of the punishment here is something that has connotations for this world. On the other hand what is meant by *jawabir* is that the punishment functions to save the criminal from torment in the hereafter. In other words, *jawabir* punishments aim to cleanse the sin of the *jarimah*. Hence, the function of the punishment has connotations for the hereafter. Nevertheless, the *ulama* differ in their opinions; some emphasize the *zawajir* function of punishment, and others emphasize the *jawabir* function.[50]

Another factor that should be kept in mind when considering the categories of punishment in Islamic criminal law, and the grouping of the enforcement of criminal law into the categories of 'Allah's right' and 'man's right', is that in Islamic criminal law some punishments are firm and other punishments are elastic in nature. 'Firm' punishments apply when the punishment must be applied if the necessary conditions have been fulfilled. 'Elastic' punishments may be adjusted in accordance with the situation and conditions, since their enforcement depends on the discretion of the judge (government) and/or the aggrieved party.

Salient questions for contemporary Muslim societies are: must 'firm' punishments be applied following a literal interpretation of the Quran and hadith; and if so, should these punishments be formally enacted in the criminal law legislation of every Muslim country? What happens if for one reason or another a 'firm' obligation cannot be realized: must we condemn this as violating or rebelling against Allah's law? In other words, how do Muslim scholars justify the fact that most Muslim countries have ignored the 'literal' implementation of Islamic criminal law? Can this phenomenon be interpreted as indicating the anachronistic nature of Islamic criminal law? Or should it merely be viewed as an indication of man's rebellion against God, as argued by conservative Muslim groups who wish to restore Islamic criminal law? Or can the texts be revisited by jurists and re-interpreted in light of changed conditions in modern times?

If one only considers the literal meaning of the Quran and hadith texts, and the analysis of some of the *ulama* in the *fiqh* books, then the answer is of course quite simple: Muslim societies must apply the injunctions of Islamic criminal law in the system of legislation or positive law, wherever and whenever! If not, the legislation that exists should be seen as not yet fulfilling the law of Allah, since it conflicts with the literal meaning of the Quran and hadith, so that Allah's words are fulfilled: 'If any do fail to judge by (the light of) what God hath revealed, they are (no better than) Unbelievers … wrong-doers … those who rebel'.[51]

However, if this way of thinking were accepted, it would assuredly have quite a serious negative impact on the existence of Islamic law itself. Islamic law would become a utopian law that only exists in sacred texts as a meaningless document, since it had not 'come down to earth' at all, because the reality has shown that this would be the case, as has been mentioned above. Professor Rudolph Peters suggests that 'the solution must be sought within an Islamic framework, for instance by reinterpreting the textual sources or by going back to the abundance of opinions found in the classical works on jurisprudence with the aim of selecting those that are most in conformity with the demands of modern society'.[52]

The discussion below will demonstrate how it is possible to reinterpret *hudud*, specifically focusing on the *hadd* for adultery and theft, as these are the crimes that occur most often, and the punishments that apply to them are quite serious. The point to be made is that it is possible to reform and reinterpret Islamic criminal law in a manner that is not only compatible with human rights principles but can also be justified under the Islamic legal tradition. If such reforms could be accepted, then one might argue that Western-inspired penal codes, which are already practised in most Muslim countries, should be considered as Islamic. Consequently, the attempts of Muslim conservatives to restore the old Islamic criminal law could not be considered to be 'Islamic' and must be rejected.

A. Reinterpretation

According to some scholars, the rules of the Islamic criminal law category of *hudud* must be applied as they are, according to the literal reading of the texts, if the necessary conditions are fulfilled. This is because these regulations are *qat'i* laws (fixed and no room for modification or adjustment). However it can be argued that it is nevertheless possible to review these conceptions through, among other things, a contextual understanding of the texts founded on the functions and objectives of punishment, and a reinterpretation of the texts that contain an *ihtimal* or possibility for an understanding that differs from the already popular understanding.

The example of how Islam has dealt with the prohibition on slavery can usefully illustrate some of these principles. When Islam arose as a religion, slavery was commonplace across the world. At that time slavery was seen as something reasonable that was approved by all parties, because the system of slavery was indeed necessary to support the needs of life, in line with the culture that then existed. This reality was accepted by Islamic teachings, since Islam did not totally eradicate slavery. On this basis, the implementation of Islamic criminal law was also in line with the system of slavery that then existed. Put clearly, the punishments that Islam enacted as Sharia were highly relevant to the culture of slavery that existed at the time.

However, it should be made clear here that at a basic level Islam intended to eradicate the system of slavery, albeit in a gradual and persuasive way. This may be seen from the various legal injunctions that require the freeing of slaves. For example, someone who kills unintentionally must pay a *kaffarah* in the form of freeing a slave, besides the *diyah* (see the Quran 4:92); this is also the *kaffarah* for someone who commits *ijma* (sexual intercourse) during the day during Ramadan.

Today the world no longer recognizes slavery, and the reality also reflects this. This fact may appropriately be made a factor that pushes Muslims to review the implementation of the regulations of criminal law that are contained in the Quran and hadith, so that they are in line with the existing reality, as a result of the end of the age and influence of the culture of human slavery. However this does not mean that these criminal law regulations should be entirely ignored, rather that they should be further examined in light of the general functions, objectives and the spirit of their enactment as Sharia. In other words, a reinterpretation of the functions and objectives of their enactment as Sharia needs to be carried out.

Taking as a foundation the discussion above concerning the functions of punishment and the general objectives of the enactment of Islamic criminal law, namely to protect the public interest, in the course of this reinterpretation, by examining the verses of the Quran and the hadith of the Prophet and also the opinions of the *ulama*, it can be affirmed that the function of punishment is both *zawajir* (to prevent) and *jawabir* (to cleanse the sins) at once. However, the *zawajir* aspect is more prominent and dominant. Instead of using the classic understanding of *jawabir–zawajir*, a new *zawajir* approach should be followed, one that protects the public interest and makes offenders aware and fearful so that another crime will not be committed or repeated. Accordingly, any kind of punishment that meets this criteria will be accepted by a modern Islamic law. Thus, the enactment of this law as Sharia becomes *ta'aqquli* (reasonable), not *ta'abbudi* (ritual only) or *gayr ma'qul al-ma'na* (non-reasonable).

Hence, the categories of punishment that are determined in the Quran and the hadith do not have to be applied literally. Any type and form of punishment may be approved, as long as it can function as *zawajir* and be capable of realizing the objective of the enactment of Islamic criminal law. On this basis, the formulation of punishment that is in line with the conditions of this day and age may also be approved. In contrast, the punishments that are determined in the Quran and hadith can be seen as only a maximum limit that needs to be applied where other forms of punishment cannot realize the objectives of the punishment. For instance, for the crime of theft, as stated in the Quran, Súra Máida 5:38, the punishment is amputation of the hand (*qat'ul yad*). Concerning this matter, the *ulama* are divided between two opinions.

The first is that this punishment must be followed literally as it is part of *ta'abbudi* (rituals that cannot be challenged). Because of this, it cannot be replaced with another punishment, with imprisonment or anything else, as was done at the time of the Prophet. This is the general view of the classic *ulama*. The second is that the punishment is *ma'qul al-ma'na*, that is, it has a rational intent and understanding. Because of this it can be replaced with a different punishment, which does not have to be amputation. Some of the modern *ulama* are of this opinion.[53]

According to the supporters of this second opinion, what is meant by 'amputation of the hand' as mentioned in the Quranic verse is 'prevention of theft'. This prevention may be brought about by detention in a prison or by other means, and does not have to be by amputation of the hand. Thus, that verse could mean: '[a]s to the thief[:] Male or female, [prevent them stealing]: a punishment by way of example'.

This group of *ulama* reasons that the word 'amputation' (*al-qat'u*) originally meant only 'prevention' (*al-man'u*), on the basis of the following:

1. According to a narration, the Messenger of Allah gave a gift to Aqra' ibn Habis at-Tamimi and 'Uyainah ibn Hisn al-Fazari of 100 camels each, whereas to 'Abbas ibn Mardas, the Prophet gave gift of less than 100 camels. Then 'Abbas started to recite a poem in front of the Prophet, that stated that his position and struggle, if not more than, could not be viewed as less than Aqra' and 'Uyainah.

When he heard 'Abbas's poem, which he repeated over and over again, the Prophet said to his Companions: '*Iqta'u 'anni lisanah*' (literally 'cut off from me his tongue'). The Companions then gave 'Abbas more camels, until he had 100, as the Prophet had given to Aqra' and 'Uyainah.[54] If the word *qat'a* meant amputation, then the Companions would surely have cut off 'Abbas's tongue, but they interpreted the Prophet's statement not according to its outward meaning, namely cutting off his tongue. Rather, they understood it as preventing 'Abbas's tongue from talking and expressing his protest, by increasing the amount of camels until it reached a hundred. Hence, the Prophet's statement was not interpreted as 'cut off his tongue', but as 'prevent his tongue'.

2. According to a narration, Laila al-Akhiliah once recited a poem to praise Commander Hajjaj. Hajjaj said to his aide, '*Iqta' 'anni lisanaha*'. Hearing this command, the aide took Laila to a blacksmith to cut off her tongue. When she saw the blacksmith taking out his knife, Laila said, 'That is not what Hajjaj meant, rather he ordered you to cut off my tongue with a gift, not with a knife'. When the aide returned to the Commander to ask him, he confirmed Laila's opinion, and the Commander then rebuked the aide for his stupidity. If the word *qat'a* was interpreted narrowly to mean 'to cut', it would not be reasonable for Hajjaj to rebuke his aide thus. Commander Hajjaj and Laila are renowned as Arab poets and literary figures during the Umayyad period, whose words may be used as evidence or argument in understanding the Arabic language. Also, the language experts are agreed that the Arabic language during the Umayyad period and the beginning of the Abbasid period up until the time of Abu al-'Atahiyah (a renowned Arab literary figure during the Abbasid period, who died in 211 AH) can be used as *hujjah*.[55] In addition, according to Abu Hanifah, as-Sauri, Ahmad and Ishak, the punishment for the crime of theft is in the form of a choice, amputation of the hand or returning (replacing) the item that was stolen to its owner,[56] or – according to other *ulama* – spending it in the path of Allah.[57]

From the above explanation, and if further detailed study is conducted, it may be possible to state that, as long as the criminal law texts contain a possibility for re-interpretation based on the wording of Quranic verses or as a result of their reading being seen as ambiguous (*mushtarak*), reinterpretation and a change of understanding remain open, alongside, of course, an emphasis on the *zawajir* function of punishment, together with the objectives (*maqasid*) and spirit of its enactment. Thus according to this, the implementation of punishment becomes elastic. Apart from the interpretation above, there are also other conditions that make it difficult, if not impossible, to implement Islamic criminal law, as will be discussed in the next section.

B. Repentance (*Tawbah*) and Intercession (*Shafa'ah*)

The *ulama* are agreed that repentance (*tawbah*) can nullify the *hadd* for the criminal offence of *hirabah* if it is done before the offender is arrested by the authorities. This is based on the revelation: 'Except for those who repent before they fall into your power: in that case, know that God is Oft-forgiving, Most Merciful' (Súra Máida 5:34).

The *hadd* for *hirabah* that is nullified by repentance is only that part of the *hadd* that concerns the right of Allah. That which concerns the rights of man, for example if the criminal who commits *hirabah* has murdered or robbed, is not nullified. The offender is still obliged to resolve the matter with the victims. In other words, this matter is given over to the discretion of the victims.[58]

The *ulama* differ in their views of whether repentance can nullify the *hadd* for offences other than *hirabah*. According to Imam Shafi'i in one of his opinions,[59] repentance can nullify all *hadd* of criminal offences, because, among other things:

1. The Quran states clearly that repentance can nullify the punishment for the offence of *hirabah*, yet this offence is more serious than other offences. If the punishment for this quite serious offence can be nullified by repentance, then surely the punishments for less serious offences can also be nullified by repentance.
2. Allah's revelation concerning the offence of adultery clearly states: 'If two men among you are guilty of lewdness, punish them both. If they repent and amend, leave them alone; for God is Oft-Returning, Most Merciful'.[60] The hadith of the Prophet in relation to the case of Ma'iz that states 'Why don't you set him free? It may be that he repents and Allah accepts his repentance', shows that the punishment for adultery can be nullified by repentance.[61]
3. Concerning the offence of theft, Allah revealed, 'But if the thief repents after his crime, and amends his conduct, God turneth to him in forgiveness; for God is Oft-Forgiving, Most Merciful'.[62] A hadith of the Prophet states: 'Someone who repents from a sin is the same as someone who has not committed a sin'. Someone who had not committed a sin would surely not be threatened with *hadd*.

The view of Imam Shafi'i has been followed by other imams, among them Imam Ahmad.[63] According to the consensus of the *ulama*, among them Imam Malik, Abu Hanifah and some Muslim jurists from the Shafi'i and Hanbali schools, repentance cannot nullify any *hadd* other than the *hadd* for *hirabah*. This is because repentance cannot nullify punishment. In addition, according to this group, the function of the punishment is to cleanse the sin of the offence (*jawabir*); and these offences are not analogous to the offence of *hirabah*.[64]

It should be expressed here that this difference of opinion only applies to criminal offences whose punishments are categorized as Allah's right. Hence, in the offence of *qazf* (which is *haqqul adami*), repentance cannot affect the punishment. The only thing that can nullify the punishment in this matter is the forgiveness of the slandered party. Thus repentance can also only have an effect if the offence has not yet been determined (*isbat*) by a judge. If the offence has reached a judge and the judge has determined it, the offender must be punished.[65]

Shafa'ah, which is an effort by a person to avert punishment from the offender before the case has been processed by a court, can nullify punishment. However, where the offence has been decided by a court, *shafa'ah* is entirely without effect,[66] and the matter is under the discretion of the judge. In relation to *shafa'ah*, the Prophet said, among other things: 'Try to forgive one another's *hadd* among yourselves, since matters that reach me must be carried out'.[67]

C. Differences of Fact or Opinion (*Shubhah*)

The *ulama*, other than those of the Zahiri madhhab, have agreed that *hudud* may be nullified by reason of the existence of *shubhah*. This is based on the well-known hadith of the Prophet, 'avoid the *hudud* with *shubhah*' ('*Idra'u al-hudud bi ash-shubhah*'). Another hadith states, 'Strive with all effort that the *hudud* do not reach a Muslim. If there is a way to release a *hadd* then leave that *hadd*, since an error by an imam (judge) in forgiving is better than an error in punishing'.[68]

Despite this, the *ulama* differ in their opinions in determining the forms of *shubhah* that may nullify a *hadd*. Something may be seen as *shubhah* by one imam, but not by others. The following section discusses some of the types of *shubhah* and examples of them in relation to the offence of adultery, according to the Shafi'i and Hanafi madhhabs.[69]

The Shafi'i madhhab mentions various types of *shubhah*, which include:

1. Shubhah fil fa'il, meaning the offender supposed or believed that what he was doing was lawful for him, for example, having sexual intercourse with a woman whom he supposed was his wife, but in fact was not.
2. *Shubhah fil jihat*, meaning a *shubhah* that occurs because of a difference of opinion regarding something's lawfulness or unlawfulness, for example, having sexual intercourse with a woman who was married without a guardian, without witnesses, or without both guardian and witnesses, or who was married in a *mutah* marriage, although the offender was certain that his act was prohibited.

The Hanafi madhhab divides *shubhah* into two types. The first is *Shubhah fil fi'l* – this is a *shubhah* for a person who is unclear about the lawfulness or unlawfulness of an act. There is actually no textual ground showing the lawfulness of the act, but the person thinks that something which is not a ground (*dalil*) is a *dalil* (that shows its lawfulness), for example, sexual relations with a former wife who is undergoing the waiting period for divorce. In this case, marriage no longer has an effect on the lawfulness of sexual relations, because it has been annulled by divorce, but there is still an effect from the obligation of the husband to provide maintenance, and the fact that the (former) wife is (temporarily) forbidden from remarrying.

Sexual relations in this situation are forbidden and are counted as adultery, which must receive a penalty unless the offenders claim that they were unclear about the legal position of their act and thought that it was lawful, because the effects of marriage, namely those relating to the obligation to provide maintenance and the temporary prohibition for the (former) wife to remarry, still exist, such that these facts produced a strong supposition that the effects of marriage relating to the lawfulness of sexual relations also still existed. Although it cannot be made a legitimate *dalil*, this supposition, because it was believed to be a *dalil*, can nullify the *hadd*.

From the above explanation it is clear that for this *shubhah* to exist, the necessary conditions are that there are no *dalil* at all showing the prohibitedness of the act, and the offender must believe (have *i'tikad*) in its lawfulness. Hence, if there is a *dalil* that makes the act prohibited, or if he or she did not believe in its lawfulness, then the view is that there is no *shubhah*. If it is proven that he or she was certain his or her act was prohibited, then *hadd* must be given.

The second type is *Shubhah fil mahall*. An example is having sexual intercourse with a wife who has been divorced by a *kinayah* (unclear words) divorce. Someone who does this cannot be given the penalty (*hadd*), even if he is certain the act is unlawful.

Abu Hanifah added one other type of *shubhah* that could nullify the *hadd* for adultery, namely *shubhatul 'aqdi*, for example, having sexual intercourse, through marriage, with (1) a woman whom it is unlawful to marry (*mahram*), (2) another person's wife, (3) a fifth wife, and (4) another person's wife who is still in her 'waiting period' (*'iddah*), as well as having sexual intercourse with a woman who has been hired for the purpose of sex. Sexual relations in this situation of *shubhatul 'aqdi* do not give rise to *hadd*, even though the offender knows or supposes that it is unlawful. However, a judge may impose punishment on a person who is certain that the act is unlawful in the sense of the politics of law (*siyasah*), not as a *hadd*.

Other than by reason of *shubhah*, the *hadd* for adultery is also nullified (meaning it cannot be imposed) for the following reasons:

1. a retraction of a confession of adultery by someone who has confessed to adultery;
2. the witnesses (to adultery) retracting their testimony;
3. one of an adulterous couple rebutting the confession of adultery by the other person, or claiming to be married;
4. a witness to adultery becomes legally unreliable (*ahliyah*) before the *hadd* is carried out;
5. a witness dies before the punishment of stoning is carried out (these last three points (3–5) are only according to the Hanafi madhhab, the other three madhhabs disagree);
6. someone who commits adultery marrying the partner in adultery – this is only the view of Abu Yusuf of the Hanafi school, by reason that this marriage can give rise to *shubhah*. The other madhhabs disagree.

These are the circumstances that can nullify the *hadd* for adultery. From the analysis above, it can be concluded that the implementation of punishment in Islamic criminal law is highly elastic. In other words, to impose a certain punishment, there are many stringent conditions. Not every offence must be given a punishment, because there may be an element of *shubhah* therein. Besides this, it needs to be stated here that, according to a number of hadith of the Prophet,[70] someone who commits an offence that does not concern a *haqqul adami* (man's rights, see above) is urged to keep quiet about it, not to tell anyone else, and repent immediately. Thus also, people who see it are urged to keep quiet about it also. This is because in reality punishment is not the main objective, rather only a deterrent so that people do not transgress the commands or prohibitions of Allah. On a final note, the matter of *qisas* or the death penalty for murder, and also for physical violence, is *haqqul adami*. This means that its implementation is based on the demands of the victim's family. It is not mandatory for someone who has killed another to be given the death sentence. Thus, in these matters of murder and physical violence, the government (rulers) can regulate according to the requirements of the common good.

4. CONCLUSION

Although over the last century Western law, international norms and policies of codification have transformed the nature of criminal law in many Muslim nations, the criminal law as contained in the Quran and Sunna has not been relegated to history, but is implemented in varied forms in several Muslim nations and is subject to on-going *ijtihad*. This chapter introduced the important elements of Islamic criminal law, including the categories of prohibition (*jarimah* or *jinayah*) and punishment (*uqubah*), the dichotomy of 'Allah's' right and 'man's' rights, and the classic rules pertaining to *hudud*, *diyah*, *qisas* and *ta'zir*. Also introduced was the concept of *kaffarah*, which applies to specific violations, including unintentional killing, and provides an atonement mechanism for cleansing the sins of the wrong-doer. In addition to this overview of the classic stance, which remains relevant in light of the re-introduction of Islamic criminal law in parts of the Muslim world, the chapter also considered ways in which the sacred texts can be revisited by jurists and re-interpreted in light of changed conditions in modern times. This was done through analysis of the *hadd* offences of adultery and theft to show that it is possible to reform and reinterpret Islamic criminal law in a manner that is not only compatible with human rights principles but can also be justified under the Islamic legal tradition.

NOTES

1. See his website http://www.tariqramadan.com/An-International-call-for,264.html?lang=fr
2. '"Stoning" woman Sakineh Mohammadi Ashtiani could be hanged instead', 26 December 2011: http://www.news.com.au/world/stoning-woman-sakineh-mohammadi-ashtiani-could-be-hanged-instead/story-e6frfkyi-1226230371831
3. Al-Mawardi, *al-Ahkam as-Sultaniyah* (Dar al-Fikr, Beirut, 1983), 219.
4. Ahmad Fathi Bahansi, *al-'Uqubah fi al-Fiqh al-Islami* (Maktabah Dar al-'Urubah, Cairo, 1961), 9.

5. 'Abd al-Qadir, *'Audah, at-Tasyri' al-Jina'i al-Islami*, Vol. 1 (Mu'assasah ar-Risalah, Beirut, 1992), 609.
6. Abu Zahrah, *al-'Uqubah fi al-Fiqh al-Islami* (Dar al-Fikr al-Arabi, Cairo, 1990).
7. 'Abd al-Qadir *'Audah, at-Tasyri' al-Jina'i al-Islami* (Mu'assasah ar-Risalah, Beirut, 1992), 343–4.
8. Adultery is considered as a crime against descendants as it is against *hifz al-nasl* or *al-nasb* (protection of lineage), as one of the five objectives of Islamic law (*maqashid al-Shari'a*). In other words, it is damage to the family unit caused directly by adulterous relationships.
9. Ibid., 634.
10. On *Zihar*, see Chapter 5.
11. 'Abd al-Qadir, *'Audah, at-Tasyri'al-Jina'i al-Islami* (Mu'assasah ar-Risalah, Beirut, 1992), 4.
12. Ahmad Fathi Bahansi, *Nazariyat fi al-Fiqh al-Jina'i al-Islami* (al-Sharikah al-Arabiyah, Cairo, 1963), 55.
13. Ibid., 56.
14. Ibn 'Abidin, *Hasyiyah Radd al-Mukhtar*, Vol. 4 (Dar al-Alam al-Kutub, Riyadh, 2003), 48.
15. Al-Mawardi, *al-Ahkam as-Sultaniyah* (Dar al-Fikr, Beirut, 1983), 229; dan Muhammad Husain al-'Aqabi, *al-Majmu' Syarh al-Muhazzab* (Matba'ah al-Imam, Egypt, 1980), 298.
16. Al-Mawardi, *al-Ahkam as-Sultaniyah* (Dar al-Fikr, Beirut, 1983), 237; Ahmad Fathi Bahansi, *Nazariyat fi al-Fiqh al-Jina'i al-Islami* (al-Sharikah al-Arabiyah, Cairo, 1963), 65; Ahmad Fathi Bahansi, *al-'Uqubah fi al-Fiqh al-Islami* (Maktabah Dar al-'Urubah, Cairo, 1961), 115.
17. Ahmad Fathi Bahansi, *al-'Uqubah fi al-Fiqh al-Islami* (Maktabah Dar al-'Urubah, Cairo, 1961), 127.
18. 'Abd al-Qadir 'Audah, *at-Tasyri' al-Jina'i al-Islami* (Mu'assasah ar-Risalah, Beirut, 1992), 663.
19. The Quran, Súra Baqarah 2:178; Abdullah Yusuf Ali, *The Qur'an: Text, Translation and Commentary* (Tahrike Tarsile Qur'an, New York, 2005), 70.
20. The Quran, Súra Máida 5:45; Abdullah Yusuf Ali, *The Qur'an: Text, Translation and Commentary* (Tahrike Tarsile Qur'an, New York, 2005), 257.
21. The Quran, Súra Baqarah 2:178; Abdullah Yusuf Ali, *The Qur'an: Text, Translation and Commentary* (Tahrike Tarsile Qur'an, New York, 2005), 70–1.
22. The Quran, Súra Nisáa 4:92; Abdullah Yusuf Ali, *The Qur'an: Text, Translation and Commentary* (Tahrike Tarsile Qur'an, New York, 2005), 209.
23. J.N.D. Anderson, 'Homicide in Islamic Law' (1951) 13(4) *Bulletin of the School of Oriental and African Studies* 811.
24. Al-Mawardi, *al-Ahkam as-Sultaniyah* (Dar al-Fikr, Beirut, 1983), 221–3.
25. The Quran, Súra Núr 24:2; Abdullah Yusuf Ali, *The Qur'an: Text, Translation and Commentary* (Tahrike Tarsile Qur'an, New York, 2005), 896.
26. Muslim, *Sahih Muslim*, Vol. 2 (Dar al-Qalam, Beirut, 1987), 108; Tirmizi, *Jami' al-Tirmizi bi Sharh Tuhfah al-Ahwazi* (Dar al-Fikr, Beirut, 1980), 704.
27. Muslim, *Sahih Muslim*, Vol. 2 (Dar al-Qalam, Beirut, 1987), 99.
28. Bukhari, *Matn al-Bukhari bi Hasyiyah al-Sindi*, Vol. 4 (Dar al-Fikr, Beirut, 1995), 4205: Sulaiman b. Buraida reported on the authority of his father that Ma'iz b. Malik came to Allah's Apostle (may peace be upon him) and said to him: Messenger of Allah, purify me, whereupon he said: Woe be upon you, go back, ask forgiveness of Allah and turn to Him in repentance. He (the narrator) said that he went back not far, then came and said: Allah's Messenger, purify me. Whereupon Allah's Messenger (may peace be upon him) said: Woe be upon you, go back and ask forgiveness of Allah and turn to Him in repentance. He (the narrator) said that he went back not far,

when he came and said: Allah's Messenger, purify me. Allah's Apostle (may peace be upon him) said as he had said before. When it was the fourth time, Allah's Messenger (may, peace be upon him) said: From what am I to purify you? He said: From adultery, Allah's Messenger (may peace be upon him) asked if he had been mad. He was informed that he was not mad. He said: Has he drunk wine? A person stood up and smelt his breath but noticed no smell of wine. Thereupon Allah's Messenger (may peace be upon him) said: Have you committed adultery? He said: Yes. He made pronouncement about him and he was stoned to death. The people had been (divided) into two groups about him (Ma'iz). One of them said: He has been undone for his sins had encompassed him, whereas another said: There is no repentance more excellent than the repentance of Ma'iz, for he came to Allah's Apostle (may peace be upon him) and placing his hand in his (in the Holy Prophet's) hand said: Kill me with stones. (This controversy about Ma'iz) remained for two or three days. Then came Allah's Messenger (may peace be upon him) to them (his Companions) as they were sitting. He greeted them with salutation and then sat down and said: Ask forgiveness for Ma'iz b. Malik. They said: May Allah forgive Ma'iz b. Malik. Thereupon Allah's Messenger (may peace be upon him) said: He (Ma'iz) has made such a repentance that if that were to be divided among a people, it would have been enough for all of them. He (the narrator) said: Then a woman of Ghamid, a branch of Azd, came to him and said: Messenger of of Allah, purify me, whereupon he said: Woe be upon you; go back and beg forgiveness from Allah and turn to Him in repentance. She said: I find that you intend to send me back as you sent back Ma'iz. b. Malik. He (the Holy, Prophet) said: What has happened to you? She said that she had become pregnant as a result of fornication. He (the Holy Prophet) said: Is it you (who has done that)? She said: Yes. He (the Holy Prophet) said to her: (You will not be punished) until you deliver what is there in your womb. One of the Ansar became responsible for her until she was delivered (of the child). He (that Ansari) came to Allah's Apostle (may peace be upon him) and said the woman of Ghamid has given birth to a child. He (the Holy Prophet) said: In that case we shall not stone her and so leave her infant with none to suckle him. One of the Ansar got up and said: Allah's Apostle, let the responsibility of his suckling be upon me. She was then stoned to death.

29. The Quran, Súra Núr 24:4; Abdullah Yusuf Ali, *The Qur'an: Text, Translation and Commentary* (Tahrike Tarsile Qur'an, New York, 2005), 897.
30. Rudolph Peters, *Crime and Punishment in Islamic Law: Theory and Practice from the Sixteenth to the Twenty-first Century* (Cambridge University Press, Cambridge, 2005), 14–15.
31. The Quran, Súra Máida 5:90; Abdullah Yusuf Ali, *The Qur'an: Text, Translation and Commentary* (Tahrike Tarsile Qur'an, New York, 2005), 270–1.
32. See Muhammad bin Isma'il al-Bukhari, *Matn al-Bukhari bi Hasyiyah al-Sindi* (Dar al-Fikr, Beirut, 1995), 196.
33. Ibn Majah, *Sunan Ibn Majah* (Maktabah Dahlan, Semarang, 1996), 859.
34. The Quran, Súra Máida 5:38; Abdullah Yusuf Ali, *The Qur'an: Text, Translation and Commentary* (Tahrike Tarsile Qur'an, New York, 2005), 254.
35. The Quran, Súra Máida 5:33; Abdullah Yusuf Ali, *The Qur'an: Text, Translation and Commentary* (Tahrike Tarsile Qur'an, New York, 2005), 252–3.
36. See also Chapter 10.
37. The Quran, Súra Baqarah, 2:217; Abdullah Yusuf Ali, *The Qur'an: Text, Translation and Commentary* (Tahrike Tarsile Qur'an, New York, 2005), 85.
38. al-Bukhari, *Matn al-Bukhari bi Hasyiyah al-Sindi* (Dar al-Fikr, Beirut, 1995), 316.
39. See Mahmoud Ayoub, 'Religious Freedom and the Law of Apostasy in Islam' (1994), 20 *Islamochristiana*, 79–85.
40. S.A. Rahman, *Punishment of Apostasy in Islam* (Kazi, Chicago, IL, 1986).

41. See Frank Griffel, 'Toleration and Exclusion: al-Shafi'i and al-Ghazali on the Treatment of Apostates' (2001) 64 *Bulletin of the School of Oriental and African Studies* 3.
42. See also Chapter 10.
43. In 2001, an Islamist lawyer accused Nawal El-Saadawi, the noted Egyptian feminist activist, physician and writer, of apostasy, and argued that she should be divorced from her husband. See Nancy Gallagher, 'Apostasy, Feminism, and the Discourse of Human Rights' (2003), accessed at http://repositories.cdlib.org/uciaspubs/edited volumes/4/1058
44. The Quran, Súra Hujurát 49:9; Abdullah Yusuf Ali, *The Qur'an: Text, Translation and Commentary* (Tahrike Tarsile Qur'an, New York, 2005), 1405.
45. Khaled Abou El Fadl, *Rebellion and Violence in Islamic Law* (Cambridge University Press, Cambridge, 2001), 4.
46. Ibid.
47. Ibid.
48. See 'Abd al-Qadir *'Audah, at-Tasyri' al-Jina'i al-Islami* (Mu'assasah ar-Risalah, Beirut, 1992), 93–6.
49. Ahmad Fathi Bahansi, *al-'Uqubah fi al-Fiqh al-Islami* (Maktabah Dar al-'Urubah, Cairo, 1961), 13.
50. Ibid., 10–12; Ahmad Fathi Bahansi, *Nazariyat fi al-Fiqh al-Jina'i al-Islami* (al-Sharikah al-Arabiyah, Cairo, 1963), 71–5.
51. The Quran, Súra Máida 5:44, 45 and 47; Abdullah Yusuf Ali, *The Qur'an: Text, Translation and Commentary* (Tahrike Tarsile Qur'an, New York, 2005), 257–8.
52. Rudolph Peters, *Crime and Punishment in Islamic Law: Theory and Practice from the Sixteenth to the Twenty-first Century* (Cambridge University Press, Cambridge, 2005), 190.
53. Ibrahim Dasuqi asy-Syahawi, *As-Sariqah* (Maktabah Dar al-'Urubah, Cairo, 1961), 9–13; Ibrahim Hosen, 'Ukhuwwah Islamiyah Jangan Menjadi Retak Dikarenakan Masalah Khilafiyah' [Let Not Islamic Brotherhood Become Fractured Because of Khilafiyah Problems] (1981) 15(6) *Studia Islamika* 15–16.
54. Ibid.
55. Ibid.
56. Imam al-Fakhr ar-Razi, *at-Tafsir al-Kabir*, Vol. XI (Dar al-Kutub al-'Ilmiah, Tehran, n.d.), 228; and Al-Mawardi, *al-Ahkam as-Sultaniyah* (Dar al-Fikr, Beirut, 1983), 228.
57. Al-Alusi, *Ruh al-Ma'ani*, Vol. 6 (Dar Ihya' at-Turas al-'Arabi, Beirut, n.d.), 135.
58. Al-Mawardi, *al-Ahkam as-Sultaniyah*, Vol. 6 (Dar al-Fikr, Beirut, 1983), 218; Ibn 'Abidin, *Hasyiyah Radd al-Mukhtar*, Vol. 4 (Dar al-Alam al-Kutub, Riyadh, 2003), 4; al-Alusi, *Ruh al-Ma'ani*, Vol. 6 (Dar Ihya' at-Turas al-'Arabi, Beirut, n.d.), 120.
59. Syafii, *Al-Umm*, Vol. 7 (Dar al-Fikr, Beirut, 1990), 51.
60. The Quran, Súra Nisáa 4:16; Abdullah Yusuf Ali, *The Qur'an: Text, Translation and Commentary* (Tahrike Tarsile Qur'an, New York, 2005), 184.
61. Ibn Hajar, *Fath al-Bari*, Vol. 15 (Mustafa al-Babi al-Halabi, Egypt, 1959), 146; al-Baihaqi, *Tuhfah al-Ahwazi*, Vol. 4 (Dar al-Fikr, Beirut, 1980), 228.
62. The Quran, Súra Máida 5:39; Abdullah Yusuf Ali, *The Qur'an: Text, Translation and Commentary* (Tahrike Tarsile Qur'an, New York, 2005), 254.
63. Ibn Taimiyah, *Majmu' Fatawa*, Vol. XVI (Idarah al-Masahah al-'Askariah, Cairo, 1404 AH), 31.
64. Al-Qurtubi, *al-Jami' li Ahkam al-Qur'an*, Vol. 6 (Dar al-Katib al-'Arabi, Cairo, 1967), 174–5; Zamakhsyari, *al-Kasysyaf*, Vol. I (Mustafa al-Babi al-Halabi, Egypt, 1966), 612; Abu Hayyan al-Andalusi, *al-Bahr al-Muhit*, Vol. III (Dar al-Fikr, Bairut, 1978), 414; al-Fakh ar-Razi, *at-Tafsir al-Kabir*, Vol. XI (Dar al-Kutub al-'Ilmiah, Tehran, n.d.), 230.

65. See, among others, Ibn 'Abidin, *Hasyiyah Radd al-Mukhtar*, Vol. 4 (Dar al-Alam al-Kutub, Riyadh, 2003), 4.
66. See, among others, al-Alusi, *Ruh al-Ma'ani*, Vol. 6 (Dar Ihya' at-Turas al-'Arabi, Beirut, n.d.), 83.
67. Abdurrahman, *Tuhfah al-Ahwazi*, Vol. 4 (Dar al-Fikr, Beirut, 1990), 688.
68. Ibid.
69. Ibn 'Abidin, *Hasyiyah Radd al-Mukhtar*, Vol. 4 (Dar al-Alam al-Kutub, Riyadh, 2003), 18–25; 'Audah, *at-Tasyri' al-Jina'i al-Islami* (Mu'assasah ar-Risalah, Beirut, 1992), 209–16; Ibn al-Humam, *Syarh Fath al-Qadir*, Vol. 5 (Dar al-Fikr, Beirut, 1977), 247–61.
70. See, among others; Abdurrahman, *Tuhfah al-Ahwazi*, Vol. 4 (Dar al-Fikr, Beirut, 1990), 690–93.

10. Contemporary debates on and within Islam

1. INTRODUCTION

> Difference amongst my community is a sign of the bounty of Allah.
>
> (Hadith of the Prophet[1])

This chapter reflects on areas of legal contention for Muslims in the modern era. The five issues selected arouse debate not only in Western countries but also in many parts of the Muslim world. At a time when several Muslim nations are undergoing reform arising from what has been called the 'Arab Spring' or are wanting to revisit the direction for their nation, as seen in Malaysia and Turkey, there are more competing interpretations of Islam than at any other period of history. Whether it is in elections, protests, campaigns, on-line sites or academic debate, the prospects of new directions, whether modernist, conservative or, textualist are the defining feature of the twenty-first century. These contrasting visions were evident in the views presented by the ten Presidential candidates in Egypt's 2012 elections, as well as in the platforms of the two final candidates for the presidency, Mohamed Mursi of the Muslim Brotherhood and Ahmed Shafik, of Mubarak's military regime.[2] The same breadth of vision is true for other Muslim nations, whether Tunisia, Indonesia or Iraq, and while this gives rise to internal tensions, the plurality of views is evidence of the vibrancy of contemporary Islam. The other contemporary dimension of Islam that is characteristic of the twenty-first century is the migration of Muslims to the West, which has fostered forms of religious and ethnic pluralism within Western countries. As Western societies review ways to better accommodate their Muslim citizens, there are particular issues on which unanimity is far from being achieved. Divergence, even tension, is intensified by the range of views Muslims too have on many of these issues. Although all Muslims share the central tenets of Islam, there can be considerable variation in their application and adherence. This variety is seen among today's 1.6 billion Muslims in the world: there are 49 nations where the Muslim population is over 50 per cent, some with a bare Muslim majority, such as Chad, which has a population that is 55 per cent Muslim, while other nations, for example, Iran, Morocco, Tunisia and Yemen, are overwhelmingly Muslim at 99 per cent of their population.[3] Some Muslim majority nations are secular republics, like Turkey, for which Sharia is not part of the legal system, while others are Islamic monarchies, like Saudi Arabia, where Sharia is pivotal to all aspects of law and governance. This heterogeneity highlights that intra-Muslim plurality is axiomatic. Events in the Islamic calendar, such as Ramadan and the *hajj*, unite Muslims everywhere, but at times bitter divisions on sectarian and ethnic lines tear Muslim societies apart. The aim of this chapter is not to highlight tensions but to canvass a range of perspectives, Muslim and non-Muslim, on some topical issues and appraise the Islamic foundation for each. It is hoped this chapter will demonstrate how Muslims using Islamic methodology can legitimately come to different conclusions on a question, as well as outlining some of the frequently articulated non-Muslim perspectives on these very same issues that at times bewilder and concern non-Muslims.

2. DEBATE ON THE BURQA

Possibly no issue gives rise to more polarization, concern and division than that of the burqa. The term 'burqa' comes from the Arabic root 'to sew up' and technically refers to a form of a loose outer garment that covers the entire woman's body including her head, where there is a mesh panel or woven grille concealing her eyes and mouth that enables her to see out, but prevents others from seeing in. Traditionally the garment was worn in Afghanistan, where it is also called a *chadri*, and in adjacent parts of Pakistan, such as the Northwest Province, and some parts of India. Today the term is used more broadly in the West to refer to any form of Muslim dress that conceals a woman's face (eyes may be excluded) in addition to covering her body. The word 'burqa' is technically incorrectly used to include the *sitar*, the long veil that covers a woman's eyes and body, in addition to all forms of face veils, the *niqab*,[4] which may be worn with an *abaya* (cloak) as in the Middle East, or with a *chador* in Iran, or a *jilbab* elsewhere. The word 'hijab' comes from the Arabic word for curtain or cover and refers to a veil or headscarf that allows a woman's face, but not hair, to be visible. Other forms of headscarves are *al-amira*, *shayla*, *tudong*, *kerudung* and *khimar*. The word 'hijab' is also used generically to mean modest Islamic clothing involving a veil or headcovering.

In discussing the issues surrounding it, the term 'burqa' will be used in its lay or popular sense to mean a body covering that includes the concealment of the face, and the generic words 'veil' or 'headscarf' will be used to describe head coverings that allow the face to be seen.

Today the angst about veiling is almost exclusively directed at Muslim women. Heath writes that it is 'a locus for the struggle between Islam and the West and between contemporary and traditional interpretations of Islam'.[5] Yet, not all Muslim women veil and women from other religions also choose to veil. Throughout history veiling was a common practice in Christianity, Judaism and Hinduism. It is rare for the Virgin Mary, mother of Jesus, to be depicted without a veil, and for centuries Catholic women who took holy orders as nuns veiled while laywomen covered their heads at Mass. These practices mainly ended in the 1960s with the Second Vatican Council's determination to 'renew and update the church', but the end to veiling in the Catholic Church was not without controversy. Fifty years later, many brides in the Christian tradition will still veil for marriage. A large number of Greek and Southern Italian women continue to wear a black headscarf, similar to Muslim women in rural Turkey.

For Muslims, the history of when and where Muslim women started veiling is not clear. One view is that, during the time of the Prophet, women did not veil but that, as Islam spread towards the Persian, Assyrian and Byzantine-Christian regions where upper class or wealthy women did veil (in contrast to peasants and slaves), the custom was also adopted into Muslim practice.[6] Another view is that forms of veiling did occur in the desert communities of pre-Islamic Arabia as a means to protect the face from the elements of the sun, sand, dust and wind, but after Allah's revelations to the Prophet it became mandatory to veil for female modesty, at first for the Prophet's wives and then, through emulation, for all Muslim women. The practice spread but took on the colours and features prevailing in different local cultures where these were compatible with the principle of covering the body and head.

Today, the headscarf in all its manifestations is the most visible sign of identification as a Muslim woman. Data shows that it is now adopted more frequently than it was 50 years ago. In the 1950s, veiling had almost disappeared in some societies where economic, political and scientific advances were accelerating, such as Egypt, as unveiling became associated with women's social advancement in Muslim societies. The exception to the general trend away from veiling was in places the historian Albert Hourani called the 'backward regions' of Saudi Arabia and Yemen.[7] Today, however, women whose mothers did not veil are choosing to do so, both in Muslim and in Western countries. The revival and popularity of the burqa is spreading to parts of the Muslim world, such as Malaysia and Brunei, where by tradition a women's face was always visible and where veiling was optional. It would seem that a sign of modern Islam is a revival of tradition. Return to traditional dress and head-coverings for women may demonstrate an explicit rejection of Western practices and values in support of Islam. In countries like Tunisia and Turkey, prohibitions on Islamic clothing are being relaxed or overturned. Muslim immigrant communities in the West adopt the burqa and headscarves as symbols of religiosity and empowerment to assert a collective identity distinct from the Western one in which they reside. It is not all one-way, however. At the other end of the spectrum is another manifestation of modern Islam: this is the woman who rejects traditional clothing, believing what is in her head is more important than what is on it, and what is in her heart counts more in the eyes of Allah than what covers her body. These Muslim women dismiss as superficial the conflation of religious piety with layers of clothing. This dimension is not just for Muslim women in the West. Some prominent Muslim women in media organizations and in parliaments choose to wear Western-style suits, at the risk of peer and public condemnation. In Kuwait and Jordan attempts were made to exclude non-hijab-wearing female members of parliament.[8]

To analyse these dichotomous positions, the starting point must be the Quran. How the Quranic passages have been interpreted by scholars, past and contemporary, gives rise to the disparity of views. This will be followed by reflections on the burqa in a political, cultural and religious context in Muslim lands and also from the non-Muslim perspective, including the rationale for several European countries imposing bans and fines for wearing a burqa in public.

A. The Quran

There are several verses in the Quran that relate to the appropriate dress for Muslim women in general and one that refers to the Prophet's wives. The most commonly cited verse is Súra Núr 24:31:

> And say to the believing women that they should lower their gaze and guard their modesty; that they should not display their beauty and ornaments except what (must ordinarily) appear thereof; that they should draw their veils over their bosoms and not display their beauty except to their husbands, their fathers, their husband's fathers, their sons … or small children who have no sense of the shame of sex; and that they should not strike their feet in order to draw attention to their hidden ornaments.[9]

The traditionalist interpretation of this verse interprets broadly the phrase 'not display their beauty and ornaments' as to encompass every aspect of a woman's body, including hands and face. Lowering 'their gaze' directs specific attention to the feature of her eyes, which makes the burqa the ideal manifestation of the Quranic passage. For traditionalists, the wearing of the burqa or *niqab* is a command of God and is an obligation (*fard*), not a mere recommendation (*mustahabb*) for women. The face is regarded not as the last, but as the first 'bodily part' that she must cover, because her face 'is the source of temptation and the source of people desiring her'.[10] Men must be protected from any desire that the sight of a woman's face could arouse while a Muslim woman can feel more secure and appear less sexual if wearing a burqa.

The modernist view is that this verse does not say a woman is to cover any particular part of the body, except for the bosom, and the words 'except what must ordinarily appear' can only be referring to the hands and face. To extend the phrase 'not display their beauty' to covering one's face, hair, hands and her entire body belies Islam's true message of modesty and humility. This is supported by the preceding verse, which calls on men to also 'lower their gaze and guard their modesty' (Quran, Súra Núr 24:30), so modesty is the key for both genders. The verse requires both sexes to 'lower their gaze'; in order to follow this requirement, the face and especially the eyes must be visible. There is no comparable juristic ruling that men should cover their faces, so it is paternalistic to interpret it to apply solely for women. What is modest should be determined in keeping with what others in the society wear and this will change over time, according to place, and also according to cultural practices and the tasks women will perform. Modernists refute that the onus should rest on women alone to curb male desire, and stress that men should develop self-control. If men and women have equal obligations to submit to God, it cannot be only women who are expected to manifest this dedication outwardly in the form of either burqa or even hijab.

The only verse in the Quran (Súra Ahzáb 33:53) where the more generic word 'hijab' (curtain or screen) is used is in the context of the wives of the Prophet. 'And when ye ask of them [the wives of the Prophet] anything, ask it of them from behind a curtain'. Scholars would extrapolate concealment by the curtain inside his home to outside places with the hijab 'a physical barrier'[11] between women and others. Modernist scholars such as Reza Aslan and Leila Ahmed[12] draw on this to show that requirements for hijab, or covering, were applicable just for the Prophet's wives because of their exalted status and special social position as the Prophet's intimate companions. On the other hand, traditionalists assert that this requirement in the Quran laid down the exemplar for all Muslim women to emulate. Yet a verse in the same chapter, Súra Ahzáb 33:32, clearly states 'O Consorts of the Prophet! Ye are not like any of the (other women)'.[13] This enables the verse following at 33:35 to be a qualifier, limiting the hijab requirement to the Prophet's wives, rather than laying down an edict for women in all places and in subsequent centuries.

i. Ahadith

There is an array of hadith relating to women's dress, and several deal with the wearing of the face-covering *niqab*. One narrated by al Bukhari is that women during *hajj* must show their face and hands, thereby making it forbidden (*haram*) to wear *niqab*, a burqa or gloves during *ihram*.[14] Literalists use this hadith to support the wearing of *niqab* at all other times on the basis that the Prophet would not have otherwise needed to spell out the *hajj* exception. The alternative view is that, if face covering was not required at this important religious ceremony, where both genders are present, then it would not be mandatory at other times. Another hadith narrated by A'isha that further supports the conservative stance is: 'When (the verse): They should draw their veils over their bosoms was revealed, (the ladies) cut their waist sheets at the edges and covered their faces with the cut pieces'.[15] Similarly, at the end of a long narration, the Prophet said: 'and if one of the women of Paradise looked at the earth, she would fill the whole space between them (the earth and the heaven) with light, and would fill whatever is in between them, with perfume, and the *veil of her face* [italics added] is better than the whole world and whatever is in it'.[16] However, there are hadith which support the less restrictive view. For example, one hadith recounts that, when the Prophet was travelling with Al Fadhl, they came across a beautiful woman who spoke to the Prophet seeking advice for her father, and Al Fadhi was impressed by her beauty until the Prophet turned Al Fadhi's head away.[17] For Al Fadhi to notice her beauty, she must not have had her face veiled, and the fact that the Prophet did not warn or chastise her for this indicates his tacit or silent approval for her unveiled state.

It can be seen from the preceding discussion how legitimate juristic differences of opinion can arise. For modernists this diversity is to be respected and admired as it gives flexibility to Muslim women to follow the interpretation that resonates with them. For textualists this diversity of views can be dangerous as it fractures the *ummah*. Yet, the burqa debate continues unabated today and remains controversial even in the Muslim heartlands. There was mixed reaction to Saudi cleric Sheikh Muhammad al-Habadan's ruling that women should not only cover their faces, but when wearing *niqab* should reveal only one eye because 'showing both eyes encourages women to use eye make-up to look seductive'.[18] There were mixed reactions also to Sheikh Mohammad Sayyed Tantawi, the Grand Imam of al-Azhar, Egypt, ruling that face covering was a pre-Islamic customary practice, and not a religious injunction. In certain contexts, notably at schools, he argued that the face must be visible and was reported telling a student wearing a *niqab* at school to immediately remove it.[19] In the West there is also division amongst Islamic scholars, with the majority of the view that, if it accords with her religious beliefs, then it is a woman's right as a Muslim to wear the burqa or *niqab*. While it is noted that in countries like Canada, for example, most scholars 'are silent'[20] on whether the burqa is obligatory or not, there are some, such as Britain's Shaykh Syed Mutawalli Darsh, who caution against women covering their face in the West. This is because face coverings may create a barrier between the wearer and non-Muslims for whom the concept has never been known. Full veiling may therefore mitigate against outreach (*da'wah*) to non-Muslims, which is an obligation on all Muslims.[21] Covering her face may also cause a Muslim woman to be harassed. Muneeb Nasr writes that a 'reasoned justification for not wearing the *niqab* in this society (Canada) is needed – one that seeks to engage others in an intra-community discussion, not alienation'.[22]

Reflecting on practices across the Muslim world, it is apparent that what women wear becomes an important index of many factors: the prevailing *fiqh*; the nation's political direction; the influence of the *ulama* at the public and personal level; and the woman's own religious conviction. Conservative Hanbali Saudi Arabia requires all women, Muslim or non-Muslim to veil and wear an *abaya* in public places. Religious police (*muttawa*) enforce the law. In Taliban-controlled areas of Afghanistan there are severe penalties for violation of the burqa dress code. The opposite is true in some secularized Muslim nations, where it is the burqa that is banned. From the 1980s liberal Tunisia banned not only the burqa but also the hijab in public schools, universities and government buildings. When the Islamist party gained office in the 2011 elections, they quickly quelled fears that Tunisian women would now be forced to wear hijab. Instead, they stated that wearing the hijab is recommended, but is not obligatory. At the political level, regime change may mean a whole different legal and religious paradigm in which what women wear is a key visual and symbolic component. This has been evident since 1925, when Ataturk prohibited not only *niqab* but all forms of veiling for women in the modernization and secularization of Turkey. The Shah of Iran followed suit, only to have the policy fully overturned by Khomeini's Islamic Revolution when the strict *chador* dress code was restored and enforced. Today there are reports of young Iranian women testing the boundaries of that law by adopting tighter fitting clothing and minimal or loose headscarves. Conversely in Turkey women are willing to risk penalties by wearing burqas and forms of hijab in public places in contravention of the law. Syria banned the *niqab* from universities in 2010 only to reverse the policy 12 months later during the uprisings and civil unrest. Even in nations like Indonesia, what Muslim women wear is at the forefront of religious and legislative debate both nationally and now in the provinces, which have the power to set and enforce their own dress codes and morality programmes.

Muslim women's dress clearly comes with political, religious and cultural messages that an observer can decode. Dress can be seen to align the wearer with a Salafi or a modernist interpretation of Islam. It can signify a political direction either in support of, or against, secularism or Islamization or against Western cultural dominance through colonization or globalization. It also can reflect a cultural identity and tradition. In Afghanistan a woman wears the light hues of the burqa and secludes herself (*purdah*) to demonstrate her and her family's honour and respect for social order.[23] On the Arabian Peninsula she wears a black *abaya* as a reflection of Salafi traditonalism,[24] which generally restricts her movements in public non-segregated spaces. In Malaysia, she wears the vibrant colours of traditional *baju kurung* with *tudong* and is not constrained by notions of *purdah* as Malay women have for centuries worked with and alongside men. However, these identifications are not static. For example, the spread of Salafi Islam from Saudi Arabia to Southeast Asia has meant that some Malaysian women who want to show their identification with that worldview don black *abaya* and *niqab*. Wearers of face coverings also believe that it brings them closer to God and personifies their piety, spirituality and the highest possible personal level of modesty.

B. Burqa Bans in the West

In Western nations with significant Muslim minorities most people accept the headscarf as a visible expression of a Muslim identity, but see the burqa as something alien and confronting. The burqa gives rise to a number of concerns in Western secular nations: rejection of the nation's culture and values; subjugation of Muslim women by Muslim men, whether fathers, husbands or imams; alignment with reactionary Islamist forces or terrorist-supporting bodies; and weakening of human rights protections through oppression and loss of female autonomy. In response to these concerns, burqa and *niqab* wearing Muslim women in the West claim that it is in fact Western women who are oppressed by their sexualization and objectification. Women who wear face coverings argue that it is their human right to cover their face in any nation that claims to enshrine freedom of religion and expression; it is completely their decision and not one imposed on them, directly or indirectly by men; that Islamist views are lawful in a democracy and, as terrorism is contrary to Islam, it can have no connection or connotation with what a woman wears. At times, supporters of a burqa take a critical stance against the laxity and permissiveness in the West. It is frequently expressed that the clothing of Western women is a sign that Western men do not value women and that women in turn have low self-esteem, dressing only to please men's carnal desires. In contrast, because Muslim women in burqas are kept hidden, they are treasured like precious jewels. This type of reasoning was evident in a well-publicized Friday sermon given by Sheik Taj Din al-Hilali, the then Mufti of Australia and one of the nation's senior clerics, in which he made the analogy that women who do not wear the Islamic veil are like meat left uncovered in the street to be eaten by cats; in effect, their immodest dress invites sexual assault and gives excuse to the man who does so.[25] His view, however, was widely criticized by other leaders of Australia's Muslim community and it shocked non-Muslims.

In liberal Western societies, it is not only non-Muslims that find the burqa confronting. Some Muslims also express angst because for them it does not evoke piety; rather they see it is as 'the signature dress of Islamism' and are concerned that extremist, militant Islam is taking root in the West in the hearts and minds of young Muslims.[26] Rather than canvass the extensive range of opinions across Western societies, the chapter will provide a brief overview of the debate over the 'burqa ban' in France – the country with the largest Muslim population (6 million) in Europe.

i. France and the burqa ban

In 2009, France's President Sarkozy said that the nation 'cannot accept that women be prisoners behind a screen, cut off from all social life, deprived of all identity'[27] and set up a commission of inquiry to investigate the wearing of face coverings. The following year, France's National Assembly passed 335–1 an 'Act prohibiting concealment of the face in Public Space'[28] (hereinafter the Act) with a fine of €150 or lessons in French citizenship, or both, for concealing one's face in a public place, which included cinemas, theatres, businesses (cafés, restaurants, shops), banks institutions, railway stations, airports and all means of public transport, as well as forests, beaches and public gardens.[29] The

Act is worded neutrally to cover men and women of any age or nationality, but specifies the wearing of *niqab* or burqa as forms of concealment along with other face-covering items such as balaclavas, helmets and masks. The rationale given to the people of France was that face-coverings prevent the clear identification of a person, which can be both a security risk and a social hindrance within a society that relies on facial recognition and expression in communication. Also, in the words of the Minister of Justice and Freedom, the 'wearing of the full veil signifies a withdrawal from national society, rejection of the very spirit of the French Republic founded on the desire for social cohesion'.[30] The Act was passed by the Senate and also found to be constitutionally valid by France's Constitutional Council,[31] on the grounds that 'such practices are dangerous for public safety and security' and 'women who conceal their face, voluntarily or otherwise, are placed in a situation of exclusion and inferiority patently incompatible with constitutional principles of liberty and equality'. In addition, the Act creates an offence in the Penal Code (art 225-4-10) of compelling another person, 'by means of threats, duress or constraint, undue influence or misuse of authority … by reason of the sex of said person to conceal their face'. This offence is punishable by one year's imprisonment and a fine of €30,000, and these punishments are doubled if the person compelled is a minor. The Act is subject to a series of cases being brought to the European Court of Human Rights on grounds that the ban is in violation of Article 9 (religious freedom) and Article 14 (discrimination) of the European Convention on Human Rights.[32]

While the Act received criticism, with public shows of defiance by some Muslim women and supporters of a Muslim's right to choose,[33] it was generally popular in France. The burqa ban was reported as having 80 per cent popular support, and Muslim members of Parliament also voted for the ban. Fadela Amara, the Muslim Algerian-born housing minister, called the burqa 'a kind of tomb, a horror for those trapped within it',[34] and 'a visible symbol of the subjugation of women', and the Mufti of Paris, Dalil Boubakeur, advised the Assembly that the *niqab* was not prescribed in Islam and he saw it as inconsistent with French secularism. However, he did caution that imposing any legislated ban would be difficult. French politicians also noted Tantawi's support for the banning of the burqa (as noted earlier in this chapter) and that of fellow al-Azhar cleric, Abdel Muti al-Bayyumi, who stated: 'I want to send a message to Muslims in France and Europe. The niqab has no basis in Islam … I personally support the ban and many of my brothers in the Islamic Research Academy support it'.[35] There have been only a handful of arrests but the law sends a message that the burqa, at this point in time, is inconsistent with French citizenship. This message is reflected in cases where citizenship for Muslim women is denied on the ground that burqa wearing is 'incompatible with the fundamental values of the French community, and notably with the principle of sexual equality'.[36] Amnesty International condemned the law as a human rights violation of the freedom of expression of the women who choose to wear it willingly. Although Sarkozy lost the Presidential election in 2012, his socialist successor, Hollande, guaranteed to the voters that, if elected, he would not seek to overturn the law.

The stance taken by France commenced a chain of similar responses across Europe regarding the burqa. Belgium and Italy have enacted similar legislation, and the Netherlands Parliament voted in support of a ban on 'concealing the face', to take effect in 2013. Austria, Spain and Switzerland are currently debating the issue. The UK and Australia have ruled out such a ban, but it remains divisive with tension points arising regularly. Australian Senator Cory Bernadi supports a ban because the 'burqa isolates some Australians from others. Its symbolic barrier is far greater than the measure of cloth it is created from'.[37] However, unlike France, where the Left and Right of politics agree, no political party in Australia has taken such an un-libertarian stance, but both the Prime Minister and Leader of the Opposition have described the sight of women in burqas as 'confronting'.[38]

Apart from the symbolism of 'them and us', the religious dimensions and human rights implications, there are practical aspects, especially in Western nations, that arise regarding the burqa. Can a burqa or *niqab* wearer give evidence in court, especially as a witness in a criminal trial, where the jury have to assess the veracity of the testimony of the witness without seeing her facial expression? An Australian Court said no,[39] whereas New Zealand allowed it.[40] When facial recognition is the basis of passports, driver licences and other forms of identification, what exceptions, if any, should be made for a Muslim woman who wears a burqa? If identification by face is not possible, should face-covered women be fingerprinted? This was an issue in Australia after a Muslim woman wearing a burqa was charged and convicted of making false accusations against the police, but had this overturned on appeal because the court could not be absolutely certain of her identification because the burqa prevented any facial identification.[41] What concessions should be made to enable fully veiled Muslim women to engage in sport including in national teams? Australia's design of the burqini for recreational swimming as well as for use in Surf Life Saving was well received amongst the wider community, and deemed 'permissible' by Mufti Hilali, but was not accepted by all Islamic clerics, as there were concerns it hugged the body and a woman's form was apparent, especially when the fabric was wet.[42] The burqini also leaves the face exposed. What degree of accommodation should be made for Muslims who wear the burqa and seek differential treatment? In response to a request for separate citizenship ceremonies for Muslim women who cover their faces, Canada not only rejected segregated ceremonies but banned Muslim women from covering their faces during such ceremonies on the ground that 'we are all becoming Canadians together and … it is only a sign of respect for your fellow citizens, when you are pledging to them your commitment to live in a community with them, to show your face and who you are and that your pledge is heartfelt and authentic'.[43]

The debate goes on – in the West and in Muslim nations, in universities, parliaments, in the media, in homes and between friends. Whether the burqa is a source of women's liberation which enables her 'to be judged not on face value' but for who she is 'as a person', or whether it empowers her by being 'in control of displaying [her] beauty to whom she chooses'[44] or whether the burqa is, simply, as Saudi journalist Maha al-Hujailan describes it, 'walking prison',[45] will remain a moot issue.

3. THE DEBATE ABOUT SHARIA AND THE STATE

After the events of 11 September 2001 world leaders wondered whether democracy could flourish in the lands where Islam prevails. The main question posed was: is Sharia compatible with democracy, the rule of law and constitutionalism? Different responses to this will be explored in this section including the views of opponents of Islamic constitutional law and the counter arguments. One group of scholars takes the view that Sharia is sufficient to meet all Muslim needs, so that a Western version of democracy, the rule of law, human rights and constitution is redundant. As the Sharia is God's law, it is above these Western and foreign concepts. In other words, according to this authoritarian view, Sharia has already provided a unique system of government or politics. Another perspective is that Sharia should have no relationship with state affairs. According to the views of this secularist group, it is misleading to enforce the Sharia through a constitution, since one contradicts the other. Although both perspectives (authoritarian and secularist) have different arguments, they share the same conclusion: that the nature and characteristics of the Sharia do not permit compatibility between Sharia and constitutionalism.

The arguments for both views will be summarized and a third view, that Sharia is compatible with democracy, constitutionalism and the rule of law, will be explained.

A. Authoritarian or Traditionalist Perspectives

The authoritarian or traditionalist perspective of Sharia argues that the immutability, divine nature and breadth of Sharia suits it for all situations, and that it is incompatible with the concepts of constitutionalism.

First, authoritarians view Islamic law as immutable because the authoritarian, divine and absolute concept of law in Islam does not allow for change in legal concepts and institutions. The Sharia is immutable, regardless of history, time, culture and location. Sharia has also never developed an adequate methodology of legal change. Muslims may change, but Islam will not. This means that the rulings pronounced by the Sharia are static, final, eternal, absolute and unalterable. In other words, the idealistic and religious, rigid and casuistic nature of Sharia leads to its immutability.[46] This position is not compatible with the nature of a constitution that can be amended, modified, reformed or even replaced by a new one.

Second, the Sharia is based on the revelation of God. The source of Islamic law is the will of God, which is absolute and unchangeable. There has always been a close connection between Islamic law and theology. This means that the laws that do exist must operate within the boundaries set by the Sharia. In other words, the real of power is in the hand of Allah.[47] This condition is in contradiction with the nature of constitutionalism, which is based on the will of people. Accordingly, in the Sharia, sovereignty belongs to God, not to the people.[48] This means that the government must act according to the Sharia. It is argued by supporters of this view that the fact that a legislative measure has been supported by a majority does not necessarily imply that it is a 'right' measure. It is always possible that the majority, however large and even well-intentioned, is on occasion mistaken, while the minority, despite being a minority in quantity, is right. What is right and what is wrong should be based on the Sharia, not on the popular vote.[49] Accordingly, democracy is not compatible with Islam.

Third, constitutionalism is not drawn originally from Islam. It is a Western product and part of its hegemony. The tension between church and state in the Western tradition is evident in all European constitutional traditions, and in the constitutions of colonial states such as the United States and Australia.[50] It is argued that adopting constitutionalism, which is outside of Islamic discourse, will lead Muslims to abandon their own religion by separating Islam from politics. Moreover, in Islam, democracy and the rule of law are alien concepts introduced by Western tradition. Unlike in a secular state, there is no distinction or separation between religion and state in the Sharia. Islam is a religion and a state (*din wa dawlah*).[51] Politics of the state is a part of Islamic teachings, in that Islam is a religion as much as it is a legal system. Secularization, or the separation of religion and politics, is seen as the product of Western conspiracy and colonialism, directed against Islam. During the colonial era, accordingly, the concept of secularization was introduced into Muslim society in order to maintain Western power. With the separation of religion and politics, the jihad would be meaningless. The term and the idea of 'secularization' became pejorative. Any Muslim scholar who supported this concept would allegedly be seen as a supporter of Western hegemony. Accordingly, constitutionalism is the product of this Western idea.[52]

Fourth, it is argued that, based on the Quran (Súra Máida 5:3),[53] Sharia is perfect and covers a broad range of topics such as ritual, social interaction, criminal law and political law. Every single problem can be answered by the Sharia because it was designed for all times and places and for universal application to all peoples. It is comprehensive and encompasses all aspects of law: personal, societal, governmental, constitutional, criminal, mercantile, war and peace and international treaties. Hence, Islam is an ideology addressing all life affairs,[54] in contrast to constitutionalism, which will not (and cannot) provide answers for all the problems of human kind.

B. Secularist Perspectives

In contrast to the views of the authoritarians and traditionalists, the secularists argue that the Sharia is not compatible with constitutionalism since the Sharia is a matter for individual compliance. States do not have the right to intervene nor to enforce Sharia law on the public. One may observe that Islamic law began with the activities of jurists guided by religious motives, and was not a creation of legislation. This results in the jurists' conviction of the independence of Islamic law free from state control. States could encourage their citizens' compliance with the Sharia, such as in paying *zakat*, fasting and going on the pilgrimage to Mecca, but a state could not force its citizenry to comply. Unlike the authoritarians' view, secularists believe the Sharia cannot (and should not) take the place of a constitution. They introduce the idea of de-politicizing Islam, and determine it to be solely a religious faith, a view articulated by the Islamic scholar 'Ali 'Abd al-Raziq.[55]

In addition, secularists argue that, owing to the fact that the Sharia was laid down 15 centuries ago, it is fit only for the conditional, political and institutional conditions of that time. The Sharia could operate only in a traditional state (or city-state) based on the personal charisma of the leader rather than a constitutional system. Fifteen centuries ago, there was no parliament, no check-and-balance system, no judicial review, no accountable governance, no separation of powers, and so on. The implementation of the Sharia therefore is in contradiction with modern institutions and concepts. Moreover, constitutions cannot be viable documents in the absence of the ideological, cultural and political prerequisites for constitutional life. How can constitutionalism emerge in societies in which liberalism and secularism are so far from hegemonic?

If constitutionalism is defined as a set of ideologies and institutions predicated on the idea of the limitation and regulation of government authority by law, the Sharia does not limit the power of governments. Accordingly, the caliph could do anything he wanted without the fear of facing the opposition party or even impeachment procedures. In this way, the implementation of the Sharia would lead to an undemocratic state. The power of the caliph was unlimited. In the words of Bassam Tibi, 'none of them was a legal ruler in the modern constitutional sense'.[56] One of the reasons for this is that there existed no institutional authority able to control the caliph's compliance with the Sharia. The received image is that Islamic law allows the ruler (king, prime minister or president) to govern as a dictator: whatever his decision, it is always right. This follows with other images that Sharia does not provide procedural regulations to control a government, does not have a clear rule on how to elect a government nor how to limit the powers of the government, and there is no judicial independence in the countries that adhere to the Sharia. The decision of the caliph would be based heavily on his discretion, or his interpretation of the Sharia, not on the rule of law.

The best model of the authoritarian view is Saudi Arabia. The Quran and the Sunna are that country's constitution and the Sharia is its basic law, implemented by the Sharia courts with *ulama* as judges and legal advisors. The head of state is a king, elected by and from the extensive Saud' family. The king, assisted by a council of ministers, supervises legislative and executive institutions, and the judiciary. Saudi Arabia has no institutions such as a House of Representatives whose members are elected by the people, and has no political parties. The best model of a secular state in the Muslim world is Turkey. The republic that Kemal Ataturk founded and subsequent leaders have shaped is radically different from the imperial society of the Islamic Ottoman Empire. Turkish law is codified, with civil and commercial law originally based on the Swiss system, administrative law based on the French system and criminal law based on the Italian system. Turkey today is a secular state. Turkey has mosques, churches and synagogues open to all, but politicians are forbidden to exploit religion for political purposes.

C. The Third Way

Do we have the third option? Contrary to the (religious) authoritarians' views, other Muslim scholars such as Abdullahi Ahmed An-Na'im and Muhammad Sa'id Al-Ashmawy advocate an emancipated understanding of the Sharia, stressing its original meaning as a 'path' or guide, rather than a detailed legal code. The Sharia must involve human interpretation. Islamic law is, in fact, the product of a very slow and gradual process of interpretation of the Quran and the collection, verification and interpretation of the Sunna during the first three centuries of Islam (seventh to the ninth centuries AD). This process took place amongst scholars and jurists who developed their own methodology for the classification of sources, and the derivation of specific rules from general principles, as was discussed in Chapter 1.

This led scholars to distinguish between the Sharia and *fiqh*. While the Sharia can be seen as the totality of divine categorizations of human acts, *fiqh* might be described as the articulation of the divine categorizations by human scholars. These articulations represent or express the scholars' understanding of the Sharia. This means that jurists or scholars in the Islamic tradition, however highly respected they may be, can present only their own personal views or understanding of what the Sharia is on any given matter. Moreover, the Quran and the Sunna cannot be understood or have any influence on human behaviour except through the efforts of (fallible) human beings.

Therefore, even though Sharia is based on the revelations of God, it cannot possibly be drawn up except through human understanding, which means both the inevitability of differences of opinion and the possibility of error, whether amongst scholars or the community in general. Khaled Abou El Fadl explains further: 'All laws articulated and applied in a state are thoroughly human, and should be treated as such. Consequently, any codification of Shari'a law produces a set of laws that are thoroughly and fundamentally human. These laws are a part of Shari'a law only to the extent that any set of human legal opinions is arguably a part of Shari'a. A code, even if inspired by Shari'a, is not Shari'a.'[57]

Since Sharia involves human understanding, the social norms of Sharia follow the nature of human beings because they are derived from specific historical circumstances. For instance, the caliphate was the product of history, an institution of human, rather than divine, origin, a temporary convenience, and therefore a purely political office. This means that most of the regulations in Islamic law, including the status of non-Muslims and women in Islamic societies, may be amended, changed, altered and adapted to social change. An-Na'im argues that the coercive enforcement of Sharia by the state betrays the Quran's insistence on voluntary acceptance of Islam. Just as the state should be secure from the misuse of religious authority, Sharia should be freed from the control of the state. State policies or legislation must be based on civic reasons accessible to citizens of all religions. An-Na'im maintains that the very idea of an 'Islamic state' is one based on European ideas of state and law, and not Sharia or the Islamic tradition.[58]

While the Quran contains a variety of elements, such as stories, moral injunctions and general, as well as specific, legal principles, it should be noted that the Quran prescribes only those details that are essential. It thus leaves considerable room for development, and safeguards against restrictive rigidity. The universality of Islam lies not in its political structure, but in its faith and religious guidance. Abd al-Wahhab Khallaf goes further by stating that the Islamic government is a constitutional government, not a tyrannical one. In other words, based on Khallaf's understanding, a government in Islam is not based on the charisma of the person. He also takes the view that Islam guarantees individual rights (*huquq al-afrad*) and provides for the separation of powers. Khallaf's views can be justified on the grounds that the Quran provided the basic principles for a constitutional democracy without providing the details of a specific system. Muslims were to interpret these basic principles in the light of their customs and the demands of their historical consciousness. Once again, this partly explains why Muslims still need a new reinterpretation or *ijtihad*.

Nathan J. Brown points out that Sharia does provide a basis for constitutionalism and that Islamic political thought is increasingly inclined towards constitutionalist ideas. While it is true that attempts to put these ideas into practice have not so far been successful, the problem could be seen to lie in the lack of attention to the structures of political accountability, rather than in flaws in the concept of Islamic constitutionalism.[59] Azizah Y. al-Hibri explains some key concepts of Islamic law in order to support the view that Sharia is compatible with constitutionalism. A state must satisfy two basic conditions to meet Islamic standards: the political process must be based on 'elections' (*bay'ah*); and the elective and governing process must be based on 'broad deliberation' (*shura*). These two principles are part of the criteria employed to determine or to judge Islamic constitutional law. According to al-Hibri, these principles, together with other factors, including that the ruler in a Muslim state has no divine attributes and that there is no ecclesiastical structure in an Islamic setting, indicate that there is, in fact, little difference between an Islamic constitutional setting and a secular one.[60]

A relevant example of the third way is Indonesia. The Indonesian founding vision, the Pancasila, sets out the five pillars (of belief) that underpin the state foundation and the Constitution: Belief in one God, Humanitarianism, National Unity, Representative Democracy and Social Justice. These pillars are basically compromises between secularism, where no single religion predominates in the state, and religiosity, where religion (especially Islam) becomes one of the important pillars of the state. An Islam-inspired agenda is welcome, to the extent that it corresponds with, and does not contradict, the Pancasila. The very fact that Indonesia is the largest Muslim country in the world does not require it to become an Islamic state, like Egypt, Iran or Saudi Arabia. In other words, it is a common belief that Indonesia is neither a secular nor an Islamic state but one that endorses belief in God. Under its 1945 *Constitution*, Indonesia was designed to stand in the middle position.[61]

4. DEBATE ON BUILDING PLACES FOR WORSHIP

The issue of building places of worship, in Islamic countries and in secular states, is important. Essentially the main questions are: can Muslims build mosques in non-Muslim societies; and can non-Muslims build their places of worship (church, temple or synagogue) in Muslim countries?

Legally, building a place of worship can be complex. In Bosnia and Herzegovina, for example, mosques have been built without official permission in the Muslim Bosnia-controlled area. In contrast, Catholic and Protestant churches and temples for Jehovah's Witnesses face years of official obstruction. In the Croat-controlled areas, especially in and around Mostar, Muslim and Protestant places of worship cannot be legally built. In the Serb-controlled areas, Serbian Orthodox churches can be built, but places of worship for other faiths can face much obstruction.[62]

In Muslim nations problems can arise for minority communities. As was seen in the Chapter 4, Saudi Arabia prohibits the building of any place of worship for religions other than Islam and a fatwa was issued calling for 'the destruction of all Christian churches on the Arabian peninsula'. Egypt, with about a 10 per cent Christian population, has the largest community of Middle Eastern Christians, the Copts. They have systematically raised concerns about state discrimination, especially as regards their right to access places of worship.[63] In Egypt, there is now a unified law that regulates the building of all places of worship. This has been a long held demand of Copts and human rights advocates, especially after several incidents of sectarian violence over church building. For example, on 23 November 2008 clashes erupted between Muslims and Christians in the Cairo district of Ain Shams after Muslim neighbours prevented the reopening of a church. Under the former regime of President Hosni Mubarak the building of a church was a security issue, but a new bill was drafted following the fall of Mubarak acknowledging the Copts' demands.

In Indonesia, on 21 March 2006, Religious Affairs Minister Maftuh Basyuni and Home Affairs Minister Muhammad Ma'aruf signed a revision of the controversial 1969 joint ministerial decree regulating the establishment of places of worship.[64] According to the 2006 regulation, a religious community that is not the local majority community needs a congregation of at least 90 people and approval by 60 local people from other religions in order to obtain permission to build a place of worship. Local officials must authenticate these lists. Additionally, written recommendations are required from the head of the Religious Affairs Ministry office for the district or municipality and from the district or municipal Communication Forum for Religious Harmony (FKUB). Article 21 of the revised decree states that any dispute concerning the establishment of a worship house is to be settled through deliberation among the local people. If consensus is not reached, the district head or mayor, assisted by the head of the local Religious Affairs Ministry office, is to settle the dispute in a fair way. In such a case the opinion or recommendations of the local FKUB is to be given consideration. In the case that a congregation of at least 90 worshippers cannot gain the needed minimum support from people of other religions for the site it chooses, the local administration 'is obliged' to help it find an alternative site. Article 8 of the revised decree directs the government to facilitate the establishment of FKUB by the local society in provinces, districts and municipalities. FKUB members are local religious leaders, and all religions are represented in the forums.

The FKUB have the task of dialoguing with religious and societal leaders, and collecting views from religious non-governmental organizations and individuals to channel policy recommendations to the governor, district head or mayor. They also are expected to disseminate laws and policies related to inter religious harmony. Theophilus Bela, a Catholic proponent of interreligious dialogue, said that the requirement to collect a minimum of 90 worshippers' names and 60 names of people of other faiths is difficult for smaller Protestant sects, who now worship in private residences or shops.[65] Rural sites like remote villages in West Papua province, which commonly have communities made up of fewer than 50 residents, will be denied a place of worship based on this 2006 regulation.

Almost as soon as the joint Ministerial Decree No. 1/2006 came into force, several Muslim groups were exploiting its rulings. On 26 March 2006, an angry mob forced Christians of a Pentecostal Church in Bogor to evacuate and close down their church. A Bethel Church community in South Jakarta suffered a similar attack on 22 March 2006.[66] In 2011, a mayor in Bogor (West Java) disregarded a Supreme Court ruling to reinstate the building permit of a church and also dismissed a recommendation by the National Ombudsman Institute to do so.

A. Mosque Building in the West

In Western countries the building of mosques can be controversial. In 2002 in Australia, Abbas Aly, a member of the Shia community in Annangrove, New South Wales, made an application to the local council to build a Muslim prayer centre on his own land. Five thousand residents wrote to the Annangrove Council saying that they opposed it because the building was 'not in keeping' with the character and amenity of the area. The site was subjected to constant vandalism, including smashed windows and a severed pig's head impaled outside the building. The Council rejected Aly's application, claiming that most of the worshippers lived outside the suburb and that such a house of worship would impact on the rural-residential character of the area. It would cause social unrest and anti-social behaviour, and would not accord with the community's shared beliefs. Aly took his case to the New South Wales State Land and Environment Court,[67] which ruled in his favour on the ground that it was the right of all Australians to practise their religious beliefs. The court supported Aly's application, ordering the council to allow the prayer centre to be built whether the residents wanted it or not.[68] The decision of the Court clearly showed that the Australian Constitution could and should protect the right of minority groups to practise their religion. As long as the proposal to build a mosque is in accordance with the regulations to build any building in terms of protecting and promoting public health, safety, welfare and peace of the inhabitants of the city, including maintaining the environment, parking space, location, water, reducing the noise level, and so on, then any proposal should be accepted and building permits issued.

However, different situations can lead to different outcomes. Another case with a different outcome occurred in Elermore Vale, Newcastle, Australia, where a proposal to build a mosque was rejected. In 2011 the local Muslim community proposed to build a mosque in the area. The proposal was rejected by a Joint Regional Planning Panel in August 2011 owing to traffic and parking limitations. The Newcastle Muslim Association said that concerns over traffic were unfounded as it is only compulsory to pray at the mosque on a Friday for congregational prayer and therefore they should not have large numbers attending during the week. The residents in the area argued that the real issues at the heart of the rejection of the proposed mosque concerned planning, the size of the project and location, and that these would be issues for any large development planned for this site. They claimed that the issue was one of planning, not of paranoia or Islamophobia.[69] They stated that they would have the same reservations regardless of the religion, if any religious group proposed a similar project. As a response, the Muslim association lodged an appeal and amended its plans for the mosque. Modifications included limiting the capacity to 250 people instead of the peak of 400 people expected during Friday prayer sessions. Traffic studies had said the mosque would require 267 parking spaces when full during Friday prayer, but the site only had room for about 160 cars. Changes to capacity would allow the mosque to conform with planning guidelines for parking. However residents were concerned that no mention had been made of revising the scale of any of the buildings planned. The plan was at odds with the 2011 Local Environmental Plan, which prohibited a place of public worship in the proposed area. On 15 March 2012, the New South Wales Land and Environment Court dismissed an appeal by the Newcastle Muslim Association.[70]

As was mentioned in Chapter 2, there was also controversy with regard to the mosque at Park51, a 13 storey Islamic community centre in Lower Manhattan.[71] The plan was for most of the centre to be open to the general public, and its proponents argued that the centre would promote interfaith dialogue. Plans included a Muslim prayer space which, owing to its location two blocks from the World Trade Center site, had controversially been referred to as the 'Ground Zero mosque', although numerous commentators argued that it was neither a mosque nor at Ground Zero.[72]

The to-build-or-not-to-build controversy grew even more intense when an American Pastor, Terry Jones, announced his intention to commemorate the terrorist attacks of 11 September 2011 by burning a Quran at his Florida church. The leader of a small congregation, Jones did not proceed after being pressed not to do so by President Barack Obama, General

David Petraeus, Defense Secretary Robert Gates and a host of others. After his plan actually provoked death-creating riots in Muslim-dominated countries and created threats directed at American forces in Afghanistan, Jones publicly retreated from his opposition to the mosque. Former Mayor Rudy Giuliani and former United States Ambassador to the UN John Bolton were among many who opposed the idea because of its proximity to what they and many others considered 'hallowed ground'. They agreed that the planners had the right to proceed, but they insisted that it would be extremely insensitive to do so.[73]

Other Americans supported the construction of the Muslim community centre. President Barack Obama acknowledged the right of Muslims to build the Islamic centre, saying, 'Muslims have the same right to practice their religion as anyone else in this country. And that includes the right to build a place of worship and a community center on private property in lower Manhattan, in accordance with local laws and ordinances'.[74] New York Mayor Michael Bloomberg strongly endorsed the project, saying that Ground Zero was a 'very appropriate place' for a mosque, because it 'tells the world' that the United States has freedom of religion for everyone. Responding to opposition to the mosque, he said, 'The government should never, never be in the business of telling people how they should pray, or where they can pray. We want to make sure that everybody from around the world feels comfortable coming here, living here, and praying the way they want to pray'.[75] Former US President Bill Clinton also supported Park51, noting that many Muslims were also killed on 11 September. He suggested that the developers could have avoided controversy if they had dedicated the centre to the Muslim victims of the attacks. More than 20,000 people signed an on-line petition for the Committee to Stop the Ground Zero Mosque, and unsuccessfully lobbied the NYC Landmarks Preservation Commission to give the location landmark status, which would have added a major hurdle to construction. On 21 September 2011, Park51 was opened to the public as 4000 square feet of renovated space in the Burlington Coat Factory building.

B. The Minaret Debate

As has been mentioned Chapter 2, the earliest mosques were built without minarets, as the call to prayer was performed elsewhere. Hadiths relay that the Muslim community of Medina gave the call to prayer from the roof of the house of Mohammad, which doubled as a place for prayer. Around 80 years after Mohammad's death the first known minarets appeared. Therefore, according to Sharia, it is not compulsory for a mosque to have a minaret. Controversy over minarets in Switzerland led to a November 2009 referendum preventing the construction of mosques with minarets in that country. The Swiss minaret controversy began in a small municipality in the northern part of Switzerland in 2005. The contention involved the Turkish cultural association in Wangen bei Olten, which applied for a construction permit to erect a 6-metre-high minaret on the roof of its Islamic community centre. The project faced opposition from surrounding residents, who formed a group to prevent the tower's erection. The Turkish association claimed that the building authorities improperly and arbitrarily delayed its building application. They also believed that the members of the local opposition group were motivated by religious bias. The Communal Building and Planning Commission rejected the association's application. The applicants appealed to the Building and Justice Department, which reversed the decision. As a consequence of that decision, local residents and the commune of Wangen brought the case before the Administrative Court of the Canton of Solothurn, but failed with their claims. On appeal the Federal Supreme Court affirmed the decision of the lower court. The 6-metre-high minaret was eventually erected in July 2009. The Swiss People's Party and the Confederate Democratic Union took up the issue. Through parliamentary motions in several cantonal legislatives, they unsuccessfully tried to prohibit the construction of minarets. However, in April 2007, the two parties launched a ballot initiative to establish a constitutional ban on minarets at the federal level.

Swiss voters passed the ballot initiative for a constitutional ban on the construction of minarets by a majority of 57.5 per cent. The ban was all the more surprising in light of the fact that Switzerland has only four minarets, and none of them are used for the Islamic call to prayer (*adhan*).[76] A minaret ban, its proponents argued, would effectively protect the Swiss constitutional order, safeguard fundamental rights and halt the spread of Sharia law. In short, it would offer a 'panacea to the ills of Islamization'.[77] This referendum fuelled the debate on Islam in Europe as Europeans had already seen the banning of the burqa in public places, along with the banning of the hijab in French public schools, the murder of Dutch filmmaker Theo van Gogh, bombings in Madrid and London, and the offensive depiction of the Prophet in a regional Danish newspaper. It seemed that Islam's growth and visibility had generated alarm across Europe. Just as churches face difficulties in non-Muslim societies, Muslims too are facing similar issues with regard to building mosques in historically Christian, now secular, countries. It is a reminder for all of us that the issue of accommodating minority religion traditions and practices is still a controversial matter.

5. THE *HALAL* FOOD DEBATE

Food is central to daily religious practice and holiday celebrations the world over. Food's presence and absence serve as distinctive religious markers. Orthodox Jews keep kosher, Muslims feast after fasting during the holy month of Ramadan, and Hindus cannot eat beef. For many, food is seen as nourishment for the body and soul. At times, food also functions symbolically, for example, when prayers before eating are said to express gratitude to God, when the Christian Eucharist[78] is conducted in church services, when the Passover meal commemorates the freeing of the Israelites, or when Arabic Muslim and Christian coffee rituals call on the divine. At other times food is offered directly to deities, for example, rice at Hindu shrines or sweets for the Buddha. Furthermore, the provision of food to the hungry is considered by many religions to be a spiritual obligation.

As such, religion plays a large part in the selection and consumption of food by some individuals and by their respective communities. Religious practices and teachings have promoted or prohibited various foods, have dictated the planting and harvesting of crops, and were an early source of information on healthy versus unhealthy food substances. Some religions have incorporated alcohol into religious ceremonies, while others have discouraged or forbidden its use altogether.[79]

In Islam, during Eid al-Adha (the Festival of Sacrifice), typically, a sheep or goat is sacrificed, although some sacrifice cattle or a camel instead. The meat is usually given as charity to the poor, in commemoration of the Sacrifice of Ismail, in which God tested the faith of Abraham (Ibrahim) by ordering him to sacrifice his son Ishmael (Ismail). During Eid al-Adha, distributing meat amongst the people and chanting the *takbir* out loud before the Eid prayer on the first day and after prayers throughout the three days of Eid are considered essential parts of this important Islamic festival.

Controversy can arise in both Muslim and Western societies regarding *halal* products. Islam identifies all food as either permitted (*halal*) or prohibited (*haram*). Prohibited foods are pork and pork-derived foods, including lard and bacon, and flesh and other products from carnivorous animals or from those that eat carrion. Meat that is *halal* must have the blood drained from it.

Islam strongly enjoins Muslims to treat animals with compassion and not to abuse them. It is forbidden to beat animals unnecessarily, to brand them on the face, or to allow them to fight each other for human entertainment. The Prophet Mohammad stated that an animal must not be mutilated while alive.[80] Mohammad is also reported to have said 'There is no man who kills [even] a sparrow or anything smaller, without its deserving it, but Allah will question him about it [on the judgment day]'.[81] In the context of food, *halal* meat is derived from animals slaughtered by hand according to methods stipulated in Islamic religious texts. One such method, called *dhabihah*, consists of making a swift, deep incision with a sharp knife on the neck that cuts the jugular vein, leaving the animal to bleed to death. However, despite the moral code outlined by the Prophet above, the ritual method of slaughter as practised in Islam has been decried as inhumane by some animal welfare organizations in Western and some Muslim countries on the ground that it causes severe suffering to animals.[82] The concern is that cutting an animal's throat while the animal is fully conscious causes significant pain and distress. Stunning, which typically uses an electrical current to render an animal unconscious and insensible to pain, is, it is argued, kinder and more in keeping with the Quran's edict to treat animals with compassion. Animal welfare legislation in Europe requires that abattoirs stun all animals prior to slaughter unless they are being ritually killed according to the practices of a non-Christian religion. Amendment 205 to the European Union food information regulations, passed by members of the European Parliament in June 2010 by a vote of 559 to 54, would have required all meat or meat products from animals slaughtered without stunning to be labelled as follows: 'Derived from animals that have not been stunned prior to slaughter'.[83] Although *halal* meat is well labelled in specialist butcher shops and food outlets, the EU regulation would have alerted non-Muslim consumers to supplies entering the mainstream food system. Muslims (and Jewish groups) were prepared to challenge animal rights campaigners over this European Union measure requiring *halal* and kosher meat products to carry such a label.

On 15 January 2002, the German Constitutional Court allowed slaughtering without pre-stunning. In an appeal by a Turkish citizen who practised Islamic ritual slaughter, the Constitutional Court struck down a former ban on ritual slaughter, holding that the German Basic Law's guarantee of religious freedom prohibited the German government from applying a law requiring stunning prior to slaughter to observant Muslims who practise ritual slaughter for religious reasons. The Basic Law's guarantee of religious freedom applies to slaughterers as well as to consumers of meat. In other words, 'Muslim butchers can be granted an exceptional permission for ritual slaughter'.[84]

Muslim scholars are divided on the issue of stunning. Both Indonesian (Majelis Ulama Indonesia) and Australian *ulama* (Australian Federation of Islamic Councils) accept stunning before slaughtering and Malaysia has issued guidelines to be followed. It is allowed on the basis that modern stunning techniques were not known at the time of the Prophet (many centuries before the invention of electricity) and that such techniques can achieve a more compassionate death for animals. Requirements that stunning be performed by a Muslim with *halal* certification, and that stunning must not kill the animal, just render it unconscious, are incorporated in the Malaysian Code.[85] Other Muslim scholars reject stunning outright, on the basis that traditional methods were the practice of the Prophet and are kind to animals, while stunning may kill an animal and thus violate the prohibition against consuming dead meat. It remains a controversial issue in Islamic societies, and in the West. However, the prohibition of stunning and the treatment of the slaughtered animal is also expressed in Shechita law in Jewish tradition. For instance, Jews in New Zealand who observe the laws of kashrut will no longer be able to purchase locally kosher-slaughtered beef or chicken, according to the country's new *Animal Welfare Code*, which went into effect on 21 May 2010. The new code, which the Ministry of Agriculture and Forestry states was implemented for humane reasons, bans the slaughter of livestock without stunning. The new law also forbids the importation of raw kosher poultry. Since Jewish law forbids the use of stunning in the slaughter process, the ban effectively prohibits the practice of kosher slaughter in New Zealand. Kosher law prohibits stunning prior to slaughter because there is a chance that the animal can regain consciousness during the slaughter. Rabbis also argue that modern stunning technologies, which include the use of a captive bolt gun, can leave a wound on the animal, which is prohibited by the laws of kashrut. Meat that is slaughtered for human consumption must be free from wounds and other abnormalities.

Despite the fact that some Muslim groups accept stunning pre-slaughtering, the controversy about *halal* food remains in the West. Non-Muslims can misunderstand the *halal* requirements. For example, non-Muslims have objected to eating *halal* food because they believe that the food has been blessed by Muslim *ulama*, and therefore refuse to consume it, as they are unaware that the classification of food as '*halal*' is due to the method of slaughtering the animal. Others, such as Australian Senator Cory Bernardi, expressed his distaste at having inadvertently consumed *halal* food, and criticized Muslims for insisting on eating *halal* food.[86] As was seen in Europe, governments in most Western countries now work closely with Islamic organizations in order to accommodation Muslim's needs and requirements for *halal* products.

6. DEBATE ON APOSTASY

The English word 'apostasy' comes from the Greek word '*apostasia*', which means to defect, rebel or depart, and was the term coined for Christians and Jews who abandoned their faith. In centuries past it was a serious crime. In many parts of Europe during the Middle Ages Christian apostates, along with heretics and blasphemers, could face terrible penalties, including execution.[87] Today there are no legal or temporal consequences for apostasy in secular or notionally Christian countries, although there are religious consequences as churches can excommunicate an apostate. However, in the seventh century, when Islam emerged, the concept of apostasy would have been known in Arabia because of its role in Jewish and Christian law and practice. In Islam, *riddah* is the Islamic equivalent of apostasy and traditionally has been classified as a criminal offence. As a *hadd* offence (one against the rights of God) and discussed in Chapter 9, it remains a serious offence in many, but not all, Muslim countries today, particularly in the few, like Saudi Arabia and Iran, where forms of Sharia criminal law are applied. In almost all Muslim nations, including Egypt, Morocco and Malaysia, *riddah* has significant legal but civil consequences as well. An apostate is deprived of the right to remain married to his or her Muslim spouse, to retain guardianship over his or her Muslim-born children, to inherit from his or her Muslim family, and all contracts entered into by the apostate are null and void post-conversion.

While the Muslim world retains a predominately traditionalist stance, modernist views have been emerging from progressive Islamic scholars revisiting the sacred sources and texts to question whether apostasy is indeed an immutable law, or one that can, and should, be re-evaluated in light of the other Quranic verses and in the historical and political context in which the revelations were received. The relevance of apostasy in contemporary times is also questioned as Islam is now the religion of a quarter of the world's people and its fastest growing religion, in contradistinction to the time in the seventh century when Islam emerged into a world dominated by other established religions and also polytheistic practices. In the last few decades, some well-publicized cases have fuelled the debate on the contemporary role for apostasy in Islam, making it a hotly contested concept for Muslim scholars and governments. In many of these cases, apostasy has been used as a tool to stifle opposition to prevailing religious and political ideology in some regimes, and in the West apostate or blasphemy accusations 'for insulting Islam' brought against high-profile individuals have caused distress, protests and threats fracturing Muslim and non-Muslim relations.

How is it possible that there can be such disparity in Islamic jurisprudence that a Muslim apostate can receive the death penalty in one Muslim country, whereas in another, will face no criminal consequences at all? In the former the apostate has turned away from 'the truth' and in so doing deserves to die, whereas in the latter, he or she is held to be expressing their Quran-given right to religious freedom, which must compass freedom to change one's religion.

A. Perspectives on *Riddah* in the Primary Sources

Riddah means 'turning back' and there are several passages in the Quran where it is used, such as at Súra Muhammad 47:25: 'Those who turn back as apostates after Guidance was clearly shown to them, – the Evil One has instigated them and buoyed them up with false hopes'.[88] 'Turning back' can occur in a range of ways other than a formal conversion to another faith tradition, such as adopting atheism; denying by word or action a belief or practice essential to Islam, including the five pillars; expressing doubts on a fundamental issue on which there is juristic consensus (*ijma*); and degrading Islam or insulting the Prophet. *Riddah* therefore is a broad term that encompasses blasphemy, heresy and hypocrisy. Excluded are matters on which there are differences between the Islamic schools of law. The Prophet reportedly said that 'difference of opinion among my community is a sign of the bounty of God'.[89] Also apostasy is Islam-specific, the majority view being that a non-Muslim who changes religion to 'embrace Islam' is not an apostate.[90] The word therefore has a pejorative connotation.

The most cited verse on apostasy is Quran Súra Baqarah, 2:217: 'And if any of you turn back from their Faith and die in unbelief, their works will bear no fruit in this life and in the Hereafter; and they will be Companion of the Fire and will abide therein'.[91] In this verse, the Quran condemns the apostate to eternal damnation but no earthly punishment is prescribed; it is a sin in this world and the punishment of hell fire awaits the apostate in the next life. A similar conclusion comes from the Quran Súra Nahl 16:106 where: '[a]nyone who, after accepting Faith in God, utters Unbelief' will receive 'Wrath from God, and theirs will be a dreadful Penalty'.[92] Yet, consensus was reached by early jurists in each of the four Sunni schools that an apostate who refuses five times the opportunity to recant should be put to death, with the Hanafi school making an exception for a woman.[93] In support of the death penalty scholars rely on other verses in the Quran, including Súra Máida 5:33,[94] which is seen as analogous in that it sets out forms of execution for those who wage war of God or the Prophet. More importantly these scholars draw on the hadith 'Kill the person who abandons his religion'.[95] While there has been considerable debate on this hadith, textualists see it as providing a clear unambiguous directive for killing an apostate. It is on this basis that jurists added apostasy to the *hadd* category of offences. For other jurists *riddah* remains a grave sin, but in the absence of a Quranic temporal penalty, *riddah* should be categorized as *ta'zir*. As a *ta'zir* offence, the punishment can change according to time, place and circumstances. Either way, the orthodox position is that, if you are born Muslim or freely accept Islam as your faith, it not possible to leave and punishment of some form must follow. This is first to deter or prevent a Muslim from committing a grave sin and thereby deter others, and second, to retain Islam's integrity and dignity.

Modern revisions for *riddah* follow three lines of thematic reasoning. First, without a Quranic mandate, capital punishment should not be endorsed. The authenticity of one hadith even with other interpretative devices can be questioned. Second, analysis of apostasy should occur in the socio-political context in which it took place. Abdullah Saeed explains:

> In the political context of the Prophet's time, a person either belonged to the community of believers (Muslims), the unbelievers (non-Muslims) who were at peace with Muslims, or the unbelievers who were at war with Muslims. If one leaves Islam and the Muslims and their allies, there is no option but to join the opposition. An apostate, therefore, was perceived to have automatically joined the non-Muslim side, becoming part of the enemy ranks and using apostasy as a means to attack and inflict maximum harm on the Muslim community.

In other words, apostasy is akin to treason. Scholars like Rahman[96] and Tariq Ramadan[97] also highlight that there is no evidence that the Prophet himself sentenced any person to death solely for renouncing Islam as he did so only when other factors were at play. The account of the tribe of Ukl supports the need for apostasy to have an additional elements not just repudiation.[98] The third theme is that Islam is a religion of tolerance as the Quran recognizes other religions and accords respect to their scriptures, as evidenced, Kamali writes, by the number of verses that 'declare not only the validity and divine provenance of other faiths, but highly compliment their teachings'.[99] For example, at Súra Máida 5:44 'It was we who revealed the Law (to Moses) [the Torah]: therein was guidance and light'.[100] Islam gives special legal standing to Jews and Christians, as people of the Book, for example, the Quran Súra Máida 5:69 states: 'Those who believe (in the Qur'an), those who follow the Jewish (scriptures), and the Sabians and the Christians, – any who believe in

God and the Last Day, and work righteousness, – on them shall be no fear, nor shall they grieve'.[101] Gomaa, Grand Mufti of Egypt, supported this reasoning, which also links to what Saeed calls the 'the strong thread of personal responsibility in the Quran, as seen in 18:29: "Say, The truth is from your Lord": Let him who will believe, and let him who will, reject (it)'. This is supported by the Quran's message on freedom of religion: 'Let there be no compulsion in religion: Truth stands out clear from Error'[102] (2: 256). Also at Súra Yúnús 10:99: 'If it had been thy Lord's will, they would all have believed, – all who are on earth! wilt thou then compel mankind, against their will, to believe!'[103] Instead of forcing conversions, Muslims should 'invite' others to come freely to Islam.[104] It was never permitted to kill a person who was an unbeliever (*kuffar*),[105] unless the unbeliever posed a threat to a Muslim or a Muslim community, so it is not logical to allow killing of a Muslim simply because he or she has joined the ranks of *kuffar*.

In addition to the long-debated issue of whether the death penalty should be imposed or another punitive measure adopted for apostasy, there is also debate on how apostasy should be dealt with in today's multi-ethnic and multi-racial societies. Malaysia is one Muslim majority country where the role of apostasy has been contentious. Another controversy surrounds the use of apostasy as a tool to silence opposition, to prevent academic analysis by revisionist Islamic scholars, or to eradicate criticism of government policies on religion. Egypt is one of several countries where apostasy charges have been used in this way. Another contentious use of apostasy is in the international arena, where writers, publishers and filmmakers living in the West receive pronouncements of apostasy if they are Muslim, or accusations of blasphemy, if they are non-Muslim, which have significant ramifications for inter-religious and community relations.

B. Apostasy in Malaysia

In Malaysia, a multi-ethnic, multi-religious and democratic country where Muslims comprise 60 per cent of the population, apostasy has become a very sensitive, even explosive, issue. Islam is the religion of the federation,[106] but freedom of religion is guaranteed in Article 11, subject to a prohibition in Article 11(4) on propagation of another religion to Muslims.[107] Several prominent cases have highlighted the difficulties that can arise in a pluralistic setting where each state of the 13 state federation[108] lays down different ways for dealing with apostasy, and where being born to Malay parents legally means you are Muslim[109] 'until your dying day'.[110] Some states criminalize apostasy,[111] but the death penalty is not imposed;[112] some require detention in an Islamic Faith Rehabilitation Centre for a six month period, others up to three years, where the apostate must undergo education and will routinely be asked to recant;[113] and one state, Negeri Sembilan, provides a procedure for renouncing Islam before a judge of the Sharia High Court, although there is also a mandatory lengthy counselling period required before the order will be made.[114]

The case of Lina Joy is perhaps the best known of the apostasy cases in Malaysia. Azlina binte Jailani was born to Malay parents, and so by virtue of her birth was Muslim. In 1998, after attending a Christian church, she was baptised in accordance with the practice of the Christian faith. She wanted her national identity card to reflect this change as she planned to marry a Christian, which would be impermissible were her card to state 'Islam' as her religion.[115] The National Registration Department allowed her to change her Muslim name to Lina Joy, but refused to delete the word 'Islam' on her identity card, which meant she could not marry. As she was no longer a Muslim, she sought a declaration from the High Court (Malaysia's civil court) to have her religion officially changed from 'Islam' to 'Christian'. The court refused on the following grounds: first, only the Sharia Court was competent to determine the question of renunciation of Islam. Second, as she was born Malay, she would remain a Malay to her dying day and it was impossible for her to renounce Islam. Third, the freedom to profess and practise the religion of one's choice guaranteed by Clause (1) of Article 11 did not include freedom of choice of religion.[116] This freedom had to be construed with other provisions, including the Islamic ban on apostasy, which must limit its scope. The Court of Appeal subsequently confirmed that exclusive jurisdiction over apostasy remained with the Sharia Court, adding: 'The Muslim community regards it as a grave matter not only for the person concerned, in terms of the afterlife, but also for Muslims generally, as they regard it to be their responsibility to save another Muslim from the damnation of apostasy'.[117] Finally, in her unsuccessful last appeal, the Federal Court also ruled that Lina Joy's religious status was a question for the Sharia Court alone as a Malay 'must comply with the practices or law of the Islamic religion … and one cannot at ones whims and fancies renounce or embrace a religion'.[118] The dissenting judge noted that, as apostasy is a criminal offence in several Malaysian states, to require a citizen to apply for a declaration of apostasy and thereby be exposed 'to a range of criminal offences under Islamic law is unreasonable'.[119] In addition, at that date the Sharia Court had not allowed any individuals to renounce Islam. The issue of apostasy remains very much in the political and religious arena in Malaysia, with public protests arising from concerns that conversions, especially to Christianity, are still occurring.

C. Apostasy in Egypt

There have been several cases in Egypt where the views of prominent Muslim scholars have resulted in a trial and conviction for apostasy. This is surprising because, until the events of 2011 and 2012 at least, statutes in Egypt were silent on the issue of apostasy. However the courts in a series of cases adopted Hanafi *fiqh* to develop a law on apostasy, as public policy allowed the courts to give effect to the essential principles of Islamic law, which are fixed and indisputable.[120] Apostasy was held to be one of these legal developments, as were *talaq* divorce and polygyny. In Egyptian jurisprudence, therefore, apostasy was prohibited. The death penalty was not imposed; instead its impact was to render a person's marriage void, sever all ties with children and family; exclude apostates from inheritance; and nullify many civil contracts. The result was what Berger describes as 'civil death'.[121] This stance on apostasy was in accordance with orthodox *fiqh* and was not per se controversial; however it was the way it was used to silence intellectuals, as with Nasr Abu Zayd, and to stifle critics of government policy, as with Nawal El-Saadawi, that fired widespread local and international debate.

Nasr Abu Zayd was a Muslim scholar and Professor at Cairo University, where he wrote and taught on Quranic Sciences. His writings, which informed the Islamic reform movement, came to the attention of the courts via a *hisbah* motion,[122] for his liberal stance on the universality of Islam, his questioning of literal meaning of texts, deeming some beliefs and practices as mere superstitions, and his arguing that a conservative perspective of Islam was hindering progress and leaving Islamic societies like Egypt reactionary and backward. Zayd always claimed to be a devout Muslim, and rejected repeatedly that he was an apostate, asserting that his writing was not an attack on Islam per se, but on the prevailing human interpretations of it. He also was critical of the actions of some Islamic investment companies in Egypt. The Court of Cassation found that his writings and statements were contrary to Hanafi orthodoxy and he was therefore an apostate. With this ruling, his marriage was annulled and he was divorced from his wife, and received threats against his life. He went in exile to Europe where he could be with his wife and continue his writings on Islam. Before his death in 2010, he wrote: 'Having been at the receiving end of such allegations – and driven from my home in Egypt to exile in the Netherlands – I can state with conviction that charges of apostasy and blasphemy are key weapons in the fundamentalists' arsenal, strategically employed to prevent reform of Muslim societies and instead confine the world's Muslim population to a bleak, colorless prison of sociocultural and political conformity'.[123]

Zayd was not alone. A former teacher of his, Hasan Hanafi, received a similar charge for positing a metaphysical interpretation of the Quran focused on its message of social justice. Nawal El-Sadaawi, a Muslim feminist, psychiatrist and physician who wrote and campaigned against the practice of female genital mutilation in Egypt, was also subjected to a *hisbah* charge. She had been a strong critic of Mubarak government, but she had also published writings and given interviews in which she argued that veiling was not compulsory for Muslim women (she did not veil), that the social justice message in Islam has been subsumed by rituals, some of which were historical and not divine (for example, kissing the black stone). Interestingly, in her court case she attacked *hisbah* as a violation of section 40 of the Egyptian Constitution, which stated: 'All citizens are equal before the law. They have equal public rights and duties without discrimination due to sex, ethnic origin, language, religion or creed'. As only Muslim men had standing to bring *hisbah*, she argued that it was discrimination on gender and religious grounds and the process thereby was unconstitutional. The charges against al-Sadawi were eventually dismissed and she remained in Egypt, where she was actively involved in the 2011 Tahrir Square uprising in Cairo.[124]

D. Apostasy in the West

Western nations have struggled to deal with the orthodox Islamic stance on apostasy, whether involving a high profile author like Sir Salman Rushdie, who was the target of the 1989 Khomeini fatwa ordering his execution for apostasy,[125] or the plight of Abdul Rahman, the Afghan convertee to Christianity sentenced to death by a rural Afghani Court in 2006. In Western eyes, freedom of religion must include freedom to change religion, and freedom of speech must allow contrary and also derogatory views of religious tenets, holy figures and religious practices, as well as the policies and actions of governments, religious or secularists. The sensitivity and hurt felt by Muslims when 'sacred' matters are dealt with inaccurately or negatively is not fully appreciated in the West. The publication in Denmark of the *Jyllands-Posten* cartoons on the Prophet, Pope Benedict's academic paper at Regensburg, the films of Dutch filmmakers Geert Wilders (*Fitna*) and Theo van Gogh (*Submission*), as well as the performance of Mozart's opera *Idomeneo*,[126] have offended Muslims across the world. While Egypt's Ahmad Al-Aswani has argued, 'I do not think that cartoons, books, or films can harm a religion or affect the faith of those who adhere to it out of conviction',[127] others disagree, including influential media mufti al Qaradawi. He held that such acts were done by 'the enemies of Islam' out of rancour and called on all Muslim governments to react with political and economic boycotts[128] and Muslims to 'stand against those who offend the Prophet'.[129] He called apostasy one of the greatest threats to Islam'.[130]

There is tension in Western countries as religious vilification and hate speech laws have been introduced in an attempt to limit the scope of free speech and also ongoing efforts have been made on efforts for 'respect for religious figures' to be added the United Nations' catalogue of human rights.[131] Getting the balance right between respect for the sacred and maintaining freedom of speech remains an ongoing challenge.

7. CONCLUSIONS

This chapter has reflected on some important and ongoing debates that touch on important matters of humanity and life for Muslims today. Of course, there are many more issues and debates to have, but these five, the burqa, *halal* foods, construction of places of worship, Sharia compatibility with democracy and apostasy, were selected to show that there is not one monolithic discourse on Islam, as a form of twenty-first century *taqlid*, but a plurality of views, in which *ijtihad* continues in and beyond the Middle East, even in the land of the infidel, where centres of Islamic scholarship are thriving free from the political and religious constraints of authoritarian regimes. Although conservative scholars cloaked in 'the mantle of religious authenticity' may seek to shut down critical inquiry, decrying modernist or revisionist views as heretical or made in error, contemporary perspectives cannot be suppressed indefinitely. Between idealizing and demonizing Islam, there is huge space for revisiting the foundational elements of Islamic law in light of socio-political contextualization and in line with principles of modern life, justice, human rights, democracy, and the dignity to be given to all humankind. Zayd writes that an

> objective historical approach to studying the law is fiercely resisted by many clerics and mullahs. Yet it is absolutely vital, if we are to liberate the 'deep substance' of the Holy Qur'an's message, which proclaims the Prophet Muhammad (and hence, by implication, Islam itself) to be 'a blessing for all creation'.[132]

The search for the contemporary significance of the Quran's profound message[133] is ongoing. It needs to come from a place of respect and tolerance for a plethora of views. The group 'Sisters in Islam' embodies this spirit, writing:

> Ignorance is never bliss. By narrowing the space for open dialogue among citizens and squashing their quest for information and to read, the government's act can be deemed as 'promoting Jahiliah' as it will push us into a more suppressed world where we will blindly follow with no questions asked, lest it disrupts our small worldview.[134]

NOTES

1. Ali ibn Abd-al-Malik al-Hindi, *Kanzul 'Umal*, Vol. 10 (Dar al-Kutub al-'Ilmiyah, Beirut, 1998), 136.
2. Mohamed Mursi was elected President of Egypt in June 2012.
3. Data from *Pew Forum on Religion and Public Life*, available at http://www.pewforum.org
4. Half-*niqabs* tie around the head leaving the eyes and forehead visible, whereas full *niqabs* completely cover the face leaving a narrow opening for the eyes. Sometimes the eyes are also covered by two or more sheer layers so that a woman can see out but her eyes cannot be seen.
5. Jennifer Heath, *The Veil* (University of California Press, Berkeley, CA, 2008), 1.
6. Jonathon Bloom and Sheila Blair, *Islam: A Thousand Years of Faith and Power* (TV Books, New York, 2002).
7. Albert Hourani, 'The Vanishing Veil: A Challenge to the Old Order', *UNESCO Courier* (January 1956), 35–7.
8. Toujan Faisal was the first female elected to Jordan's Parliament. In Kuwait, Rola Dashti and Aseel Al-Awadhi were among four women elected in 2009. Richard Spencer, 'Kuwaiti Women MPs Refuse to Wear Hijab in Parliament', *The Telegraph*, 12 October 2009.
9. Abdullah Yusuf Ali, *The Qur'an: Text, Translation and Commentary* (Tahrike Tarsile Qur'an, New York, 2005), 904–905.
10. Islam's Women Q&A Fatwa No. 1173 issued by Shaikh ibn Uthaimin, available at http://www.islamswomen.com/qa/question.php?qid=1173
11. Susan A Spectorsky, *Women in Classical Islamic Law* (Brill, Leiden, 2010), 50.
12. Leila Ahmed, 'The Veil of Ignorance' (12 June 2011) *Foreign Policy*.
13. Abdullah Yusuf Ali, *The Qur'an: Text, Translation and Commentary* (Tahrike Tarsile Qur'an, New York, 2005), 1115.
14. This is the term for the sacred state of purity a Muslim must be in, in order to perform the *hajj* rituals. Some scholars also hold that the face should not be covered during the five daily prayers.
15. Sahih Al-Bukhari, Vol. 6, Book 60, hadith No. 282.
16. Ibid., Vol. 8, Book 76, hadith No. 572.
17. Ibid., Vol. 8, Book 74, hadith No. 247.
18. This comes from the authority of Ibn Jarir from an authentic chain of narrators from Ibn Abbaas', available at http://www.ahlalhdeeth.com/vbe/archive/index.php/t-6000.html; 'Saudi Cleric Favours One-eye Veil', *BBC News*, 3 October, 2008.

19. 'Niqab at the Centre of Raging Controversy in Egypt', *Islamic Voice*, available at http://www.islamicvoice.com/March2010/THEMUSLIMWORLD/. Al Qaradawi, another prominent Egyptian Islamic scholar and media mufti, stated that in his view 'the niqab is not obligatory'.
20. Muneeb Nasr, 'The Niqab Furore', *The Muslim Presence*, 5 November 2009, available at http://muslimpresence.com/?p=3089
21. Ibid.
22. Ibid.
23. Dinah Zeiger, 'That (Afghan) Girl' in Jennifer Heath (ed.), *The Veil* (University of California Press, Berkeley, CA, 2008), 273.
24. Up until the 1960s and 1970s women in Saudi Arabia and Oman wore colourful traditional Arab dress, but the shift on conservative thought, especially after the Iranian Revolution, has made black *abaya* dominant. Susan Mubarak, 'Why the Black Abaya?' *Muscat Daily*, 7 February 2011, available at http://www.muscatdaily.com/Archive/Stories-Files/Why-the-black-abaya
25. Sheik al-Hilali advised that 'If you take out uncovered meat and place it outside on the street, or in the garden or in the park, or in the backyard without a cover, and the cats come and eat it … whose fault is it – the cats or the uncovered meat? The uncovered meat is the problem. If she was in her room, in her home, in her hijab (veil), no problem would have occurred'.
26. Leila Ahmed, 'The Veil of Ignorance' (12 June 2011) *Foreign Policy*.
27. Sarkozy: Burqas, '"Not Welcome" in France', *CBS News*, 22 June 2009, available at http://www.cbsnews.com/stories/2009/06/22/world/main5103076.shtml
28. See http://www.diplomatie.gouv.fr/en/IMG/pdf/Q_A-ENG_2_.pdf
29. *Code Penal* (France) Article 131-13.
30. Michèle Alliot, Minister of Justice and Freedom, speech given in the Senate on the Bill on Concealment of the Face, Paris, 14 September 2010, available at https://pastel.diplomatie.gouv.fr/editorial/actual/ael2/bulletin.gb.asp?liste=20100920.gb. html
31. Decision No. 2010-613 DC of 7 October 2010.
32. See generally, Shaira Nanwani, 'The Burqa Ban: An Unreasonable Limitation on Religious Freedom or an Unjustifiable Restriction?' (2011) 25 *Emory International Law Review* 1431–75.
33. Financial support was offered by several organizations and Muslim individuals to pay the fine of any Muslim charged with an offence under the anti-burqa law.
34. William Langley, 'France's Burka Ban is a Victory for Tolerance', *The Telegraph*, 11 April 2011.
35. 'The Niqab Debate', available at http://thedebateinitiative.com/2012/05/04/the-niqab-debate-banning-freedom/
36. Shaira Nanwani, 'The Burqa Ban: An Unreasonable Limitation on Religious Freedom or an Unjustifiable Restriction?' (2011) 25 *Emory International Law Review* 1431.
37. Cory Bernadi, 'For Australia's Sake we Need to Ban the Burqa', *The Brisbane Times*, 6 May 2010, available at http://www.brisbanetimes.com.au/opinion/society-and-culture/for-australias-sake-we-need-to-ban-the-burqa-20100506-ubun.html#ixzz1yC3IpIgU
38. Joel Gibson, 'Burqa Decision Ripples Across World', *The Sydney Morning Herald*, 20 August 2010.
39. Ibid.
40. *New Zealand Human Rights Commission's Annual Race Relations Reports, 2004–2010: Religious Diversity in New Zealand.*
41. 'Appeal Upheld in Sydney Burka Case', *ABC News*, 20 June 2011.
42. Fatwa 83702, *Islamweb*, available at http://www.islamweb.net/emainpage/index.php?page=fatwa

43. Interview with Canada's Citizenship and Immigration Minister Jason Kenney; Stewart Bell, '"Widespread Support for Burka Ban" Jason Kenney says; Muslims Salute Minister for "Courageous" Move' *National Post*, 23 January 2012.
44. Jacqueline Maley, citing Umm Jamaalud-Din, in 'It's un-Australian – Rally Condemns Push to Ban the Burqa', *Sydney Morning Herald*, 20 September 2010.
45. Maha Al-Hujailan, 'The Nature of the Abaya', available at http://trueislam.tribe.net/thread/6ba1df7d-a03f-4907-9dd2-001b67e78eb5
46. See the discussion in Muhammad Khalid Masud, *Shatibi's Philosophy of Islamic Law* (Kitab Bhavan, New Delhi, 1995), 17.
47. Ahmad Syalabi, *al-Hukuumah wa al-Dawlah fi al-Islam* (1958), 23.
48. See M. Abd al-Qadir Abu Faris, *al-Nizam al-Siyasi fi al-Islam* (1984), 15–40.
49. Muhammad Asad, *The Principles of State and Government in Islam* (University of California Press, Berkeley, CA, 1980).
50. See Said Amir Arjomand, 'Religion and Constitutionalism in Western History and in Modern Iran and Pakistan', in S.A. Arjomand (ed.), *The Political Dimensions of Religion* (SUNY Press, Albany, NY, 1993), 69–99.
51. See Muhammad Salim al-'Awwa, *Fi al-Nizam al-Siyasi li al-dawlah al-Islamiyyah* (al-Maktab al-Misri al-Hadis, Cairo, 1983).
52. Ahmad Husain Ya'qub, *al-Nizam al-Siyasi fi al-Islam: ra'y al-sunna, ra'y al-shi'a, hukm al-shar'* (Mu'assasah Ansariyan, Iran, 1312 AH), 250.
53. 'This day, have I perfected your religion for you, completed my favour upon you, and have chosen for you Islam as your religion' (Quran, Súra Máida 5:3); Abdullah Yusuf Ali, *The Qur'an: Text, Translation and Commentary* (Tahrike Tarsile Qur'an, New York, 2005), 240.
54. Taqiyuddin al-Nabhani, *Nizam al-Islam*, available at http://www.hizb-ut-tahrir.org/arabic/kotobmtb/htm/01ndam.htm
55. 'Ali 'Abd al-Raziq (1888–1966) was the most controversial Islamic political thinker in the twentieth century. His book *al-Islam wa Usul al-Hukm*, written in 1925, invited widespread criticism from Muslim world. He was then condemned and isolated from the *ulama* council of al-Azhar, and also dismissed from his position as judge and prohibited from assuming a position in the government. Raziq disagreed with many *ulama* who considered the establishment of the caliphate as obligatory for Muslims and therefore that it would be sinful if it were not carried out. He could not find any strong foundation to support this belief.
56. Bassam Tibi, *The Challenge of Fundamentalism: Political Islam and the New World Disorder* (University of California Press, Berkeley, CA, 1998), 160.
57. Khaled Abou El Fadl, 'Constitutionalism and the Islamic Sunni Legacy' (2002) 1 *UCLA Journal of Islamic and Near Eastern Law* 67.
58. Abdullahi Ahmed An-Na'im, *Islam and the Secular State: Negotiating the Future of Shari'a* (Harvard University Press, Cambridge, MA, 2008). See also Noah Feldman, *The Fall and Rise of the Islamic State* (Princeton University Press, Princeton, NJ, 2008).
59. See Nathan J. Brown, *Constitutions in a Non-constitutional World: Arab Basic Laws and the Prospects for Accountable Government* (State University of New York Press, Albany, NY, 2002), 162.
60. Azizah Y. al-Hibri, 'Islamic Constitutionalism and the Concept of Democracy' in Fred Dallmayr (ed.), *Border Crossings: Toward a Comparative Political Theory* (Lexington Books, Lanham, MD, 1999), 63–87.
61. Nadirsyah Hosen, 'Indonesia: A Presidential System with Checks and Balances' in T. Röder and R. Grote (eds) *Constitutionalism in Islamic Countries: Between Upheaval and Continuity* (Oxford University Press, Oxford, 2011).
62. See Drasko Djenovic, 'Bosnia: To Legally Build a Place of Worship ...', available at http://www.unhcr.org/refworld/pdfid/468919af2.pdf

63. Ahmed Zaki Osman, 'New Places of Worship Law Leaves Much to be Desired', *Egypt Independent*, 17 June 2012, available at http://www.egyptindependent.com/news/new-places-worship-law-leaves-much-be-desired
64. Moerkekaq Senggotro, 'Indonesian Christians Sceptical about New Decree on Places of Worship', *Asia News*, 3 August 2006.
65. 'Catholic Church OKs Indonesian Gov't Revised Worship Decree', *Catholic Online*, available at http://www.catholic.org/international/international_story.php?id=19233
66. Ibid.
67. *New Century Developments Pty Limited v Baulkham Hills Shire Council* [2003] NSWLEC 154.
68. Claire O'Rourke, 'Jihad Declared on Residents Opposed to Prayer Centre, Court Told', *Sydney Morning Herald*, 14 May 2003.
69. Ben Smee, 'Elermore Vale Mosque Plans No More', *Newcastle Herald*, 15 March 2012.
70. *Newcastle Muslim Association v Newcastle City Council* [2012] NSWLEC 1056.
71. The Muslim prayer space is planned to occupy two floors of the 13 storey building. Besides the prayer space, the Initiative's plan includes a 500-seat auditorium, theatre, performing arts centre, fitness centre, swimming pool, basketball court, childcare services, art exhibitions, bookstore, culinary school and a food court serving *halal* dishes.
72. See Imam Feisal Abdul Rauf, *Moving the Mountain: Beyond Ground Zero to a New Vision of Islam in America* (Free Press, New York, 2012).
73. John F. McManus, 'Mosque at Ground Zero, or Elsewhere?' *The New American*, 11 October 2010.
74. Dan Gilgoff, 'Obama Throws Support Behind Controversial Islamic Center', *CNN* 13 August 2010, available at &http://edition.cnn.com/2010/POLITICS/08/13/obama.islamic.center.support/index.html#fbid=qlMj9FlaYim&wom=false
75. Javier C. Hernandez, 'Planned Sign of Tolerance Bringing Division Instead', *The New York Times*, 13 July 2010.
76. Todd H. Green, 'The Resistance to Minarets in Europe' (2010) 52(4) *Journal of Church and State* 619.
77. Lorenz Langer, 'Panacea or Pathetic Fallacy? The Swiss Ban on Minarets' (2010) 43(4) *Vanderbilt Journal of Transnational Law* 863.
78. Also known as Holy Communion. It is a sacrament in which consecrated bread and wine are ritually taken 'in remembrance' of Jesus Christ and the Last Supper.
79. Beth Dugan, 'Religion and Food Service' (1994) 35(6) *The Cornell Hotel and Restaurant Administration Quarterly* 80.
80. Tirmidhi, *Sunan al-Tirmidhi*, hadith No. 1480.
81. Al-Nasa'i, *Sunan al-Nasa'i*, Vol. 7, hadith No. 239.
82. Ven. Alex Bruce, 'Do Sacred Cows Make the Best Hamburgers? The Legal Regulation of Religious Slaughter of Animals' (2011) 34(1) *NSW Law Journal* 351.
83. See Annex III of Position of the European Parliament in which it adopted a legislative resolution on the Council position at first reading with a view to the adoption of a regulation of the European Parliament and of the Council on the provision of food information to consumers, amending Regulations (EC) No. 1924/2006 and (EC) No. 1925/2006 and repealing Directives 87/250/EEC, 90/496/EEC, 1999/10/EC, 2000/13/EC, 2002/67/EC, 2008/5/EC and Regulation (EC) No. 608/2004.
84. Full text of the Court's Decision 1 BvR 1783/99 of 01/15/2002 (in English) can be read at: http://www.bundesverfassungsgericht.de/en/decisions/rs20020115_1bvr178399en.html
85. Department of Standards Malaysia, *Halal Food Production, Preparation, Handling and Storage* (2004).

86. Cory Bernardi, 'The Failure of Multiculturalism', available at http://www.corybernardi.com/2011/02/the-failure-of-multiculturalism.html
87. The Spanish Inquisition was designed to find and punish apostates and heretics. Many Jews were forced to convert to Christianity or leave Spain.
88. Abdullah Yusuf Ali, *The Qur'an: Text, Translation and Commentary* (Tahrike Tarsile Qur'an, New York, 2005), 1385.
89. Noel Coulsen, *The History of Islamic Law* (Edinburgh University Press, Edinburgh, 1984), 102.
90. The contrary view is discussed in Mohammad Hashim Kamali, *Freedom of Expression in Islam* (Islamic Texts Society, Cambridge, 1997).
91. Abdullah Yusuf Ali, *The Qur'an: Text, Translation and Commentary* (Tahrike Tarsile Qur'an, New York, 2005), 85.
92. Ibid., 685.
93. The justification for this is that execution is to prevent the person joining the enemies of Islam, and as women generally would not engage in fighting, they should be exempt from such a severe punishment.
94. 'The punishment of those who wage war against Allah and His Messenger, and strive with might and main for mischief through the land is: execution, or crucifixion, or the cutting off of hands and feet from opposite sides, or exile from the land: that is their disgrace in this world, and a heavy punishment is theirs in the Hereafter'.
95. Sahih Bukari 14:395–6.
96. Modernist views including Rahman are discussed in Mohammad Hashim Kamali, *Freedom of Expression in Islam* (Islamic Texts Society, Cambridge, 1997), 93.
97. Tariq Ramadan, 'Moratorium on Death Penalty', *The American Muslim*, 24 March 2006, available at http://theamericanmuslim.org/tam.php/features/articles/moratorium_on_death_penalty/
98. Sahih Bukari 82: 794. The Ukl had embraced Islam, and given the Prophet their allegiance. When they became ill, the Prophet gave them a place amongst his camels, providing food and support to aid their recovery. When well, the Ukl denounced Islam, killed the shepherds and stole the Prophet's camels. On the Prophet's orders they were deemed apostates, and were captured and killed. They violated the Prophet's trust, and inflicted harm on Muslim property, in addition to being apostates.
99. Mohammad Hashim Kamali, *Freedom of Expression in Islam* (Islamic Texts Society, Cambridge, 1997), 101.
100. Abdullah Yusuf Ali, *The Qur'an: Text, Translation and Commentary* (Tahrike Tarsile Qur'an, New York, 2005), 256. Also see the Quran verses 5:48, 3:84; 5:46–8.
101. Abdullah Yusuf Ali, *The Qur'an: Text, Translation and Commentary* (Tahrike Tarsile Qur'an, New York, 2005), 265.
102. Súra Baqarah, 2:256; Abdullah Yusuf Ali, *The Qur'an: Text, Translation and Commentary* (Tahrike Tarsile Qur'an, New York, 2005), 103.
103. Abdullah Yusuf Ali, *The Qur'an: Text, Translation and Commentary* (Tahrike Tarsile Qur'an, New York, 2005), 509–10.
104. Quran, Súra Nahl 16:125: 'Invite (all) to the Way of thy Lord with wisdom and beautiful preaching; and argue with them in ways that are best and most gracious: for thy Lord knoweth best, who have strayed from His Path, and who receive guidance'. Abdullah Yusuf Ali, *The Qur'an: Text, Translation and Commentary* (Tahrike Tarsile Qur'an, New York, 2005), 689–70.

105. *Kuffar* is divided into levels: a 'major' *kuffar* is denying God and the Prophet; the 'lesser' *kuffar* is not appreciating what God has provided. Susanne Olsson, 'Apostasy in Egypt: Contemporary Cases of Hisbah' (2008) 98 *The Muslim World* 95, 100.
106. Article 3 (1): 'Islam is the religion of the Federation; but other religions may be practised in peace and harmony in any part of the Federation'.
107. Article 11(4): 'State law and in respect of the Federal Territories of Kuala Lumpur and Lubuan, federal law may control or restrict the propagation of any religious doctrine or belief among persons professing the religion of Islam'.
108. Malaysia is a federation of 13 states, nine of which have hereditary rulers (the Sultans), plus the federal territories of Kula Lumpur, Putrajaya and Lebuan. Islam is the religion of the federation but each state legislature has jurisdiction for Islam, Islamic law and for Sharia courts.
109. Article 160 (2).
110. *Lina Joy v Majlis Agama Islam Wilayah Persekutuan & 2 Ors* [2004] CA.
111. Melacca, Perak, Teregganau.
112. This penalty falls outside the jurisdiction of state Sharia courts. Two states under *Parti Islam Se-Malaysia* [Pan-Malaysia Islamic Party] enacted Hudud Legislation, but it could not be implemented as criminal law is a federal not state matter.
113. Kelantan and Sabah allow detention for rehabilitation for up to 36 months.
114. Section 90A Administration of Islamic law (Negeri Sembilan) Enactment, 1991.
115. Malaysia's Civil Registry of Marriages refused to register her marriage to a Catholic while Islam appears on her identity card. *Law Reform (Marriage and Divorce) Act 1976* (Malaysia).
116. *Lina Joy v Majlis Agama Islam Wilayah Persekutuan & 2 Ors* [2004] 2 MLJ 119 (High Court).
117. *Lina Joy v Majlis Agama Islam Wilayah Persekutuan* [2006] 6 MLJ 193, 208 (Court of Appeal).
118. *Lina Joy v Majlis Agama Islam Wilayah Persekutuan* [2007] CLJ 557, 587 (Federal Court).
119. *Lina Joy v Majlis Agama Islam Wilayah Persekutuan* [2007] CLJ 557, 614 (Federal Court).
120. Maurits Berger, 'Apostasy and Public Policy in Contemporary Egypt: An Evaluation of Recent Cases from Egypt's Highest Courts' (2003) 25 *Human Rights Quarterly* 720, 726.
121. Ibid.
122. *Hisbah* gives Muslims or state officials the right to file lawsuits in cases where it is alleged an exalted right of God has been violated. In Zayd's case, seven Islamist lawyers brought the *hisbah* action. See generally, Susanne Olsson, 'Apostasy in Egypt: Contemporary Cases of Hisbah' (2008) 98 *The Muslim World* 95.
123. Nasir Abu-Zayd, 'Renewing Quranic Studies in the Contemporary World' in Paul Marshall and Nina Shea (eds), *Silenced: How Apostasy and Blasphemy Codes are Choking Freedom Worldwide* (Oxford University Press, New York, 2012).
124. 'The Feminists in Tahrir Square', *Newsweek* 6 March 2011, available at http://www.thedailybeast.com/newsweek/2011/03/06/the-feminists-in-the-middle-of-tahrir-square.html
125. Ayatollah Khomeini issued his fatwa against Salman Rushdie, an Indian Muslim, and the publishers of his novel, *Satanic Verses*, in 1989, for its 'poisonous and insulting subject-matter concerning Islam, the Koran and the blessed prophet'. The fatwa called on 'all zealous Moslems to execute [Rushdie and others involved with the novel] quickly, wherever they find them, so that no one will dare to insult Islamic sanctity'. He offered a reward of $2.6 million for an Iranian and $1 million

for a foreigner, and guaranteed that anyone who was killed fulfilling the fatwa would go straight to paradise.

126. 'Muslims Agree that it was Wrong to Silence Opera', *The Daily Mail*, 28 September 2006.
127. 'Arab Columnists: Islam Has Been Harmed More by Muslims Than by the West', MEMRI Special Dispatch No. 1951, 6 June 2008.
128. Jytte Klauson, 'The Danish Cartoons and Modern Iconoclasm in the Cosmopolitan Muslim Diaspora' (2009) 8 *Harvard Middle Eastern and Islamic Review*, 86–118. At 91, Al Qaradawi also is cited as warning Western governments against being silent about 'crimes' that offend the Prophet, which causes terrorism by making Muslims take the defence of the Prophet into their own hands.
129. 'Qaradawi Outlines Jihad Against Danish Cartoons', *The Global Muslim Brotherhood Daily Report*, 8 March 2008, available at http://globalmbreport.org/?p=606
130. Al Qaradawi, 'Apostasy Major and Minor', available at http://www.slideshare.net/IslamicBooks/apostasy-major-minor-by-dr-yusuf-al-qaradawi-2777415
131. Jytte Klauson, 'The Danish Cartoons and Modern Iconoclasm in the Cosmopolitan Muslim Diaspora' (2009) 8 *Harvard Middle Eastern and Islamic Review* 86, 91.
132. Nasir Abu-Zayd, 'Renewing Quranic Studies in the Contemporary World' in Paul Marshall and Nina Shea (eds), *Silenced: How Apostasy and Blasphemy Codes are Choking Freedom Worldwide* (Oxford University Press, New York, 2012).
133. Ibid.
134. Sisters in Islam, 'Banning of the Book on "Muslim Women and the Challenge of Islamic Extremism"', press statement, 21 August 2008, available at http://www.sistersinislam.org.my/index.php?option=com_content&task=view&id=769&Itemid =1

Epilogue

Throughout this book, the recurring message has been that Islamic law continues to be dynamic and evolving. Since the dawn of Islam, Muslim scholars have debated the nature of revelation, the Prophethood and the Islamic legal principles to be derived from two unassailable divine sources, the Quran and Sunna, and while there have been times of ebb and flow throughout 15 centuries of debate, the dialogue remains ongoing and vibrant today. For most of these centuries, scholars and jurists were custodians of the law authorized to give meaning to and apply the revelations. Such exclusivity has been challenged in modern times and *ijtihad* democratized so that mainstream Muslims can now use its tools, including applying their personal reasoning, in their social interactions. A feature of modern Islamic law is that, across the globe, there are literate, highly educated, globally interconnected Muslims, of both genders, who engage in *ijtihad*, many of whom live and work outside the heartland of the Middle East in pluralist societies like Malaysia and Indonesia, where 60 per cent of the world's Muslims reside, or in the West. These challenges to the erstwhile monopoly over *ijtihad* have not always been welcomed in every quarter, but the dimension of human agency in different cultures and centuries has ensured that the dynamic nature of Islamic law remains at the fore. Scholars today continue the tradition of the early jurists who developed the principles of jurisprudence (*usul al fiqh*), as is shown to be true for both the public and private sphere. Dynamism is found not only in the beliefs and practices of individual Muslims, but also in the operation of political entities and in Islamic public institutions: Islamic councils (*shura*), the judiciary (*qada*), mosque (*masjid*) and schools (*madrasa*).

In reflecting on modern perspectives on Islamic law, one is drawn both to the consensus on the theological underpinnings of Islamic law and the unity arising from the concept of the *ummah*, demonstrating the inherent variation and diversity within Islamic law. Many writers have tried to capture this inter- and intra-religious plurality through notions of 'Islams' rather than 'Islam',[1] or by using 'Muslim jurisprudence', rather than 'Islamic jurisprudence'.[2] The co-existence of these two dimensions need not be a tension but can be a strength. This is captured in the Indonesian concept of 'unity in diversity' (*Bhinneka Tunggal Ika*), which recognizes that, by acknowledging plurality or diversity, the outcome can unify rather than fracture a heterogeneous population. Related to diversity is the concept of what is 'modern'. 'Modern' perspectives, as outlined earlier, mean perspectives present today in the world, and so can, in fact, be an old or orthodox perspective that has been retained, or revisited and revived in a similar, or even a quite different, format. Revision can result in a reversion to a past practice or early concept, not necessarily a reformed one. This trend was evident in the chapter on Islamic law and economics, where the displacement of Islamic law in this field by Western systems and concepts is currently being pared back. Some Muslims return to the basic Islamic teachings on commerce and trade to reject all Western accretions. Others have revived Islamic principles of socio-economic justice to create a range of new financial instruments, like *sukuk*, or to infuse the operation of banks and other Western-style institutions with the Islamic prohibitions in business dealings. Although such instruments and institutions were unknown in the time of the Prophet, their Sharia-compliant character now better aligns with principles laid down in the Quran and Sunna.

In many ways, this book is a study in comparative law. There are comparisons between different times and places; between different schools and sects; between Islamic scholars of the same or different eras; between the early communities of Islam with their knowledge of the Prophet and the later eras of caliphates and nation-states; and between cultures. There are also comparisons to be drawn between Muslim and non-Muslim perspectives. What is clear is that some concepts and laws from the earliest days of Islam in the seventh century can endure unscathed while others are revised, revisited and reformed. The traffic is not all in one direction; nor is it uniform. Islamic criminal law has been abandoned in many countries, retained in some form in others nations, while a small minority of Muslim states have restored or are seeking to restore Islamic criminal laws in order to champion the realization of a fully committed Islamic state. Even those states that apply Islamic criminal law are continuously reforming and modifying their criminal law systems.

Two particularly important recent developments are the presence of strong Muslim communities in the West, and the role of non-Muslim scholars contributing their own scholarship on Islamic law. Muslims are now at home in the West, able and willing to live in harmony with Islam and maintain their Muslim culture while participating in their respective Western societies as fellow citizens. We devoted a chapter to seeing a Western nation through Muslim eyes and throughout many chapters in the book we consider how Muslims in the West manage adherence to particular aspects of Islamic law. Family law and inheritance are particularly relevant given that these create important individual and shared identities for Muslims as minorities within the larger entity of the nation-state, and also connect Muslims in the West with the greater *ummah*. Apart from the greater presence and influence of Muslim communities in Western nations, another important modern phenomenon is the entrance of non-Muslim scholars into scholarship on Islamic law. Legal scholars, whether comparativists or positivists, from a range of different legal and faith traditions as well as from non-Muslim cultures located in every continent, are engaged with Islamic law. They bring an 'outsider' analysis to the debate. This 'outsider' interest in Islamic law also has its roots in globalization, and in the application of notions of universality of norms and human rights independent of religious tradition and national practice. The growth in non-Muslim interest is also a response to the burgeoning Muslim diaspora in lands once categorized as '*dar al-Islam*'. These factors mean that the on-going debate on Islamic law today is no longer the sole preserve of Muslims. The West has had to enter dialogue with Muslims in order to better understand its Muslim citizenry and to ensure that their societies develop as ones in which all feel a sense of belonging and are valued regardless of faith and ethnicity. This is a challenge too for the West. Each country goes about it differently, but the intention should be inclusionary, not exclusory, although, as is seen in Chapter 10, decisions made in the West are often viewed as 'attacks' on Islam and motivations are brought into question. This includes the burqa ban in some parts of Europe, approval for the building of mosques and places for worship, and the application of *halal* certification. These issues, however, are also ones on which there remains dissent between Muslim jurists and widespread variation between Muslim countries. Lastly, the burgeoning interest of non-Muslims scholars in the laws and legal institutions of Islam embodies a new-found respect for the Islamic legal system as a major force in the world, and one that is coherent and instructive. Some years ago American Professor David Forte wrote, 'I have known many experts in Islamic Law, though none would seek to claim the title. All of us, fascinated by one of the great legal systems in the world's history, and standing in awe of some of the most creative legal minds, can only be students'.[3]

NOTES

1. H. Patrick Glenn, *Legal Traditions of the World*, 2nd edn (Oxford University Press, New York, 2004), 203.
2. Said Ramadan, *Islamic Law, its Scope and Equity* (A.S. Noorudeen, Kuala Lumpur, 1970), 62.
3. David F. Forte, *Studies in Islamic Law: Classical and Contemporary Application* (Austin & Winfield, Lanham, MD, 1999), 2

Index